A Record in Bone breathes vibrant new life into the study of organic technologies and the central role they played in Indigenous lifeways. In this masterpiece volume, Langley highlights how tools and ornaments made from bones and teeth are central to understanding major themes in Australian archaeology, including the dynamics of reciprocity, identity, and cultural complexity over 65,000 years.

LAUREATE PROFESSOR PETER VETH, FAHA, MAACAI
THE UNIVERSITY OF WESTERN AUSTRALIA
AUSTRALIA

This meticulously researched book presents the first comprehensive account of the tools and ornaments crafted from bone by Australia's First Peoples, offering unparalleled insights into a rich, dynamic, and enduring material culture. Discover the wealth of information which has been compiled about the skills and knowledge needed to make these items and find out how they were used in everyday tasks or in the rituals and ceremonies that sustained people's lives. For all those interested in the crafts of Australia's First Peoples, this is an invaluable companion to *A Record in Stone: The study of Australia's chipped stone artefacts*.

ASSOCIATE PROFESSOR NICOLA STERN, FAHA
LA TROBE UNIVERSITY
AUSTRALIA

Embark on a captivating journey through time and culture with *A Record in Bone*. This awe-inspiring masterpiece showcases bone and tooth artefacts from Australia's Indigenous people, offering rich iconography, detailed descriptions, and methodological rigour. Unveil the evolution of technology and the cultural legacy preserved within, fostering appreciation for our profound interconnectedness as humans. This timeless book empowers anthropologists, archaeologists, and curious readers to analyse and interpret this unique cultural heritage, celebrating the diversity that defines humanity.

DIRECTOR OF RESEARCH FRANCESCO D'ERRICO
CENTRE NATIONAL DE LA RECHERCHE SCIENTIFIQUE
FRANCE

Michelle C Langley

A RECORD IN BONE

Exploring Aboriginal and Torres Strait Islander bone and tooth objects

ABORIGINAL
STUDIES PRESS

First published in 2023
by Aboriginal Studies Press

© Michelle C Langley 2023
© Foreword: Lesley Head 2023

All rights reserved. No part of this book may be reproduced or transmitted in any form or by any means, electronic or mechanical, including photocopying, recording or by any information storage and retrieval system, without prior permission in writing from the publisher. The Australian *Copyright Act 1968* (the Act) allows a maximum of one chapter or 10 per cent of this book, whichever is the greater, to be photocopied by any educational institution for its education purposes provided that the educational institution (or body that administers it) has given a remuneration notice to Copyright Agency Limited (CAL) under the Act.

The opinions expressed in this book are the author's own and do not necessarily reflect the view of AIATSIS or ASP.

Aboriginal and Torres Strait Islander people are respectfully advised that this publication contains names and images of deceased persons and culturally sensitive information. Readers should also be aware that some sections describe material culture made on human skeletal remains.

Aboriginal Studies Press is the publishing arm of the Australian Institute of Aboriginal and Torres Strait Islander Studies.

GPO Box 553, Canberra, ACT 2601
Phone: (61 2) 6246 1183
Fax: (61 2) 6261 4288
Email: asp@aiatsis.gov.au
Web: www.aiatsis.gov.au/asp/about.html

 A catalogue record for this book is available from the National Library of Australia

ISBNs: 978 0 85575 128 9 (pb); 978 0 85575 142 5 (ePub)

Cover design: Sarah Evans
Cover images: Adam Black
Text design and typesetting: Typography Studio
Photographs: The author, unless otherwise credited
Illustrations: Adam Black
Maps: The author
Printed in Australia by Ligare Pty Ltd, Sydney

The author and publisher acknowledge the financial support of the Australian Research Council, through its Discovery Early Career Researcher Award, in the publication of this book.

Foreword

Scholars have long contrasted the complexity of social systems in pre-invasion Indigenous Australia with the simplicity of material culture. Michelle Langley's overview of the richness and abundance of bone and tooth objects and technologies suggests that the idea of this as *simple* material culture needs rethinking. Bones, teeth, quills, shells, beaks, claws, and barbs were made into toggles, awls, skin-workers, charms, combs, containers, drills, eating utensils, fighting tools, fishhooks, knives, musical instruments, pipes, spear points, toys, beads, pendants, circlets, headbands, necklaces, and earrings.

Drawing on archaeological and ethnographic evidence plus museum collections, Langley argues that even archaeologists—who uncover mostly stone remains at the sites they study—are not aware of the abundance of bone artefacts in the records. They will be grateful she has taken the trouble to look, document, and compile objects that she argues have been 'hiding in plain sight'. Her detailed summary brings to life the importance of Indigenous technologies made from organic materials and shows that bone or tooth artefacts are found at 129 archaeological sites in Australia, including many of the best known.

The early chapters pay tribute to archaeologists who are less well known than those who have worked on the oldest records, entwined as the latter are with records in stone. For example, Ron Lampert, who in 1966 excavated almost 500 artefacts made on short-tailed shearwater bone from a sea cave at Durras North in New South Wales.

With the permission of many Indigenous communities and the Indigenous advisory boards of museums, Langley has viewed tools and ornaments and provides a respectful acknowledgement of the importance and wonder of these objects. She is an advocate for the distinctive mechanical qualities of bone—strength and stress-resistance, but also flexibility—reflecting how different skeletal elements have evolved to serve an array of functions in the original animal. These were made use of in many parts of the world as well as in Australia. Langley is careful both to distinguish her contribution from that of Indigenous knowledge, and to consider the spatial and preservation limitations of the record.

Structured clearly as an undergraduate text, the book situates the Australian record in even deeper time, examining the roles of bones and teeth in human evolution, long before people arrived in Australia. It outlines a range of methods used in bone-tool analysis and discusses how to identify and describe them.

Everyday lives spring from these pages; for example, through the poignant summary lists of things found in women's and men's bags across the continent. Bone awls appear as standard contents in these bags, suggesting that many people carried at least one finished awl and often several blanks for spares; in turn, the awls evoke clothing and skin working, and on ongoing cycle of manufacture and repair.

FOREWORD

While writing for a general audience, Langley does not shy away from imprinting her own conceptual insights into the work. She argues that the study of Indigenous Australian bone and tooth artefacts can help us understand important themes such as the practice of reciprocity and the impact of alternate 'ways of doing'. One example of the latter is that bones as ornaments were combined with other organic materials, including feathers, string, and resin, but perforated beads and pendants were almost completely absent. Distinctive Aboriginal and Torres Strait Islander modes of attachment that do not rely on perforation are another important element of the book's argument, challenging archaeological interpretations that have relied on the presence of perforation to identify adornment.

A record in bone will be an important archaeological reference work and a companion to Holdaway and Stern's *A record in stone: the study of Australia's flaked stone artefacts* (published by Aboriginal Studies Press in 2004).

Written with clarity and verve, this book will be accessible to a wide audience. It is beautifully and profusely illustrated. Langley encourages us all to take another look at the breathtaking richness of material cultures expressed in bones.

Emeritus Professor Lesley Head
University of Melbourne
May 2023

Contents

Foreword   v
List of figures   xi
List of tables   xiv

• • •

Preface   xv
Acknowledgements   xvii

Chapter 1.
Why study bone and tooth artefacts?

Introduction	1
A brief overview of bone and tooth artefacts through deep time	2
A historical overview of Australian bone and tooth artefact finds	5
What types of materials are worked?	15
Products of Australia: tools and ornaments	17
What is in this book	18
Summary	19

Chapter 2.
Bone tool analysis: identifying materials and production processes

Introduction	20
Archaeozoology and osseous tool analysis	20
Undertaking a new analysis	21
Raw material properties	21

Identifying osseous (or keratin) artefacts	26
Types of bone- and tooth-working	26
Wear and damage from use	33
Lying on the ground: biting, gnawing, and weathering	37
While in the ground	40
During excavation and analysis	42
Osseous artefact studies to date	42
Summary	56

Chapter 3.
Attributes in describing tool types

Introduction	57
Terms for describing tools	57
Identifying raw material	58
Active edge	59
Hafted or handheld?	59
Orientation	59
Cross-section	61
Microtraces: traces from manufacturing, use, and taphonomic processes	62
Defining 'types'	63
Summary	64

Chapter 4.
Attributes in describing ornament types

Introduction	65
Terms for describing ornamentation	65
Raw material and shape	67
Orientation and metrics	68
Manufacturing traces	69
Attachment and use traces	70
Summary	72

CONTENTS

Chapter 5.
Tools

Introduction	73
Defining types	73
Awls	74
Burnishers	87
Ceremonial tools	88
Charms	88
Combs	90
Containers	91
Death Pointers*	92
Drills	96
Eating utensils	98
Fans and fly-flicks	99
Fighting tools	100
Fishhooks	102
Groovers/smoothing boards	109
Handles	110
Harpoons	111
Housing	112
Knives	113
Medical or surgical tools	114
Murder weapons	116
Musical instruments	118
Needles	119
Pins or fasteners	120
Skin-working tools	122
Smoking pipes	123
Spear points	123
Spearthrower pegs	133
Stone-working tools	135
Toys	136
Woodworking tools	137

CONTENTS

Material culture made on human bone	144
Summary	150

Chapter 6.
Ornaments

Introduction	151
Ornaments worn on the head	151
Ornaments worn around the neck	194
Ornaments worn on the torso	204
Ornaments worn on the arms and hands	205
Summary	205

Chapter 7.
From artefacts to understanding the human story in Australia

Introduction	206
Recurring themes from Australian bone and tooth artefacts	206
The future of Australian bone and tooth artefact studies	208
Conclusion	210
Summary	210

References	211
Index	239
About the author	245

CONTENTS

List of figures

FIGURE 1.1.	A beautiful example of a macropod incisor necklace, as worn by 'Yarruun Parpur Tarneen (Victorious), Chiefess of the Morrporr Tribe'	2
FIGURE 1.2.	Archaeological sites at which bone or tooth artefacts have been found (site names in Table 1.1)	6
FIGURE 1.3.	Distribution of muduk, after McCarthy (1940:Fig. 2)	12
FIGURE 1.4.	The most popular bones for making tools on the Australian continent are the long bones of macropods—especially the fibula, tibia, and ulna	16
FIGURE 1.5.	The long leg bones (tibiotarsus and tarsometatarsus) of emus have been used extensively in Indigenous material culture	17
FIGURE 1.6.	The size of the dots on this map correlate with how many tools or ornaments have been collected from particular locations and that are now housed in the studied museum collections	19
FIGURE 2.1.	Different kinds of bone and their characteristics	23
FIGURE 2.2.	Along with macropod incisors, keratin-based claws, stingray barbs, and the cassowary casque are used in creating tools and ornaments	*colour section*
FIGURE 2.3.	The creation and use life of a bone tool may have followed one of these possible pathways	27
FIGURE 2.4.	Examples of chop marks, cut marks, saw marks, and scrape marks	*colour section*
FIGURE 2.5.	Examples of drilling, grinding, polish, and flaking	*colour section*
FIGURE 2.6.	This large unipoint found at Riwi Cave on Mimbi Country in south-central Kimberley was created on a macropod tibia some 35,000 years ago	*colour section*
FIGURE 2.7.	Examples of use wear developed from cutting, digging, handling, and hafting	*colour section*
FIGURE 2.8.	Examples of use wear developed from projectile impact and repetitive piercing activities	*colour section*
FIGURE 2.9.	Examples of abrasion, digestion, gnawing, and tooth marks	*colour section*
FIGURE 2.10.	Example of a fracture from trampling, marks from root etching, and manganese staining	*colour section*
FIGURE 3.1.	Determining the active edge of the tool will allow you to orient the artefact	58

CONTENTS

FIGURE 3.2.	Determining the distal (active) and proximal extremities on projectile points can sometimes be tricky. For these two examples from Madjedbebe, located on Mirarr Country, identifying the distal tip relies on the presence of impact fractures	*colour section*
FIGURE 3.3.	Terms for describing Australian pointed bone tools	61
FIGURE 3.4.	Terms for describing fishhooks	62
FIGURE 3.5.	This 1000-year-old bone jabbing fishhook from Madjedbebe was made using a combination of flaking, gouging, and grinding	*colour section*
FIGURE 3.6.	Further terms for describing bone-pointed tools	*colour section*
FIGURE 4.1.	Terms used to describe pieces of ornamentation, including those that describe bead perforation (following Beck [1928] and Werner & Miller [2018])	68
FIGURE 4.2.	An example of a 'point of attack' (left) and keyholing (right), both indicated by an arrow	*colour section*
FIGURE 4.3.	Different modes of attachment create distinctive types and distributions of wear	71
FIGURE 5.1.	This map indicates those regions with many tools curated in the studied museum collections (darker colours) through to regions that are least well represented (lighter colours)	74
FIGURE 5.2.	Two main types of bone awl are found in Australia	75
FIGURE 5.3.	A *Zygomaturus* tooth embedded in vegetable resin and fixed to a length of human hair string, collected by Kim Akerman in the west Kimberley region	89
FIGURE 5.4.	A drill tipped with a kangaroo incisor and hafted using ligature overlaid with resin	97
FIGURE 5.5.	Two examples of spoons made on the long bones of macropods	99
FIGURE 5.6.	Shark-tooth fighting knives utilise the natural capacity of shark teeth to cause severe flesh wounds	101
FIGURE 5.7.	Most non-marine shell-based fishhooks are 'jabbing' hooks	104
FIGURE 5.8.	The construction of composite wood and bone bipoint jabbing hook. Redrawn after Thomson (1936)	108
FIGURE 5.9.	Smoothing boards or groovers are an essential maintenance tool used in Cape York	109
FIGURE 5.10.	Harpoons made on the West Cape are used to take large fish as well as dugong	111

CONTENTS

FIGURE 5.11.	Whalebone houses were observed in Encounter Bay, South Australia	*colour section*
FIGURE 5.12.	'Yam knives' are made using the scapula of macropods, with use over time wearing the blade down	113
FIGURE 5.13.	The eyed needle made on a large feather quill known as a tatti	119
FIGURE 5.14.	Bipoints are used to create the bone-tipped spears.	127
FIGURE 5.15.	Whole macropod mandibles, sometimes with their processes covered in resin haft, are used for a range of woodworking	137
FIGURE 5.16.	Portrait of Tasmanian man, Malapuwinarana, painted by Thomas Bock (Oc2006,Drg.70, the British Museum)	*colour section*
FIGURE 6.1.	Some regions are better represented (more pieces of ornamentation have been collected) in Australian museums than others	152
FIGURE 6.2.	Broad forms of ornamentation worn on the head in Indigenous Australia	152
FIGURE 6.3.	Two broad forms of hair pins have been found	155
FIGURE 6.4.	Portrait of an unnamed man at Ooldea, South Australia, c. 1919 (photograph by AG Bolam, B45287/47 SLSA)	155
FIGURE 6.5.	Circlets could incorporate any number of teeth or small animal bones, though macropod incisors remain a favourite material	159
FIGURE 6.6.	The three broad types of headbands that incorporate hard animal materials	162
FIGURE 6.7.	Types of forehead pendan	170
FIGURE 6.8.	Sidelock pendants are attached to a lock of hair so they fall just in front of the ear	175
FIGURE 6.9.	Types of nose bones found across the Australian continent	181
FIGURE 6.10.	Eaglehawk talons are used as a feature piece on headbands and necklaces worn by women in Central Australia	197
FIGURE 6.11.	Eel rays create a neckline from the Rainforest region	198
FIGURE 6.12.	Fish vertebrae necklaces could be coloured with pigment or left plain	199
FIGURE 6.13.	Macropod incisors are attached to the red leather band by folding short strips of leather over the tooth root and then wrapping the end over using sinew	200

CONTENTS

List of tables

TABLE 1.1.	Archaeological sites at which bone or tooth artefacts have been found, as shown in Figure 1.2	7
TABLE 2.1.	Terminology for bone flaking (after Vettese et al. 2020)	31
TABLE 2.2.	Examples of experimental programs undertaken on osseous artefacts around the globe	47
TABLE 3.1.	Definitions of attributes used in describing hard animal material tool types	60
TABLE 3.2.	Common terms used in describing traces resulting from manufacture, use, and post-depositional damage	63
TABLE 3.3.	Terms used in describing bone-pointed tools (distal extremity) (after Langley 2018)	64
TABLE 4.1.	Definitions of major attributes used in describing beads and pendants (following Beck [1928] and Werner and Miller [2018])	66
TABLE 5.1.	Summary of information available from ethnographic sources, museum collections and archaeological reports regarding the characteristics of awls utilised in Australia	76
TABLE 5.2.	Currently known characteristics of Death Pointers ('pointing bones') from ethnographic reports and museum collections	93
TABLE 5.3.	Overview of (non-marine shell) fishhooks present across the Australian continent	103
TABLE 5.4.	Characteristics of spears pointed with hard animal materials from ethnographic reports and museum collections	124
TABLE 5.5.	Woodworking tools identified in museum collections and ethnographies	142
TABLE 6.1.	Presence of head ornaments recorded in museum collections	153
TABLE 6.2.	Presence of hair pins recorded in museum collections	156
TABLE 6.3.	Presence of circlets recorded in museum collections	160
TABLE 6.4.	Presence of headbands recorded in museum collections	164
TABLE 6.5.	Presence of forehead pendants recorded in museum collections	171
TABLE 6.6.	Presence of sidelock pendants recorded in museum collections	178
TABLE 6.7.	Presence of nose bones recorded in museum collections	183
TABLE 6.8.	Presence of necklace types recorded in museum collections	194

Preface

This volume, *A record in bone*, is intended to be both a standalone reference for Australian bone and tooth artefacts and a companion to Simon Holdaway and Nicola Stern's (2004) *A record in stone: the study of Australia's flaked stone artefacts*, published by Aboriginal Studies Press and Museum Victoria.

Bone tools and ornaments have been made by Australia's First Peoples for at least 46,000 years and, despite their beauty, sophistication, and ubiquity, have largely been ignored by archaeologists in favour of their stone counterparts. In fact, it is a common misperception that bone artefacts are rare in the archaeological record and, consequently, of little use in reconstructing Australia's deep history. This idea has resulted in the accumulation and publishing of very little knowledge about how these items were made and used in the past and how communities across space and time differed in their use of hard animal materials.

This book changes that situation.

Stemming from research conducted as part of an Australian Research Council project, this volume draws together all published information regarding Indigenous osseous (bone, tooth) and keratin (claw, quill) technologies and integrates it with data that have been hiding in museum databases for too long. It also outlines how these artefacts are studied archaeologically, providing a guide for students of archaeology, anthropology, and museum curation, as well as for professionals already working in consulting and research.

Written for the undergraduate student or interested public, this work raises awareness of Australia's unique and innovative industries in bone, tooth, quill, and claw and serves as a starting point for connecting current archaeological understandings of osseous technology with Indigenous knowledge about these organic objects.

It is hoped that, in a small way, this volume will help to give back knowledge about these vibrant living technologies.

Acknowledgements

This book came from a desire to demonstrate that bone technology is just as vibrant and interesting as stone technology in Australia—but even I did not anticipate the enormous array of material culture created from bone, tooth, claw, quill, and casque. The richness of the museum collections, ethnographic accounts, and oral histories have shown tenfold just how important these artefacts have been—and continue to be—to Indigenous communities across the continent.

The work presented in this volume is the culmination of four years of research and writing, funded initially by a Discovery Early Career Researcher Award from the Australian Research Council. This award gave me the financial resources to travel to museums across Australia and focus on research for a period of almost three years.

This book would not have been possible without the time and knowledgeable assistance of museum staff from across Australia. In particular, I would like to thank Allison Djanovich and Rebecca Jones at the Australian Museum (Sydney); Tara Collier, Alice Beale, and Jacinta Koolmatrie at the South Australian Museum (Adelaide); Melanie Raberts at Museum Victoria (Melbourne); and Annie Carson and Moya Smith at the Western Australian Museum (Perth). Each of these women fielded many emails, facilitated visits to museum spaces, and actively helped me find examples of tools or ornaments made from hard animal materials in their respective collections. At the Queensland Museum (Brisbane), Geraldine Mate gave up several hours of her time so that we could make sure that Queensland was well represented, sitting with me to sift through yet another unwieldy database full of local quirks. Thank you.

Similarly, this book would not be as full without my having been allowed to view numerous tools and ornaments curated in these museums. As such, I give many thanks to the Quandamooka, Jinibara, Mithaka, Mirarr, Mimbi, Bunuba, Taungarung, Wiradjuri, Willandra Lakes, and Batemans Bay communities, as well as the museums' Indigenous advisory boards who gave me permission to see their material culture. Thank you for trusting me with your heritage. I hope that you find this book worthy of that trust. Here it should be noted that there are two portraits in this book of Aboriginal individuals who are now deceased. Permission to include these images was provided by the family of the deceased and the institutions that curate (SLSA and SLV) the original photographs.

Colleagues have also been generous with their time and thoughts. Discussions and correspondence have helped me to identify what form this book should take and make sure that it contains useful information for a range of readers. Kim Akerman, with his wealth of knowledge on Indigenous Australian technologies, has been fielding emails from me regarding unknown or unfindable information for the past few years and generously shared photographs of artefacts he had previously gathered. I also bothered a

ACKNOWLEDGEMENTS

number of colleagues with drafts: Eva Martellotta, Jillian Huntley, and Lynley Wallis. Thank you for your precious time and honest feedback.

I would like to thank my family for giving me as much thinking and writing time as possible among unsettling global circumstances. Your support meant that this book could be not only written but also completed without too much delay.

Finally, the hand-drawn illustrations found throughout this book were created by Adam Black. These images were based on photographs and descriptions of ornaments collected for this project and it is hoped that they will allow readers to better understand the unique technology of Australia.

CHAPTER 1
WHY STUDY BONE AND TOOTH ARTEFACTS?

Introduction

Upon reaching the Australian continent, Europeans observed that more than 95 per cent of the Indigenous technology was made from organic materials. Hardwoods yielded timbers not only for making excellent spears, spearthrowers, and shields but also for boomerangs, bowls, and digging sticks. Baskets and nets for catching game and fish were woven from plant fibres, kangaroo and possum skins created warm covers, and spinifex gum provided an easy-to-use glue. Similarly, the bones, teeth, shells, and quills of the native fauna were utilised to make a multitude of everyday tools, personal ornaments, and sacred objects (see Figure 1.1). Thus, while stone was important for making technology on this continent, as it has been to humanity everywhere for the past 3.3 million years (Harmand et al. 2015), most of what people owned was made from something other than stone. And frequently it was the bones and teeth of wildlife that formed the basis of material culture.

When metal and glass tools flooded into the continent, making (by hand) new tools from the traditional materials of stone and bone became an increasingly rare occurrence. Today, the knowledge of how these items—once a mainstay of everyday Australian life—were made and used is hidden, secreted away within European writings of early settlements, museum collections, and the ground itself. Few people remember making these technologies or seeing them made by their elders. Few hold onto knowledge that has been passed down for thousands of years. Consequently, those interested in the 65,000-year-long (or longer) human story on the Australian continent must reconstruct the lives and technologies of all those who came before from that which is left behind in the archaeological record, the ethnographic record (written or illustrated observations), museum collections, and oral histories.

This book presents an overview of what is currently known about the bone and tooth technologies made and used in Indigenous Australia from the archaeological and ethnographic evidence, joined by that which can be gleaned from major Australian museum collections. It provides a starting point for exploring the richness and diversity of tools created using bone, tooth, quill, and turtle shell, as well as a pathway for future research into Indigenous material culture practices. But before delving into the Australian evidence, understanding the enormously long history of bone and tooth technologies throughout the human experience is necessary.

FIGURE 1.1. A beautiful example of a macropod incisor necklace, as worn by 'Yarruun Parpur Tarneen (Victorious), Chiefess of the Morrporr Tribe'. Reproduced from the frontispiece of Dawson (1981[1881]) with permission from Yarruun's closest known descendant, Titta Secombe, and the State Library of Victoria.

A brief overview of bone and tooth artefacts through deep time

Because bone tools are susceptible to decay, identifying the origin of bone technology has a restriction that stone technology does not. Despite this setback, however, we know that pre-*Homo sapiens* hominins were able to understand the usefulness of hard animal materials and that they began using them early on in our evolution. Currently, the earliest known use of bone for tools dates back some 2–1.7 million years at Swartkrans and Drimolen in South Africa. Here, large shaft pieces were used to break open termite mounds to gather insects for food, as were horn cores and an ulna, which display evidence of shaping and use (Backwell & d'Errico 2001, 2008). Significantly, these artefacts indicate that whoever made them did not just pick up a bone lying around and momentarily use it but had the cognitive abilities to modify the pieces so that they became more effective to use (d'Errico & Backwell 2003b). This evidence also indicates that bone technology has a greater antiquity, probably at least as old as its stone counterparts, as *unshaped* bone or horn would likely have been the first used as tools.

Around this same time, further north at Olduvai Beds I and II in Tanzania, bones and teeth from a range of animals (including hippopotamus, suids, elephants, and

1. WHY STUDY BONE AND TOOTH ARTEFACTS?

giraffes) were flaked to create early forms of soft hammers, a tool used to make stone tools (originally reported by Mary Leakey 1971; Backwell & d'Errico 2004). Interestingly, *Paranthropus robustus* has been suggested to have made the South African digging tools, while *Homo erectus* may have made the bone hammers in the north (Pante et al. 2020), though we do not yet know for certain who was making what, or where, in this very early period of humanity.

From about 1.4 million years ago, pieces of bone—especially those from elephants—began to be utilised to make handaxes (Beyene et al. 2013; Sano et al. 2020). This Acheulean technology, thought to be originally designed for stone, was transposed onto particularly large bones at several sites in both Africa and Eurasia. This utilisation of large bones, as if they were nodules of stone, to create distinctive handheld tools appears as an interesting development in how hominins were interacting with bony materials and one that continues over the next million years (Zutovski & Barkai 2016).

Use of bone for toolmaking continued in both Africa and Eurasia during Marine Isotope Stage 9 (MIS 9), which stretched between 337,000 and 300,000 years ago. However, the types of tools made diversified with smaller pointed tools, soft hammers, and retouchers (these last two for making tools in stone) identified at Gran Dolina and Bolomor Cave in Spain as well as Qesem Cave in Israel (Rosell et al. 2015). Other sites that produced carefully shaped bone tools from this Lower Palaeolithic period include Castel di Guido (Radmilli & Boschian 1996), Fontana Ranuccio (Bidittu & Celletti 2001), and Polledrara (Anzidei 2001), all in Italy; Bilzingsleben in Germany (Mania & Mania 2005); and Vertesszöllös in Hungary (Dobosi 2001). Similar bone hammers were also found at the famous English Lower Palaeolithic site of Boxgrove (Roberts & Parfitt 1999). At these sites, the artefacts were frequently made on proboscidean bones, with researchers suggesting that the use of this raw material was in response to a lack of appropriate lithic raw material in the surrounding area (Anzidei 2001; Dobosi 2001; Gaudzinski et al. 2005). Importantly, bone hammers continued to be made alongside smaller, more delicate bone retouchers through the Middle (c. 300,000 to 45,000 years ago) and Upper Palaeolithic (c. 45,000 to 11,750 years ago) across the Old World (see Pante et al. 2020 for a summary).

With the arrival of Neanderthals and *Homo sapiens* on the scene, osseous technology became increasingly complex and diversified. In Europe, Neanderthals created large, pointed tools from mammoth ribs (function currently unknown) at the German site of Salzgitter-Lebenstedt, which dates to somewhere between 100,000 and 48,000 years ago (Gaudzinski 1999) and retouchers from bear bones in Belgium during the Weischselian Early Glacial (MIS 5d to 5b, between about 130,000 and 80,000 years ago) (Abrams et al. 2014).

By around 50,000 years ago, Neanderthals had developed a type of bone tool called a *lissoir* or burnisher—a tool used to work animal skins (Soressi et al. 2013). These leather- or fur-working tools (which are still used today) are then joined by bone awls, which are known from later Neanderthal cultures such as the Châtelperronian at Grotte du Renne, France (d'Errico et al. 2003). A remarkable find of a three-ply bark fibre string found in 52,000 to 41,000-year-old levels at Abri du Maras, France, demonstrates that Neanderthals also had string technology for use in conjunction with their bone awls (Hardy et al. 2020). In addition, analysis of Neanderthal dental wear suggests that they also used their own teeth as vices to hold materials—such as leather hides—while they worked them (Krueger et al. 2019).

Back in Africa, *Homo sapiens* were producing a range of pointed bone tools, which may have functioned as projectile point tips or awls, from 78,000 years ago (Henshilwood et al. 2001; Shipton et al. 2018). There is also tantalising evidence that barbed points, perhaps used in fishing, may be as old as 930,000–800,000 years at Olduvai (Pante et al. 2020), even though the previous Katanda finds dated to 90,000 years ago have been seen as controversially early since their publication (Brooks et al. 1995). Barbed points (often called 'harpoons' in the archaeological literature), like many forms of osseous implements, have long been seen as particularly advanced forms of technology. Thus, their appearance tens (and now hundreds) of thousands of years earlier than the European Upper Palaeolithic (starting around 45,000 years ago) has caused consternation among researchers who thought they were a relatively late invention.

A tool type that does appear to be quite recent is eyed bone needles. These tools have been found in a number of Upper Palaeolithic sites across Western Europe as well as northern and central Asia, including from 50,000- to 36,000-year-old contexts at Denisova Cave in the Russian Altai (Shunkov et al. 2020), 39,000- to 34,000-year-old contexts at Zhoukoudian in China (Li et al. 2018), the Epi-Gravettian (around 21,000 years ago) site of Bistricioara-Lutărie III in Romania (Anghelinu et al. 2017), and Solutrean (around 22,000 years ago) through to Magdalenian contexts across Western Europe (Stordeur-Yedid 1979). Of course, eyed needles were not the only solution to threading fibres for sewing (as shown in Chapter 5)—sharp points can also work. If we consider such pointed tools, bone points identified as having been used as 'awls' some 70,000 years ago at Blombos Cave in South Africa can be included here (Henshilwood et al. 2001), as well as bone and antler awls, spear points, chisels, and other items found in the Ahmarian and Aurignacian levels in Manot Cave dating to between about 41,000 and 33,000 BP (Tejero et al. 2016).

Among the earliest evidence for the use of bony materials to decorate the human body is the use of eagle talons by Western European Neanderthal communities for a span of about 80,000 years at the end of their reign (Rodríguez-Hidalgo et al. 2019; Romandini et al. 2014). For *Homo sapiens*, the earliest evidence comes from the Kimberley region of Western Australia, where an ochre-stained nose bone dated to at least 46,000 years ago was found at Carpenters Gap 1 (Langley et al. 2016).

Back in Europe, the first *Homo sapiens* on that continent made extensive use of animal bones and teeth, as well as mammoth ivory and deer antler, to produce a range of beads and pendants (Vanhaeren & d'Errico 2006). Interestingly, from what has been found so far, the earliest *Homo sapiens* populations in Africa appear to have preferred using marine shells and ostrich eggshell over bone or ivory to produce their adornment (d'Errico et al. 2005; Shipton et al. 2018).

Other tools that played an important role in developing human symbolic expression are musical instruments. Possible instruments made on bone have been reported for a number of similarly aged contexts falling around 40,000 years ago across the Old World. These finds include bone aerophones in Later Stone Age deposits at Klasies River Main site and Matjes River Rock Shelter on the very south coast of South Africa (Kumbani et al. 2019), aerophones from Natufian contexts in Israel (Shahom & Belfer-Cohen 2017), and bird and mammoth bone flutes in Aurignacian contexts in Germany (Morley 2013).

Small, portable carved artworks also become more common in the archaeological record after 50,000 years ago, the oldest such example being created by a Neanderthal

1. WHY STUDY BONE AND TOOTH ARTEFACTS?

artist some 51,000 years ago (Leder et al. 2021). This piece was made on a giant deer phalanx and was found at the north German site of Einhornhöhle. Though it is not clear what the artwork represents exactly, the intentional carving of the piece is indisputable. Among *Homo sapiens*, the oldest examples of carvings also come from Germany, this time at sites located in the Swabian Jura. These include a woman carved from mammoth ivory some 35,000 years ago (Conard 2009), as well as the famous 'lion man' of Hohlenstein-Stadel, dated to about 38,000 years ago. Whether this last mammoth ivory figure depicts a man with a lion's head or a standing bear is a matter of continuing debate (Clifford & Bahn 2018).

Along other lines, one of the oldest forms of technology invented by humanity was likely containers (see Langley & Suddendorf 2020 for discussion). Some of the oldest containers, at least that have survived to discovery, made use of natural concave surfaces such as those provided by ostrich eggshell (dating back 65,000 years in South Africa; Henshilwood et al. 2014; Texier et al. 2010), as well as tortoise shells, which were used at Kebara in Israel by Neanderthals between 60,000 and 48,000 years ago (Speth & Tchernov 2002).

In general, after about 40,000 to 30,000 years ago, osseous materials, as well as other hard materials that could be collected from animals (quills, claws, shells), became increasingly evident within archaeological sites the world over. Some of this temporal patterning is owing to the shorter amount of time artefacts have had to survive to be recovered by archaeologists, but some of it may also reflect the ability of humans to assess the opportunities that such resources had to offer and turn them into a reality.

In Australia, preservation conditions have made the survival of osseous finds dating to the first 40,000-odd years of human occupation exceedingly rare. Despite these circumstances, artefacts made from bone and teeth have been found in the most ancient sites and demonstrate that First Australians were creating tools and ornaments just as spectacular as anything found elsewhere in the Old World.

A historical overview of Australian bone and tooth artefact finds

Despite bone implements being recovered from the very first scientific excavation undertaken on the Australian continent (at a site called Ngaut Ngaut on the Lower Murray River, discussed below), only a handful of researchers have paid any focused attention to these artefacts. What follows is an overview of those archaeologists who did more than just briefly report the appearance of 'bone tools' in their excavation.

1930s–1940s: Tindale and McCarthy

Bone artefacts were a very visible part of early Australian archaeology. In 1929, Herbert Hale and Norman Tindale undertook the first systematic archaeological excavation in Australia, investigating two sites located not too far from Nildottie on the Lower Murray River (South Australia) (see Figure 1.2). This excavation presented a clear break from the rough and ready digs of the past to the systematic, carefully controlled, and carefully recorded excavations of the future.

Ngaut Ngaut (published as 'Devon Downs shelter', though Tindale emphasised that it should be referred to by its local Aboriginal name—Ngaut Ngaut—in his notes;

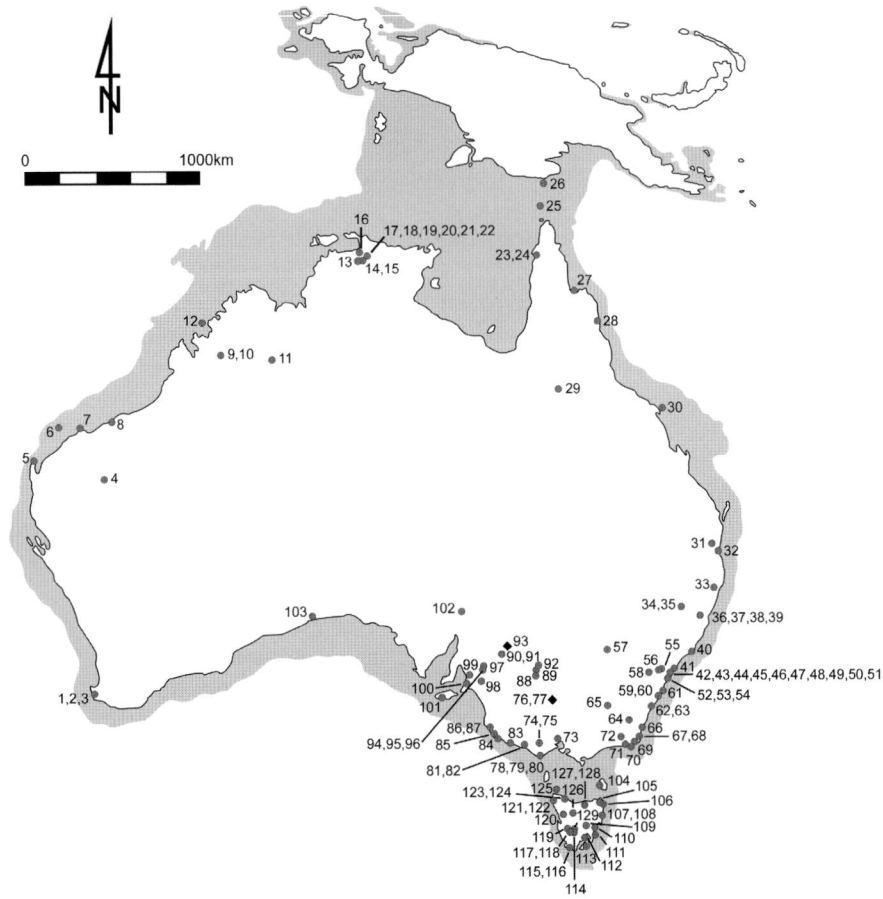

FIGURE 1.2. Archaeological sites at which bone or tooth artefacts have been found (site names in Table 1.1). Black diamonds indicate sites from which beads have been recovered.

Smith 2000) was found to contain some six metres of rich faunal assemblages along with a variety of stone and bone technologies. Tartanga, on the other hand, was an open burial site down on the banks of the river and included a shell midden with a few stone implements (Hale & Tindale 1930). Based on the well-stratified layers of Ngaut Ngaut and the older context found at nearby Tartanga, Hale and Tindale (1930) defined five cultural phases (moving from oldest to youngest): Tartangan, Pre-Pirrian, Pirrian, Mudukian, and Murundian. These 'archaeological cultures' were defined using the European tradition of 'type fossils' (*fossils directeur*)—that is, they used the presence of a particular distinctive artefact to identify a particular period or people. Bone artefacts feature in these descriptions, with Hale and Tindale (1930:204) speaking of 'coarse bone implements', 'scant bone industry', and 'double-pointed bones (muduk)' being present or absent within each phase. The muduk, in particular, played an important role, being the type fossil for the 'Mudukian'. Smith (2000) studied Tindale's field notes, finding that Tindale experimented with a variety of terms for this phase, including 'Kankomuda' (bone,

1. WHY STUDY BONE AND TOOTH ARTEFACTS?

TABLE 1.1. Archaeological sites at which bone or tooth artefacts have been found, as shown in Figure 1.2. Site names are as presented in their original publication.

NUMBER IN FIGURE 1.2	ARCHAEOLOGICAL SITE	REFERENCE
1	Devil's Lair, Western Australia	Balme 1979; Dortch & Merrilees 1973
2	Mammoth Cave, Western Australia	Dortch 1979
3	Tunnel Cave, Western Australia	Dortch 1996
4	Juukan 2, Western Australia	Slack et al. 2009
5	C99, Western Australia	Veth et al. 2014
6	Haynes Cave, Western Australia	Veth et al. 2014
7	Burrup Peninsula, Western Australia	Vinnicombe 1987
8	FMGP04-023, Western Australia	Harrison 2009
9	Carpenters Gap 1, Western Australia	Langley et al. 2016
10	Djuru, Western Australia	Maloney et al. 2016
11	Riwi, Western Australia	Langley et al. 2021a
12	High Cliffy Shelter, Western Australia	O'Connor 1992
13	Kina, Northern Territory	Brockwell & Akerman 2007
14	Anbangbang I, Northern Territory	Brockwell & Akerman 2007
15	Burial Cave, Northern Territory	Brockwell & Akerman 2007
16	Birriwilk Rockshelter, Northern Territory	Shine et al. 2013
17	Arguluk Hill, Northern Territory	Brockwell & Akerman 2007
18	Malangangerr, Northern Territory	Schrire 1982
19	Nawamoyn, Northern Territory	Schrire 1982
20	Ngarradj Warde Jobkeng, Northern Territory	Brockwell & Akerman 2007
21	Paribari (Padypady), Northern Territory	Schrire 1982
22	Djawumbu-Madjawarrnja, Northern Territory	Wright et al. 2016
23	Kwamter Shell Mound, Queensland	Bailey 1993
24	Weipa Shell Mounds, Queensland	Wright 1971
25	Tigershark Rockshelter, Torres Strait	McNiven et al. 2008
26	Sokoli Midden, Torres Strait	Carter 2001
27	Endaen Shelter, Queensland	Beaton 1985
28	Jiyer Cave, Queensland	Cosgrove & Raymont 2002
29	Micky Springs 34, Queensland	Morwood & Godwin 1982
30	Nara Inlet, Queensland	Barker 1991
31	Platypus Rockshelter, Queensland	Francis 2002

NUMBER IN FIGURE 1.2	ARCHAEOLOGICAL SITE	REFERENCE
32	Broadbeach Burial Ground, Queensland	Haglund 1976
33	Seelands, New South Wales	Matthews 1966
34	Graman Area B, Site 1, New South Wales	McBryde 1968
35	Graman Area B, Site 4, New South Wales	McBryde 1968
36	Clybucca 3, New South Wales	Connah 1975
37	Connection Creek 1, New South Wales	Connah 1975
38	Maguire's Crossing, New South Wales	Connah 1975
39	Stuarts Point 1, New South Wales	Connah 1975
40	Birubi, New South Wales	Sheppard Brennand 2018
41	Angophora Reserve Rock Shelter, New South Wales	McDonald & Ross 1990
42	Connells Point Rockshelter, New South Wales	Wade 1967
43	Curracurrang Shelter, New South Wales	Lampert 1971
44	Gymea Bay, Lower Rock-Shelter, New South Wales	Megaw & Wright 1966
45	North Cronulla, New South Wales	Lampert 1966
46	Port Hacking, New South Wales	McCarthy 1940
47	Skeleton Cave, New South Wales	Megaw 1969
48	Spring Cove, New South Wales	Stockton 1977a
49	Watering Place, New South Wales	Megaw 1969
50	Inscription Point, Botany Bay, New South Wales	Lampert 1971
51	Parramatta, New South Wales	Balme & O'Connor 2019
52	Bass Point, New South Wales	Bowdler 1976
53	Stanwell Park, New South Wales	McCarthy 1976
54	Wattamolla, New South Wales	Lampert 1971
55	Bird Tracks, New South Wales	Attenbrow 2003
56	MacDonald River Site (MR/1), New South Wales	Moore 1976
57	Wee Jasper, New South Wales	Theden-Ringl & Langley 2018
58	Shaws Creek KII Rockshelter, New South Wales	Kohen et al. 1984
59	Currarong, New South Wales	Lampert 1971

1. WHY STUDY BONE AND TOOTH ARTEFACTS?

NUMBER IN FIGURE 1.2	ARCHAEOLOGICAL SITE	REFERENCE
60	Burrill Lake, New South Wales	Lampert 1971
61	Lake Wollumboola, New South Wales	Lampert 1966
62	Durras North, New South Wales	Langley et al. 2021b
63	Murramarang Point, New South Wales	Lampert 1971
64	Cooma, New South Wales	Feary 1996
65	New Guinea II, Victoria	Ossa et al. 1995
66	Pambula Lake Midden, New South Wales	Sullivan 1984
67	Greenglade Rockshelter (Site 63-3-63), New South Wales	Murray-Wallace & Colley 1997
68	Lake Wonboin, New South Wales	McCarthy 1940
69	Captain Stevensons Point, Victoria	Coutts 1976
70	Point Hicks, Victoria	Coutts 1976
71	Clinton Rocks, Victoria	Coutts et al. 1977
72	Cloggs Cave, Victoria	Flood 1974
73	Keilor, Dry Creek, Victoria	Gallus 1970
74	FM/1, Victoria	Coutts and Witter 1977
75	KP/1, Victoria	Coutts and Witter 1977
76	Kow Swamp, Victoria	Dortch 1979
77	Nacurrie, Victoria	Balme & O'Connor 2019
78	Aire River, Shelter II, Victoria	Lampert 1966
79	Cape Otway (Seal Point), Shelter 2, Victoria	Lourandos 1976
80	Glen Aire, Victoria	Coutts 1976
81	Koroit, Victoria	Lampert 1966
82	Tower Hill Beach, Victoria	Gill 1974
83	Bridgewater Caves, Victoria	Head 1985
84	Port McDonnell, Victoria	Lampert 1966
85	Koongine Cave, Victoria	Frankel 1986
86	Five Mile Concaves, Victoria	McCourt 1975
87	Five Mile Knob, Victoria	McCourt 1975
88	Lake Mungo, New South Wales	Mulvaney 1974
89	Lake Garnpung, New South Wales	Johnston & Clark 1998

NUMBER IN FIGURE 1.2	ARCHAEOLOGICAL SITE	REFERENCE
90	Lake Victoria, New South Wales	Pardoe 1993
91	Wallpolla Island, New South Wales	Gallus & Gill 1973
92	Lake Mulurulu, New South Wales	Clark 1987
93	Lake Nitchie, New South Wales	Macintosh et al. 1970
94	Ngaut Ngaut, South Australia	Hale & Tindale 1930
95	Fromm's Landing, Rockshelter 2, South Australia	Edwards 1968
96	Tartanga, South Australia	Hale & Tindale 1930
97	Roonka, South Australia	Pretty 1977
98	Swanport, South Australia	Pretty 1977
99	Salisbury Burial, South Australia	Owen & Pate 2014
100	Kongarati, South Australia	McCarthy 1949
101	Seton, South Australia	Stockton 1977b
102	Warratyi Rock Shelter, South Australia	Hamm et al. 2016
103	Allen's Cave, South Australia	Marun 1972
104	Mannalargenna, Tasmania	Brown 1993
105	Mount Cameron West, Tasmania	Jones 1971
106	Ansons Bay, Tasmania	Jones 1971
107	Piccanini Point, Tasmania	Jones 1971
108	Seymour, Tasmania	Jones 1971
109	Oatlands, Tasmania	Jones 1971
110	Little Swanport, Tasmania	Jones 1971
111	Maria Island, Tasmania	Jones 1971
112	South Arm, Tasmania	Jones 1971
113	Adventure Bay, Tasmania	Jones 1971
114	Bone Cave, Tasmania	Webb & Allen 1990
115	Louisa Bay, Tasmania	Gilligan 2007
116	LR-1, Tasmania	Vanderwal 1978
117	M86/2, Tasmania	Webb & Allen 1990
118	Wareen, Tasmania	Allen et al. 1989

1. WHY STUDY BONE AND TOOTH ARTEFACTS?

NUMBER IN FIGURE 1.2	ARCHAEOLOGICAL SITE	REFERENCE
119	Kutikina, Tasmania	Allen et al. 1988
120	Bottle Creek, Tasmania	Jones 1971
121	West Point Midden, Tasmania	Jones 1965
122	South of the Arthur River, Tasmania	Jones 1971
123	Blackman's Cave, Tasmania	Jones 1965
124	Rocky Cape, Tasmania	Jones 1971
125	Cave Bay Cave, Tasmania	Bowdler 1975
126	Parmerpar Meethaner, Tasmania	Cosgrove 1995
127	Flowery Gully, Tasmania	Jones 1971
128	West Head, Tasmania	Jones 1971
129	Beginners Luck Cave, Site P, Tasmania	Goede et al. 1978

pointed), 'Kankomuna' (bone, old), 'Munnaroo' (old, ancient), and 'Mudukanka' (bone point)—before finally settling on 'Mudukian'. These phases were much criticised by contemporary Frederick McCarthy; however, Tindale defended his chronology staunchly and applied it widely, including at sites found intestate and even in Indonesia. Although these phases and phrases are no longer used by archaeologists today, Tindale's attention to the bone industry at the start of Australian archaeology is significant.

Unfortunately, after this initial attention at Ngaut Ngaut, bone technology disappeared from the developing chronologies of Australia's human history. Frederick McCarthy produced a schema for eastern New South Wales based on his 1936 excavation of Lapstone Creek Rock Shelter, a site that had such poor organic preservation that there 'was the almost entire absence of animal bones and mollusc shells' (McCarthy 1948:21). Not surprisingly, then, his schema focused on stone tools, moulding the 'Bondaian' (after Bondi points) and 'Elourean' (after a type of adze flake). McCarthy summarised the then-current archaeological evidence for this two-phase chronology, stating that 'the Bondaian culture is associated with raw-ochre drawings, paintings and stencils in five rock-shelters' (McCarthy 1948:29)—no mention of bone artefacts. Similarly, the Elouerean culture includes no mention of bone artefacts despite 'split kangaroo bones' being listed as found at North Harbour (Port Jackson), '3 bone awls' found at North-west Arm (Port Hacking), and 'several bone awls' from Woolwich (Port Jackson) (McCarthy 1948:30). Instead, the Elouerean was stated to 'embrace ... outline rock engraves, stone cairns, fish-hooks and files' (McCarthy 1948:30). In a later paper, McCarthy did include 'bone points' among specific tool types he argued represented distinctive 'lithic cultures' of Australia (McCarthy 1961), though they received little mention in the accompanying discussion.

Tindale and McCarthy also went head-to-head regarding the function of muduk. The small bone bipoints (an implement with a point at both ends) were argued by Hale and Tindale (1930:205) to have been a 'fishing-bone' or gouge, as seen used in fishing

FIGURE 1.3. Distribution of muduk, after McCarthy (1940:Fig. 2).

along the Murray River and southeast coast (and, specifically, as reported by Brough Smyth 1972[1878]a). McCarthy, on the other hand, stated that they were more likely to have functioned as a 'dual spear point and barb' on fishing spears (McCarthy 1940:313).

From his review of the ethnographic literature and museum collections, McCarthy (1940) further argued that wherever muduk were found along the southeast coast, it was 'probably correct to assume' that the pronged fishing spear was used (McCarthy 1940:317). His assertion extended the known use of such bone-barbed fishing spears from northern Queensland (where they were prevalent) to a 'new known range in south-east Australia ... from the Brisbane District to the Murray River mouth, Lower Darling and Murray Rivers, and at Devon Downs and Swan Hill on the Murray River' (McCarthy 1940:318). He argued that future research would probably fill the gaps along the coast of New South Wales and Queensland and noted that 'mammal bones, bird bones, fish teeth and bones, and stingray spines were used for making *muduk*' (McCarthy 1940:318). He finished his paper by noting the presence of muduk outside Australia, notably in 'Bougainville and Buka, Solomon Islands. On New Hebridean spears ... and in prehistoric Toalian culture of Celebes and southern Java' (McCarthy 1940:318) (see Figure 1.3). Massola (1956) followed suit, using the term 'muduk' to describe small bone bipoints from the Sulawesi Toalean, as well as those found in European Palaeolithic archaeological contexts and modern cultures in North America, Africa, Polynesia, and Micronesia.

From these last works, it is evident that the term 'muduk' was used to describe any small bone barb initially used to tip spears in Australia but was then extended out into the wider Oceania and Australasian regions and even further. Indeed, 'muduk' was commonly used to describe any small bone bipoint until the 1970s (Davidson 1937; Massola 1956; McCarthy 1936, 1940, 1965, 1976; Megaw & Wright 1966; Mulvaney 1960; Pretty 1977) and still finds mention today (e.g. Langley 2018; Perston et al. 2021).

1. WHY STUDY BONE AND TOOTH ARTEFACTS?

1960s–1970s: Lampert, Jones, Bowdler, and Balme

The 1960s, and particularly the 1970s, saw a flurry of bone and tooth artefacts being reported in the Australian archaeological literature, as well as a revival of discussions articulating bone tool data to broader questions surrounding Australia's deep past.

In 1966, Ron Lampert excavated a two by two metre pit in the back of a small sea cave not far from Batemans Bay called Durras North. Here, he found himself with almost 500 artefacts made on short-tailed shearwater bone. Such a large assemblage of bone technology was hitherto unheard of in the Australian context, and Lampert put significant effort into attempting to understand the industry. He developed a classification system based on artefact length, tip shape, and tip length, before expanding it with reference to bone artefacts from his excavation at Currarong, also in New South Wales (Lampert 1971). In this second publication, Lampert suggested a single class of bipoints alongside four types of unipoints (those that are only pointed at one end), with these latter artefacts being classified according to their raw material (e.g. bird bone, macropod fibula) and/or traces of use (e.g. gum from hafting, spatulate-form tips). This careful description of the Durras North and Currarong assemblages became the standard by which all other bone points were defined thereafter. For example, on finding a bone point, authors would say they found artefacts 'within the range of "unipoints" as recently extensively studied by Lampert' (Megaw 1969:17) and similar turns of phrase.

At the same time that Lampert was excavating sites in New South Wales, Rhys Jones was exploring Tasmania. After excavating at Rocky Cape and West Point on the northwest coast of Tasmania, Jones realised that bone technology had been part of the Tasmanian toolkit before being abruptly abandoned about 3500 years ago (Jones 1971). Indeed, further excavations by Richard Cosgrove, Jim Allen, Harry Lourandos, and others found bone tools in archaeological sites (e.g. Warreen Cave) dating back to 27,000 years ago (Cosgrove 1999), but nowhere across Tasmania has anyone found tools younger than 3500 years. Why?

Even more intriguing, Jones' excavations found that at about the same time that bone tools disappear, so too does fishbone, despite this food source having previously been consumed for thousands of years (Jones 1971). Indeed, subsequent excavations along the coast and interior of Tasmania never found fishbone in sites dated to less than 3000 years, suggesting that this change in behaviour was island-wide. But was the abandonment of bone points and fishing connected? Jones states in his PhD thesis that while he had initially seen the two as being connected, he changed his opinion to the apparent association being a

> fortuitous one, in that both were practised during an early phase, and that both were eventually discontinued approximately the same time. Even if the possibility be conceded that one of the uses of bone tools was in fishing, I don't think that it was the major use. (Jones 1971:510)

This change of view was prompted by the apparent poor suitability of the found bone unipoints for tipping fishing spears and the fact that although most bone tools had been recovered from coastal shell middens, some had been found inland where fishing was not conducted (Jones 1971). Sandra Bowdler (1979), however, convincingly argued that 'it is likely that there was a central function which dominated the bone artefact industry and once this dominant function ceased to be necessary the entire industry became defunct' (Bowdler 1984:125). She therefore argued that the 'coincidence' of fish-eating and bone tool–making could not be a coincidence and that the bone unipoints had been used in the construction of fishing nets. As an activity that would be conducted at the coastal shell middens (where many of the broken tools were recovered) but required raw materials collected from the interior to create (macropod long bones), this explanation neatly tied together the evidence found on both the coast and interior (Bowdler 1979, 1984). To explain the island-wide behavioural change, she suggests the following:

> In Tasmania, selective pressures in the north-west in mid-recent times may have led to the cessation of fishing ... A cosmology may have been erected to sustain this apparently aberrant decision, which spread to other parts of Tasmania where fishing was, in any case, of little importance. (Bowdler 1980:339)

This tradition of fish avoidance was still in effect at the time of European arrival, when it was noted with much interest. Indeed, the new arrivals were fascinated that while people would eat sea mammals, shellfish, crustacea, and stingrays, they would not consume scaled fish, even when offered (see discussion in Gill & Banks 1956).

If the bone tools were not used in constructing fishing nets, then what other functions may they have served? Jones (1971:522–4) suggested that they were used in making fur cloaks based on ethnographic comparison and visible use wear to the tips, an idea widely taken up by others (Cosgrove 1993; Gilligan 2007; Webb & Allen 1990). In 1990, Catherine Webb and Jim Allen published the results of a use wear study on the bone tools excavated from M86/2 and Bone Cave. Through comparison with experimentally produced use wear by Webb in 1987, Webb and Allen suggested that the M86/2 and Bone Cave unipoints were used 'for spearing furred animals, scraping the inner surface of skins and piercing dry skins' (Webb & Allen 1990:77). They also suggested that some artefacts were used as cloak toggles. This connection to skin-working and cloak toggles was continued by Gilligan (2007), who explored the presence and later absence of bone tools in Tasmania as tied to the manufacture of garments needed to protect the human body in extreme cold conditions. In an argument similar to Bowdler's (1979, 1984), Gilligan (2007) suggested that warmer climatic conditions after 10,000 years ago led to a reduction in the use of fur garments, as a result of which, 'in the absence of any other important function for these tools, their manufacture was gradually abandoned' (Gilligan 2007:107).

One of the few scholars to focus on the use of kangaroo incisors in technologies is Jane Balme. In her 1979 study of the fauna recovered from the famous southwest Western Australian site of Devil's Lair, Balme determined that there was a significant discrepancy between the number of upper and lower incisors from kangaroo found—that is, far too few lower incisors were present. She argued that this absence of evidence can be explained by the well-known and widespread use of macropod lower incisors in both tool and ornament manufacture—something that is clearly evident in Chapters 5 and 6 of this book. As such, her study provides an excellent example of how understanding the use of bone and tooth materials can help explain archaeological patterns without direct evidence for the technology itself being present.

1. WHY STUDY BONE AND TOOTH ARTEFACTS?

1990s–2010s: Akerman

No review of work on the use of hard animal materials in Indigenous Australia would be complete without acknowledging the enormous contribution of Kim Akerman. An anthropologist and archaeologist with extensive experience working with Indigenous communities, particularly in the Kimberley region, Akerman has been a touchstone for many researchers seeking to understand Indigenous technologies.

Akerman has produced numerous academic papers and books on different aspects of Indigenous Australian economic, material, and spiritual culture, his published works also including papers focused on bone and tooth artefacts (Akerman 1973, 1995, 2011, 2018). Three of these papers give a broad overview of the use of bone, tooth, and shell to create material culture in Australia (Akerman 1995, 2011, 2018), while his 1973 paper describes the unique 'charms' incorporating fossil giant marsupial teeth collected in Western Australia.

While bone and tooth artefacts continued to be regularly reported throughout the 1980s and beyond, it was not until the new millennium that a revival of interest in bone technologies was evident. This interest was driven by a new generation of researchers entering Australian archaeology, resulting in museum-curated archaeological collections being re-examined and published in several honours and PhD theses (Basiaco 2018; Francis 2002; Hutchinson 2012), as well as the postdoctoral work of this book's author (Langley 2018; Langley et al. 2016, 2021a, b).

At this time, with new archaeological sites being exposed every year and new methods and technologies that increasingly allow for the non-invasive study of often precious artefacts becoming available, we are now gaining unprecedented understanding of bone and tooth technologies on this ancient continent.

What types of materials are worked?

Most hard parts of an animal can be used for making artefacts. Bones, beaks, shells, teeth, quills, and claws have all found a use as either tools or ornaments in Australia. Some species are used commonly, and some are reserved for special objects, but all require precise knowledge of the animal and the pros and cons of working specific parts of their anatomy.

Usually, the largest animals in a landscape are those most frequently used by human inhabitants. Not only do such targets provide a great meal for a good number of people, but their bones and teeth come in large packages, making them exceptionally useful for making things. Upon reaching the Australian continent some 65,000 or more years ago, people were faced with eight to 14 types of megafauna (Wroe et al. 2013)—large-bodied animals such as the wombat-like *Diprotodon*, which was the size of a modern-day white rhino. Also roaming about were the giant kangaroos *Sthenurus* and *Protemnodon*, some of which were twice as large as those remaining today, and the giant birds known as *Mihirungs* or *Genyornis*. However, archaeologists are yet to find archaeological proof that these animals were hunted and artefacts were made from their bony parts. The only exceptions are two charms collected by anthropologist Kim Akerman during 1966–67 from the Kimberley in Western Australia. These charms incorporate fossil megafauna teeth, one from a *Zygomaturus* (wombat-like marsupial the size of a pygmy hippopotamus), which was set into a resin mount and attached to a string made from human hair. The other is a small emu feather wallet containing four

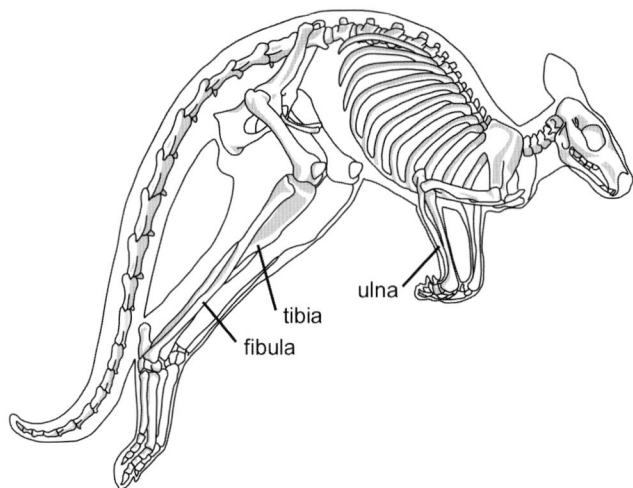

FIGURE 1.4. The most popular bones for making tools on the Australian continent are the long bones of macropods—especially the fibula, tibia, and ulna.

Sthenurus teeth (Akerman 1973). As these teeth were collected already fossilised (not fresh from hunted individuals), we continue to ask: where are the megafauna-based artefacts? Did cultural sanctions on the hunting and/or use of these animals exist? Have they not survived to discovery? Or have we simply just not found them yet?

We do know that kangaroo—which is currently the largest terrestrial animal on the Australian continent—bones have long been used to create tools and ornaments. The 46,000-year-old nose bone from Carpenters Gap 1 mentioned above provides the earliest example of an artefact made on kangaroo fibula. Indeed, kangaroo and wallaby ('macropod') long bones (see Figure 1.4)—their lower leg bones (fibula and tibia) and their lower arm bones (ulna)—are the most favoured bones for making artefacts through time and space on the Australian continent. As will be seen in Chapters 5 and 6, a great number and range of tools and ornaments have been and continue to be made on macropod long bone. And it is not surprising that it has found such widespread popularity. The sudden and frequent hard impacts that these bones endure throughout the life of the animal make them resilient—enabling people to make tough, long-lasting tools.

Another animal that provides large and long bones that have seen common use is the emu. As with macropods, it is their lower leg (tibiotarsus and tarsometatarsus) bones that are most useful (see Figure 1.5). In fact, the bones (both leg and wing), as well as the claws and beaks from a range of large birds, are commonly used to make various pointed tools and ornaments, as they are both lightweight (great for ornaments) and hollow (often useful).

Marine and freshwater animals are not ignored either. Stingrays are constantly growing and shedding their barbs, providing a ready-made barbed point. Jawbones of fish, as well as their spines, were identified as useful, as were the bones and shells of turtles and tortoises. Dugongs were hunted in the north, and their bones were incorporated into important social rituals. Whales that beached themselves along the coast were not wasted, their bones being used to create houses and large tools. Both individual

1. WHY STUDY BONE AND TOOTH ARTEFACTS?

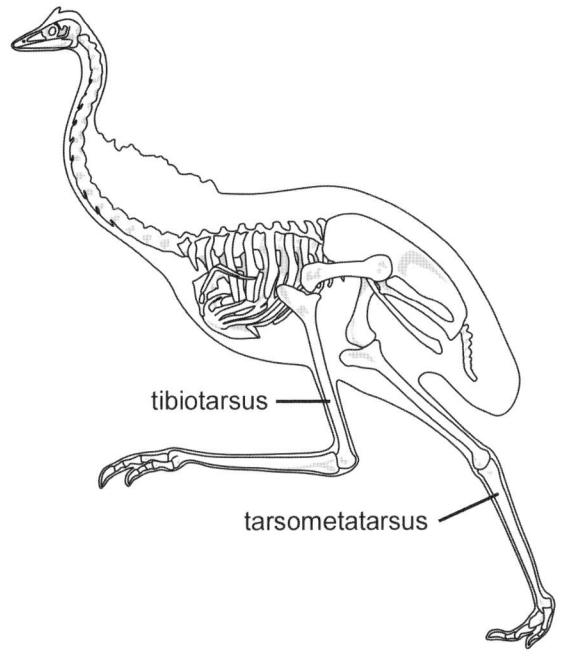

FIGURE 1.5. The long leg bones (tibiotarsus and tarsometatarsus) of emus have been used extensively in Indigenous material culture.

teeth and whole jaws of a range of mammals, reptiles, and fish became woodworking tools and attractive bright and shiny jewellery. These were set into plant-based resins and attached to plant, fur, or hair string for adorning the human body. Human bone was not left out. People used their teeth as vices in working both soft and hard materials, while arm bones were sometimes collected from the deceased and turned into powerful sorcery instruments (see 'Material culture made on human bone' in Chapter 5).

All in all, any hard material (osseous or keratinous) that could be turned into something useful, was turned into something useful.

Products of Australia: tools and ornaments

In an archaeological understanding of the past, anything made and used by humans might be classified as a 'tool'. A 'tool' is a device or implement used to conduct a particular function, which can be primarily economic, spiritual, or other. We usually think of handheld implements such as gardening shears or screwdrivers when we think of tools, but tools could also describe jewellery because it too has a purpose. For example, everyone from a Western background understands that a ring worn on the left hand is an indicator of marital status. That ring is sending a message to all those around us that we have made a commitment to our spouse and are no longer available to others as a life partner. As such, it is a device for sending social information. Having said this, most archaeologists and anthropologists divide a culture's 'techno-complex' (everything made and used by them) into 'tools' and 'ornaments' for ease of reference and discussion. This volume will do the same for one main reason: the jobs that ornaments do are often (but not always) quite different from the jobs performed by the tools used in catching, collecting, and preparing food, for example. Hence, separating them allows us to focus on issues specific to each grouping and facilitates a meaningful comparison of similar items in the chapters that follow.

What is in this book

The information presented in this book draws together all available archaeological data (artefacts recovered from archaeological sites), Australian museum collection data, and written observations by early European arrivals (ethnographic data) about bone, tooth, quill, and claw artefacts. Specifically, this work presents an archaeological view of bone and tooth material culture to support future studies into the hard animal material technologies of Indigenous Australia. Much is missing from this work—most obviously, the knowledge of the Indigenous communities and peoples. As such, it needs to be recognised that this volume is simply a starting point for investigating and understanding the hard animal material technologies of Australia.

It is important to note that, wherever possible, permissions were sought from Indigenous communities and representatives on museum advisory boards to view the information held by museums on their material culture. In most cases, the objects themselves were not viewed—only photographs and written data held in museum-curated databases.

Readers should be aware that some of the described material culture was made on human skeletal remains. These items are described in a separate section at the end of Chapter 5, 'Material culture made on human bone'.

The collections housed in seven Australian museums—the Australian Museum (Sydney), Museum Victoria (Melbourne), the South Australian Museum (Adelaide), the Queensland Museum (Brisbane), the Western Australian Museum (Perth), the National Museum of Australia (Canberra), and the Tasmanian Museum and Art Gallery (Hobart)—form the basis of the museum-based knowledge presented herein. These collections are far from being a comprehensive representation of the material culture that was and is utilised by Indigenous Australians from 1788. Instead, they reflect the movements of Europeans who took an interest in collecting the distinctive tools and ornaments of the land in which they lived and worked, with these gathered objects later forming the basis of the museum collections. As such, some places, peoples, and regions are better represented than others (see Figure 1.6).

To better understand this inherent bias, and to look for spatial patterns in the use of hard animal material tools and ornaments, the regions established by the Australian Institute of Aboriginal and Torres Strait Islander Studies (AIATSIS) for *The encyclopaedia of Aboriginal Australia* (Horton 1994) was utilised. These regions combine watershed basins with then-current knowledge of language, tribal, or nation groups. While some differences in regional representation are noted when only focusing on ornaments versus tools (see the start of Chapters 5 and 6), in general, central and far north Australia are much better represented in museums than is the very south. Tasmania, in particular, is under-represented in museum collections and, as such, most information regarding the use of osseous or keratin-based items for this region comes from ethnographic and archaeological data.

1. WHY STUDY BONE AND TOOTH ARTEFACTS?

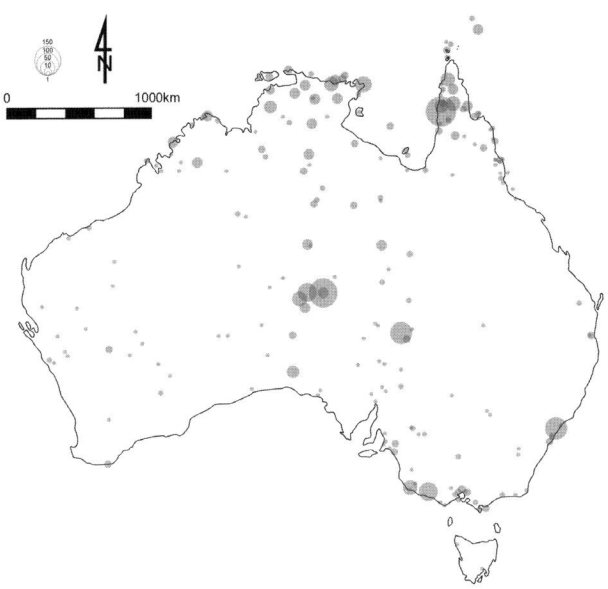

FIGURE 1.6. The size of the dots on this map correlate with how many tools or ornaments have been collected from particular locations and are now housed in the studied museum collections.

SUMMARY

- Osseous materials include bone, tooth, antler, and ivory.
- 'Hard animal materials' is a broader term that includes anything produced by an animal that might be called 'hard' and includes bone, tooth, quill, shell, horn, and claw.
- Bone and tooth tools and ornaments are the most abundant organic artefacts found in archaeological deposits, as they resist decay longer than 'soft' organic materials.
- A huge range of tools and ornaments was made on osseous materials around the globe, and archaeologists can use these forms to identify changes in human behaviour and populations. Bone and tooth technologies date back to more than 1.7 million years ago.
- Multiple types of humans, starting with some of our earliest ancestors, have utilised bone as tools.
- On the Australian continent, more than 95 per cent of Indigenous technologies were made from organic materials.
- Kangaroo and wallaby long bones have been most extensively used across the continent to make tools and ornaments.

CHAPTER 2
BONE TOOL ANALYSIS: IDENTIFYING MATERIALS AND PRODUCTION PROCESSES

Introduction

Objects made from hard animal materials such as bone, antler, teeth, quills, and claws have played an important and often central role in human cultures since hominins first realised their utility. To explore how this behaviour first developed and then became varied across space and time, archaeologists must be able to identify when an animal part has been intentionally modified or used by people. This chapter describes how osseous or keratinous artefacts are identified and their use and taphonomic histories determined.

Archaeozoology and osseous tool analysis

Archaeozoology or zooarchaeology is the analysis of animal bones, shells, scales, or any other part of an animal recovered from an archaeological context. Through the study of these remains, archaeologists can identify the past diets of the human inhabitants, explore animal domestication, and reconstruct the environment that surrounded the site. Frequently, it is during faunal analysis that potential tools and ornaments made from animal parts are first identified, whereupon they are sent to an osseous tool specialist for verification and study. On receiving a possible bone or tooth artefact, the specialist works to identify exactly what animal part the object is made on, how it has been modified by humans (or if, in fact, it has been modified by people at all), and what happened to it after it was deposited into the archaeological record. While both of these analysts work with hard animal materials, osseous tool specialists are focused more on how past people have selected and worked animal parts into technologies, while archaeozoologists explore the wider interaction of humans with the animals in the surrounding landscape.

By identifying the animals that worked bones originate from—what species and the age of the particular individual taken—we can learn about not only the types of animals that were favoured for sustenance and toolmaking but also what the environment was like at different periods in the past. Some species are able to live across multiple types of habitats, while others have very specific needs. It is these fussy others that are particularly useful, as their presence or absence in an archaeological site can indicate if the local environment was dry, wet, cold, hot, or somewhere in between.

Knowing something about what animals people were able to catch also helps us to understand the development of human behavioural complexity. Many animals are very fast or very dangerous, requiring hunters to know a lot about their behaviour to safely catch one; this capture often required several people working together. Working together involves complex social interactions to achieve something for the good of all those involved—and this capacity was not always present in the human mind. At the moment, it appears that while our bodies became anatomically modern around 300,000 years ago (Richter et al. 2017), it took at least 100,000 years for our minds to catch up (Marean et al. 2007).

We can also use the way things were made or their particular style to track the development and spread of ideas and populations (as discussed at the end of this chapter). The power of this type of information is well recognised by archaeologists and has, for example, allowed us to track the migration of *Homo sapiens* out of Africa and into Europe and Asia (Armitage et al. 2011; Cortés-Sánchez et al. 2019). It also allows us to identify ancient trade routes across and between continents. In Australia, we can use the appearance of artefacts made of particular raw materials—such as scaphopod or baler shells—to trace networks thousands of years old (McCarthy 1939). Being able to visualise these networks allows us to understand more about how past peoples understood and utilised the landscape and the resources it held.

Undertaking a new analysis

Most things that entered the archaeological record were no longer considered useful by those who discarded them. As things wore out and were thrown away, accidentally lost, or intentionally left behind, they decayed and completely disappeared—or they were buried, becoming the artefacts that archaeologists discover today. As such, it is very rare for archaeologists to find something that was made but not used, and so we are often working to understand the purpose of an artefact that looks very different from when it was newly created.

The key to unlocking the 'life history' of each artefact—from the selection of the raw material, shaping for use, use, repair, re-use, through to its being discarded—is understanding why someone would select a particular raw material, how that material behaves when worked or used in particular ways, and how it then decomposes over time in different environments. In the following sections, the different raw materials and processes that they commonly undergo when being transformed into and used as a tool, those that occur when they are left in the ground, and then those which happen after they are excavated are overviewed. This information is organised alphabetically for ease of reference.

Raw material properties

Anthropogenic or cultural alterations to osseous materials usually occur soon after the death of the animal because fresh bone and teeth are easier to work than older, dried specimens. However, older bone is sometimes preferentially selected and finished tools will require resharpening or repair as they dull or break. Fossilised bone and teeth are sometimes also collected, and determining whether a material was sourced fresh, aged, or already fossilised is important for understanding each technology.

Indeed, understanding the properties of each raw material utilised to make the tools and ornaments of Indigenous Australia is essential for understanding not only the people who made them but also the history of each individual artefact. Characteristics of raw materials are best learned through firsthand experimentation. Such knowledge would have been collected as the materials were initially found, and then passed down over generations within communities. Today, researchers essentially reinvent this knowledge base by working with the materials themselves wherever possible and by speaking with modern artists and toolmakers who hold such information.

Among archaeologists, there has been a tendency to regard organic materials, including bone, as inferior substitutes for stone (and later, metal). However, the mechanical properties that these organic materials possess are in many ways unique and remarkable and, frequently, supremely suitable for the tool that has been created. The material properties of different skeletal elements are diverse because these hard animal materials have evolved to serve an array of functions in life. In Australia, antler and ivory—raw materials that were hugely popular for creating tools, ornaments, and portable art pieces in Africa and Eurasia—were unavailable. Instead, the unique Australian environment provided ample hardwoods, as well as bizarre bounding animals with stress-resistant bones, perfect for making weapons and heavy-duty containers.

Not all the raw materials described below are *osseous*. The word 'osseous' comes from the Latin word for bone—*os*—and refers to the fact that the material contains osteons. Osteons are tube-like structures that contain blood vessels and are only found in areas of harder compact bone where they are aligned in the same direction along lines of stress to help the bone resist bending or fracture. Archaeologists use the term 'osseous' to refer to antler, bone, ivory, and teeth—all of which contain osteons—and they use the phrase 'hard animal materials' when including other keratin-based materials (horn, claw, quill). Below, each raw material commonly found in archaeological sites and museum collections of Australian Indigenous material culture is considered.

Bone

The light colour, light weight, and ability to be worked into almost any shape has seen bone widely used throughout the human past, including into the very recent manufacture of bone buttons, combs, hair pins, and the like by numerous European peoples (MacGregor 1985).

Bone tissue consists of organic (about 95 per cent collagen fibres) and inorganic (calcium phosphate mineral) components, which are intimately combined to create a solid but responsive structure. These two elements create the distinct mechanical properties that make bone most impressive as a raw material, with the collagen providing tensile strength while stiffness and compressive force are contributed by the calcium phosphate. Bone is actively constructed and remodelled throughout life as part of natural growth and in response to injuries. Within any bone, the tissue is woven into two main patterns: cortical bone and cancellous bone. 'Cortical bone' is the hard outer layer that is visible and accounts for most of the bone's mass. 'Cancellous bone', on the other hand, is often called 'spongy bone' and is a less dense network found at the ends of long bones, near joints and

2. BONE TOOL ANALYSIS

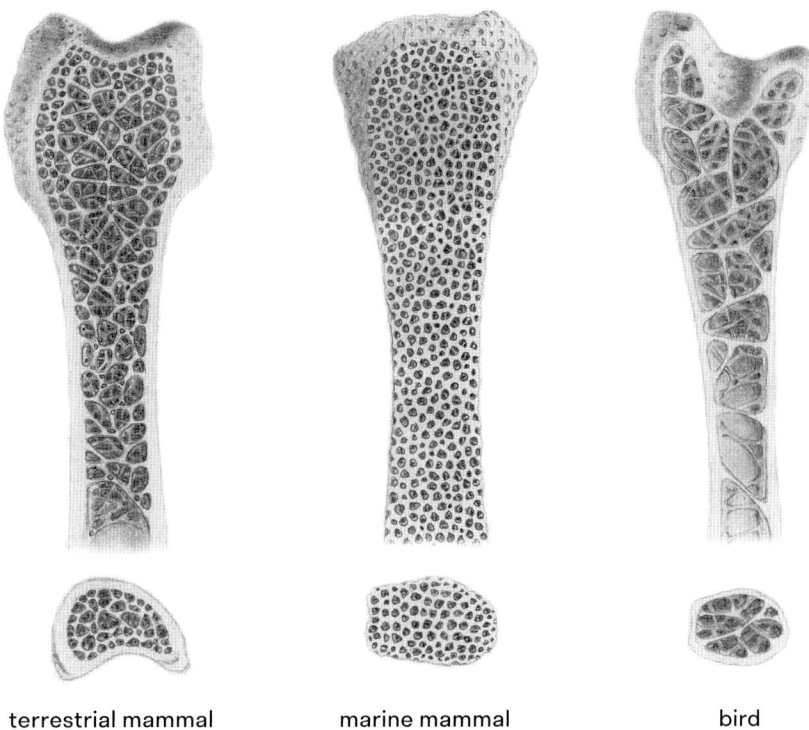

terrestrial mammal   marine mammal   bird

FIGURE 2.1. Different kinds of bone and their characteristics.

in the interior of vertebrae (Currey 2002; MacGregor 1985) (see Figure 2.1). As the spongy cancellous bone is weaker and net-like, it is the denser cortical bone with its hard and smooth surfaces that is typically targeted for the creation of material culture.

A classic 'in-field' method for identifying a fragment of bone previously taught in archaeological field schools was to lightly touch the piece to your tongue. If it sticks, it is bone. If not, it is stone or something else. Obviously, now it is known that residues and ancient DNA can survive many thousands of years and contaminating potentially important artefacts by testing them in this manner is unacceptable. Further, in contexts in which there is a high likelihood that the bone may be human, excavators need to be cognisant of respectfully interacting with that record. As such, the visual structure and weight of the piece should be utilised for initial in-field identification of raw material. While colour is often helpful in this regard, it can be deceptive, for if a bone piece has been burned (even incidentally) in the right conditions, it can appear black, grey, or blue rather than the white to light brown colour usually expected (Fernández-Jalvo & Andrews 2016). Similarly, what was originally a relatively smooth cortical surface can be pitted, scratched, and crumbly depending on the processes it has undergone in its depositional environment (see below).

Marine mammal bone is different from that of terrestrial animals, reflecting its aquatic adaptation and need for buoyancy control. It has no clear distinction between cortical and cancellous tissues and instead is almost completely homogeneous throughout its mass (Felts & Spurrell 1965). Visually, this type of bone has an appearance that is somewhere between the smooth cortical and spongy cancellous bone of terrestrial animals—having small cavities distributed equally across the surface (see Figure 2.1). Significantly, the degree of porosity found in the cancellous tissue can vary considerably across a single skeletal element (Buffrénil & Schoevaert 1998). Marine mammal bone is lighter than terrestrial bone of a similar size, a characteristic adapted for buoyancy and another useful indicator when attempting to identify species origin. Their light but strong and homogeneous characteristics make marine mammal bone particularly useful for making larger objects, as the 'module' (the basic package or core) is naturally thicker than what is usually found in land-based animals.

Bird bone is different again, usually being hollow with crisscrossing struts (see Figure 2.1). However, there are differences between types of birds: soaring birds have the most hollow bones, diving birds' bones are less hollow, and some species do not have many hollow bones at all (like penguins) (Kaiser 2007). However, even flightless birds, like the emu, still have hollow femurs and cervical vertebrae. Despite bird bone being thin-walled (one attribute to look for), it is structurally strong and stiff as a result of the internal struts designed to withstand bending and torsional stress during flight (Pennycuick 1967). Avian wing bones with their hollow interior have long been used by toolmakers as ready-made tubes. They have also been found particularly useful for tools required to be used with pressing and twisting motions, motions similar to movement in flight.

Fishbone is lighter and more fragile again (Szpak 2011). Even quite large fish hold some very small bones that are easily broken and can pass easily through archaeological sieves if a careful methodology is not implemented. Most commonly, it is the vertebrae that are used in material culture production in Australia (see Chapter 6). These bones are some of the most durable parts of fish skeletons and generally consist of a large disc-shaped central structure with a natural, centrally located perforation (which protected the spinal cord). This perforation can be used to create ready-made beads for some fish species, while others need to be widened to accommodate a string.

Bird beak

Although beaks vary significantly in size, shape, and colour, they all share a similar structure: two bony projections—the upper and lower mandibles—covered with a thin keratinised layer of epidermis (rhamphotheca). Most species of bird have two holes in their beak known as nares that lead to the respiratory system (Kaiser 2007). Luckily, the shapes and lightness of beaks often allow for easy identification among other skeletal elements.

Claw

Animal claws are not osseous but, rather, are made from keratin. Being keratinous, they are more susceptible to wear and post-depositional processes than similarly sized osseous parts, making them a very rare find in archaeological contexts. Along with various mammals and reptiles, birds also have claws; those found on birds of prey typically called 'talons'. Talons are particularly long and sharp, as they are the animal's primary tool for hunting.

As with bird beaks, the size, shape, and colour of claws and talons vary across species and reflect their use by the animal. In general, claws will appear to be black or a dark colour and weigh much less than an equal-sized osseous-based material (see Figure 2.2, colour section). If lightly dropped on a tabletop or against each other, they will make a high-pitched 'tinkling' sound.

Cassowary casque

Like claws, the large rudder-like crest that is so distinctive of the cassowary is made of keratin. The casque has an extensive network of blood vessels, which play a key role in keeping the bird cool in the hot and humid environments of North Queensland (see Figure 2.2, colour section). Identification of this element is based primarily on its size and overall form, but if broken into small parts, it may be difficult to determine without further intrusive analyses.

Echidna quill

The quills (or spines, spikes, etc.) of the echidna are incredibly sharp. These creamy-coloured and dark-tipped spines reach 50 millimetres in length and are made of keratin. While the quills are under neuromuscular control (the animal can make them stand up to protect itself from a predator), they are fixed and do not readily fall out. Consequently, the gathering of these spikes must be from a deceased animal.

Stingray barb

The spinal barb of stingrays is known by a number of terms, including 'barbs', 'spines', and 'stingers'. On a stingray, this barb may be located at the base of the tail (where it meets the body) or halfway down the tail. Stingrays continuously grow barbs, with barbs being shed as they get old and new ones growing in their place. Some stingrays will have between five and six barbs stacked on top of each other, with the new growing underneath the old. Barbs are covered with vasodentin, a cartilaginous material that can easily cut through skin, and typically feature two longitudinal grooves on the underside which store venom (see Figure 2.2, colour section). The overall morphology of barbs differs between species, varying in length as well as the presence and density of serrations down each side of the barb (Schwartz 2008, 2009).

Tooth

As teeth are structurally quite different from the rest of the skeleton, they are considered here separately. Teeth are a hard, calcified structure found in many vertebrates. Unlike bone, teeth are made up of multiple tissues of varying density and hardness that originate from the central germ layer (ectoderm) (Chauvière 2013). It is the outer, white and shiny dentin layer that appeals to our aesthetic sense, as well as their often-pleasing shapes and hard-wearing nature. Teeth are not only distinctive (making them valuable for identifying species present at a site) but also long lasting, even when they have been dislodged from their jaw. It is worth noting that in some contexts animal teeth have been referred to as 'ivory', particularly when talking about hippopotamus teeth, deer teeth, or whale teeth. Identifying the species origin of found teeth can be achieved through comparison with zooarchaeological collections.

Turtle shell

Turtle scutes, part of the hard upper carapace of the animal, are made from keratin and act to protect the underlying bony shell from scrapes and bruises. This keratinous section is the part of the turtle shell that has been primarily targeted for use in Indigenous Australia, though parts of the bony lower plastron are occasionally also found. Turtle scutes are somewhat translucent when held up to light and display varying shades of brown. Their extremely light weight relative to their size can also be used to identify this raw material. Turtle shell is widely available across Australia, with 28 species of freshwater turtle found on the continent and an additional six marine species found in coastal waters (Cogger 2014).

Identifying osseous (or keratin) artefacts

When determining if a hard animal material is in fact a piece of organic technology, the analyst must establish that at least one human has altered the piece either purely through use or by deliberate modification to create a certain form (both known as 'anthropogenic modification'). Modifications that transform a material into a tool or ornament can range from very minor alterations through to major working that completely transforms the piece into something physically unrecognisable from its original form. In some cases, an individual may simply have picked up a bone fragment left over from a meal, which fortuitously displayed a point or sharp edge, to use for a single task. Such tools are commonly known as an 'expedient technology' (see Figure 2.3). However, not all minimally altered tools are truly expedient. Some tools do not need to be heavily worked—or worked at all—to function as desired. At the other extreme, the creator may have had to extensively plan their actions to just obtain the desired raw material. In such cases, the resulting tool or ornament may then experience extra care ('curation') by its owners, resulting in a very long 'use life'. Both types of tools can be used by the same people, and both can tell us a great deal about how the community interacted with their environment and each other.

In any case, bone-working, like stone-working, is a 'reductive' technology: a tool is made through successive stages of material being removed either through use or to shape it into the desired form. Fragments flaked, cut, or scraped away are known as 'debitage', with these waste products appearing in the archaeological record alongside finished objects. By studying the debitage, as well as finished tools, archaeologists can reconstruct the whole sequence of actions required to make the object from start to finish. They are able to effectively get inside the mind of the person/s who made it and learn about the problems they were troubleshooting as they created the tool.

Types of bone- and tooth-working

Finding evidence for human interaction with a hard animal material requires a thorough examination of its surfaces for marks that may be attributed to manufacture and/or use ('microtraces'). For the most part, archaeologists are now able to differentiate these traces from each other and from those caused by natural agents, owing to extensive research programs conducted in the last few decades by archaeologists all over the globe. Initially developed by Sergeĭ Semenov (1964), 'use wear analysis' took off during the 1980s and has allowed us to understand the development of a huge range of

2. BONE TOOL ANALYSIS

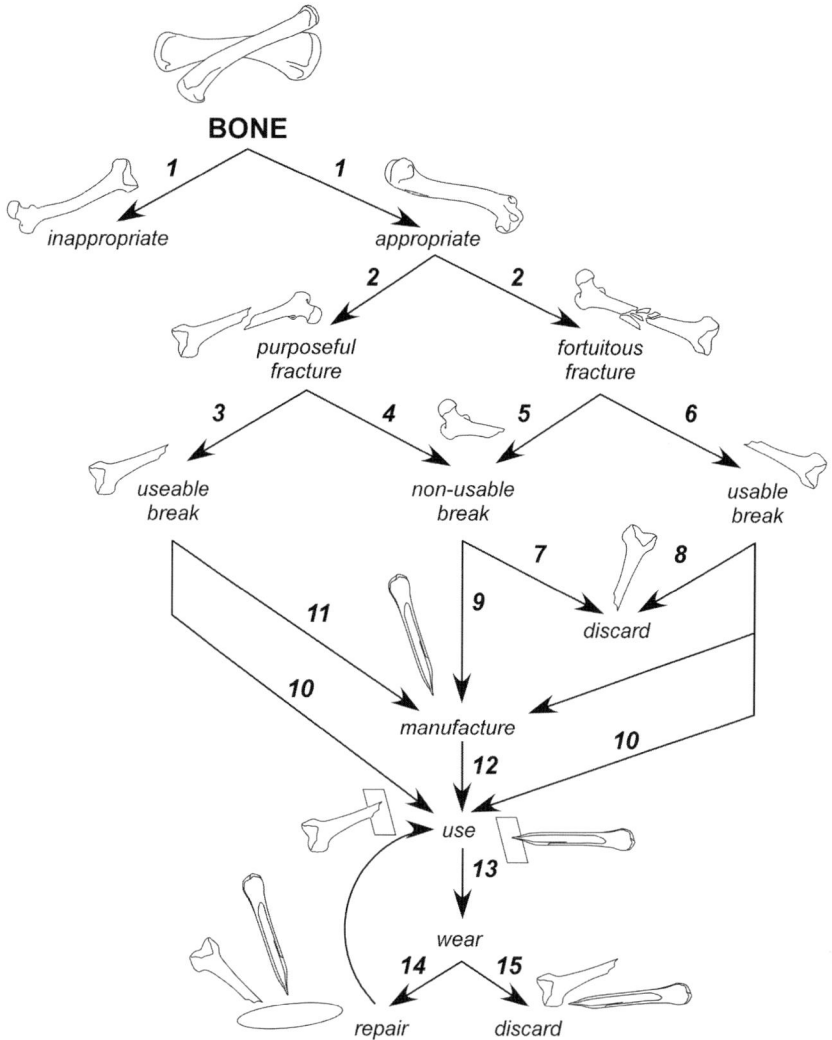

FIGURE 2.3. The creation and use life of a bone tool may have followed one of these possible pathways (altered after Lyman [1984:316]).

macroscopic and microscopic marks commonly observed on artefacts. Indeed, these studies have focused on understanding exactly how traces from manufacture and wear develop on different types of surfaces and why similarities or differences between raw materials and actions occur (e.g. Fernández-Jalvo & Andrews 2016; Fisher 1995; LeMoine 1994; Olsen & Shipman 1988; and in the Australian context: Fullagar 1986, 1991; Kamminga 1978). While archaeologists have made great strides in being able to separate anthropogenic from natural origins for different marks, identifying anthropogenic traces remains challenging in many respects. As such, research into this field continues and now constitutes an important line of evidence for investigating a variety of archaeological, paleoanthropological, and taphonomic issues.

The following sections outline characteristic marks that result from different methods of working and utilising bone. However, before moving through this information, the term 'striation' must be defined. Striations are a common feature of many types of manufacturing traces, use wear, and post-depositional damage, and 'striation' is a term utilised frequently in the archaeological literature. While a precise definition is debated, it is used here in the most general way to refer to any clear linear feature left as a result of material dislocation (after LeMoine 1991). Put another way, a 'striation' is a linear mark observed on a surface and caused by particles moving across that surface under some force. The length, depth, form, orientation, density, and arrangement of striations are all important aspects to note, and of all these features, it is the arrangement, distribution across the tool surface, and morphology of the individual striations that are the most diagnostic for ascertaining origin.

Chop marks

Chop marks differ from cut marks (see 'Cut marks' below; see Figure 2.4, colour section). A chop mark is characterised by a broad, relatively short linear depression that has a V-shaped cross-section (Binford 1981; Cook 1986; Fisher 1995; Noe-Nygaard 1989). They are sometimes described as 'notches' or 'clefts' (Perez et al. 2005). The main mark will often be surrounded by adhering or hinged flakes, have associated fracture lines, and reflect the removal of a significant amount of bone (Perez et al. 2005). Chop marks are usually repeated several times in one concentrated area and display transverse striations running down from the top of the mark towards the deepest section of the mark—reflecting the movement of the chopping implement (Greenfield 1999; Olsen & Shipman 1988). The morphology of a chop mark will depend on the chopping implement's striking edge, the force used, and the surface being struck (Fisher 1995). Differences in bone thickness result in different fracture patterns during percussion and must be kept in mind when comparing a series of marks (Bartram & Marean 1999). Chop marks can be confused with percussion pits (see 'Flaking' below).

Cut marks

Cut marks are created on an osseous surface by a sharp-edged implement cutting through or otherwise removing attached soft tissues (Fisher 1995; Potts & Shipman 1981; Shipman & Rose 1983a). Cut marks will only be created when a cutting implement comes into direct contact with an osseous surface, and experiments have shown that the periosteum (the dense fibrous membrane that covers the surfaces of bones) can impede the creation of cut marks (Shipman & Rose 1983a). This fact means that cutting away an animal's flesh will not always leave cut marks on its bones. A cut mark will travel along a flat surface but miss depressions or lower areas of bone. As such, you may observe a cut mark up to the edge of a depression and then see it pick up again on the other side.

Cut marks appear as an elongated, relatively narrow linear striation (Fisher 1995) (see Figure 2.4) and will reflect the shape of the implement's cutting edge, as well as the angle and force that the tool was applying to the bone (Greenfield 2006; Shipman & Rose 1983a). Indeed, in addition to it being possible to distinguish between different blade edges that were used, studies have suggested that the cross-section size and morphology of a cut mark may be able to indicate whether it was made using a particular type of

2. BONE TOOL ANALYSIS

tool (e.g. an unmodified flake, a retouched flake, a handaxe, or another specific type of stone tool) (Bello et al. 2009; Greenfield 2006; Jones 1980; Juana et al. 2010; Pobiner & Braun 2005).

Cut marks made with stone tools are typified by an asymmetrical V-shaped cross-section, with fine, parallel striations found within the cut mark boundaries (termed 'internal microstriations') (Shipman & Rose 1983a). They will also often display 'shoulder effect', 'barbs', and/or 'splitting' (Eickhoff & Herrmann 1985; Shipman & Rose 1983a), though these marks may be absent. Importantly, the absence of these marks does not necessarily signal that it is *not* a legitimate cut mark. Shoulder effect can be explained as small Hertzian cones that have chipped off the boundary of the cut mark, caused by contact between the bone surface and the 'shoulder' of the cutting implement. These Hertzian cones generally only appear on one side of the cut mark (usually the shallower side) but can occur on both (Bromage et al. 1991). Displaced bone may build up to form a raised shoulder alongside the cut. A barb is a striation or set of closely spaced parallel striations that diverge at an acute angle from the end of an associated striation. Barbs can occur at either the beginning or the end of a cut mark and appear to be formed by 'small, inadvertent motions of the hand either in initiating or in terminating a stroke' (Shipman & Rose 1983a:66). Splitting, on the other hand, can take various forms though it often 'expresses itself as one or more lines that originate from the main mark and take a diverging course' (Eickhoff & Herrmann 1985:267-9). Splitting, unlike barbs, usually occurs at just one end of a cut mark. All these characteristics result from the harder stone surface removing and displacing bone material as it travels. The direction in which the cutting edge was dragged can be determined by examining the interior walls and floor of the cut mark, where small flakes or smears of bone will have lifted in the opposite direction of the cut (Bromage & Boyde 1984). Finally, cut mark size may be influenced by the effort necessary to skin, disarticulate, and deflesh differently sized animals (Merritt 2012).

Experimentation by Buc (2011) found that cut marks made by a shell tool differ slightly from those made with a stone implement. Shell blades will create a cut mark whose walls are smooth and staggered with an open V-shaped cross-section. Some types of shell may produce a 'double-track groove' (Choi & Driwantoro 2007). Different again are bamboo knife cut marks, which are usually faint with the smooth outer surface of the bamboo creating a groove and displacing bone material to the outside of the cut mark (Spennemann 1986, 1987; West & Louys 2007). The opposing fibrous side of the bamboo knife does not cut into the bone as deeply, creating an asymmetrical cross-section to the cut mark. Within the boundaries of the cut mark, a series of step-like striations on the shallow side of the cut (corresponding with the fibrous side of the bamboo knife) will be evident (West & Louys 2007). Metal knives similarly present different characteristics (Blumenschine et al. 1996; Greenfield 1999; Olsen 1988). In their case, cut marks tend to have deeper profiles that are steeply sided and present a V-shaped cross-section, unless the knife is dull, in which case the cross-section will be ⊔-shaped (Greenfield 1999). The cut mark can be deep and narrow or deep and wide depending on the type of blade used and may present no striations within the cut mark boundaries or striations of very uniform depth and spacing if the knife is serrated (Greenfield 1999). In general, a metal cutting edge will produce a cleaner cut mark than that produced with stone, shell, or bamboo knives.

Important to note is that linear striations produced by trampling can be confused with cut marks without careful examination (Olsen & Shipman 1988). Similarly, very fine vascular grooves on bone surfaces, created by contact between the bone and tiny blood vessels and sometimes accompanying nerves, can be confused macroscopically with cut marks. Vascular grooves can be identified from their U-shaped cross-section, smooth walls, and high variability in their form on a single bone piece (d'Errico & Villa 1997; Shipman & Rose 1984). Their occurrence at anatomical positions that feature major blood vessels is also a giveaway (Morlan 1984). From this brief overview, it should be evident that identifying true cut marks can be a difficult endeavour. As such, the application of new and developing 2D and 3D techniques is essential to accurate cut mark identification and description (see Courtenay et al. 2018 for discussion).

Drilling

Drilled holes in osseous materials can be achieved with either stone or tooth-tipped drills, the drill head moving back and forth while constant downwards pressure is applied. Holes produced by drilling with a stone point exhibit characteristics that distinguish them from holes made by natural processes that produce pits or punctures (see sections below).

Drilling can be achieved unifacially (from one side) or bifacially (from both sides), with the cross-section of the perforation indicating which may be the case. Unifacially drilled perforations will exhibit a wide U-shaped cross-section, while those drilled from both sides will appear as an hourglass (sometimes called a 'biconical perforation') (Olsen 1979). The U and hourglass shape is produced by a tapering drill tip, and concentric striations running around the inside of the perforation reflect the turning of the implement. These concentric striations are the key characteristic that indicates the use of a rotating drill. Werner and Miller (2018) found in their experiments that you can differentiate hand drilling (when a tool is held directly in the hand and used by twisting the wrist back and forth) from rotary drilling (using a mounted drill bit rolled between the hands or using a bow) by the specific traces left behind. Hand drilling is characterised by striations that do not form complete circles, the presence of a notch within the aperture, and the presence of 'waving' inside the aperture (see Figure 2.5, colour section). This type of drilled aperture has been called 'perforation by demi-rotation' by White (2007). Rotary drilling, on the other hand, can be distinguished by crisp, even cup perimeters, smooth cup walls, and concentric and complete striations within the aperture. These shapes will not only be dictated by the profile of the drill used to create the perforation but also be altered by different degrees of use wear. More specifics regarding drilling terminology are provided in Chapter 3.

Flaking

The simplest way to flake bone is to snap it between the hands ('flexion') if it is thin enough to do so. Often, this straightforward approach removed the desired section—called a 'blank'—from its 'parent bone', allowing it either to be put into immediate use (if no other changes were required) or to move through to additional modifications (see Figure 2.6, colour section).

Additionally, bone, like stone, can be shaped using direct percussion. That is, it can be struck with a hard object to remove flakes. This approach has been extensively studied in terms of determining how humans extracted bone marrow and broke up carcasses for consumption throughout human evolution (e.g. Pickering & Egeland 2006), as well as how people used unmodified cobbles or hammerstones to break apart and

2. BONE TOOL ANALYSIS

TABLE 2.1. Terminology for bone flaking (after Vettese et al. 2020).

TERM	DEFINITION
adhering flake	A flake whose fracture line is incomplete and is thus still attached to the parent bone.
	The flake has a semicircular shape visible on the critical surface and can sometimes show an inner conchoidal or semicircular scar.
crushing mark	A roundish lesion in the cortical bone formed by multiple dented-in adhering flakes.
flake	Bone flakes generally share the same characteristics as lithic flakes. Bone flakes may display a platform at the impact point, a percussion bulb below the platform, some ripple or hackle marks originating at or near the bulb, greater breadth than length, or absence or reduction of the cortical surface.
percussion notch	Found on a fracture edge and is the negative flake scar.
percussion pit	Roughly round or linear superficial pits that appear on the cortical surface.
	Percussion pits may appear as ovoid pits (with a round shape) or triangular or linear pits.
percussion groove	Superficial grooves to the cortical bone surface that are more elongated that percussion pits.

shape osseous materials for technology manufacture (e.g. Pétillon & Ducasse 2012; Sano et al. 2020; Zutovski & Barkai 2016).

'Percussion marks' are caused by uneven surfaces on the hammerstone. 'Percussion notches' occur as part of the flaking process and can be used to determine the anthropogenic origin of bone flakes (Binford 1981; Blumenschine & Selvaggio 1988; Capaldo & Blumenschine 1994; Pickering & Egeland 2006).

Depending on the type of bone being worked (terrestrial mammal, bird bone, marine mammal, etc.), the force which is brought to each strike, and the condition of the bone when it is being flaked, differently sized and shaped flakes will be produced (Davis 1985; Pickering & Egeland 2006). It is important to note that it is not only 'fresh' bone that can be flaked but also bone that has undergone either slight or moderate weathering (Bonnichsen 1979; Haynes 1991; Morlan 1984). Flakes produced on these latter types of bone will slightly differ from those made on fresh ('green') bone. When a bone is fresh, it is somewhat flexible and resilient to impact, though when rested on an anvil and sharply struck with a hard object, it still fractures in a predictable fashion (Bonnichsen 1979; Bonnichsen & Will 1980; Morlan 1983; Pickering & Egeland 2006). These fractures are conchoidal (smooth, rounded, and dome-shaped) and produce both a 'flake' and a corresponding 'flake scar'. These flakes, like those found in stone, will usually have a 'platform' at the impact point and a corresponding 'bulb of percussion', the flake scar displaying the negative image of the flake removed (Fisher 1995). As is sometimes the case with stone, these characteristics may be absent or not clearly identifiable (Morlan 1980). The tube shape of long bones (which are most commonly utilised for tool manufacture) influences the shape of the bone flake. Typically, the flake will expand laterally (sideways) below the impact point and along the interior wall of the tube to a width that exceeds the flake length. As such, bone flakes are typically wider than they are long, with the flake scar having a semicircular shape (Fisher 1995) (see Figure 2.5, colour section).

Recently, bone technology analysts have been working to standardise how each of these marks is described for flaked bone (see Table 2.1) (Vettese et al. 2020).

The more precise the working needs to be, the more skill that is required by the toolmaker. Indeed, some bone points are so small and finely worked that a different approach to flaking is used. By holding the bone blank in the hand and using a pointed bone (usually made from macropod ulna), tooth, or stone tool called a 'pressure-flaker' in the other hand, the worker can press the tip of the pressure-flaker against the bone edge they want to adjust and slowly increase the force applied until a tiny flake snaps off. This 'pressure-flaking' method is used to create the iconic stone Kimberley points of North West Australia and is just as effective at making miniature bone points for fishing spears (see Chapter 5).

Grinding

Grinding—where the bone or tooth is repeatedly rubbed against a hard and coarse surface (like a sandstone block)—is a very common technique for shaping tools into their final form. Easy to do, grinding can create both exceptionally sharp points and regularly shaped curves. The use of grinding to shape an osseous surface is identified by the presence of characteristic fusiform (long, spindle-shaped) striations whose breadth, depth, and cross-section depend on the hardness and topography of the grinding material, whether an additional abrading agent (such as ochre or sand) was used and how much pressure was applied by the toolmaker (d'Errico et al. 1984) (see Figure 2.5, colour section).

A different grinding method, observed and reported in Australia, is to repeatedly thrust a flaked bone point into sandy soil until it becomes even and smooth (Bird & Beeck 1980). In such cases, the sand grains are then acting as the grindstone, with finer-grained sands able to smooth the bone surface until it is smooth and glossy.

Polishing

Polish is created by extensively smoothing a surface (Fullagar 1991). Polish, strictly speaking, is a special case of abrasion, though analysts tend to restrict the term 'abrasion' to natural processes (see 'Abrasion: sediments, water, and tongues'). Humans can create polish both intentionally and unintentionally. Intentional polish is usually achieved by rubbing the bone item between the hands (where your sweat and the dirt on your hands act as an abrasive) or by rubbing powdered ochre, fine sand, or another light abrasive agent against the bone until all surface irregularities have been reduced to a common level. In experimental studies, the polishing of bone has been achieved by using a leather cloth in conjunction with ochre powder (Nivens 2020; Pargeter & Bradfield 2012), while Heckel (2009b) found that using a leather cloth in conjunction with wet hematite powder polished a small surface area, including the erasure of shallow tool marks, in about 20 minutes. Polish can also be created by taphonomic agents (discussed below), and as such, it is important that other indicators of shaping are present to confirm an anthropogenic origin for polish.

Sawing

Where more controlled sectioning of a bone or tooth blank is required, the toolmaker may select sawing or 'persistent cutting' (Fisher 1995:17). Saw marks are characterised by multiple, closely spaced, parallel or near-parallel cut marks that cumulatively create a single, deep incision (Fisher 1995) (see Figure 2.4). Sawing usually travels around the circumference of a long bone (for example) until the bone surface is thin enough to be snapped.

Scraping

Scraping is often used to remove the periosteum from an area of bone to be flaked. Removing the periosteum is required, as it creates a slippery surface causing the cutting or sawing tool to slip over the bone surface. Further, the periosteum is removed to achieve greater control over breakage (Binford 1981). Scraping is also used to shape osseous surfaces as an alternative to grinding. Scrape marks are produced by the dragging of a sharp-edged (usually stone) tool across the surface being worked. Scrape marks can be identified by their set of multiple, closely spaced, parallel or near-parallel striations that are elongated, linear, and relatively narrow (Fisher 1995; Noe-Nygaard 1989; Potts & Shipman 1981) (see Figure 2.4). Scrape marks will often display 'chattermarks' or 'chattering', which are a series of regular undulations that run perpendicular to the striation but are found within the bounding of the scrap mark (Newcomer 1974).

Wear and damage from use

As an osseous object is used, its surfaces will accrue wear and damage. The types and severity of this wear depend on the specific use/s of the tool and the intensity of that use. Four main processes are thought to be involved in the development of wear (LeMoine 1994): (1) abrasive processes, (2) adhesive processes, (3) fatigue, and (4) chemical or corrosive wear. More than one of these processes may—and usually does—impact an osseous artefact, complicating the story that its surfaces tell. Abrasive wear is caused by friction between two surfaces, one harder than the other, which results in the removal of material from the osseous surface. Adhesive wear is effectively the opposite of abrasive wear. In this second process, material from one surface is transferred to the other (usually onto the tool surface, but transfer can go both ways). Fatigue is the failure (breakage) of an artefact owing to repetitive stress over time. And finally, chemical or corrosive wear is the result of chemical reactions between the artefact surface and its environment. Experimental programs designed to differentiate wear patterns left behind by different (and specific) activities have found that wear patterns can be identified with more or less certainty (e.g. Backwell & d'Errico 2001; Buc 2011; Gates St-Pierre 2007; LeMoine 1994). The most common causes of wear and damage to bone and tooth technologies are outlined in the following sections.

Cutting

Using an osseous or keratin blade to cut softer materials (which can include meat, vegetable matter, skins, etc.) commonly results in micro-flaking (tiny flakes), rounding (high edges of material smoothed over), and polishing (creating a homogeneous surface) of the working edge (see Figure 2.7, colour section). While the faces of the blade may be in contact with the material being cut, it is the working edge that bears the brunt of the force applied. Thus, the sides (faces) of the knife will accrue wear much more slowly than the working edge and there is usually a clear demarcation between worn and unworn areas of the cutting implement (LeMoine 1991, 1994). As wear accrues, the cutting edge dulls, requiring that it be resharpened regularly. Resharpening may remove most, if not all, traces of previous use, in which case, the overall morphology of the artefact may be the only clue as to the extent of its use life.

Digging

Digging activities, whether digging out termite mounds or digging out tubers, produces a localised wear pattern that includes a single rounded extremity that is smoothed and polished, with striations covering the worn tip (including in concavities) running parallel or sub-parallel to the long axis of the tool (see Figure 2.7, colour section). These striations decrease in density as you move away from the digging tip towards the proximal (held) extremity (Backwell & d'Errico 2001; Langley et al. 2021a; Semenov 1964). How far the striations travel up the shaft of the tool will depend on the depth to which it was repeatedly plunged into the sediment, with striation characteristics dependent on the particle sizes and coarseness of the sediment in which it was used (Backwell & d'Errico 2001).

Direct pressure

Here, the action of carefully placing an osseous edge against a harder material to alter that surface—that is, pressure-flaking—is referred to specifically. Pressure-flaking results in some of the same use wear described below for both impact and piercing activities, specifically crushing, chipping, and rounding. This damage will be restricted to the tip or working edge of the implement.

Handling

Simply handling a tool will create wear. Handling or 'prehensile' wear on osseous tools generally consists of a polish developing on the part that is in extended contact with the hand. In this case, the polish develops unintentionally. Friction from the hand in conjunction with sweat, particles from dirt, and whatever substance the tool is working against together work to smooth and round uneven surfaces of the tool surface (Frison 1982; Shipman & Rose 1988) (see Figure 2.7, colour section). Polish can appear in two forms: as 'invasive' and as 'non-invasive'. Invasive polish covers all or most of the worn surface, including the sides and even bottoms of striations. Invasive polish is usually produced by a soft material that is able to conform to the contours of the surface. A non-invasive polish is just the opposite, being a polish that does not conform to the tool surface and instead only affects high points. As the polish develops, it can wear these high points down until it covers the surface evenly. Non-invasive polish is produced most often by hard, rigid materials (LeMoine 1991). Some discolouration or staining of the handheld portion of the tool may be present.

2. BONE TOOL ANALYSIS

Hafting

When an osseous tool is set into a fixed haft or handhold, the part of the tool covered by that haft will accrue wear different from that experienced by the exposed and active edge. Specifically, the raw materials used to construct the haft, along with how strong the hold is, will result in the smoothing of the hafted portion with isolated striations (Buc 2011). Compression of the hafted area may also be present if a ligature was used to bind the extremity of the tool (Langley et al. 2021b) (see Figure 2.7, colour section). Frequently, the resin, wax, or other types of mastic used to haft an artefact incorporated colourants like ochre or were themselves colourful and therefore often leave detectable staining on the hafted surface (Allain & Rigaud 1986; Langley et al. 2021b).

Impact

'Impact' is the damage sustained by projectile points. Projectile points can be defined as the distal extremities (tips) of weapons that are launched at a target in either hunting or conflict. Projectile points can be hafted using a fixed (as in a spear tip) or mobile (as in a harpoon) fashion, with the force of impact creating wear on both the distal (active) and proximal (hafted) extremities. For osseous projectile points, the distal extremity will suffer crushing, chipping, mushrooming, rounding, and larger impact fractures that may appear as bevel, step, cleavage, or splinter fractures (see Figure 2.8, colour section) (Arndt & Newcomer 1986; Bradfield & Lombard 2011; Pétillon 2006; Pokines 1998; Stodiek 2000). The proximal extremity, on the other hand, suffers crushing, chipping, mushrooming, and rounding owing to the proximal edge being jarred against the wooden (or other material) foreshaft or shaft on impact (Bradfield & Lombard 2011; Langley et al. 2021b; Pétillon 2006; Stodiek 2000). 'Crushing' is the displacement of bone material, often where the cortical bone has been displaced into the spongy bone (Pétillon 2006; White 1992b). 'Chipping' refers to the micro-fracturing of the tip edge (Buc 2011; Legrand 2007; Pétillon 2006), while 'mushrooming' occurs when the extremity becomes deformed under pressure from impact and takes on a flattened aspect (Pétillon 2006). Generally, bone (as a raw material) does not exhibit mushrooming. Finally, 'rounding' is the result of repetitive wear, which compacts material down to form a smoothed surface (Buc 2011; Legrand 2007; Semenov 1964). Projectile points can exhibit none, one, or several of these wear traces at any one time. Larger fractures of the proximal edge can also occur, especially if the point is not fixed adequately and shifts on impact (Bergman 1987; Knecht 1991a, 1993, 1997; Stodiek 2000).

Piercing

Piercing of materials can use a longitudinal motion of the tool, which results in striations following the longitudinal orientation of the tool (Gates St-Pierre 2007) and may also include a rotating motion (to help it pierce), which results in transversally oriented striations (d'Errico et al. 2003) (see Figure 2.8, colour section). The repeated pressure on the distal tip results in step and bevel fractures, as well as small (less than six millimetres long) unifacial spin-offs (Bradfield & Brand 2015). In experiments, Bradfield and Brand (2015) found that dry, brittle bone was more susceptible to fracture, a finding supported by experiments undertaken by the author with Quandamooka artist Kyra Mancktelow, where surface-collected kangaroo fibulae were much easier to work but accrued wear and fractured much faster than fresh kangaroo fibula.

Experiments using bone or antler points to pierce a range of raw materials, including fresh and dry skins and a range of different plant fibres, have determined that the raw material pierced can be narrowed down somewhat according to the wear pattern presented. This identification is possible because raw materials generally differ in their abrasive properties, these properties producing the use wear on the bone awls at different rates and extents. Piercing of hides or plant fibres is found to produce rounding and polishing of the distal extremity (Bradfield & Brand 2015; Buc 2011; Gates St-Pierre 2007; Legrand 2007; LeMoine 1991), with Bradfield and Brand's (2015) experimental series finding that polish generally did not extend below about 50 millimetres from the tip, nor erase traces of manufacture. Buc (2011) found that for both skin and rush piercing, the sides and face of the bone point became rounded, though fresh and dry skins produced different patterns of striations (also shown by LeMoine 1991 and Legrand 2007). Piercing of dry skins produced deep and closely spaced striations, while piercing of fresh skins produced shallower and more dispersed striations. Importantly, Buc demonstrated that a bone awl used to pierce fresh skins for an extended period began to display a striation pattern more similar to that seen in awls used on dry skins, highlighting the fact that confidently identifying the specific use of a tool with an extended use life may be complicated. Another important insight is that the lubrication provided by wet materials (like fresh skins or plant fibres) will reduce the amount of wear that builds up on the tool surface (LeMoine 1991). These factors complicate the rebuilding of implement use histories; however, in general, skin-working produces striations that are long, deep, and crossed, whereas plant-working (with its softer surfaces) produce striations that are shorter, shallower, and more parallel in aspect (Buc 2011; d'Errico et al. 2003).

Scraping, stretching, and smoothing

A large part of skin-working is the scraping away of the inner membrane, stretching the skin for drying, and the smoothing of its surface during the drying process to make it pliable. These actions result in the same types of use wear observed for piercing instruments, as essentially the same forces are applied to the osseous point, though over a wider surface area, and as such, assessing the morphology of the active edge is important. Skin-working tools will generally present a spatulate-form distal extremity that has been flattened and smoothed. Experimental studies have found that the working edge of a skin-working tool will exhibit a flattened and smoothed edge some two to three millimetres wide (Backwell & d'Errico 2004) and exhibit either deep, crossed, and closely spaced striations (more likely dry skins) or shallower, sub-parallel, and dispersed striations (more likely fresh skins) (Buc 2011; Legrand 2007; LeMoine 1991). If the tool has been used in flaying, the working edge will present a smooth edge with polishing of the prominent areas, along with individual sub-parallel grooves on the flat underside of the tool (Backwell & d'Errico 2004).

Various plant stems and leaves are also processed by scraping their surfaces, and these activities create striations very similar to those made in scraping skin: very narrow striations that are smooth, straight, and largely parallel (Buc 2011). Backwell and d'Errico (2004) similarly found that using a bone tool for bark removal created a smooth surface covered by individual sub-parallel striations. One difference that may be helpful in determining whether it was skins or plant fibres being worked is that the demarcation between the worn and unworn areas on tools used on plant fibres is usually sharp, whereas for a tool used to scrape and stretch a skin it is less obvious owing to the tool being pressed into the surface of the skin with more force (LeMoine 1994).

Lying on the ground: biting, gnawing, and weathering

It is not only the deliberate actions of people that alter the organic surfaces of bony materials. A range of natural processes will act to mark surfaces, including while lying on the ground surface, during the process of burial, while buried in the ground, during excavation, and even during analysis by researchers. An artefact may bear the marks of some or all these processes, and each must be recorded and identified if researchers are to reconstruct the history of each object. Similarly, natural agents can shape hard animal materials in ways that make them appear superficially like human-made tools or ornaments, and as such, separating real artefacts from 'pseudotools' is a crucial part of analysing an osseous assemblage.

Abrasion: sediments, water, and tongues

Abrasion can be defined as the erosion of a surface by a harder material through physical force (Bromage 1984). For osseous artefacts, abrasion is characterised by the rounding, smoothing, and polishing of surfaces and edges (Behrensmeyer 1982) (see Figure 2.9, colour section). Striations, sometimes visible to the naked eye but usually with the help of a microscope (Andrews & Cook 1985; Shipman & Rose 1983b), along with near-universal rounding and smoothing of the piece in question, are the most prominent evidence for abrasion. Polish may or may not be present on abraded pieces and is created by the smoothing of the bone surface via the removal of particles on high surfaces or the compaction and smearing of bone, resulting in a gloss or sheen (Bromage 1984; Shipman & Rose 1988). This process results in the loss of surface detail (Behrensmeyer 1990) and can superficially appear to be use-related wear to an untrained eye.

The most common cause of abrasion for artefacts lying on the ground (as opposed to within the ground; see 'Abrasion (again)' below) is wind-borne particles that effectively 'sand blast' the surface (Shipman 1981). Similarly, artefacts within streams, rivers, or other bodies of water will suffer abrasion as sediment particles within the water move past them (Behrensmeyer 1982; Bromage 1984; Rick 2002). Carnivores licking the surfaces of bones also cause abrasion, and bones located within their dens that are incidentally kicked about again suffer abrasion (Haynes & Stanford 1984; Oliver 1994). Determining these origins of visible abrasion requires consideration of the find context and comparison to the rest of the recovered faunal assemblage.

Digestion

Bones ingested by mammals, raptors, and other animals will be abraded as a result of stomach acids. Digested bones can enter sites after being regurgitated or having completely passed through an animal's digestive tract, with such bones typically exhibiting widespread abrasion, dissolving, scalloping, smoothing, thinning, perforations, and polish (e.g. Andrews & Evans 1983; Cruz-Uribe 1991; Fisher 1981; Hockett 1996; Marshall & Cosgrove 1990; Rensberger & Krentz 1988) (see Figure 2.9, colour section). Typically, it is smaller bone fragments that will have been subjected to these processes, owing to their need to fit within the animal's digestion system. While some of these modifications may superficially resemble human alteration of the bone, digestion is usually identifiable by the extent of damage and the presence of several of the above-mentioned attributes (Fisher 1995; Villa & d'Errico 2001).

Fracture

Organic materials can be fractured by agents other than humans and animals. Skeletal elements moved around the landscape in floods, landslides, rockfall, and even volcanic eruptions can all result in fractures, with fracture types mimicking deliberate blows from a human (d'Errico & Backwell 2003a; Lyman 1984; Oliver 1989). Indeed, volcanic eruption was found to mimic anthropogenic rounding and chipping of flaked long bones (Lyman 1984), and as such, fractured bone requires careful examination of its context and the presence of additional use-related traces to identify its anthropogenic origin.

Gnawing by rodents and herbivores

Rodent gnawing is one of the easiest traces to identify on osseous materials, owing to distinctive dentition anatomy and the well-understood feeding behaviour of these animals. The characteristic dragging use of their paired incisors along bone surfaces results in paired, broad, U-shaped grooves, with a rodent typically beginning to gnaw at one focal point before expanding outwards, creating a large scalloped-out area (Lyman 1994) (see Figure 2.9, colour section). Chattermarks can also sometimes be present within rodent toothmarks (Shipman & Rose 1983a). The size of the grooves can indicate the overall size of the rodent actor, with numerous tiny to very large rodents all known to gnaw on bones.

Herbivores also frequently chew on bones (known as 'osteophagia') to consume minerals (Hutson et al. 2013). The bones that are picked up by a herbivore are found on the surface, with the resulting damage including grooving, pitting, crushing, and polish to the bone surface (Cáceres et al. 2011; Haynes 1991; Hutson et al. 2013). Herbivore toothmarks typically do not closely resemble cut marks or other human modifications to bone and are typified by sinuous lines with U-shaped cross-sections that frequently overlap (Hutson et al. 2013; Langley 2020).

Insect activity

Insects can create striations, grooving, pitting, and perforations in bone surfaces as part of their search for nutrients or nesting behaviour (Backwell et al. 2012; Behrensmeyer 1978; Go 2018; Roberts et al. 2003; Watson & Abbey 1986). The appearance of these traces depends on the type of insect at work, with much research still required to confidently tell many of these agents apart (Backwell et al. 2012). Insect-created perforations usually exhibit dozens of tiny grooves leading into the hole (Fernández-Jalvo & Andrews 2016), while termites are known to create striations and 'star-shaped' pits (Backwell et al. 2012; Pomi & Tonni 2011). Insect damage is often visible to the naked eye and is usually quite easy to distinguish from anthropogenic processes.

2. BONE TOOL ANALYSIS

Tooth marks from carnivores

Unlike gnawing, tooth impressions and punctures can be harder to identify on bone surfaces and can be (and have been) mistaken for anthropogenic cut marks, percussion marks, or perforations (d'Errico & Villa 1997). Tooth marks are typically characterised by scores, pits, punctures, and furrows, though the exact shape and size of each mark vary according to the shape of the tooth cusp that created the mark, which in turn varies by tooth type (incisor, canine, premolar, molar) and by species (Binford 1981; Haynes 1983; Shipman & Rose 1983a). 'Scores' are marks whose length is about three times longer than their width (Domínguez-Rodrigo & Piqueras 2003), have a high breadth to depth ratio, a U-shaped cross-section, and rarely have microstriations present within their boundary (Blumenschine et al. 1996). Tooth scores tend to have a uniform depth, display small sideways deviations, and follow the surface contours of a compact bone, making them appear quite different from cut marks, which tend to be deeper on convex areas and shallower on concave areas (Binford 1981; Eickhoff & Herrmann 1985; Morlan 1984). 'Pits' are small depressions caused by the cusp of a tooth and can be difficult to distinguish from percussion pits produced by a hammerstone (Blumenschine & Selvaggio 1988). However, White (1992b) has argued that the outline and internal topography of hammerstone percussion pits are generally more irregular than tooth pits because of the presence of irregularities on the surface of hammerstones. For 'tooth impressions', identification of the species that left the tooth marks can be gleaned from the size and configuration of the cusp pattern where adequately preserved (e.g. Domínguez-Rodrigo & Piqueras 2003; Haynes 1983; Langley 2020; Pickering et al. 2004) (see Figure 2.9, colour section). When an animal bites down hard enough, this impression becomes a 'puncture'. Punctures may leave only a pit or penetrate either partially or completely through a bone. The shape of these punctures can vary highly owing to the huge range of carnivores that can produce them (Cook 1986). Punctures are often accompanied by tooth impressions, pits, and scoring left by the animal moving the bone around in its mouth (Blumenschine 1988; Fisher 1995).

The number of carnivore tooth marks on a gnawed bone can range from zero to many, depending on the species and its hunger (Haynes 1983). Something else to look out for are edges featuring crenulated or ragged fractures, which carnivores produce when chewing along a focused area (Binford 1981; Blasco et al. 2008). These fractures can be confused with anthropogenic flaking (Fisher 1995), so looking for evidence for tooth marks on the bone in question can help shed light on what processes were at work.

Weathering

'Weathering' refers to modifications a skeletal element suffers between the time of an animal's death and the time of its burial and which are a combination of physical and chemical processes (Behrensmeyer 1978; Collins et al. 2002). Weathering occurs as exposed bones undergo gradual breakdown, resulting in bleaching, cracking, splitting, exfoliation, and disintegration of the osseous element (Fisher 1995), with the degree of weathering sometimes allowing rough estimates of how long they have sat on the ground (Behrensmeyer 1978). The rate of weathering differs according to the environmental context, however, and climatic or anthropogenic-induced events (such as burn-offs) can make such estimates unreliable (Andrews & Armour-Chelu 1998; Andrews & Cook 1985; Lyman & Fox 1989; Pokines & Ames 2015; Tappen 1994). Weathering can alter or completely eliminate anthropogenic traces (such as cut marks) as the bone surface degrades and falls apart. Conversely, anthropogenic processes such as burning can superficially mimic the effect of weathering (White 1992b).

While in the ground
Abrasion (again)
Abrasion again appears as a major cause of surface alterations once an artefact has been buried in the ground. In this context, pressure on or within deposits causes sediments to move across the bone or vice versa, creating striations (Olsen & Shipman 1988). The size and orientation of striations can be highly variable owing to differences in the size and type of particles in the deposit and the forces acting against them. Even on the same specimen, the effects of sedimentary abrasion can appear in several different forms and can consist of anywhere from a single striation to many hundreds (Behrensmeyer et al. 1986; Fisher 1995; Haynes 1988; Olsen & Shipman 1988; Shipman & Rose 1983a). Sedimentary abrasion can be confused with cut marks and scrape marks, though microscopic comparison is usually able to separate the anthropogenic from the taphonomic. Specifically, striations caused by sedimentary abrasion will generally be shallow and short and lack anthropogenic features such as chattermarks (Blumenschine & Selvaggio 1988).

While various geological and biological processes can cause movement of the soil—including freezing and thawing cycles, the swelling and shrinking of clays, trees being uprooted and animals digging burrows—a major cause of sedimentary abrasion is trampling.

Trampling
Trampling of artefacts (by humans and animals) already embedded into a deposit is a major cause of artefact damage and displacement (Behrensmeyer et al. 1986; Olsen & Shipman 1988; Pargeter & Bradfield 2012; Schiffer 1987; Stockton 1973). Through experimentation, it has been determined that most trampling-induced damage occurs when the artefact lies on or just under the surface, with damage potential decreasing as it migrates lower in a deposit (see summary in Olsen & Shipman 1988; Pargeter & Bradfield 2012).

Trampling damage generally comes in two forms: macro-fractures and surface marks. Regarding macro-fractures, trampling has been demonstrated in experimental studies to produce step fractures, particularly on thinner sections of bone artefacts (such as a distal extremity on a point; see Figure 2.10, colour section) (Pargeter & Bradfield 2012). Pargeter and Bradfield (2012) and Arndt and Newcomer (1986) found that the surfaces of these snap fractures were smooth, perhaps suggesting that this attribute can be used to identify the fracture as having occurred post-deposition. Additionally, dry bones have been found to usually fracture at right angles and produce scalariform morphologies (Villa & Mahieu 1991), while notches are commonly produced on bones with oblique angles (Blasco et al. 2008).

Regarding surface marks, the occurrence of abrasion was touched on above and has been recorded to produce a polish on bone surfaces in experiments and field collections (Oliver 1989; Olsen & Shipman 1988; Pargeter & Bradfield 2012). Much research has been devoted to understanding the development of striations on bone surfaces resulting specifically from trampling, as it was noted early on in bone artefact studies that they could be easily mistaken for butchery marks (Behrensmeyer et al. 1986; Olsen & Shipman 1988). Experimentation has found that striations produced by trampling can be isolated, very shallow striations; groups of randomly oriented striations of variable length and breadth; or sets of parallel striations that mimic scrape and cut marks (Andrews & Cook 1985; Behrensmeyer et al. 1986; Olsen & Shipman 1988). As described in 'Abrasion (again)' above, the type of striation depends on the substrate in which the artefact is embedded and may be restricted to a certain area on the artefact's surface or be found universally across the specimen (Behrensmeyer et al. 1986). In Behrensmeyer et al.'s (1986) experiment, they found that trampling marks differed from stone tool scraping marks in several aspects, including the fact that trampling marks were generally shorter than most scraping marks, were not located in anatomically meaningful areas, were very superficial, lacked chattermarks, and showed no pattern in orientation. It is important to note that these attributes do not occur in all cases of trampling, and as such, analysts recommend considering the proportion of bones in the assemblage that are similarly marked, the range of striation shapes exhibited, association with other surface modifications (such as polish or punctures), and the geological context of the deposit (Andrews & Cook 1985; Behrensmeyer et al. 1986; Fisher 1995; Oliver 1989, 1994; Olsen & Shipman 1988).

Finally, abrasion, fractures, and striations caused by trampling are known to alter pre-existing (ancient) cut marks and other anthropogenic modifications to bone (Behrensmeyer et al. 1986). Specifically, they begin to erase the features of these marks and can make them indistinguishable from trampling marks.

Root etching and chemical erosion

Root etching appears as long, sinuous lines that are thin and shallow and present a U-shaped cross-section (see Figure 2.10, colour section). These etchings are created by plant roots growing against the surface of organic artefacts, with acids either emitted by the roots or associated fungi creating the mark (Andrews & Cook 1985; Behrensmeyer 1978; Binford 1981; Lyman 1994). Multiple etched lines are typically present and are usually macroscopically visible. Root etching can also create small pits that may or may not be associated with the linear variety and may be confused with other agents or processes. Extensive root etching may erode a surface to such an extent that individual root marks are not clearly defined.

Similarly, wider surfaces or entire osseous artefacts can be chemically eroded when subjected to acidic deposits (Lyman 1994; Schiffer 1987). During their burial, osseous materials undergo various diagenetic alterations depending on the burial conditions, including hydrology, temperature, geochemistry, biological factors, and mechanical pressure. These changes in general include the uptake of groundwater solutes, the dissolution of soluble components, the breakdown and leaching of collagen, an increase in crystallinity, and alterations caused by microorganisms. How these factors affect the artefact's appearance depends on how long the artefact is exposed to them and their intensity. Extensive research has been undertaken to try to understand all these processes in different environmental conditions (e.g. Fernández-Jalvo et al. 2010; Hedges et al. 1995; Reiche et al. 1999).

During excavation and analysis

Organic artefacts can be easily damaged. Back at the lab, they are also not entirely safe unless the right analytical tools are used. In this regard, it is critical that metal tools are never used to handle an osseous artefact, as metal can leave scratches on or crush the surface depending on the condition of the piece. In excavation, once an osseous item has been identified, the excavator should proceed carefully using bamboo or plastic tools while trying to touch its surfaces as little as possible. Metal sieves can also scratch the surface of organic artefacts, with metal tweezers and calipers similarly able to mark the new find. Swapping out metal tools for bamboo or plastic ones is preferable, though you can also cover the working ends of your metal tools with a plastic layer to achieve the same end.

It is important to take these measures in artefact handling, as striations and other marks left on an artefact from excavation or analysis can later be misinterpreted as having originated from ancient human activity (White & Toth 1989). However, if damage has occurred, it can often be recognised, as new marks tend to exhibit a lighter colour than surrounding surfaces (White & Toth 1989). Colour differentiation is not always clear though, in which case reference to its find context is important. For example, the presence of a metal tool mark on an artefact found in a known stone tool context will be incongruous and will point to a modern origin. On the other hand, if the find context includes metal tools, this determination will not be straightforward. Overall, minimising factors that can confuse the interpretation of an osseous artefact's history is imperative for creating the most robust understanding of the past.

Osseous artefact studies to date

Now that the range of processes that may transform hard animal materials into tools and ornaments has been described, it is possible to provide an overview of osseous artefact studies. Research into osseous technologies around the globe has followed a similar path to that laid out by investigations into stone technologies. Researchers have wanted to learn why people chose particular raw materials, how they transformed them into a tool or ornament, how well they worked in comparison to similar objects from other raw materials, how to identify past behaviour from tiny traces, and why different cultures chose to do things differently. To answer these questions, archaeologists have primarily focused on defining artefact types and their spatio-temporal limits and developing more insightful analytical methods. Each of these major themes is outlined.

Form and style

Archaeologists (and humans in general) like to organise things into categories. Such classification systems ('typologies') allow us to organise large bodies of data into something that is easier to understand and that may allow meaning to be drawn out. Osseous technologies, like their stone counterparts, were organised early on into types according to their overall form and style. The first such systems were created for European Upper Palaeolithic collections of bone, antler, ivory, and tooth artefacts—with these classification systems forming the basis for how osseous artefacts are studied and understood both there and in contexts very far away in space and time. Some of the earliest classification systems were presented by Edouard Lartet and Henry Christy (1864), who grouped the extensive assemblages they excavated from numerous sites in Southern France according to apparent function, an approach also taken by Gustave Chauvet in 1910 for the Le Placard (France) collection. For Le Placard, Chauvet split the assemblage into three main groups: *cutting* objects, *piercing* objects, and *other* objects (the category 'other' hides all kinds of artefacts archaeologists do not understand). Subsequent systems followed along similar lines, separating artefacts by functional categories that were generally hunting weaponry, 'domestic' tools (such as awls and spatulas), and ornamentation. Within each category, analysts created smaller subcategories ('types') based on more and more specific aspects of function, morphology, and decorative style—and according to the aspects in which they were most interested.

As various types of tools and ornaments were described, it was noticed that projectile points, in particular, differed considerably between archaeological layers in European sites. As such, these osseous weapon tips became *fossiles directeurs*—key indicators for recognising specific archaeological cultures. The overall form of these *fossiles directeurs*, as well as any others recovered alongside them, was pored over to explore subsistence practices, technical systems, social systems, and even the cognitive abilities of the subject population/s.

During the late 1970s, researchers began to recognise that the shape that tools and ornaments took was not completely dictated by the need for them to function efficiently. They realised that the 'design' of objects (along with all aspects of their use and discard) was part of a complex social world that resulted in choices being made by the tool creator and user. In particular, Sackett (1973) argued that the 'style' of a tool—which was the product of choices made by the artist who selected from a variety of possible solutions influenced by the taste and views of their community—had the most potential to allow archaeologists to learn about past communities. For it was these 'stylistic attributes' that allowed insight into how that community believed things should be done.

Understanding how technical traditions are formed, maintained, and changed by the populations who produced them requires understanding how communities developed 'ways of doing things' (Hodder 1990:45). As Dobres and Hoffman (1994:214) put it:

> technologies are not practiced in a cultural vacuum where physical laws take precedence. Objects are made, reused, repaired, and deposited at a variety of sites, and the associated activities and social interactions that took place in these contexts form a meaningful and structuring set of background conditions.

Technological choices are dynamic operations that can (and often do) reflect the social identity and affiliations of the manufacturer and user of a tool (Lave & Wenger 1991; Lemonnier 1993). As such, the stylistic attributes of a tool can be used to learn about interactions between communities by mapping their distribution across space (Sackett 1973). There are two main theories that archaeologists have used to explain spatial and temporal patterning in artefact style: 'social interaction theory' and 'information exchange theory'.

Social interaction theory has its origins in the 'culture area studies' of the 1930s and considers style as an indicator of the degree of cultural affinity among social groups. This theory defines style as 'repetitive behavior that acts as a kind of psychological "filter" to constrain variety and reduce information overload' (Barton et al.

1994:186). Style is argued to function on the level of the individual and acts passively, having been unconsciously learned as the individual grows up in their community. The design of artefacts is therefore the result of passively shared group norms and values that are similar within spatial and temporal boundaries of identity-conscious social units (Clark 1993).

Information exchange theory, on the other hand, originated with the work of Martin Wobst and Polly Wiessner during the late 1970s and early 1980s. This approach views style as the result of a conscious act of social communication aimed at various levels of society and therefore as an active process. Style is argued to have its basis in fundamental human behaviour, where people create personal and social identities through comparison. According to this theory, the volume of style witnessed in the archaeological record indicates the amount of information flowing across the landscape. Put another way, style is the vehicle by which information about the identity of the maker/owner of an artefact is transmitted to observers, and the amount of style invested into artefacts and increased deposition of these artefacts into the archaeological record indicates the quantity of information being communicated between groups of people in the social network (e.g. Gamble 1980, 1982; Wiessner 1983, 1984, 1985; Wobst 1977).

This use of artefacts to transmit messages to others is thought to be most useful when used to communicate information to people in 'the middle distance'—that is, to those people who are not so close to the emitter that the messages are already known but who are not so distant that the meaning of the message cannot be understood. This 'middle group' are generally people who are not encountered every day but frequently enough that they understand the meaning of displayed symbols, such as neighbouring groups, trading partners, and other alliance members. As Wobst (1977) explained, because stylistic messages are primarily aimed at 'the middle distance', these messages will mostly concern social integration and social differentiation. Further, as complex messages or messages that are only infrequently emitted require more energy to both make (emit) and interpret (receive), only simple and frequently used messages will normally be encoded in material culture. Messages sent will therefore revolve around emotional state, identification (class affinity, social group affiliation, religious affiliation, rank, etc.), authorship, and ownership.

Through the study of modern peoples, it has been found that the types of artefacts heavily involved in this messaging include both body ornamentation and hunting weaponry, owing to their high visibility on the landscape (Tostevin 2007). Imagine you are walking between camps and see another group of people at a distance. The first things you are likely to notice about them are the weapons they are carrying and what they are wearing on their upper bodies, especially their heads and chests. This is what is meant by high visibility on the landscape and allows the identification of friendly or non-friendly others before getting too close.

It is because of these theories that researchers have focused on weapons and ornaments made on osseous and other hard animal materials to explore issues surrounding identity, community, social networks, and when a group or groups were under environmental and/or social stress in the deep past (e.g. Bahn 1982; Barton et al. 1994; Conkey 1980; Gamble 1982; Jochim 1983; Vanhaeren & d'Errico 2006).

2. BONE TOOL ANALYSIS

Ethnographic analogies and experimental programs

While comparing modern hunter-gatherer cultures with peoples that lived thousands of years ago can be problematic (Hiscock 2008:2–8), it has been argued that 'ethnographies' provide the only glimpse of particular technologies (such as those made on stone or bone) in an ongoing cultural context (Dibble 1995)—a cultural context that is usually very foreign to the researcher. As O'Connell (1995) put it, archaeologists have only two sources of information from which to explore past human behaviour: (1) the artefacts and patterns within the archaeological record itself and (2) the knowledge of present-day human behaviour and the consequences of these behaviours on the materials they use and discard. Focusing only on the former allows for little more than mere description of artefacts and their spatial and temporal distribution. Integrating the latter, on the other hand, provides insights into the processes that led to the appearance of these patterns in the archaeological record in the first place. Understanding these processes then allows the researcher to build stories around data.

Ethnographies that describe the manufacture, use, and discard of osseous items have been generated for cultures in numerous regions around the world, though probably the most extensive is provided by Osgood's (1940) account of the Ingalik (in Alaska). In this paper, he detailed the material, construction, place and time of manufacture, manufacturer, method of use, place and time of use, use, and length of life of a range of Ingalik implements. Such detailed information for bone, antler, and tooth items is invaluable for understanding a 'lifeway' centred around reindeer—an animal that was immensely important for many Palaeolithic peoples in Europe. Works for other regions and lifeways provide similar insights into what it is like living and working in a way very different from that to which most of us in modern Australia (or Europe, or America, etc.) are accustomed.

Unfortunately, accounts of 'traditional' lifeways as detailed as Osgood's are quite rare, as most anthropologists were making their observations during the 19th and early 20th centuries when communities had already been significantly altered by contact with Europeans and other groups who introduced alternative 'ways of doing'. For example, communities that hunted reindeer had their osseous weaponry quickly replaced with metal tools, and as such, their hunting methods changed to suit the use of steel traps and shotguns. Additionally, these early ethnographers were often men who were either more interested in understanding and recording men's activities and tools or restricted from observing and speaking to other genders and children. Thus, while ethnographic information can provide us insights into technologies of which a large proportion of researchers have no firsthand knowledge, it has its restrictions.

Nevertheless, the application of ethnographic analogies to archaeological finds has enabled a number of osseous artefacts that were originally a mystery to the scientific community to be identified. For example, working out the function of the beautifully made *bâtons percés* found in Western European Upper Palaeolithic sites relied heavily on comparison to reindeer hunting communities in North America. By comparing the reindeer antler *bâtons* that have one or more perforations with common tools from North America, it was found that the former are very similar to 'shaft-straighteners' used in the latter region. Given that Palaeolithic peoples would also have needed to straighten wooden shafts for their weaponry, this interpretation is considered a good possibility for the ancient artefacts (see Peltier 1992 for a discussion).

Now to experimental archaeology. Experimental archaeology generates and tests archaeological hypotheses by replicating or approximating the feasibility of ancient cultures performing various tasks and is used to explore everything from how a single type of tool was used to how Stonehenge was constructed during the Neolithic. The usefulness of re-creating and testing out the efficiency of bone and other types of hard animal material tools cannot be overstated for archaeology. In numerous cases, it has been these experiments that have provided the best (and sometimes only) evidence for how artefacts were used in the past. Indeed, so useful is this method that large working groups—such as the International Council for Archaeozoology Worked Bone Research Group—meet regularly to share the outcomes of their respective experimental projects.

Table 2.2 provides an overview of just some of the experimental studies that have focused on archaeological osseous technologies. Looking at this table, it should be evident that while a few early experiments were reported in the archaeological literature, it was not until the 1970s that this form of investigation gained momentum. Today, experimentally reproducing and using osseous artefacts to understand their manufacture and use is a staple of archaeological investigation into past technologies.

Identifying raw material

Selecting the right raw material to make a particular tool or ornament is an essential part of technological decision-making. This choice can mean the difference between an effective and long-lasting tool and one that barely does the job, given the unique properties and technological potentials inherent in each raw material. Practical, functional, and symbolic choices play a role in raw material selection. Indeed, it is known from modern societies that animals (and plants) are entangled with all parts of our economic, social, and spiritual life. Consequently, the hard animal materials chosen to make tools and ornaments are not always as straightforward as 'this material works the best'. Ancient toolmakers and craftspeople would have been influenced not only by the shape, strength, plasticity, and availability of materials but also by other factors such as prestige or symbolism. Products of animal origin are inevitably linked to the way human groups culturally perceived the animal world in general, and the specific species in particular.

Until relatively recently, identifying the type of raw material used to make a particular artefact was largely dependent on being able to make this identification from observation with the naked eye. First, the analyst would try to discern the gross type of raw material (antler, bone, ivory, etc.) before moving to species and the specific skeletal element. Much of this identification relied on diagnostic morphological markers being present. Where tell-tale markers were missing, archaeologists were forced to largely assume that the piece was most likely selected from one of the species present in the economic fauna (i.e. the fauna collected for food). Today, a range of analytical tools are available to identify raw material origins.

This increasing ability to identify the species from which a particular bone artefact originated began with improved visualisation methods for looking at bone cross-sections (histological analysis). Although most histological studies originally used thin section micrographs, the need to cut into the artefact to get a sample (not popular with museum curators) has been eliminated with the development of micro X-ray computed tomography (known as micro-CT). Micro-CT allows the researcher to see the distinctive micromorphological (histological) features of bone, ivory, and antler without breaking the artefact (Reiche et al. 2011).

2. BONE TOOL ANALYSIS

TABLE 2.2. Examples of experimental programs undertaken on osseous artefacts around the globe.

REFERENCE	TOOL OR ORNAMENT STUDIED	RAW MATERIAL/S	ASPECTS INVESTIGATED	CULTURAL ASSOCIATION
Tyzzer 1936	projectile point	bovid long bone	hafting possibilities, use effectiveness, morphological change with use and rejuvenation cycles of 'simple bone points'	Algonkian
Clark & Thompson 1953	projectile point	antler	reproduction of groove and splinter technique of blank production	Upper Palaeolithic & Mesolithic Europe
Semenov 1964	multiple tool types	bone, antler, mammoth ivory	reproduction of manufacture and use of multiple tool types	Multiple contexts
Newcomer 1974	awl/projectile point	bovine and sheep long bone, red deer antler, elephant ivory, hippopotamus tooth	manufacture of osseous projectile points (bipoints) and awls from Ksar Akil	Upper Palaeolithic Lebanon
Newcomer 1977	multiple tool and ornament types	reindeer antler, ox metacarpal, ox scapula, turkey and chicken wing bones, rabbit long bone	reproduction of longitudinal debitage of bone and antler; manufacture of *bâtons percés*, spearthrowers and projectile points; manufacture of bone discs, pendants and beads	Upper Palaeolithic & Mesolithic Europe
Flenniken 1978	needle	jackrabbit tibias	replication of bone needles	Paleoindian
Frison & Zeimens 1980	projectile point	bison femur	manufacture and use efficiency of bone projectile point	Folsom
Guthrie 1983	projectile point	caribou antler	performance characteristics of caribou antler compared with their organic materials in use as projectile points	Paleoindian

REFERENCE	TOOL OR ORNAMENT STUDIED	RAW MATERIAL/S	ASPECTS INVESTIGATED	CULTURAL ASSOCIATION
Allain & Rigaud 1986	projectile points, *bâtons percés*, chisels, navettes	reindeer antler	use efficiency of notches and grooves for hafting and prehension	Magdalenian
Arndt & Newcomer 1986	projectile point	reindeer antler, Père David's deer antler, ox bone, fallow deer bone, elephant ivory	impact damage on antler, bone and ivory of double-bevelled base; bipoint projectile points	Magdalenian
Bergman 1987	projectile point	*cervus* and *dama* antler, *bos*, *dama* and *capreolus* bone	use efficiency of replicated Ksar Akil points as projectiles	Upper Palaeolithic Lebanon
LeMoine 1989	multiple tool types	deer and antelope bones, caribou antler	development of use wear from a variety of activities	Mackenzie Delta area
Stodiek 1990	soft hammer	reindeer antler	use wear for soft hammer use of antler tines	Solutrean
Bosinski 1991	spearthrower	reindeer antler	manufacture and assessment of use effectiveness of antler spearthrowers	Upper Palaeolithic Europe
Knecht 1991a	projectile point	caribou antler, domestic cow bone	manufacture of split-based points with 'tongued pieces', hafting design and use efficiency	Aurignacian
LeMoine 1991	multiple tool and ornament types	deer and antelope bone, caribou antler	document build-up of use wear on a range of bone and antler tools put to a variety of activities	Mackenzie Delta area
Stodiek 1991	projectile point	reindeer antler	use effectiveness and durability of single- and double-bevel-based points	Magdalenian
Wilke et al. 1991	'bone rods'	elephant femur, walrus tusk, moose and caribou antler	reproduction and use to determine function of 'bone rods'—as pressure-flaker	Clovis

2. BONE TOOL ANALYSIS

REFERENCE	TOOL OR ORNAMENT STUDIED	RAW MATERIAL/S	ASPECTS INVESTIGATED	CULTURAL ASSOCIATION
Rozoy 1992	projectile point	*bos* femur	manufacture of single-bevelled points and use efficiency when used with a spearthrower	Magdalenian
Knecht 1993b	projectile point	caribou antler, domestic cow bone	use effectiveness and patterns of damage of spit-based, simple-based, lozenge-shaped, single-bevelled and spindle-shaped points	Aurignacian & Gravettian
LeMoine 1994	multiple tool and ornament types	caribou antler, bone	development of use-related wear	Mackenzie Delta area
Knecht 1997	projectile point	caribou antler, domestic cow bone	use effectiveness, durability and damage patterns of spit-based, lozenge-shaped and spindle-shaped points	Aurignacian
LeMoine 1997	multiple tool types	deer and antelope bones, caribou antler	development of use wear from a variety of activities	Mackenzie Delta area
Pokines & Krupa 1997	projectile point	elk antler	use effectiveness of self-barbed projectile points as fishing implements	Lower Magdalenian
White 1997	ornamentation	elephant and mammoth ivory	working properties of ivory	Aurignacian
Lyman et al. 1998	'bone rods'	elephant tibia	reproduction and use to determine function of 'bone rods'—as Clovis point hafting-wedge mechanism	Clovis
Nuzhnyi 1998	projectile point	elk antler	use efficiency of split-based points	Aurignacian
Pokines 1998	projectile point	elk antler	use efficiency and durability of single-bevel-based points from Cantabria	Lower Magdalenian
Bertrand 1999	projectile point	deer bone, antler	use efficiency of several types of Upper Palaeolithic European projectile point types	European Upper Palaeolithic

REFERENCE	TOOL OR ORNAMENT STUDIED	RAW MATERIAL/S	ASPECTS INVESTIGATED	CULTURAL ASSOCIATION
Stodiek 2000	projectile point	reindeer antler	use efficiency and durability of hafting methods, use efficiency and impact damage patterns for single- and double-bevel-based points	Magdalenian
Hoffman 2002	needle	ptarmigan long bones	reproduction and use efficiency of bone needles	Eastern Aleut
Backwell & d'Errico 2004	soft hammers	elephant limb bones	reproduction of possible flaked tools from Olduvai	Lower Palaeolithic
Buc 2005	awls and smoothers	*P. granulosus* bone, sheep long bone	development of use-wear patterns on bone tool surfaces through a variety of activities	Buenos Aires area
Backwell & d'Errico 2005	bone flakes	elephant limb bones	development of use wear from cutting meat, working hides, digging in soil and removing bark from trees	1–2 mya Africa
Brownlee 2005	multiple tool types	beaver incisors, caribou and moose antler, moose metatarsal	use efficiency of rodent incisors for bone; antler working; use efficiency of antler picks, chisels, adze; use efficiency of harpoons, fishing spears, and more	Nisichaway-asihk Cree Nation, Manitoba
Pétillon 2005	projectile point	reindeer antler	use efficiency and development of use wear on fork-based and double-bevel-based points and fore shafts	Magdalenian
Redmond & Tankersley 2005	projectile point	bison long bone	use efficiency of 'bone rods' as projectile points	Paleoindian
Van Gijn 2005	multiple tool types	*Bos* metapodia, antler, bone	identification of manufacturing versus use traces and use efficiency of adzes, axes, and flake tools	Mesolithic

2. BONE TOOL ANALYSIS

REFERENCE	TOOL OR ORNAMENT STUDIED	RAW MATERIAL/S	ASPECTS INVESTIGATED	CULTURAL ASSOCIATION
Pétillon 2006	projectile point	reindeer antler	use efficiency and development of use wear on fork-based and double-bevel-based points and foreshafts	Magdalenian
Boldurian 2007	'bone rods'	elephant femur	manufacture of 'bone rods'	Clovis
Gates St-Pierre 2007	awls	buck deer leg bones	identification of function of bone awls	St Lawrence Iroquoians
Letourneaux & Pétillon 2008	projectile point	reindeer antler	impact traces of osseous points on bones of target animals using fork-based points	Magdalenian
Heckel 2009a	sculpture	mammoth ivory	flaking, carving, and polishing properties of mammoth ivory	Aurignacian
Heckel 2009b	sculpture	mammoth ivory	flaking, carving, and polishing properties of mammoth ivory	Aurignacian
Elliot & Milner 2010	projectile point	red deer antler	reproduction of barbed points from Star Carr	British Mesolithic
Buc 2011	multiple tool types	red deer antler, shell long bones, catfish spines	development of use wear from a variety of activities	Low Paraná wetland, Argentina
Pétillon et al. 2011	projectile point	reindeer antler	manufacture and use efficiency of composite antler and lithic points	Lower & Upper Magdalenian
Rosell et al. 2011	retoucher	*B. taurus* radius	development of microtraces from use as bone retoucher for comparison to Gran Dolina artefacts	Lower Palaeolithic
Azema & Rivière 2012	'bone disc'	deer shoulder blade	reproduction of bone disc to determine use function	Magdalenian
Keddie 2012	'ulna bone tools'	mammal	identification of function of 'ulna bone tools'	North America
Tartar & White 2013	projectile point	caribou antler	manufacture of split-based points	Aurignacian

REFERENCE	TOOL OR ORNAMENT STUDIED	RAW MATERIAL/S	ASPECTS INVESTIGATED	CULTURAL ASSOCIATION
Cristiani et al. 2014	beads	cyprinid pharyngeal teeth	reproduction of teeth beads found in Vlasac burials	Late Mesolithic
Heckel & Wolf 2014	blanks	mammoth ivory	manufacture of ivory flakes	Aurignacian
Romandini et al. 2015	retouched bone	red deer radius	reproduction of retouched bone shaft from Fumane cave	Mousterian
Lbova & Volkov 2016	portable art	mammoth ivory	reproduction of portable artworks recovered from Mal'ta and development of manufacturing microtraces	Upper Palaeolithic Siberia
Gates St-Pierre 2018	tattooing points	white-tailed deer metapodial bones	development of microtraces from use in experimental tattooing	St Lawrence Iroquoians
Girya & Khlopachev 2018	blanks	mammoth ivory, reindeer antler	manufacture of ivory and antler flakes using direct percussion	Upper Palaeolithic Eurasia
Mărgărit et al. 2018	ornamentation	cyprinid pharyngeal teeth	reproduction of teeth beads found in iron gates	Mesolithic
Marítn et al. 2018	needles	*Sus scrofa* femur	manufacture of needles and microtraces developed using stone and metal tools	Xochimilca
Wojtczak & Kerdy 2018	multiple tool types	red deer metapodial, cattle, sheep and pig ribs	development of microtraces from a variety of uses	Late Neolithic
Bradfield & Wurz 2020	'notched bones'	cow rib	use functionality of 'notched bone artefacts' from South African sites	Middle Stone Age & Later Stone Age
Hohenstein et al. 2020	multiple tool types	bovid long bone	use effectiveness of Italian Copper Age pointed tools and development of microtraces from various activities	Copper Age
Osipowicz et al. 2020	ornaments	*Sus scrofa* teeth	development of use wear on pendants worn in differing modes	Sub-Neolithic

2. BONE TOOL ANALYSIS

Another approach uses chemical analysis by means of micro-proton-induced X-ray and gamma-ray emission spectroscopy (micro-PIXE/PIGE for short) and began to see use in identifying osseous materials around 1999 (e.g. Christensen 1999). Bone is a composite material composed of a mineral (carbonated hydroxyapatite) and an organic fraction (collagen type I), with the chemical composition relatively similar except for minor and trace elements. These distinctive elements can be used to distinguish between different bony materials, though they can disappear over time, making analysis more complex for older samples (Müller & Reiche 2011).

Partly destructive studies—those that require a small sample—include DNA, isotopic, and collagen peptide analyses (Bocherens et al. 2006; Buckley et al. 2010). While ancient DNA analysis is accurate, it is expensive and often time consuming (Matisoo-Smith & Horsburg 2012). DNA also needs to have preserved sufficiently in the bones to be analysed and is susceptible to contamination by modern sources (Hagelberg & Clegg 1991). Collagen peptide analysis has several advantages over traditional DNA studies in that it can survive for longer periods and is less susceptible to contamination (Buckley et al. 2009; Hounslow et al. 2013; Rybczynski et al. 2013).

From 2009, a new method was developed by Mike Buckley and has seen widespread use in archaeology. Zooarchaeology by mass spectrometry (ZooMS) uses the unique spectra of collagen peptides found inside bone to differentiate species (Buckley et al. 2009). All bones contain collagen, and the peptides within that collagen have slightly different masses from species to species—resulting in a recognisable species-specific 'fingerprint'. By analysing the collagen found in archaeologically recovered bones, researchers can at least narrow down what kind of animal it came from (cetacean, cervid, primate, etc.), if not determine the specific species (Buckley et al. 2009). Preservation is again a major issue for this method, though Bouchard et al. (2019) have found that portable Fourier-transform infrared (FTIR) spectroscopy can be used as an in-field screening method for ZooMS; however, this screening method is minimally destructive (needing one milligram of bone powder).

ZooMS can sometimes produce unexpected results, such as the first known human to be a hybrid of two different species: Neanderthals and Denisovans. This individual was a teenage girl who lived 90,000 years ago in Denisova Cave, Siberia (Slon et al. 2018). Similarly, ZooMS analysis of the bags in which artefacts are kept (rather than the fragile artefacts themselves) allowed Martisius et al. (2020) to discover that Neanderthals at two sites in south west France were selecting aurochs or bison ribs to create their hide-working tools, rather than what had previously been assumed to be reindeer bone. Another recent example is provided by McGrath et al. (2019), who conducted a ZooMS analysis on the storage bags of bone points from Pre-Contact St Lawrence Iroquoian village sites in southern Quebec, Canada. In this study, it was found that black bear and human bone was used for making the recovered bone points—results that allowed the authors to identify and explore tangible material traces of the symbolic relationship between bears and humans in this part of the world.

Researchers have also used stable isotopes to help identify species. Stable isotopes record dietary and environmental inputs into the tissues of plants and animals and provide a means to investigate human diet and mobility, as well as to explore the ways in which people exploited wild and domesticated plant and animal resources in ancient societies. An example of the use of stable isotopes to identify species origins is provided by Sayre et al. (2016), who investigated unusually large and elaborately worked bone artefacts recovered from the central highland of Peru. At Chavín de Huántar, a site considered a trading point between the Pacific coast and the Amazon jungle, analysis of the carbon, nitrogen, sulphur, and oxygen isotopes in these unusual bone artefacts found that they were likely from a cetacean or large pinniped.

Identifying what raw material artefacts are made from can afford insights into past lifeways that are often out of reach of their lithic counterparts. For example, an added bonus with antler artefacts is that they are able to indicate the season of collection and manufacture of technologies. Studies of manufacturing waste at several Magdalenian (c. 21,000 to 14,000 years ago, Western Europe) sites have indicated that an annual cycle of raw material collection and tool manufacture was tied to the type of antler required and its availability (Averbouh 1999; Chauchat et al. 1999). Averbouh (2005) found that during winter, when adult male reindeer moult, Magdalenian people would collect the large shed antler to make a range of projectile points. During spring, however, shed antler from female reindeer (which is smaller in size and does not have as dense a layer of compacta) was collected for manufacturing spearthrowers and *bâtons percés*. In addition to these two main manufacturing phases, Averbouh also suggested an 'intermediate production period' between the end of winter and the beginning of spring, when antler from young males and adult females constitutes the material available, and which might provide the raw material for producing items that were required to be replaced before the appropriate raw material became available again. Along similar lines, Julien (1982) found that the antler originating from different types of animals (males, females, juveniles) may have dictated the type of projectile point manufactured: unilaterally barbed points from the antler of smaller dimensions (female or juveniles) and bilaterally barbed points from the larger antler of adult males. The most insightful implication of this research is the indication that projectile points appear to have been manufactured only once a year (during winter) and were expected to last (at least) from one production season to the next.

Microtraces

Archaeologists have long been interested in understanding how the artefacts they recover were used in the past. Microtrace or traceological analysis, on both osseous and stone artefacts, is based on 'the belief that the study of damage patterns resulting from utilization is the most useful method in assessing the function of prehistoric artefacts' (Odell 1975:226). This approach allows researchers to 'connect the static archaeological record with the dynamic cultural context in which people operated in the past' (Yerkes & Kardulias 1993:100). Using microtraces—the striations, chipping, polishes, and other small traces outlined above—to interrogate artefacts requires experimentation by the archaeologist with newly made replicas in laboratory conditions to identify what marks are caused by exactly what movements and raw material interactions. Additionally, the study of tools used in 'real-world' conditions (i.e. tools used by artists and toolmakers in contexts where the tool user has experience in the technology under study) provides the best possible dataset for artefacts that develop complex patterns.

Until the development of microtrace ('use wear') analysis in the 1970s, researchers principally relied on using the form of a tool to determine its probable function in the past. This approach compared the shapes of tools from both modern Western and various Indigenous cultures with those that were recovered from archaeological sites. While archaeologists would note use-related wear that was clear to the naked eye

2. BONE TOOL ANALYSIS

and often use this evidence to support their conclusions as to their function, generally, microtraces (those needing examination using microscopes) were not included.

The first steps towards modern traceological work were 'efficiency studies' that tested the ability of a particular artefact type to effectively complete a particular task. In addition to assessing performance, the wear developed during the experiment on the replica tools was compared with that found on the archaeological specimens (e.g. Tyzzer 1936). If the tool was found to be able to effectively complete the set task and similar use-wear patterns were created, this experimental evidence then supported the hypothesised function of that tool in the past.

These early comparative approaches saw archaeologists describing wear patterns visible to the naked eye, as well as sometimes utilising hand lenses and low-powered microscopes. Time saw more and more scientifically designed experimental programs developed (see Table 2.2), though these studies, overall, lacked the detail required to reproduce the experiment reported, and as such, very little progress was made in utilising microtraces for the first 30 or so years. In fact, it was not until Sergeĭ Semenov's *Prehistoric Technology* (1964), which summarised his extensive experiments undertaken throughout the 1930s to 1950s, was published in English that microtraces really came to the fore. Semenov laid down the standard for how the analysis of microtraces should be conducted, discussing the importance of lighting, surface treatments, and photography in reporting results. Through describing the development of wear on modern metal tools, tools he used as comparators for stone and bone tools from numerous archaeological contexts, and standardising the use of low-powered microscopes and higher powered metallographic microscopes, Semenov demonstrated the power of this approach—this 'traceology'—to inform on past tool function.

Despite Semenov's book being available to Western archaeologists, it took until after 1975 for this more scientific approach to be taken up widely. It began with a number of zooarchaeologists located in Central and, later, Western Europe beginning to persistently study and report osseous technologies recovered from prehistoric contexts.

During the 1970s and 1980s, developments in osseous tool analysis closely paralleled those in lithic studies. Major conferences began to be held to advance osseous technologies and traceology. In April of 1974, Henriette Camps-Fabrer (1975) organised a major conference at the Abbaye Notre-Dame de Sénanque in Provence, France. This symposium included scholars from across Western Europe and focused on advancing the study of prehistoric bone technologies. Similarly, the first major meeting regarding 'microwear' in archaeology occurred in 1977 (Vancouver, Canada), and while this meeting was focused on stone tools, many leading researchers attended and, consequently, microtrace analysis started to rapidly grow widely in archaeological science. At this Vancouver conference, three significant issues were identified for focused investigation: (1) the mechanisms responsible for wear, (2) the effects of post-depositional modification of stone tools, and (3) the reliability and reproducibility of lithic microwear analysis. These three issues became central to microtrace studies on both stone and bone that were conducted over the next 20 years—and in many cases, continue to be investigated today.

Subsequently, experimental programs started to become more popular in both lithic and osseous microtrace studies (for stone: e.g. Fullagar 1986; Kamminga 1978; Keeley 1980; Odell 1975, 1977; for osseous: Newcomer 1974; Olsen 1979, 1980, 1984) (see Table 2.2). The 1980s saw these analyses develop again, with studies by Campana (1989), Choyke (1983), and Runnings et al. (1989) utilising light microscopy and scanning electron microscopy

(SEM) in the study of bone industries from the Near East and Europe. While the technology that examined experimentally produced use wear was becoming more sophisticated, comparison of archaeological finds with tools collected from modern Indigenous communities continued. Working with Indigenous communities provided a number of important insights, highlighting that (among other things) the tool types created by archaeologists did not necessarily correlate with the categories created by people in real life.

The next decade (the 1990s) saw the uptake of higher-powered microscopy and the full integration of microtrace observations, experimental data, and ethnographic data (e.g. d'Errico 1993; d'Errico et al. 1995; LeMoine 1991, 1994, 1997; Maigrot 1997). In particular, LeMoine's (1991, 1994, 1997) exploration of how different materials (such as plant fibres, stone, and animal hides) created distinctive wear patterns on bone surfaces was seminal in demonstrating our ability to tell such wear apart. Similar studies published at this time by d'Errico et al. (1995), Maigrot (1997), and Choyke (1997), who advocated for differentiating traces created by manufacturing, use, and handling of a bone tool, advanced this growing understanding of microtrace analysis even more. Alongside these efforts, issues surrounding the identification of taphonomic damage to osseous surfaces, and specifically being able to tell them apart from human-induced manufacturing and use traces, saw increased interest from archaeologists as older and older bone tools were coming to light.

In the new millennium, microtrace analysis began to be characterised by the use of multiple methods to achieve the clearest possible picture of past behaviour. Low- and high-powered microscopy was used in conjunction with SEM—and later 3D scanning—as such desktop technologies became increasingly available to archaeological researchers (e.g. Buc 2011; Stone 2011). These new analytical technologies—and improvements in the quality of the microscope imaging—allowed unresolved issues surrounding the development of use wear and post-depositional damage to be revised and, in some cases, better understood.

The last decade has seen analysts working to refine and standardise the methods used in traceology to improve the reliability of the method within the wider scope of archaeological science. Currently, there is general agreement over a number of microtraces found on hard animal materials and how they can be differentiated, though just as many traits continue to be heavily debated. In all, traceology has grown to be a sub-speciality within archaeology that is valued for the insights it can provide into past tool manufacture and use.

SUMMARY

- The natural properties of different osseous- and keratin-based raw materials lend themselves to being transformed into different types of tools and ornaments.

- Identifying the origin of surface marks on osseous artefacts is essential to determine if it is an artefact, how it was made, and how it was used.

- Correctly identifying the origin of a mark requires both macroscopic and microscopic analysis, along with a comparison with previously developed datasets.

CHAPTER 3
ATTRIBUTES IN DESCRIBING TOOL TYPES

Introduction
An important part of archaeology is letting everyone know what you found and its place in our current understanding of the past. As such, once an artefact made from osseous or keratinous material has been found, it then needs to be carefully recorded and described. These detailed descriptions allow the artefact to be interpreted by researchers and compared to similar finds elsewhere. In this chapter, the basics of how to analyse major categories of Australian bone and tooth tools are outlined to provide guidance for new tool analysts and in preparation for the deep dive into the vast array of implements presented in Chapter 5.

Terms for describing tools
Standardising terms is necessary if researchers are to make meaningful comparisons between implements and assemblages. Archaeologists have highlighted the importance of the terms used to describe tools being restricted to morphologically describing the artefact in order to avoid assigning functions to implements based solely on their appearance (e.g. Odell 1981; Pétillon 2006; Weniger 1995). Using the alternative approach, wherein a tool may be called an 'awl' simply because it has a point, can not only lead to misidentifying implement function (through assumption) but also create misunderstandings surrounding both the technology and the site from which it was recovered.

The terms suggested here follow those with a long history of use in the study of Eurasian osseous tools (Table 3.1). While initially developed to describe Western European Palaeolithic technologies (e.g. Julien 1977, 1982; Knecht 1991a, 1991b; Langley 2015; Pétillon 2006), they have been successfully employed to describe prehistoric tools from North America (e.g. Guthrie 1983; O'Brien et al. 2016; Tyzzer 1936), the Middle East (e.g. Arndt & Newcomer 1986; Bergman 1987; Newcomer 1974), and Africa (e.g. Backwell & d'Errico 2016; Bradfield 2016). They have also begun to be applied to Australian assemblages (Langley 2018). The benefits of adopting European terms for Australian bone and tooth artefacts is that the terms not only have undergone more than 50 years of development but also continue to see extensive use in describing technologies from a broad range of temporal and spatial contexts, allowing for Australian traditions to be understood on the world stage (Tables 3.1–3.3).

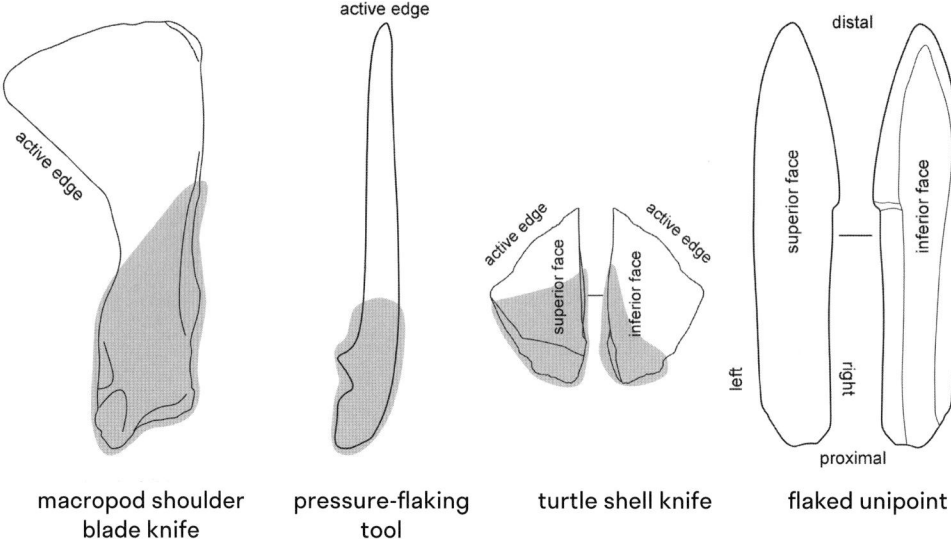

FIGURE 3.1. Determining the active edge of the tool will allow you to orient the artefact. The shaded area indicates the area hafted or handheld.

Identifying raw material

When beginning your analysis, the very first factor that you want to determine is the raw material from which your artefact is made. In making this identification, you will primarily rely on the size, colour, texture, weight, and shape of the piece. For some materials, such as echidna quills, turtle shell, and teeth, these identifications can be made quickly owing to inherent physical properties and unique appearance (see Chapter 2).

Most challenges come from attempting to identify the skeletal element and species origin for a bone tool or ornament. For larger bone artefacts, this identification is generally easier, as they tend to retain more of the natural characteristics that allow us to distinguish between elements and species. However, pieces can be so heavily worked that characteristic attributes of the raw material (like condyles) have been altered or entirely removed, making raw material identification only possible in the broadest of terms (such as 'mid-sized terrestrial mammal'). Even without tell-tale condyles (etc.), however, narrowing down the options for larger artefacts is usually straightforward with the use of a skeletal reference collection.

With smaller bone artefacts, just determining whether a piece is made from terrestrial, avian, or aquatic species can be difficult. The first clue is usually the thickness and weight of the cortical bone—bird bone will be thinner and lighter than that of a mammal, for example. Studying what species were recovered in the accompanying economic faunal assemblage (that is, remains from animals caught for food) at the site can help narrow possibilities. You should provide the most accurate raw material identification possible given the evidence available. This identification could be down to a specific element and species (e.g. 'left ulna of an eastern grey kangaroo [*Macropus giganteus*]') or only a very high-level identification (e.g. 'terrestrial mammal bone').

Active edge

The next step is to determine which part of the tool was the 'active' or 'working edge'. This edge is the extremity or other part of the artefact that cut, pierced, scraped, or otherwise acted to alter another object (see Figure 3.1). The active edge will be primarily evident by the presence of use wear and/or residues, though these traces may only be visible under a microscope. Identifying the active edge is important not only for orienting the tool for description (see 'Orientation') but also for beginning to understand its design and function.

Hafted or handheld?

After having identified the active edge—or even if the active edge is not clear—determining whether the tool was hafted or held directly in the hand is extremely useful for understanding function. Bone and tooth tools in Australia could be used directly in the hand (with no additions), hafted into a rounded mount of resin or wax (for ease of handling), or hafted with ligatures and/or mastics onto a shaft or other component (as in a projectile point). Each of these ways of handling the tool produces microtraces, which can indicate its use history. Indeed, even if the tool was only held directly in the hand, this point of contact may be evident in the form of polish restricted to a defined area. Items mounted directly into a haft of spinifex resin or beeswax may retain part of that haft or more subtle residues. Luckily, the mastics commonly used in Australia were dark in colour and often mixed (e.g. Parr 1999; Pitman & Wallis 2012) or painted over with bright ochre colourants, making them more likely to leave a visible trace of their presence.

Orientation

Orienting the artefact is important for recording and describing the tool in a consistent manner across assemblages, sites, and regions. Without consistency in this most basic of recording tasks, building an understanding of the various technologies across the continent (and the world) is impossible.

In the osseous tool literature, the distal extremity of a tool is typically the active edge, while the proximal extremity is the 'butt', 'base', or held part of the tool (following standardisation set out by Camps-Fabrer & Stodeur 1979). Often, the base is clearly identifiable owing to the raw material and overall design of the tool. For example, unipoints made on long bones that retain the condyle will display a distal tip with signs of having been used to pierce, puncture, press, or strike another object, while the proximal end will show signs of having been held in the hand (polish), mounted in a resin haft (residues or staining), or fixed-hafted to a shaft (residues from mastics, crushing and chipping to the proximal edge). Similarly, a bone or turtle shell knife may have an obvious proximal extremity or spine—the part that was held in the hand—and will be opposed by the active edge, itself displaying signs of use. In other cases, such as on bipoints, determining which extremity is which can only be determined through microscopic examination to identify subtle differences in the distribution and severity of wear types accrued across the artefact (see Figure 3.2, colour section). Extensive experimental studies on what kinds of use wear accumulate on osseous and other hard animal material artefacts used in different functions and hafted in different configurations is key to these identifications.

TABLE 3.1. Definitions of attributes used in describing hard animal material tool types.

TERM	DEFINITION
Elongated tools (unipoints, bipoints, drills, handles, etc.)	
distal	The active edge of the implement—the tip that is used to pierce, cut or otherwise alter another object (see Figure 3.3).
mesial	The middle section of the implement (see Figure 3.3).
proximal	The base of the implement—can be either held in the hand or hafted (see Figure 3.3).
left side	The edge of the implement that appears on the left when the dorsal surface is facing up (see Figure 3.3).
right side	The edge of the implement that appears on the right when the dorsal surface is facing up (see Figure 3.3).
face	A surface of the implement.
superior/exterior face	The surface of the implement that is made from cortical (dense outer surface) bone (see Figure 3.1).
inferior/interior face	The surface of the implement that is made from cancellous (spongy) bone (see Figure 3.1).
condyle	The rounded protuberance at the end of long bones.
diaphysis	The shaft or central part of a long bone.
Knives and scraping tools	
spine	The back of the knife and/or the section that opposes the active edge.
blade	The section that is defined by the active cutting edge and that may be worked back during resharpening or use.
Additional terms for fishhooks	
shank	The long stem between the bend and the section where the line is connected (see Figure 3.4).
bend	The curved portion of the fishhook (see Figure 3.4).
throat	The depth between the tip and the top of the bend (see Figure 3.4).
gape	The distance between the tip and the shoulder of the shank (see Figure 3.4).
tip	The pointed end that punctures and enters the fish (see Figure 3.4).

Once the distal end of a tool has been determined, you can then identify the left and right sides (see Figure 3.3). For tools made on split bone, it should also be possible to identify the 'superior' or 'exterior' (the outside, compact surface of bone) and 'inferior' or 'interior' (the inner, spongy surface of the bone) faces. Identification of these faces is an important step, as it will allow you to determine if that surface has been altered and to what extent.

3. ATTRIBUTES IN DESCRIBING TOOL TYPES

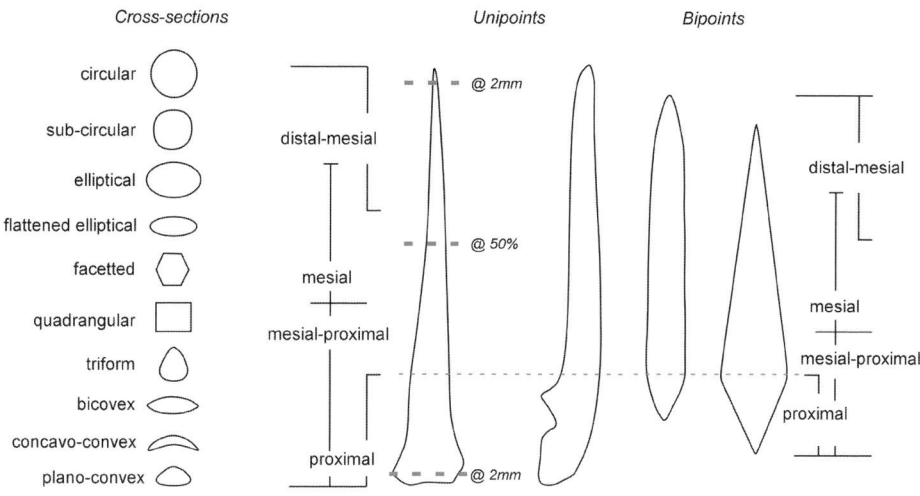

FIGURE 3.3. Terms for describing Australian pointed bone tools.

Cross-section

Recording and reporting cross-sections of several different areas (i.e. distal section, mesial section, proximal section) of the tool is a great way to communicate the form of the artefact. A cross-section is essentially the shape made when making a straight cut through the implement at a right angle to the axis (see Figure 3.3). Obviously, you do not actually cut the implement to make these determinations but instead hold the tool at eye height and assess the form at a certain point. Alternatively, you can utilise 3D technologies, scanning the artefact and then virtually cutting through the item using the software.

For elongated artefacts, like unipoints or handles, reporting the cross-section at three points is most informative. Recording the cross-section at two millimetres from the distal tip edge, at the midpoint (at 50 per cent) and at two millimetres from the proximal edge should be completed if possible (see Figure 3.3). Recording the distal and proximal dimensions two millimetres from the edge is suggested because it gives a true representation of the morphology of the extremity being described, whereas collecting these same measurements and attributes at the very edge (at 0 per cent and 100 per cent) can misrepresent the artefact's overall characteristics owing to the amount of damage these edges accrue in use. These 'absolute metrics' are the measurements you take to determine the maximum length, width, and thickness of the artefact.

For more compact implements, such as macropod shoulder blade knives, reporting cross-sections may only be informative for the active edge. Ultimately, the analyst must make a series of decisions regarding what attributes are most useful to describe in words the shape of the artefact to a future reader.

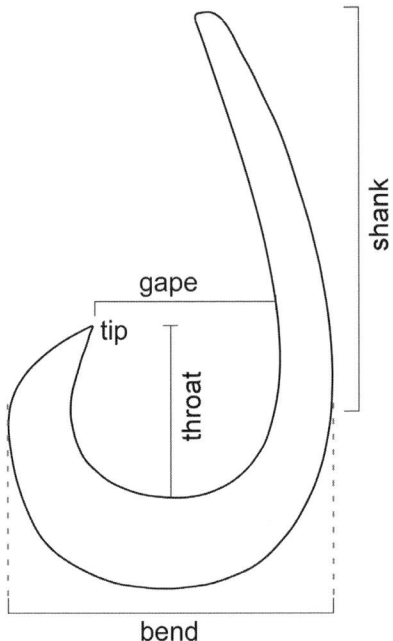

FIGURE 3.4. Terms for describing fishhooks.

Microtraces: traces from manufacturing, use, and taphonomic processes

Recording and describing all the microtraces, whether created by people or natural processes, is important for accurately reconstructing the history of the artefact (see figures 3.5 and 3.6, colour section). Chapter 2 outlined how different traces left behind by a wide range of manufacturing, use, and taphonomic factors commonly appear. As with tool morphology, the terms for describing anthropogenic microtraces have been largely standardised in the archaeological literature so that an analyst who never saw the artefact in person is able to clearly understand that item as if they did. Tables 3.2 and 3.3 provide terms that are most commonly required for describing bone and tooth tools found in the Australian context.

In practice, initial inspection of surfaces using the naked eye should be augmented with a hand lens and usually requires the use of microscopes at various magnifications for certainty. Further, some traces will only become evident under a microscope. Directional lighting is important in highlighting marks of interest and frequently illuminates traces that are almost invisible in bright light. As such, the analyst should rotate the item in directional lighting to make sure all angles have been examined.

Knowledge of trace creation needs to be joined with a good understanding of the cultural context from which the objects were recovered, the preservation conditions of the organics at the site, and the integration of previously collected data relating to similar finds elsewhere. Comparing worked and possibly-worked material with the wider faunal assemblage will allow the identification of whether the worked items form a discrete population in terms of species, skeletal part, degree of preservation, or size.

3. ATTRIBUTES IN DESCRIBING TOOL TYPES

TABLE 3.2. Common terms used in describing traces resulting from manufacture, use, and post-depositional damage.

TERM	DEFINITION
use fracture	A break caused during the use of the implement.
impact fracture	A break caused by a sudden impact with another object.
post-depositional fracture	A break that has occurred after the end of the implement's use life—once it has entered the archaeological record. Such fractures can be caused by trampling, degradation of the bone, etc.
post-depositional damage	Damage that has occurred after the end of the implement's use life—once it has entered the archaeological record.
utilised	The implement—or section of the implement—has been used.
use wear	Alteration to an implement that accrues as a result of its use.
ground	Shaping through grinding with an abrasive surface (grindstone, sea urchin spine, sand, ochre, etc.), leaving localised parallel to sub-parallel striations.
flaked	Shaping through the removal of chips through either direct or pressure-flaking with a hard edge.
polished	Part or all of the implement has been rubbed or lightly abraded to produce a smooth and shiny surface.
unaltered	Part of the implement retains its natural form and has not been deliberately altered for use.
hafted	Fitted or equipped with a hilt or handle.
handheld	The tool was held directly in the hand without any additions to create a comfortable hold (i.e. a haft).

Defining 'types'

One method archaeologists use to organise their data and attempt to bring out patterns and meaning is to group together like artefacts into 'types' (see Figure 3.6, colour section). Types can be based on morphological attributes, ethnographic observations of tool use, presence or distribution of certain use wear, presence of particular residues, or any other factor that may be of interest to the researcher. It is important to note that developed types may or may not reflect how the original creators and users of the technology viewed their toolkit, and different analysts may create different types depending on their research questions (see Adams & Adams 1991 and Lyman 2021 for discussion). As such, it is important that how and why certain artefacts have been placed together as a 'type' is clearly explained and that researchers remain flexible in regard to analysts exploring alternative groupings.

The tool types presented in Chapter 5 have been grouped together primarily on the basis of known function followed by gross morphological attributes. For some tool categories, types are more reliant on the raw material/s utilised in the tools' creation, and often the boundaries between one type and another are blurred. The typology used in this book is kept as simple as possible while also highlighting differences that may be significant for identifying the community of origin.

TABLE 3.3. Terms used in describing bone-pointed tools (distal extremity) (after Langley 2018).

TERM	DEFINITION
unipoint	Implement with only one pointed extremity.
bipoint	Implement with two opposing (one distal and one proximal) pointed extremities.
parallel mesial	The left and right sides of the implement are parallel in its mesial section.
sub-parallel mesial	The left and right sides of the implement are slightly angled either towards or away from each other in its mesial section.
lateral	The extremity appears sideways to the axis of the mesial section.
modified base	The proximal section of the implement has been intentionally modified from its natural form.
blunt-based	The proximal section of the implement has been altered into a square or rounded form with no protuberances.
conical-based	The proximal section of the implement has been altered into a cone-shaped form. The proximal edge can be either acute (sharp) or blunt.
triangular-based	The proximal section of the implement has been altered to have a triangular shape when viewed from the superior or inferior face.
convex-based	The proximal section of the implement has been altered to have a concavo-convex cross-section.
geometric	The implement—or section—is characterised by a regular (often symmetrical) shape.
spatulate tip	A broad, rounded extremity that is elliptical, flattened elliptical, or plano-convex in cross-section.
acute tip	An extremity that comes to a sharp tip.
concave tip	An extremity that has a concave-convex cross-section.
flaked tip	An extremity formed through percussion or pressure-flaking.

SUMMARY

- Using a standardised set of terms for describing bone and tooth artefacts is important for clearly communicating the morphology of the artefact and observed microtraces.
- The terminology used to describe bone and tooth artefacts was primarily developed for Eurasian technologies but can be successfully applied to other contexts, including Australia.

CHAPTER 4
ATTRIBUTES IN DESCRIBING ORNAMENT TYPES

Introduction

This chapter covers the basics of describing bone and tooth ornaments. The practice of adorning or ornamenting the human body is the most prevalent feature of all human societies and has been practised for over 100,000 years. From study of modern societies, researchers have found that ornaments are heavily associated with symbolic systems, being used to convey information about personal and group identity (Strathern 1979; Vanhaeren 2005; Wiessner 1982), and archaeological data have determined that this communication aspect has a deep history (Abadía & Nowell 2015; Kuhn & Stiner 2007a, b; Vanhaeren et al. 2013; White 1992a). Indeed, it is comparing beads and pendants both within and between sites that allows us to gather insights into the social status of buried individuals, cultural preferences for adornment, interactions between peoples, and more (e.g. Cristiani et al. 2014; Vanhaeren & d'Errico 2006).

To explore such issues, researchers must understand the complex technological processes behind ornament creation. As such, precise technological data must be collected to identify the behaviour involved in the acquisition of the raw materials, the transformation of those materials into items of adornment, their mode of use, and what happened to them after they were lost or abandoned. In short, the analyst is looking to identify the behaviours behind the ornament.

Terms for describing ornamentation

As with bone or tooth tools, ornaments must be recorded and described using consistent methods and terms. Objects that archaeologists have typically grouped together under the label of 'ornaments', 'personal adornment', or 'body ornamentation' include a huge variety of forms: shell beads, perforated teeth, carved pendants, rings, bracelets, bangles, anklets, or any other item that has been suspended or attached to the human body. In recent times, the way that humans decorate their bodies is almost endless, and they use a huge range of raw materials to create (and re-create) their ornaments. Unfortunately, the only parts of this ornamentation that archaeologists typically recover are those resistant to decay—parts made on inorganic or hard animal materials. Most of the hard animal material ornaments discovered are either 'beads' or 'pendants' (though sometimes archaeologists get lucky and find a partial or whole bangle). Beads are small, perforated items that can be threaded onto string or sewn onto fabric. Pendants, on the

TABLE 4.1. Definitions of major attributes used in describing beads and pendants (following Beck [1928] and Werner and Miller [2018]).

TERM	DEFINITION
Terms from Beck (1928)	
axis	An imaginary line through the centre of the perforation.
transverse section	The section at right angles to the axis that has the largest area.
longitudinal section	The section along the axis that includes the major radius—the section that shows the greatest distance from the axis to the profile.
perimeter	Line or lines bordering the transverse section.
diameter	Maximum width of the transverse section.
end	If the surface at the end of the perforation is approximately flat or is concave, it is called an end. If, however, it is so convex or conical as to form a feature of the bead, it is considered part of the bead profile.
apex	When the bead has no 'end', the point where the profile meets the perforation is called the apex of the bead.
profile	The line or lines bordering the longitudinal section, joining the two ends or apexes of the bead.
Terms from Werner and Miller (2018)	
aperture	The perforation point, including the cup, the point of restriction and the cup perimeter.
cup	The passage between the two faces of the beads.
cup perimeter	Top edge of the cup.
edge	Continuous side of the disc-shaped bead.
face	Flat surface of the disc-shaped bead. Each bead has two faces.
position of restriction	Usually the narrowest point of the aperture. The location where the drill initially breaks through to the opposite surface.
Additional terms	
labial	Surface of the tooth closest to the lips.
lingual	Surface of the tooth closest to the tongue.
root	Part of the tooth that was covered by cementum rather than enamel and attached to the jaw.
crown	Part of the tooth that is covered by enamel and acted as the cutting and/or grinding surface in use.
distal	Extremity of the pendant from which it originally hung. Usually where a perforation, groove or other form of attachment fixed to the item.
proximal	Extremity of the pendant that opposes the distal extremity.

4. ATTRIBUTES IN DESCRIBING ORNAMENT TYPES

other hand, are usually larger, can be perforated or not, and typically hang from one or two points of suspension.

As outlined succinctly by Beck (1928:1), 'to describe a bead fully it is necessary to state its form, perforation, colour, material, and decoration'. Each of these aspects is dealt with below. Procedures for analysing and describing beads and pendants have largely been developed by researchers reporting archaeological finds and defining terms used in their study, and then these approaches and terms are taken up by later studies. However, in 1928, Beck proposed a system of terminology specifically for reporting beads. While this system was developed to better understand a large corpus of stone, metal, and glass beads, the first order of general description is useful for any form of bead, including those made on organic materials. Those of Beck's (1928) terms that are recommended here are defined in Table 4.1 and Figure 4.1 and include bead axis, bead perimeter, and bead profile.

Beck's terms are joined here by terminology recently suggested by Werner and Miller (2018) for disc-shaped beads (see Table 4.1 and Figure 4.1). These terms include the 'aperture', which refers to the perforation point, and the 'cup', which is the passage between the two faces of the bead. The cup has concave or inward-facing walls, with the narrowest point of the aperture termed the 'position of restriction'. The position of restriction is usually the location where the drill initially breaks through the opposite surface, and the widest part of the cup indicates the direction from which drilling was initiated. The top edge of the cup is referred to as the 'cup perimeter'. Table 4.1 also includes terms commonly seen in the archaeological ornament literature and that are not covered by either Beck (1928) or Werner and Miller (2018). These terms cater to describing tooth ornaments as well as wholly-worked pendants.

Recording every single attribute listed in Table 4.1 for each bead or pendant found is not required (nor always useful). The analyst should select those attributes that are most useful in clearly describing the artefact and how it compares with similar finds from the same site as well as elsewhere. In general, the basic attributes that should be recorded are raw material, maximum length, width, and depth, as well as particulars regarding the attachment mechanism. Additions to this list will depend on the type of ornament found and the research questions being asked.

Raw material and shape

Ornament types are usually first classified by the raw material on which they are made. As with the analysis of tools, raw material identification will be based on the shape, size, colour, weight, surface texture, and any other visual aspect that might provide a clue to its origin. With archaeological and ethnographic data showing that beads and pendants can be made on marine and freshwater shells, animal teeth, bone, antler, and ivory, along with a multitude of other hard animal materials, it will be necessary to know what options were available in the find context. The goal is to narrow identification as much as possible—hopefully to species, but frequently only a very broad identification (such as 'terrestrial bone') can be achieved. Comparison with reference collections and previously published papers is useful for helping narrow down the options.

The overall shape of a bead or pendant is often dictated by the natural form of the raw material. Selection of raw materials for their shape is common, as seen by the widespread use of round 'basket-shaped' *Nassarius/Tritia* shells and deer canines across

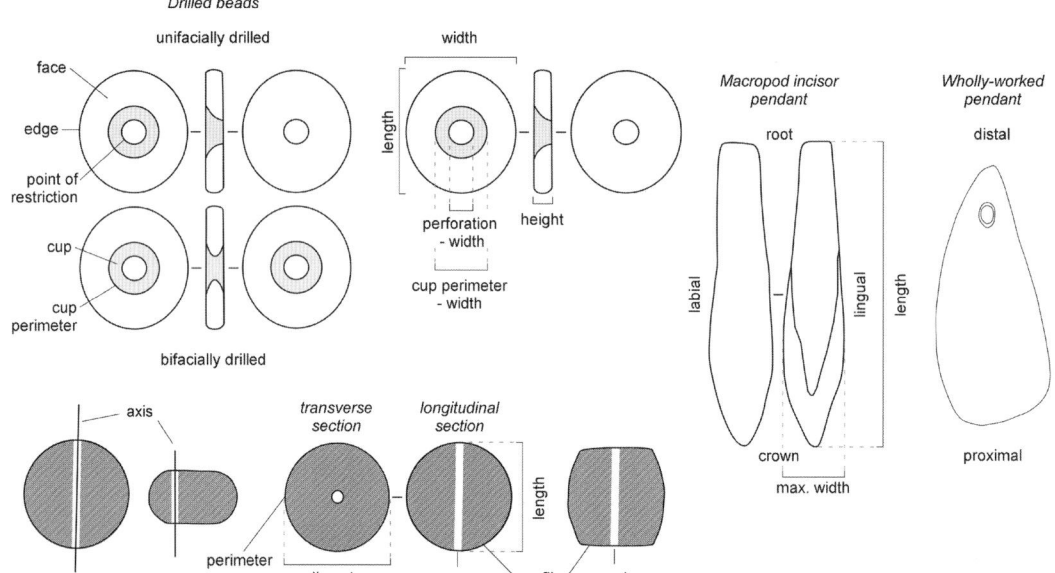

FIGURE 4.1. Terms used to describe pieces of ornamentation, including those that describe bead perforation (following Beck [1928] and Werner & Miller [2018]).

Eurasia and Africa (Vanhaeren & d'Errico 2006; Rigaud et al. 2019; Stiner 2014; Vanhaeren et al. 2013). As such, even where someone has not altered the gross form of a bead/pendant, the overall shape should still be considered and recorded. In describing shape, if the bead or pendant is made on a whole or near-whole tooth, simply stating which tooth (incisor, molar, etc.) from what animal provides the required information. If, on the other hand, it has been significantly altered, a description of these modifications is required, along with a description of the created shape along its axis and perimeter (see Table 4.1 and Figure 4.1).

Orientation and metrics

Orienting beads and pendants depends on the raw material and overall form of the piece. For disc-shaped beads, there is no obvious 'top' or distal section, whereas whole shell or tooth beads/pendants clearly present which section facilitated attachment (through either the presence of a perforation or use wear or residue distribution). Analysts usually orient beads/pendants with the attachment area at the top in illustrations, though orienting the item according to what was the apex or top of the raw material in life is also common (e.g. Taborin 1993; Vanhaeren & d'Errico 2006). If the artefact has been heavily worked and the distinctive features of the raw material are missing, analysts tend to revert to technological terminology (distal, proximal, face, etc.) to describe the artefact (e.g. Shunkov et al. 2020; White 2007). Whichever convention is used, it is necessary to be consistent and clear about which end of the artefact was strung or otherwise attached to the human body. If unsure, looking at whether there is a particular convention in general use for the specific type of bead being reported is useful.

4. ATTRIBUTES IN DESCRIBING ORNAMENT TYPES

Gathering metrics on the overall size of the ornament as well as perforations or other significant landmarks is important for not only clearly describing the artefact but also comparing it to other finds. The overall length, width, and height of each bead is essential information, as is the location of perforations or notches in relation to the closet edge. If perforations are present, recording the maximum width and length of these features is useful for assessing manufacture techniques and use intensity (see Figure 4.1). Just as the form of beads and pendants is vast, so too is the number of measurements that can be collected, and as such, the focus should be on data that will not only clearly describe the technology but also answer the posed research questions.

Manufacturing traces

Osseous ornaments can be ground, cut, sawn, drilled, or otherwise modified using any of the alteration methods described in Chapter 2. Which techniques are used depends on the cultural context in which the ornament is made, and how these marks appear on a bead or pendant will be expressed differently depending on a number of factors, including the difficulty in working the raw material, the technology used to alter the ornament, the experience of the manufacturer, the intentions of the manufacturer, the mode of attachment, the intensity of use, and the degree of post-depositional damage it suffers. These factors are understood thanks to careful observation of microscopic traces on archaeological specimens and experimental programs where researchers have effectively reverse-engineered beads and pendants to better understand them (e.g. d'Errico et al. 1993; Francis 1982; Tátá et al. 2014; White 2002).

In the manufacture of beads and pendants made on osseous materials, often the only deliberate modification to appear is a perforation or groove to facilitate attachment. An examination of archaeological finds dating back to about 45,000 years ago finds that a range of approaches can be used to perforate or groove a tooth or bone piece for it to be transformed into an ornament (White 2007), each of these processes leaving distinctive marks. First, people may scrape and gouge away material to thin a section of bone or tooth so that a hole may be drilled more easily, or they may simply scrape until enough material has been removed and a hole appears. These approaches leave traces of cutting and scraping (see Chapter 2) and were common approaches to perforating and notching animal teeth in the European Palaeolithic (e.g. White 2007).

Another common approach to creating a perforation was to use a stone-tipped drill. The drill could be applied to one ('unifacially drilled') or both ('bifacially drilled') sides of the tooth or bone or other material until it broke through to the opposite side. Yet another approach is the use of direct or indirect percussion to puncture through a tooth or other object. In such cases, the initial 'attack point'—exactly where the perforating tool was crushing the surface—sometimes remains visible (White 2007) (see Figure 4.2, colour section). A similar type of trace can also sometimes be found on drilled perforations, with the attack point being a scratch or shallow groove cut into the surface to give the drill purchase at the very beginning. Without such a cut or groove, the drill tip slides across a (usually convex) surface and is unable to bite into the raw material being worked.

The perforation or groove or other mark type (drilled, scraped, pressure, percussion), the size of the alteration, and its location on the bead/pendant should all be noted. If the ornament is on a whole tooth, shell, or similar, the analyst will typically specify through what anatomical section the perforation travels (root, crown, etc.).

In some cases, the surfaces of the bead or pendant have been further altered with incised or painted decorations. In each case, these additions should be carefully described in relation to their location on the ornament, as well as any clues as to how they were created. Finally, colour should be mentioned. Again, the raw material of the bead or pendant will often tell the reader what colour the piece is (teeth are white or cream, for example), but noting any apparently intentional alterations to the surface appearance is an important aspect of their design.

Attachment and use traces

Identifying how an ornament was attached to the human body is one of the most important aspects of its analysis, as this information can give you insights into the way it was worn and for how long. Differences in the 'mode of attachment' and use intensity can indicate changes over time in how a type of bead or pendant was used by the people who made them. Again, experimental programs have helped develop our understanding of how beads were 'strung' or otherwise attached, as well as how wear develops through the use life of the ornament (e.g. d'Errico 1993; Langley & O'Connor 2016; Vanhaeren et al. 2013; Werner & Miller 2018). Similarly, careful examination of ethnographic ornaments and ornamented clothing and tools provides data on beads that were attached in particular formations using particular types of ligatures (hair string, plant fibre strings, leather straps, sinew, etc.) and mastics and how use wear appears on these beads from 'real-world' conditions (Cristiani et al. 2014; Guzzo Falci et al. 2019; Langley & O'Connor 2016). Further, understanding how different raw materials wear over time is essential, as it is evident from experiments that some materials develop wear and break much faster than others (e.g. Mărgărit 2016). Comparison of data collected from ethnographic collections as well as experimental programs allows for the best possible understanding of how use wear and residues build up on different bead types and uses, allowing for robust interpretations of archaeological finds.

Ornaments build up different patterns of wear, which allows the identification of how each ornament was suspended (e.g. Cristiani et al. 2014; Guzzo Falci et al. 2019; Langley & O'Connor 2016; Vanhaeren et al. 2013). These modifications include changes in the original colour of the raw material, polish, the creation of facets, rounding, the creation of grooves, compression, and indentations (Bonnardin 2009). While it cannot always be absolutely determined how a particular ornament was worn in the past (unless we find it in a burial context; Cristiani & Borić 2012), these wear patterns do narrow down the possibilities. However, it needs to be remembered that ornaments can have complex use lives in which they are used not only on one necklace by one person but also perhaps restrung, incorporated into other pieces of accoutrement, exchanged, heirloomed, or hidden away for long periods, all of which will create complex use patterns on their surfaces (e.g. Ewart 2012; Lillios 1999; Wiessner 1982).

The location, directionality, and intensity of use wear and residues on each item must be carefully recorded to allow how they were used in the past to be confidently reconstructed. Creating maps—basic outlines of the ornament surfaces—onto which observed modifications can be drawn is perhaps the most effective way of not only identifying a pattern of use but also communicating this information to others. On these

4. ATTRIBUTES IN DESCRIBING ORNAMENT TYPES

maps, use wear should be recorded, as should any observed residues or taphonomic alterations. A correlation between use wear and anthropogenic residues can corroborate these two details, while differences can highlight issues that need to be addressed.

Colourant residues can be deposited on beads in a number of ways, including the use of ochre in the manufacturing process (such as to polish bead surfaces) (Nivens 2020), deliberate staining or painting of the beads (d'Errico et al. 2005), incidental accumulation through rubbing against stained threads or materials (Bouzzougar et al. 2007; Langley & O'Connor 2015, 2016), rubbing against painted bodies (Langley et al. 2016), or the use of mastics that include colourants as an ingredient (Cristiani et al. 2014; Rigaud et al. 2014). Colourants and other residues can also come to be present on bead surfaces as part of processes unrelated to the beads themselves, such as the use of a grindstone previously used to create ochre powder (Orton 2008) or by the beads rubbing up against colourant nodules while in archaeological deposits.

Care needs to be taken not to attribute taphonomic residues, such as mineral staining or incidental burning, to anthropogenic actions. The most commonly found staining (especially in cave environments) is manganese oxide staining, which first appears as small black 'flowers' and can grow to cover the entire bone in a black colour (López-González et al. 2006) (see Figure 2.10, colour section). Similarly, organic items resting in soil underneath or close to a fireplace will result in the raw material changing colour from its original whites and creams to golds, browns, and solid black (Shahack-Gross et al. 1997; Shipman et al. 1984). With black pigments being popular among past human groups, being able to determine the origin of black colours is an important part of the analysis. Each of these processes, taphonomic and anthropogenic, must be considered to determine how residues or other forms of colour change should be interpreted.

Finally, a type of use wear that is particular to suspended objects should be discussed. Beads or pendants that are perforated and have seen intensive use will frequently display a 'keyhole'. This 'keyholing' appears as a small notch into the aperture

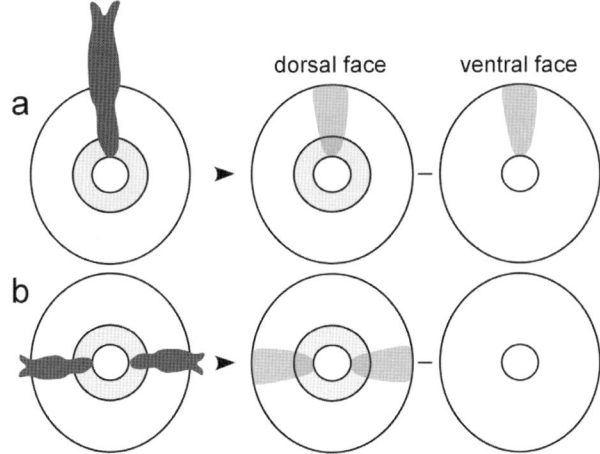

FIGURE 4.3. Different modes of attachment create distinctive types and distributions of wear.

wall and is formed by the string repeatedly rubbing in a very localised manner (White 2007) (see Figure 4.2, colour section). This notch within a perforation appears very much like an old keyhole in its profile, hence the name. If keyholing is present, it allows the analyst to determine how the bead/pendant hung with reasonable certainty. Similarly, some items (such as teeth) will not be perforated for stringing but rather will have been tightly wrapped using ligatures (and often also glued) to one extremity. In such cases, the strings with abrasives from the mastic or particles caught up in the strings in use will wear striations, polished areas, and notches into a localised area of the bead surface (Cristiani et al. 2014; Rigaud et al. 2014) (see Figure 4.3).

Through bringing all this information together on raw material selection and modifications made either intentionally or unintentionally for each ornament recovered, insights into the social world in which they were once a vibrant part is gained.

SUMMARY

- The standardisation of terms used to describe bone and tooth beads and pendants is important for clearly communicating descriptions of archaeological finds.
- The careful examination of alterations to the raw material can determine exactly how an ornament was prepared for use.
- Recording the location, type, and intensity of use wear and residues is important for identifying how beads and pendants were suspended or otherwise attached to the human body.
- Not all residues or colour changes are the result of intentional human behaviours to decorate the ornament.

CHAPTER 5
TOOLS

Introduction

This chapter provides descriptions of bone, tooth, quill, claw, and turtle shell tools made and utilised across the Australian continent. Some of these tools were so ubiquitous or they so fascinated the European observer that they are well recorded in European diaries, letters, and official reports and have a strong presence in museums both in Australia and abroad. For these objects, researchers have a basic understanding of their manufacture and use in different parts of the continent, though these understandings are frequently much less detailed than their stone or hardwood counterparts. Some of the tools described below are not mentioned in European writings at all and have only become known to the author through their rare presence in museum collections. Often, these objects are nondescript, and it is therefore not entirely surprising that they were missed or ignored by the early European observer. Elucidation of how these tools were used requires conversations with the communities from which they were taken and possibly a series of experiments to learn about their functionality.

The information below is far from complete. It represents what has been gathered from the literature and museum records over a period of four years, and new insights are likely to occur as researchers and communities continue to engage with such artefacts. It should also be noted that while specific localities or peoples are mentioned wherever that information is available, this representation reflects the travels of early Europeans across the continent and may not be truly representative of a particular artefact's spatial distribution (see Figure 5.1). Similarly, archaeological examples are included in this discussion where their form or function has been described.

Defining types

For ease of reading, tools have been grouped into major categories or 'types' to organise the available information. Future study of these technologies may divide tools grouped together here, find reason to separate them, or organise them in an entirely different fashion. Presented below is just one way to start talking about this amazing array of technologies.

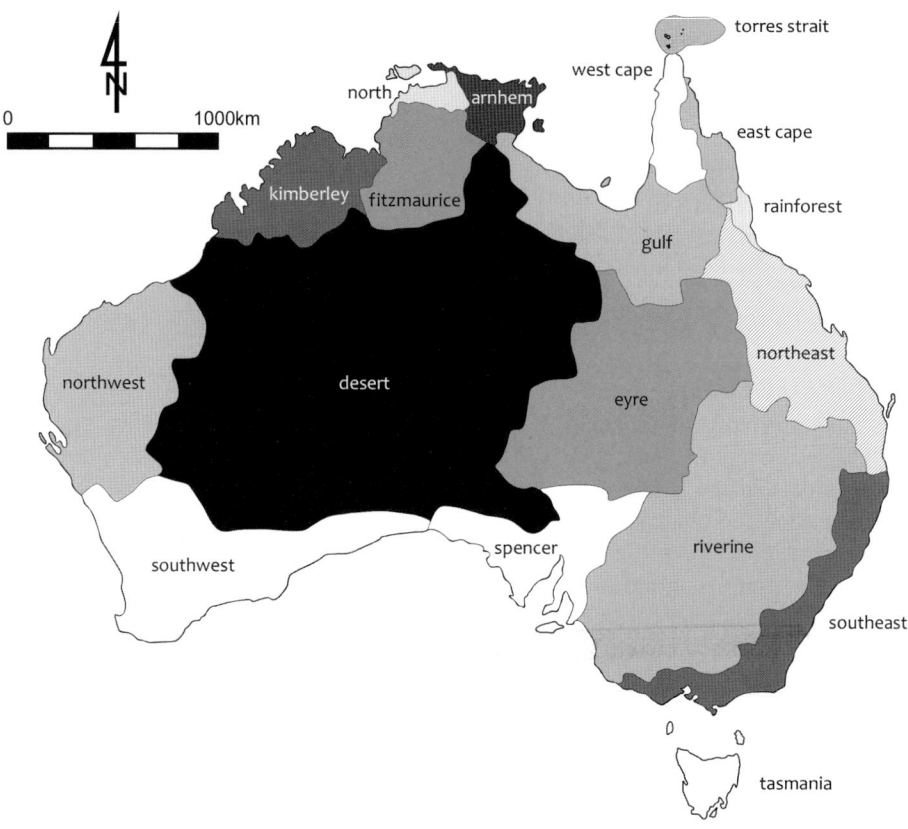

FIGURE 5.1. This map indicates those regions with many tools curated in the studied museum collections (darker colours) through to regions that are least well represented (lighter colours) distributions of wear.

Awls

Description

An awl is a handheld pointed tool commonly used for piercing—or otherwise working—surfaces of soft raw materials such as skins, barks, or plant fibres. In the Australian context, awls are most commonly made on macropod fibulae, though emu, cassowary, and other large bird long bones are also widespread (Table 5.1). These tools were used both unhafted and with a handhold made of resin or resin overlaid with plant fibre twine, which was sometimes woven (see Figure 5.2). Donald Thomson (1936:72) mentions that for the countries of North Queensland, beeswax was used instead of resin, as beeswax 'is not brittle, when displaced with use it does not crack like resin, and it can be rendered plastic by heating, and thus replaced in position without permanent damage'. Bone awls appear to have been (and continue to be in many cases) multifunctional and utilised over most, if not all, of the continent.

Broadly speaking, two types of awl are evident, here called Type 1 and Type 2 Awls. Type 1 Awls are those often referred to as 'stilettos' in museum archives and ethnographic

5. TOOLS

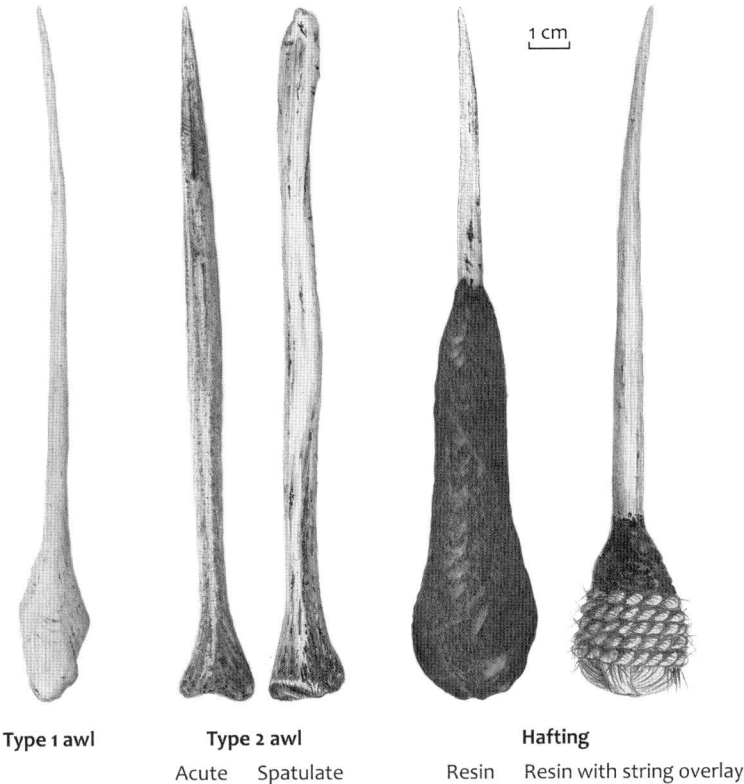

Type 1 awl   Type 2 awl   Hafting
              Acute   Spatulate   Resin   Resin with string overlay

FIGURE 5.2. Two main types of bone awl are found in Australia. Type 1 Awls are characterised by a sharply attenuated point, while Type 2 Awls are thicker and feature a shorter acute or spatulate tip. Hafting of both types appears to have been common, using dark resins or beeswax sometimes overlaid with woven fibres.

accounts, with this term stemming from the sharply tapering blade with a very acute distal extremity (see Figure 5.2). Type 1 Awls are most commonly made on the fibula of large birds (emu, cassowary, wading birds).

Type 2 Awls are much more common in both museum and archaeological collections and are usually made on macropod fibulae (see Figure 5.2). The condyle of the fibula can be entirely intact or deliberately rounded, with the distal point acute or spatulate in form, probably resulting from the most common use of the tool. Dark residues and staining from having been hafted in resin or beeswax are common on both Type 1 and 2 Awls held in museum collections.

Manufacture and use

Identification of awls recovered from the archaeological record rests mainly on their overall morphology and the presence of use wear consistent with having been accrued through repetitive piercing of skins or plant materials. Numerous pointed bone implements recovered from archaeological contexts across the continent have been summarily

TABLE 5.1. Summary of information available from ethnographic sources, museum collections and archaeological reports regarding the characteristics of awls utilised in Australia. **Bold** = museum presence; *italics* = ethnography indicated only; underline = archaeological presence.

REGION	RAW MATERIALS	TYPES	DISTAL MORPH-OLOGIES	EVIDENCE FOR HAFTING
Kimberley	macropod fibula; large bird long bone; fishbone	Type 2	acute; spatulate	dark resin covering proximal section
Fitzmaurice				
North	macropod fibula	**Type 2**	spatulate	dark resin covering proximal section
Arnhem	macropod fibula; large bird long bone	**Type 2**	acute; spatulate	a number with dark resin traces covering proximal two-thirds of the point; one example has remnants of woven wool or fur string covering; red colourant traces; intact haft made from plant fibre string and dark resin; proximal section (just below condyle) wrapped with vegetable fibre and resin
Desert	macropod fibula; macropod (?) rib	**Type 2**	acute	dark resin covering proximal section; red colourant traces
Gulf	macropod fibula	**Type 1**; **Type 2**	spatulate	red colourant traces; dark resin covering proximal section
Torres Strait	[none identified]			
West Cape	macropod fibula; macropod tibia; emu or cassowary fibula; emu or cassowary ischium	**Type 1**; **Type 2**	acute; spatulate	dark resin covering proximal section
East Cape	macropod fibula; emu fibula	**Type 2**	acute; spatulate	dark resin covering proximal section

5. TOOLS

REGION	RAW MATERIALS	TYPES	DISTAL MORPH-OLOGIES	EVIDENCE FOR HAFTING
Rainforest	macropod fibula; macropod femur; cassowary or emu leg bone	**Type 1**	acute	yellow resin traces; dark resin covering proximal section
Northeast	macropod fibula; emu fibula	**Type 2**	acute	dark resin covering proximal section; red colourant traces
Southeast	emu fibula; macropod fibula; human fibula	**Type 1; Type 2**	acute; spatulate	
Tasmania	macropod fibula; bird long bone; seal (?) bone	Type 2	acute; spatulate	
Riverine	macropod fibula; emu fibula	**Type 2;** Type 2	acute	dark resin covering proximal section
Spencer	emu bone; macropod fibula	**Type 1;** Type 2	acute	red colourant traces
Eyre	macropod fibula; emu fibula	**Type 1; Type 2**	acute; spatulate	red colourant traces; dark resin covering proximal section
Southwest	macropod fibula	*Type 2*		
Northwest	macropod fibula	**Type 2**	acute	dark resin covering proximal section

described as 'awls', though whether these artefacts were in fact an awl—as opposed to any other pointed bone tool or ornament of similar size and appearance—requires a thorough review (see discussion in Langley 2018). As images of archaeological bone tools have been rarely published, it is currently impossible to determine the 'oldest' example of this tool. However, given that awls are essentially the same form as Type 1 Nose Bones (see Chapter 6)—for which an example dating to beyond 46,000 years ago is known (Langley et al. 2016)—it follows that awls were possibly one of the oldest types of bone tools created in Australia. Certainly, early European inhabitants were under the impression that such tools had been around for a long time. Brough Smyth, describing Victoria, stated that:

> The bone and wooden awls and nails (*min-der-min*), still in use where European nails and needles are not to be had, are very ancient implements. The bone-awls are found

in the long disused *mirrn-yongs* and shell-mounds with stone tomahawks and chips of basalt. They are not ornamented in any way. (Brough Smyth 1972[1878]a:liii)

Brough Smyth, reporting investigations of the mirrn-yong heaps between Cape Otway Lighthouse and Parker River in the Southeast region by Mr Henry Ford, reports that:

> Mr. Ford opened two, and found in them one stone tomahawk, about four inches in length and three inches in breadth, and one, one inch in thickness, sharpened at one end, and composed of hard, fine-grained siliceous sandstone; numerous chips of chert or flint, black and white, such as occur along the coast, and used probably for cutting, skinning animals, cleaning skins, &c.; bone-awls, six inches in length, some round and some triangular, carefully ground and smoothed; bone nose-ornaments (apparently), about two inches in length, round and polished, and bluntly point at both ends; charred bones of the wallaby, opossum, kangaroo-rat, birds, fish, seal (ribs, vertebrae, and jaw-bone), dog (jaw-bone); mutton-fish shells; fresh and salt water mussel-shells; and limpet, whelk, periwinkle, and buckie shells. (Brough Smyth 1972[1878]a:240)

He continues on the next page talking about how Mr Reginald AF Murray, Geological Surveyor, collected at the mouth of Coal Creek near Cape Paterson (Southeast region):

> four chips of chert and two well-polished bone-awls from a shell-heap made up principally of shells of the mutton-fish, limpet, periwinkle, &c. The awls appear to be very old, and, judging from the appearance of the heap, it is probably that it is long since the spot was frequented. (Brough Smyth 1972[1878]a:241)

The Type 1 or the 'stiletto' form of awl are evident from the Gulf, West Cape, Rainforest, Eyre, Spencer, and Southeast regions (Table 5.1). Fibula from large birds—particularly emu and cassowary—are favoured for their construction, perhaps owing to their ability to be worked to a sharper point, though other factors not tied to raw material properties cannot be ruled out. Apart from their longer and sharper distal point, no other factors distinguish them from the more common Type 2 Awls. Finally, it is possible that some of these points—catalogued as 'awls' in collections—functioned more as weapons (daggers) than as utilitarian tools (see 'Murder weapons' below). Roth (1904:25) notes that the 'stilettos' he observed for North Queensland were '6 to 8 1/2 inches long, and made either of bone (kangaroo, wallaby, emu) or of "iron-wood": when of the latter material, it is usually discarded after use'.

By far and large, most of the awls described in written documentation and held within museum collections worldwide are those here brought together as Type 2 Awls. These awls are found across the continent, with museum collections holding examples from every region except for the Torres Strait, Southwest, Rainforest, and Fitzmaurice regions. Ethnographic accounts, however, suggest a wider distribution of this tool.

The Type 2 macropod fibulae examples (which are the vast majority) can be more or less worked. Most exhibit an intact condyle, with a not uncommon presence of those worked down to a blunted proximal extremity (either deliberately or incidentally from ongoing use). Spatulate distal tips appear to be more common, though acute versions are far from absent. The creation of the distal extremity (whether acute or spatulate) appears to be from a combination of flaking and grinding. An intact macropod fibula can

5. TOOLS

be easily snapped in half between the hands, then only requiring the shaping of the new distal end into the desired form. Roth (1904:11) states that in North Queensland, the 'bone may be chipped or ground in the manufacture of awls, and ground in the making of a stiletto: the grinding process can be effected both dry and wet'. A similar approach is described for people at Moorundie (Riverine region) on the Murray River by Eyre, who states that awls were made:

> from the fibula of the emu or kangaroo, and are pointed at one end by being rubbed on a stone, they are used in sewing as we use a shoemaker's awl, the hole is bored and the thread put through with the hand; the thread is made of the sinews of the emu and kangaroo. (Eyre 1845:310)

Perusal of Type 2 Awls from Yirrkala, Arnhem region, revealed that about half as many had acute distal tips as spatulate tips—which may indicate points further along the use-wear continuum or awls simply put to different uses. Discussions with Noongar-speaking peoples of South West Western Australia during the 1970s and 1980s shed light on the presence of both acute and spatulate tips within the museum collections (Bird & Beeck 1980). Caroline Bird and Colin Beeck's informants noted that kangaroo fibula was the preferred raw material to make most of their pointed bone tools, with this bone referred to using the Noongar word djung or djung bone. In their demonstration of how the tools were made, the bone was snapped between the hands about two-thirds along its length. One man elected the distal end to make a djung needle and the other (proximal) end to make a birnd. The djung needle was a shorter tool with a more spatulate tip, while the birnd was longer with a more acute tip. The use of the word 'needle' here appears to reference its sharp tip and use—which are that of an awl. After snapping the bone in two, the shafts of the bone implements were cleaned and smoothed, and the tips sharpened. Both European (such as bottle glass and sandpaper) and locally available materials (sand, grinding stone) were used in this process of shaping, with one informant—Mr Riley—stating that if the bone were fresh, he would be able to remove the remaining meat easily if it were placed in hot ashes for a short period, but in this instance, he cleaned the bone by repeatedly thrusting the bone into sandy ground. Mr Riley is also reported to have taken a 'handful of wet sand and rubbed the shaft, working the broken end of the bone with wet sand sticking to his fingers' (Bird & Beeck 1980:170). An unnamed woman commented to Bird and Beeck that she would have used sand held in a rag to make the tool. Archaeological items used to shape bone tools are rarely reported (if bone residues found on the edges of stone tools are not included); however, Isabel McBryde found sandstone blocks more than 2000 years old with 'smaller narrow grooves presumably for sharpening bone artefacts' at Graman on the New England Tableland (McBryde 1968:81).

In southwestern Australia, people remembered the djung needle being used in preparing kangaroo hides for cloak- or bag-making. Specifically, it was used to remove the inner membrane from the pelt using the spatulate-tipped point before being used to pierce holes. A firsthand account provided by Mr Jackson described that his grandmother would push the needle through the skin to make a slit before turning the tool 90 degrees to open the slit wider. Wet kangaroo sinew was then pushed through the slit using the concave face of the awl. Another account of sewing skins in southwestern Australia is provided by Hassel and Davidson while listing items found in a woman's bag:

> One or more awls of kangaroo bone. These were about seven or eight inches long and one-eights of an inch thick. One side was flattened, the other rounded... Sewing was performed by holding the sides of two skins together and forcing a hole through them with an awl. Dry sinew was then threaded through the hole and drawn tight. The holes were spaced about [a] quarter of an inch apart, but since the stitches were over-sewn the seam was very strong. It was dampened when finished and set very firmly. (Hassel & Davidson 1936:693)

A similar use of bone awls is described for both Victoria and Queensland, with Tom Petrie describing that in Moreton Bay (Northeast region):

> possum skins were greatly prized as coverings when the nights were cold. They were sewn together, and so made nice rugs. They were sewn with string, which was really kangaroo-tail sinew. This sinew was kept on purpose for sewing, and when wanted was damped to make it soft. The holes for the string were pierced either with hedgehog [echidna] quills or sharp bones. (Petrie 1904:87)

Similarly, William Buckley spoke of the use of bone awls by the community west of Port Phillip (Southeast region) with which he lived for some 17 years: 'their only covering being skin rugs, sewn together with sinews—using as needles fine bones of the kangaroo. These rugs serve them also to lay upon' (Flannery 2009:113).

In preparing the furs for sewing, people stretched them out to dry. Along the south coast, Schürmann spoke of the peoples of Port Lincoln (Spencer region), having caught a kangaroo or wallaby, as practising the following procedure:

> As soon as the skin is taken from the animal it is firmly stretched on a level spot of ground by means of pegs inserted round the edge, the flesh side being upwards; when it is dry all fleshy substances that adhere to the skin are gently pulled or shaved off with a sharp-edged piece of quartz[;] it is then rubbed with the rough surface of an ironstone, which makes it both soft and pliable. The skins are then sewn together with the sinews from a kangaroo's tail, holes for this purpose being made with a thin pointed bone. (Schürmann 2009[1879]:210)

A similar description is given for skin-working in Victoria, in that:

> the awls or nails used by the Aborigines for fastening the skins of animals to bark or wood when they are put out to dry in the sun are of various sizes. Those used for pegging down a late skin are long, and those for the skins of opossum, native cat, &c., much smaller. They are usually made of the leg-bones of animals. Those made of bone are smoothed, polished, and brought to a fine point... The native name for the nail is *Min-der-min* or *Min-dah-min*... Those used in Victoria are similar to the nails in use in Queensland. The basket lent to me by the late Mr. Matthew Hervey, which was dropped by a woman of the Burdekin tribe, contained amongst other things what appeared to be a hussy. I found in it six bone-awls, one wooden awl or nail, and three pieces of bone shaped like a spatula. The bone awls or nails were used to pierce holes in the skins of which, when sewn together, they make rugs, and the spatula-like instrument perhaps for flattening and smooth the seams. The hussy was a piece of opossum

5. TOOLS

skin tied together with twine spun from the fort of the opossum, and again fastened securely with stronger wine made of some fibre. (Brough Smyth 1972[1878]a:350)

Finally, Aiston (1928:13) noted that the:

Kokatha and Parnkalla . . . over about Tarcoola and along the coast from Port Lincoln to Fowler's Bay on the west coast of South Australia [would have] the skin . . . torn off the animal, not cut off, there was never any flesh adhering, the skin was pegged out with wooden pegs in some shady place until dry, and was then sewn into the shape required with a bone awl.

Brough Smyth (1972[1878]a) similarly noted that bone awls in Victoria were used 'for fastening the skins of animals to bark or wood when they are put out to dry', while Bennett (1967[1834]:175–6), reporting his travels in New South Wales, described the use of possum, kangaroo, and other animal skins sewn together with the dried, split tendons of kangaroos to make cloaks for use in inclement weather. The skins had been dried and scraped prior to sewing with a bone 'needle'.

Museum notes attached to awls collected from the Desert region similarly mention their use to pierce or drill holes in skins and other materials, with one from Roebourne (Northwest region) specifically stating it was used for sewing. Archaeological finds on Seton Island by Stockton (1977b) of two macropod fibulae unipoints with polished distal extremities were suggested by the excavator to have been used in skin-working.

Who undertook this skin-working and sewing is mentioned by Curr when describing Bangerang people of the Goulburn River area of Victoria:

the men hunted opossums during the day, skinned them on their return to camps, and, after feasting on their flesh, pegged out the skins, each on a small sheet of bark, which were then placed in front of the fire, so as to dry gradually. This done, the skins were scored with a mussel-shell in various ornamental patterns, and were then fit for use. When enough had been collected they were sewn together, a sharp bone being used as an awl to pierce them with; the sinews of the animal itself, or of a kangaroo serving very well for thread. This pegging out of opossum skins was a very favourite occupation, and the tap, tap, tap of the dusky workman, as he sat at his fire chanting his monotonous corroboree, might often be heard far into the night. (Curr 1965[1883]:131)

Bennett also observed men working possum skins near Goulburn River plains, stating that:

I went up to one who was busy engaged in making an opossum-skin cloak: he sewed the skins together with the fibres of the bark of the 'Stringy Bark' tree for thread, by first perforating holes in it with a sharp piece of bone, and then passing the thread through the holes as he proceeded. (Bennett 1967[1834]:322–3)

From these various descriptions of the working of furs, it appears that awls were commonly used to peg down the skins to be stretched and dried, not just for removing the inner membrane, piercing holes, and threading. The efficiency of these tools for sewing may be supported by Haydon's (1846:64) observation that for Port Phillip and surrounds (Southeast region), 'although common English needles can be procured in most parts of the settled districts, the natives still adhere to the old method'.

Another commonly mentioned use for bone awls (usually Type 2) is the boring of holes in wooden or other plant-based material culture. For example, Basedow (1913:304) noted that a bone awl was used to make the holes during the construction of a bark canoe, with the awl stated to be 'made out of the leg-bone of a wallaby'. Roth (1904:25, 1907:7) also noted the use of bone awls for perforating bark sheets in canoe-making in North Queensland, and they were also used for removing the cortical layer from the fibres of the *Livistonia* palm (cabbage tree palm) in making twine on the Musgrave River, hollowing out earring tubes on the Pennefather River, boring the holes in the Wimmera for fixing the peg (Endeavour River) and removing rough outer bark on water carriers and bark blankets in the Atherton district. He also notes that a 'stiletto' (Type 1 Awl) was used in picking off the inner surface of melaleuca bark in preparation for making blankets, canoes, and certain water carriers on Keppel Island (Northeast region) (Roth 1904:9) and 'for piercing the edges of bark before threading them in the manufacture of canoes (Pennefather and Tully Rivers)' (Roth 1904:25). Thomson (1936:74) similarly noted for Cape York Peninsula that bone awls were 'employed in the manufacture of water vessels made from the sheathing leave base of the *Archontophoenix* palm, and for the seams of the bow and stern of bark canoes', a practice also noted for eastern Arnhem Land in museum archives. Examples of both macropod and cassowary bone from the Rainforest region (Cairns) are stated in the Australian museum record as being used for making bark water bags, while in Noongar country (Southwest region), awls were used in making the hollow in the butt end of the spear to accommodate the hook of a spearthrower, along with making holes to hold the drill in fire-making (Bird & Beeck 1980). Moore (1884:23) also recorded that kangaroo fibula awls were used for the purpose of drilling holes in the butt of spears and were known as '*Djunong*'—*Djung-o* in the north, and *Djung* at King George's Sound'. Indeed, ethnographic accounts for North Queensland note that these tools were 'always carried in men's dilly bags' (Roth 1904:25) and were a common tool found wherever spears made with a distal (tip/shaft) morticed into a proximal (butt/haft) position were located.

Another common use for bone awls is in weaving plant fibre baskets. Artefacts hundreds to thousands of years old and that present use wear consistent with having been used in weaving and/or skin-working have been recovered from archaeological contexts quite removed from each other, including Durras North on the southeast coast (Langley et al. 2021b); Wee Jasper, deep within the Riverine region (Theden-Ringl & Langley 2018); and Malangangerr (Schrire 1982), Nawamoyn (Schrire 1982), Paribari (Schrire 1982), and Madjedbebe (Langley et al. 2023), all in the very northeast of the continent. Other archaeological examples may have been recovered from Fromms Landing on the Lower Murray River by Mulvaney (1960:66), who described finding 'polished awls made from bird bone' among other bone unipoints in Levels 6 and 7, dated to about 3500 years ago. Other possible bone awls of mammal bone are reported for these and lower levels of this same site. Another example was found in Cloggs Cave in East Gippsland, dating to the Pleistocene deposits retained there (Flood 1974). Whether these archaeological awls were used in basket-making or working with skins is currently unknown.

Bone awls are also commonly cited as being used in the modification of the human body, including to cut the scalp in mourning practices, to pierce the nasal septum

5. TOOLS

(discussed in Chapter 6), and to knock out teeth. This last practice was widespread across the southeast and interior of the continent (at least) (see, e.g. Augustus Robinson 1844 in Clark 2000d; Bennett 1967[1834]; Collins 1975[1798]; Curry 1965[1883]; Hunter 1963[1793]), including among the 'Murrumbidgee, Murray, Ovens, and Goulburn tribes', where a young man would have one of his front teeth knocked out as part of growing into an adult:

> this was done by first loosing the flesh from round the tooth with a piece of sharp bone, then one kicked it out with a piece of wood, used as a punch. (Brough Smyth 1972[1878]a:64–5)

Gason (2009[1879]:266–7) gives a detailed account of the event for the Dieyerie (Diyari) tribe, while Mitchell (1965[1839]a:218, 1965[1839]b:345) reports that for communities on the western side of the continent, it was not only men but also women and children who lost a front tooth.

Frequently observed on museum-curated awls is dark staining affecting the proximal one- to two-thirds of the artefact. This staining is found across raw material types (macropod, emu, large bird, etc.) and on items from many different regions (Table 5.1). After viewing the museum specimens, it became evident that this staining originated from the tool originally having been hafted within a dark resin (such as spinifex) handhold. Awls still retaining their resin handhold are also present in museums, with some featuring a plant fibre twine overlay (twine being wound round over the resin repeatedly) or, more rarely, a one-piece woven fabric piece. Such examples include two large stingray barbs from the 'Northern Territory' (no further provenance in museum notes provided), while an example with plant fibre twine overlay was collected from Milingimbi (Arnhem region, held in the Australian Museum). Such plant fibre overlays—whether twine wrapped or with a woven fabric piece—would have created a comfortable and long-lasting handhold. This method of hafting bone awls is rarely mentioned in written accounts of awl construction and use in Australia, though Eyre (1845:Plate I) does provide an illustration of what appears to be an awl hafted with resin and string from the Riverine region. From the disproportionate amount of stained (that is, previously hafted) tools compared with still resin-hafted tools curated in museums, it would seem that removing and recycling the resin from an exhausted awl was a regular part of retooling.

Finally, it is interesting to note that bone awls appear to be a ubiquitous tool found in collected or otherwise inspected women's bags. For example, a basket collected from a woman on Melville Island (North region) contained 'a single animal bone sharpened to a point and a number of other such bones wrapped in bark' (Item X020688 notes, Museum Victoria), while Mitchell (1965[1839]a:337) for the Bogan River (Riverine region) states that the:

> women usually carry besides their children, thus mounted, bags containing all the things which they and the men possess . . . pins for dressing and drying opossum skins, or for net-making.

Similarly, Hassell and Davidson for Wheelman (Wiilman) and surrounding peoples of the Southwest region describe how:

a bag or *coot* was made from a young male kangaroo skin prepared like the skins for cloaks. It was doubled up so that the hind legs formed the band which went around the neck, while the neck of the animal served as the flap to cover the mouth of the bag . . . A bag is used to carry all the household goods and food . . . The typical contents of a *coot* may be listed as follows.

- One or more awls of kangaroo bone. These are about seven or eight inches long and one-eights of an inch thick. One side was flattened, the other rounded.
- A bundle of dried kangaroo tail sinews rolled in a ring.
- A women's knife.
- A *cobal*, or small bag made from the paunch of the opossum, scraped and turned inside out. It was usually filled with plucked opossum fur for spinning.
- A spindle whorl.
- One or more magic stones. (Hassell & Davidson 1936:693)

Yet another account of a woman's bag, this time by Grey on the western coast of Australia, states that:

the contents of a native woman's bag are:—A flat stone to pound roots with; earth to mix with the pounded roots; quartz, for the purpose of making spears and knives; stones for hatchets; prepared cakes of gum, to make and mend weapons, and implements; kangaroo sinews to make spears and to sew with; needles made of the shin bones of kangaroos, with which they sew their cloaks, bags, &c.; opossum hair to be spun into waist belts; shavings of kangaroo skins to polish spears, &c. The shell of a species of muscle to cut hair, &c. with; native knives, a native ratchet, pipe clay; red ochre, or burnt clay; yellow ochre; a cup of paper bark to carry water in; waistbands, and spare ornaments; pieces of quartz, which the native doctors have extracted from their patients, and thus cured them from diseases; these they preserve as carefully as Europeans do relics. Banksia cones (small ones), or pieces of a dry white species of fungus, to kindle fire with rapidly, and to convey it from place to place; grease, if they can procure it from a whale, or from any other source; the spare weapons of their husbands, or the pieces of wood from which these are to be manufactured; the roots, &c. which they have collected during the day. Skins not yet prepared for cloaks are generally carried between the bag and the back, so as to form a sort of cushion for the bag to rest on. (Grey 1841:266)

The less inspected men's bags are also found to contain bone awls, with an example called a nerti from Port Lincoln stated to contain:

all the above weapons and implements are with other things packed in the knapsack which is carried under the left arm, being by one or more strings run over the shoulder. It is either a mere kangaroo skin, drawn together by a string like a purse, or a coarse net, manufactured of the fibres of rushes. The smaller articles contained in the knapsack are:—a large flat shell for drinking, a round smooth stone for breaking the bones of animals, one or more kinds of paint, a wooden scoop used in roasting roots, some

5. TOOLS

pieces of quartz, and the whole skin of some animal which answers for a purse to keep minute things in, such as kangaroo sinews and pointed bones of various sizes (serving for needles and thread), sharp-edged thin bones to peel roots with, tufts of feathers, tips for beards, strings, spear-bars, &c. (Schürmann 2009[1879]:215)

In a second rare account of a man's bag, Brough Smyth describes from the River Murray:

The large kangaroo bag, *Bool-la-min-in* or *Moo-gro-moo-gro*, is used and carried by the males only. When not engaged in hunting, the Aboriginal keeps his tools and implements in this bag, his *Leange-walert*, teeth of animals, mussel-shells, bits of quartz and black basalt, &c., &c. (Brough Smyth 1972[1878]a:273)

From its description, this bag appears to be very similar in construction to that reported from the Southwest region:

the ends are wound together and tied with strings made of grass, and a grass rope is attached to the ends, so as to enable him to sling the bag over his shoulder. (Brough Smyth 1972[1878]a:273)

Donald Thomson collected a number of containers from the Arnhem region, with bone awls commonly listed as part of their contents. In one from Darbilla Creek, seven 'pointed bone implements' were found together with four firesticks sheathed together in melaleuca bark, while another pack from Howard Island contained 10 fire sticks and 'four unmodified kangaroo fibulae and one bone tool' bundled together with hair string (Item DT001200 notes, Museum Victoria). Another example, this time from Caledon Bay (Arnhem region), consisted of a loop stick bag holding three bone awls wrapped in melaleuca bark and a small string bag containing finger bones (relics to remember family members or friends; see 'Material culture made on human bone' below). In another example, the bag contained a finished bone awl as well as unworked fibulae. Augustus Robinson similarly notes in his journal that on 17 April 1841, he stumbled upon some baskets left cached near Lake Elingermite (Riverine region) and that the:

parcels . . . were carefully bound up. They consisted of the small leg bones of the kangaroo, some sharpened into a point—and which are used for piercing the kangaroo and opossum skins for making rugs. Two I brought away. (Clark 2000b:134)

From these bags, it appears that people in many parts of the continent commonly carried at least one finished awl and often several blanks for future needs.

Bone for the production of awls appears to have been a subject of trade in some areas, with Roth noting that the Cape Bedford (East Cape region) community:

send out or export iron tomahawks, iron digging-sticks, nautilus-shell, different kinds of dilly-bag, pearl-shell chest ornaments and Melo-shells. In return, they obtain forehead-bands, kangaroo-tail sinew, kangaroo bones (of a certain kind to be specially used for making bone awls) . . . They travel in barter along the Northern Coast-line as far as, very probably, the Flinders River. (Roth 1910a:18)

This movement of bony raw materials for use in technology production is an area sorely in need of study.

Macropod fibula unipoints with either acute or spatulate distal extremities have been reported for a number of Tasmanian archaeological sites, including early finds from shell middens on the northwest and western coast (Little Swanport) (Crowther 1924, 1926). From their spatulate morphology, Crowther (1926:264) suggested that they may have been used in 'extracting the contents of such edible types as turbo, &c.', though more recent researchers have suggested use in net-making (Bowdler 1979, 1984). Meston (1956:193) reported collecting unipoints from a number of sites, including Cape Sorell, Rocky Cape, Arthur River, and Tiger Creek on the northwest and western coast of Tasmania—he described them as being 'of two distinct types, points and spatulas, and all are formed from parts of the long bones of mammals and, in one case, a bird'. From the size and cross-section of the bird bone, Meston (1956:193) suggests that it is likely from a 'blue crane' (*Notophoyx novaehollandiae*) owing to the bird being fairly common in Tasmania. Meston (1956) suggests, as did Crowther before him, that these acute and spatulate-tipped points were used to 'remove molluscan food from the shell', as there 'are no eyewitness accounts of the use of bone implements by the Tasmanians' (Meston 1956:195). Unipoints described by Jones (1971) and recovered from archaeological sites from across Tasmania have mostly spatulate tips, though little information about their particulars is available, including those he excavated himself from Rocky Cape. These awls are of some antiquity, at least 3500 years old based on archaeological findings surrounding the use of bone technology on this southern island. Tasmanian archaeological sites that have produced bone artefacts are shown in Figure 1.2 and listed in Table 1.1.

Several of the more unusual examples of bone awls that are currently curated in museums should be noted to finish this overview of their use across Australia. These awls include a particularly long example made on the leg bone of a brolga (or other large wading bird), as well as three smaller examples (all under 10 centimetres in absolute length) made on fishbone from the Kimberley region (Item 491, Western Australian Museum). An artefact in Museum Victoria (stated only as having come from 'Central Australia') is unique. It appears to be a small rib bone and is accompanied by a note that it was 'used when sewing skins together' (Item X098947 notes, Museum Victoria). This rib bone awl is the only example that was come across during this study. A particularly interesting archaeological find is an intact Type 2 Awl made on the tibiotarsal of a bird, possibly a scrub turkey, which was recovered from Jiyer Cave south of Cairns (Cosgrove & Raymont 2002).

Local names recorded for bone awls (in general) include:

- bingal (Yirrkala, Arnhem region; Item E080884 notes, Australian Museum)
- yan-gul (Arnhem region; Meehan 1975)
- barrakalla karritjambal (Millerpilling, Darbilla Creek, Arnhem region; Item DT002892 notes, Museum Victoria)
- bar'gi (East Arnhem; Item DT007309 notes, Museum Victoria)
- parra-kalla (East Arnhem; Item DT002879 notes, Museum Victoria)
- pringal (Milingimbi, Arnhem region; Item DT002880 notes, Museum Victoria)

5. TOOLS

- rté-uma (Pennefather River, West Cape region; Roth 1904)
- o'on'o pi'wo (East Cape region; Item DT003391 notes, Museum Victoria)
- chegeal (Cairns, Rainforest region; Item E010124 notes, Australian Museum)
- min-der-min (Yarra River, Southeast region; Brough Smyth 1972[1878]a)
- pinki (Lower Murray River, Riverine region; Item X001578 notes, Museum Victoria)
- djunong, djung-o or djung (King George Sound, Southwest region; Moore 1884)
- djung (spatulate tip, Noongar, Southwest region; Bird & Beeck 1980)
- birnd (acute tip, Noongar, Southwest region; Bird & Beeck 1980).

Type 1 Awl specific names include:
- katjim (West Cape region; Item DT003938 notes, Museum Victoria)
- olpo nampi (East Cape region; Item DT003392 notes, Museum Victoria).

Burnishers

Description

A burnisher is a long tool featuring a hard, often bevelled, active edge that is rounded through use. This tool is used in smoothing or polishing softer surfaces—namely skins or plant fibres—through repeated scraping and rubbing.

Manufacture and use

While awls were the main bone tool used to work skins (as described above), other implements also appear to have been utilised. A kangaroo femur tool collected from 'Victoria' (no further provenance; Item E017186 notes, Australian Museum) features a long concavo-convex—spoon-like—distal extremity. This active end is rounded and highly polished, and the surface is covered with fine striations. A dark red residue is clearly visible on both distal and proximal extremities, which may indicate that this substance was incidentally caught up in the hand while the tool was in use. The museum notes that this tool is a 'skin finisher . . . used after skin has been roughly dressed with rasp of lava' (Item E017186 notes, Australian Museum).

While this tool is thus far unique, possible burnishers have been found in archaeological contexts. These archaeological examples consist of lengths of animal long bone that have been halved or otherwise had a concave-convex extremity created, this section featuring significant rounding and polishing from use. Such examples may include artefacts from Currarong (Lampert 1971), Madjedbebe (Langley et al. 2023), and Durras North (Langley et al. 2021b), along with artefacts described as 'spatulate tools' from a number of archaeological contexts in Tasmania and the southeast of the mainland.

Ceremonial tools
Description
Hard animal materials are known to have played more than just a small role in ceremonies around the continent. The form that these items take depends very much on the community involved and their surrounding environment. Below are examples of items held in Australian museums that might be described as 'ceremonial' in nature.

Manufacture and use
Whole parts of an animal were sometimes incorporated into ceremony. For example, the South Australian Museum holds five turtle skulls, each carefully painted in red and white pigment, from Stanley Island (East Cape region), which represent the first turtle killed by young initiates. Along similar lines, the hyoid bone of a long-necked tortoise is carefully removed and revealed to a young man at his initiation in parts of Western Australia. These hyoid bones—and the animal from which they come—are considered special because the bone resembles a Wanjina figure (Akerman 2018).

Other bone items linked to ceremony in museum archives include long bipoints. One such example from the Eyre region is stated by its accompanying notes to have been used during ceremony to increase the number of lizards present on the landscape (Item X023556 notes, Museum Victoria), while another made on emu bone is stated to have been used for piercing arms during ceremony in the Eyre region (Item X042745 notes, Museum Victoria). Long unipoints, such as the awls described above, are also known to have been used in ceremony. Often, Type 2 Awls were used by mourners at a funeral to 'gash themselves on the head and on other parts of the body to draw blood, the women using stones and sharpened bones or digging sticks' (Berndt & Berndt 1977:455). The use of bone points or splinters for piercing participants in ceremonies is well documented ethnographically, but specifics will not be provided here out of respect.

Finally, several long unipoints stated to be from Cairns in the Rainforest region made on cassowary leg bone display a high polish and deeply engraved decorations. Such a high polish is suggestive of a ceremonial or otherwise special use (see 'Death Pointers' below), but no notes regarding the use of these very beautifully made points accompany them.

Charms
Description
Charms are small trinkets or amulets that hold power or protection through magical properties.

Manufacture and use
Some of the most interesting charms incorporate teeth from extinct megafauna. Two examples are known, both from the west Kimberley region of Western Australia. The first is an upper right permanent premolar of a diprotodontid, *Zygomaturus trilobus*, embedded in vegetable resin and fixed on a length of human hair string (see Figure 5.3). The second charm consists of a feather bundle containing a left upper permanent premolar

5. TOOLS

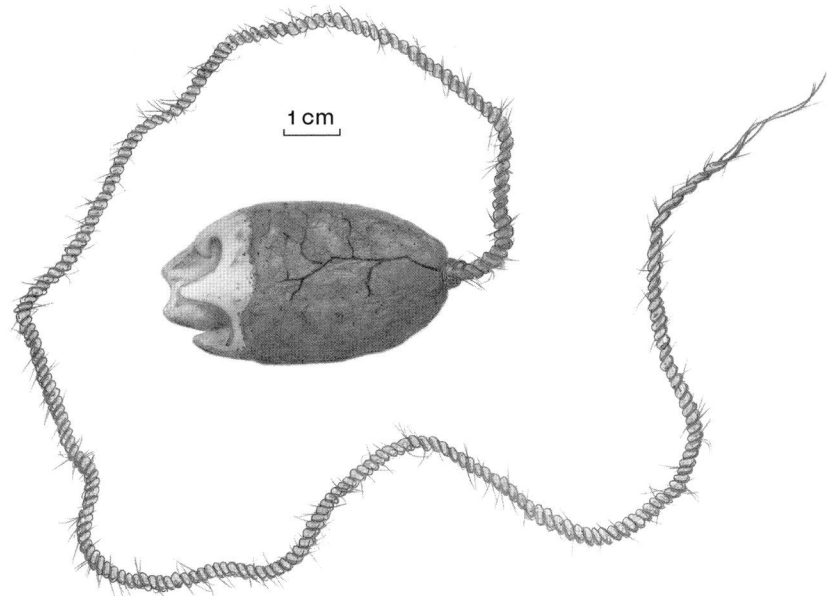

FIGURE 5.3. A *Zygomaturus* tooth embedded in vegetable resin and fixed to a length of human hair string, collected by Kim Akerman in the west Kimberley region. Drawn after a photograph in Akerman (1973).

and three upper left molars of the extinct large macropod *Sthenurus brownei* (Akerman 2011). These two artefacts are incredibly rare and offer insight into the continued relevance of fauna to communities long after becoming extinct.

Another charm currently registered within Australian museums consists of a group of small bones stated to be used for enticing caterpillars. These charms were collected from Cooper Creek, Eyre region (South Australian Museum), while a dugong tooth charm collected from Sunday Island (Kimberley region) features a high polish over its entire surface, indicating frequent handling or having been heirloomed over generations. In the ethnographies, Roth (1903a:37) describes a type of charm called a manda-kuya from the western districts of Queensland:

> a flattened spindle-form, about 5 or 6 inches long, made of emu feathers which, after being placed lengthways and bundles, are wound round and round with opossum-string, and then coasted all over with red-ochre grease: a slender piece of bone of some sort is occasionally enclosed in its centre. Originally, in the olden days throughout the Boulia district, this was used as a sign of good faith to be forwarded to some other friendly tribe whose assistance was required in fighting a common enemy: in those times there was but one of them in each camp, and the preview individual used to wear it on his chest, over which it would hang by means of a string passing round the neck. Subsequently this *Manda-kuya* came to have remedial properties attitude to it, and worn, in similar position, has been gradually imitated and supplied by the more common *woraka*. (Roth 1903a:37)

Perhaps also suitable to mention here is the arrangement of dugong bones along the northern coastlines of Queensland. Roth (1903a:27) reports that at Princess Charlotte Bay, communities carefully heap together the skeletal remains of dugong, and if this practice is not adhered to, no more will be caught in the future (see McNiven & Bedingfield 2008 on this activity).

Combs

Description
Combs are tools for personal grooming characterised by a row of teeth for pulling through the hair.

Manufacture and use
A number of intact fish jaws, specifically the palatine bone of *Sphyraena barracuda*, wrapped in a paperbark sheath are recorded as having been 'possibly used as combs' in their accompanying Australian Museum notes (Items E013865-8 notes, Australian Museum). These jaws were collected from Bentinck Island (Gulf region) and range from between 5.6 and 6.3 centimetres in absolute length. While the details of these artefacts are quite ambiguous, Roth (1907) makes mention of such personal items, stating that fish mandibles were used as combs in the far north, leading Best (2012) to interpret a group of fish mandibles (identified as *Sphyraena barracuda* or *Sphyraena obtusata*) and a bark bundle also containing fish mandibles from Bentinck Island in the Wellesley Islands as possible combs. Tom Petrie also mentions that men in Moreton Bay (Northeast region) always owned a small dillybag in which they carried their belongings:

> a piece of white clay, red paint, a lump of fat, a honey rag and a hair comb. The latter was a small bone from a kangaroo's leg, like a skewer; it was sharpened at one end by rubbing on sandstone, and was used to comb out a man's hair. (Petrie 1904:107–8)

Such combs may have been found in several burials of young men buried at the Broadbeach burial ground on the Gold Coast (Northeast region) (Haglund 1976). In these southeast Queensland cases, it sounds like awls (described above under 'Awls') found yet another use in personal grooming, which was also observed by Betty Meehan (1975) in Arnhem Land.

Also of interest here is a report by Roth (1903a:21), who states that along the Proserpine River (Rainforest region), 'young men can make their whiskers grow quickly by rubbing over the surface the teeth from a carpet- or black-snake', while Mason (1909:47) similarly states for the interior of Western Australia that when young men are 'desirous of growing whiskers [they] have the unique method of rubbing over the surface the teeth of the carpet or black snake'.

5. TOOLS

Containers
Description
Containers, objects for holding and/or transporting other items, are ubiquitous in human cultures globally. In the Australian context, containers—made from animal skins, woven plant fibres, bark, carved wood, and shells—are all present. Here, focus is on those incorporating hard animal material elements.

Manufacture and use
Beginning with those containers that take advantage of natural concavities, a singular example was found in the museum collections and consists of a turtle plastron from Bentinck Island in the Gulf region. This container features a large stain of red ochre in its centre and is recorded as a palette used in rope-making by the South Australian Museum. A similar use of a tortoise shell is noted for Narrinyeri (Ngarrindjeri) people (Riverine region) by Taplin (2009[1879]:42), who states that 'their vessels at that time were the shells of the fresh water tortoise (emys)'.

The use of hollow long bones appears to be common in the southern regions and the Arnhem region. A container collected from Cooper Creek (Eyre region) made from a section of pelican humerus some 19.5 centimetres long has been plugged at both ends with wax or resin and was used as a receptacle for pituri (South Australian Museum). Two further examples of pelican humeri are curated in Museum Victoria, with these examples also featuring wax or resin plugs to cap the ends. The long wing bones of other large birds appear in collections—an example from Cooper Creek (Eyre region) some 15 centimetres long is recorded as being used for carrying seeds, while a wing bone of a jabiru from Darbilla Creek (Arnhem region) was a tobacco container. The local name for this last implement is recorded by the South Australian Museum as waimbal kanji. The ends of these bird bone containers feature cleanly cut extremities. Finally, macropod long bones also saw use as containers, with an example from the Arnhem region stating that they have acted as a sheath for holding a Death Pointer (see 'Death Pointers' below).

Sheaths or containers for keeping awls were also present. One example from Wergaia (Southeast region) curated in Museum Victoria consists of a macropod awl kept within a 'bone scabbard with emu feather plume', while a kangaroo fibula awl from the Lower Murray River, Victoria (Riverine region), comes together with a bird wing bone sheath. Another woman's bag or 'work box' that included a hollow bone case in which a bone awl was kept is described by Bonwick (1870:410). This last example is curated in the Christie Collection at the British Museum. Edwards (1968) reported finding a bone point still within its hollow bone container sticking out of the ground within Rockshelter 2 at Fromms Landing on the Lower Murray River, while Schrire (1982:94) found a bird limb bone 'with one article end intact [and] the other end . . . broken and . . . ground inwards in the saw way as the bone tubes' at Malangangerr, as well as three others at Paribari, which she reports are ground on at least one end with 'the grinding . . . overlain by a high gloss' (Schrire 1982:62).

Another type of container is bone pins onto which kangaroo tail tendons or other sinews were wound for storage. Examples of these tools collected from Hermannsburg in the Desert region are recorded as having the name liurkna. They measure between nine and 18.5 centimetres in length.

Death Pointers*

*Indigenous readers should note that this section contains potentially harmful information. Details regarding the use of Death Pointers have been kept to a minimum, and the focus is kept on how to identify them.

Description

Death Pointers—also known as 'pointing bones'—make up a large proportion of the Australian bone technology curated in museums worldwide. This weapon saw widespread use across the continent at the time of European incursion (Spencer & Gillen 1904) and fascinated early observers to such an extent that they are the most mentioned bone tool in the Australian ethnographic literature (Table 5.2). Despite this notoriety, the identification of these weapons—in comparison to other unipoints used as awls, cloak pins, nose bones, etc.—in museum collections remains difficult.

From the examination of a great number of Death Pointers, it appears that this weapon can be distinguished from secular tools and ornaments by the following characteristics.

Death Pointers will typically feature:

- a high polish over their entirety
- a very acute distal point
- incised decorations on their shaft—particularly for the Desert region. These decorations may be burned in (Spencer & Gillen 1904) and typically are a series of short parallel lines cut horizontally across the shaft. However, not all known examples of Death Pointers (even those from the Desert) are incised
- a knob of resin at their proximal end onto which human hair string is attached
- decorations such as feathers (eagle down) and eagle talons attached to the hair string.

Death Pointers can be made on macropod or emu fibula, as well as human long bone (personal observation; Howitt 2001[1904]). Of these characteristics, the high polish is the most telling aspect that a unipoint may be a Death Pointer rather than another secular item. The presence of several of these factors increases the likelihood of an artefact being a Death Pointer.

Manufacture and use

In the interests of cultural safety, exactly how these tools were utilised will not be described here other than to state that death would be meted out by 'pointing the bone', 'striking with the bone', or 'giving the bone' (Howitt 2001[1904]). In some communities, only specific individuals could use this weapon, while in others, any individual was able to command this tool (Gason 2009[1879]; Spencer & Gillen 1904).

Taplin provides a good description of the creation of a Death Pointer as observed among Narranyeri (Ngarrindjeri) people (Riverine region):

5. TOOLS

TABLE 5.2. Currently known characteristics of Death Pointers ('pointing bones') from ethnographic reports and museum collections.

REGION	PRESENT	DESCRIPTION	INCISED DESIGNS
Kimberley	yes	resin or beeswax knob at proximal end	incised chevrons and opposed arcs
Fitzmaurice	yes	eagle down	
North	yes		
Arnhem	yes	string attached	
Desert	yes	kangaroo fibula; acute distal tip; blunt proximal end; red, black or white ochre; high polish; spinifex resin or beeswax knob at proximal end; human hair string; eagle talons; sinew binding; emu feathers; eagle down; Forehead Pendant Type 4	incised line winds down the length of the shaft; incised series of short parallel lines cut across the shaft
Gulf	yes	human long bone	
Torres Strait	no		
West Cape	yes	human long bone; emu fibula; spear form	
East Cape	yes	human long bone; emu fibula; spear form	
Rainforest	yes		
Northeast	no		
Southeast	yes	kangaroo fibula	
Tasmania	no		
Riverine	yes	human fibula; kangaroo fibula; emu fibula; polish; red ochre; human hair string	
Spencer	yes		
Eyre	yes	kangaroo fibula	
Southwest	Yes		
Northwest	Yes		

when a man has obtained a bone—for instance, the leg bone of a duck—he supposes that he possesses the power of life and death over the man, woman, or child who ate its flesh. The bone is prepared by being scraped into something like a skewer; a small round lump is then made by mixing a little fish oil and red ochre into a paste, and enclosing in it the eye of a Murray cod and a small piece of the flesh of a dead human body. This lump is stuck on the top of the bone and a covering tied over it, and it is put in the bosom of a corpse in order that it may derive deadly potency by contact with corruption. After it has remained there for some time it is considered fit for use, and is put away until its assistance is required. (Taplin 2009[1879]:24)

A RECORD IN BONE

A similar description for a Death Pointer also in the Riverine region is given by Howitt (2001[1904]:360), who reports that it is made out of the 'fibula of a dead man's leg, which is scraped, polished, and ornamented with red ochre, and a cord of the dead man's hair is attached to it', while Cameron (1885:361) noted that in New South Wales:

> a string about six feet long is made of human hair taken from the dead. This is attached to the small bone of a kangaroo, and the power of the spell is considered to be increased by having previously anointed the bone with human kidney fat.

Spencer (1928:253) noted that paired eagle claws were attached by hair string to a number of pointing bones. Just such a weapon appears to be curated by the British Museum. This artefact is stated as being collected from Arrernte people (Desert region) and consists of a group of five pointing bones, each with a resin knob on its proximal end. Human hair string stems from these resin knobs, with the string tying the group together. Also attached to this bunch is an apparent forehead ornament (Forehead Pendant Type 4; see Chapter 6), which is stated to be a 'sorcerer's hand' in the museum note (Item Oc1933,1012.6 notes, British Museum). This item is illustrated in Spencer and Gillen (1904:456) and is there noted to be called an injilla ungakura, used by the peoples living on the Erlitthera Creek.

Palmer describes for the peoples of the Gulf region that the:

> They are much afraid of having the *Thimmool* pointed at them. It is said to be a human leg-bone, about 6 inches long, ground to a point. (Palmer 1884:293)

Palmer (1884:293) also describes another similar type of interpersonal weapon, this time called a marro: 'The *Marro* is the pinion bone of a hawk, a double piece of bone in which hair of an enemy is fastened with wax ... to make him only sick or to kill him'. Another type of Death Pointer was found in the Australian Museum's catalogue. From Cape York (no further provenance), this item is more like a spear in appearance—a single bone point attached to a wooden shaft and foreshaft with two-ply twisted plant fibre string secured with dark resin adhesive. The accompanying notes state that it is an om-bo. Roth describes these charms, stating that:

> on the Pennefather River the death-charm or *om-bo* consists of a long thin bone-needle fixed into a wooden shaft—a spear in miniature. The bone from the emu's or human leg is considered more efficacious than any other. (Roth 1903a:32)

He continues, 'another pattern consist[s] of three or four small bone-needles stuck into a longer handle: it works more effectively' (Roth 1903a:32). Roth (1903a:34) also describes a separate tool known as the mangani, which could cause sickness, accident, or death:

> the charm may be said to consist of a pointer ... connected by twine ... with an elongate cylindrical receptacle ... from 3 to 5 inches long, [it] is made usually from one of the human fore-arm bones, or an emu bone, ground down from the blunt extremity to a gradually tapering point: among the Kalkadun [Kalkatungu], the sharpened end of this pointer is sometimes fashioned into the shape of a fish-hook ... The twine ... is made of human hair or opossum-fur, or both plaited together, and varies from 3 to 4 to

5. TOOLS

as much as 12 or 15 feet long: by means of cement-substance (beef-wood or spinifex) it connects the blunt extremity of the pointer with the internal surface of the base of the receptacle. The receptacle is generally formed of a piece of human arm- or shin-bone cut to a length of 3 or 4 inches and hollowed or scraped out so as to form a kind of cylinder. A human bone however, though most appreciated for the purpose, is not always at the moment obtainable, and under such circumstances may be substituted by a portion of kangaroo or emu leg-bone . . . One extremity, the base, of this receptacle is closed in with the usual cement-substance, to which passing down the inside, the connecting-string is attached. Though a layman can manufacture this death-charm, it is only the medicine-man who has the power of using or 'pointing' it successfully. (Roth 1903a:34)

Spencer and Gillen (1904) noted that a knob of spinifex resin on the proximal end is a common feature of Death Pointers in the Desert region, with the pointer kept safely in a hollow bone (bringing into question those found in such containers mentioned above). This container is capped with another knob of resin. Envelopes of grass stems (Gulf region), emu feather sheaths (Desert region), and paperbark sheaths (Fitzmaurice region) are also recorded within museums.

Local names recorded for this tool include:

- kurewa (Melville and Bathurst Islands, North region; Harney & Elkin 1943:233)
- njalla (Hermannsburg, Desert region; Item A14748 notes, South Australian Museum)
- intjala (Charlotte Waters, Desert region; Item E018559 notes, Australian Museum)
- injilla (Arunda (Arrernte) and Ilpirra, Desert region; Spencer & Gillen 1904)
- irna (Arunda (Arrernte) and Ilpirra, Desert region; Spencer & Gillen 1904)
- takula (Arunda (Arrernte) and Ilpirra, Desert region; Spencer & Gillen 1904)
- tjinpila (near Finke River, Desert region; Spencer & Gillen 1904)
- inwania (Kaitish (Kaytetye), Desert region; Spencer & Gillen 1904)
- unqurlia (Kaitish (Kaytetye), Desert region; Spencer & Gillen 1904)
- therpera (Desert region; Spencer & Gillen 1904)
- atnilinga (Desert region; Spencer & Gillen 1904)
- pirritthi (Desert region ; Spencer & Gillen 1904)
- thimmool (Gulf region; Palmer 1884)
- om-bo (Pennefather River, West Cape region; Roth 1903a)
- mangani (North West Queensland; Roth 1903a)
- yertung (Kurnai, Riverine region; Howitt 2001[1904])
- yulo (North Western Victoria, Riverine region; Howitt 2001[1904])
- dulu-durrai (groups along the Murray and the Murrumbidgee rivers, Riverine region; Howitt 2001[1904])
- naria-moku, kutimara, panji (Cooper Creek, Eyre region; Item A44115 notes, South Australian Museum)
- gimu (Southwest region; Item A1361 notes, South Australian Museum).

Drills

Description

A drill is a tool equipped with a cutting tip, which when rotated with pressure produces a round hole through another surface. The most common form of drill encountered on the Australian continent is the kangaroo tooth–tipped variety, with shell- or bone-tipped examples also appearing. Indeed, McCarthy (1976) notes that these organic-tipped drills were more widespread than the stone variety. For this type of drill, a single macropod incisor (or bone or shell fragment) is hafted to a long wooden shaft with the aid of a sinew ligature and/or resin/wax (see Figure 5.4).

Manufacture and use

Only a handful of drills appear to be curated in Australia's museums and consist of those armed with a single macropod incisor. These tools were collected from the East Cape, where they are described as having been twirled between the hands with downwards pressure (in the same fashion as a firestick) and used to drill holes in shells and wood (Roth 1904). Roth states that at Princess Charlotte Bay (East Cape region), the tooth drill:

> is made with an incisor, from any of the larger species of kangaroo, which is stuck into a short handle, and fixed in position with twine and cement. The exact method of fixation consists in splitting (with shell) the extremity of the handle into four, by means of two cuts at right-angles, tying a piece of string around some little distance beyond, to prevent the splits from extending, and inserting the base of the tooth in the double edge so produced: the extremity of the handle is next firmly wound round with string twine, and covered with 'iron-wood' cement, while the string beyond, which, of course, is no longer required after once the resin has set, is finally removed. (Roth 1904:24–5)

The same type of drill has also been collected from the West Cape—Roth (1904) outlining that they were used to drill holes in spearthrowers for placing the peg, as well as holes in shells in constructing necklaces (presumably the *Nautilus* shell necklaces for which the region is known) (also observed by Thomson 1936:74). Additionally, they were used in the construction of coconut and turtle shell fishhooks. Roth (1904:25) further adds that on the coast between the 'Mitchell and the Staten [rivers] the constituent pieces of the shell necklaces or fore-head circlets were to be pierced with an opossum-tooth drill', indicating that it was not only the teeth of macropods put to this specific use. Hale and Tindale (1933) observed people at Princess Charlotte Bay (East Cape region) re-edge the tooth by biting off the blunt end.

Also worth mentioning here is the archaeological recovery of a tiger shark tooth with use-related wear, recovered from Tigershark Rockshelter in the Torres Strait (McNiven et al. 2008). The excavators of this artefact, which is dated to about 500 year ago, suggest that it was utilised to perform 'cutting/scraping functions' (McNiven et al. 2008:26), perhaps linked to Haddon's (1912) observation that shark teeth were used to inscribe designs or drill perforations in pearl shell pendants in the area.

5. TOOLS

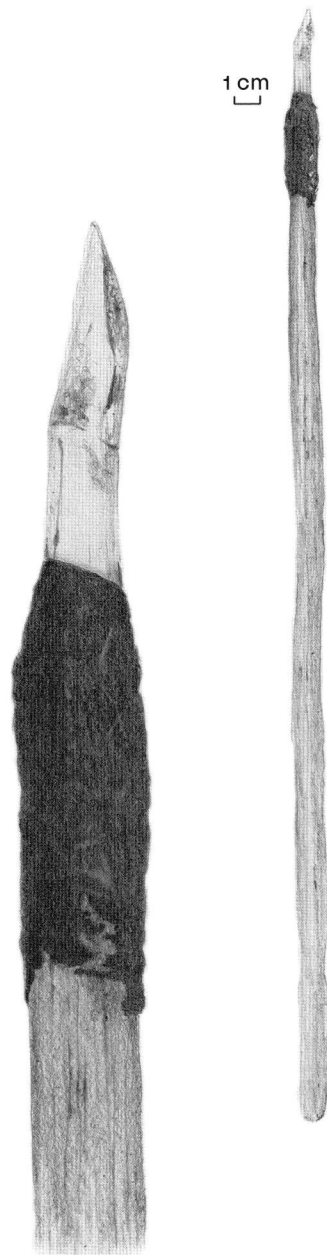

FIGURE 5.4. A drill tipped with a kangaroo incisor and hafted using ligature overlaid with resin.

Eating utensils

Description

Eating utensils may be defined as implements used for cutting or otherwise handling food in the process of consumption. There are three types of eating utensil currently evident in the Australian record: (1) long bone points used to skewer food morsels, (2) bone spoons made on macropod long bone (see Figure 5.5), and (3) macropod bone straws for drinking.

Manufacture and use

The most common eating utensil appears to have been a bone unipoint—a Type 2 Awl. Betty Meehan (1975:158) describes the use of such a tool to extract the meat from shellfish in Arnhem Land, a method also mentioned by Brockwell and Akerman (2007), in use by people living at Blyth River (also in the Arnhem region). On the Queensland coast, Type 2 Awls were similarly used for removing the flesh of black nerites after boiling. Here, the tip of the bone point was hooked into the flesh at the opening of the shell, and then the shell was rotated in the opposite direction so that the flesh came out as a complete spiral (Isaacs 1987:178). In Moreton Bay (Northeast region), people watched out for signs of the crowned melon shell, which was much esteemed for its beauty. When its tracks were seen, 'a bone skewer' was used to probe for and dig up the shell (Backhouse 1967[1843]:369). This tool is also cited as being used to pick out the nuts from roasted pandanus (Hale & Tindale 1933:114; Roth 1907), something also recorded for a particular kangaroo fibula awl made by Nawulandji Wunungmurra at Yirrkala (Arnhem region) held in the Australian Museum. This tool is recorded to have been used to cut through ganyawu (native cashew) skin to get to the nut inside.

A similar artefact was found at the Sokoli midden in Torres Strait, where an 'intricately carved hollow bone implement (probably a lime spatulate for betel nut)' was reported (Carter 2001:50). This artefact was dated to about 2280 years ago.

The next implement is typified by three artefacts collected by Donald Thomson from Bare Hill in East Cape York. Made on macropod long bone, one extremity is chipped away to create a spoon-like end. The local name for this implement is recorded as marpi, and while it is catalogued as an 'eating utensil', no further detail as to its use is provided (see Figure 5.5). Possible archaeological examples of such 'spoons' include wide spatulate split-bone unipoints, the likes of which are present in 3500-year-old deposits at Fromms Landing on the Lower Murray River (Mulvaney 1960) as well as shell midden sites that are at least this old along the west and north western coast of Tasmania (Crowther 1924, 1926; Jones 1971) and Currarong in New South Wales (Lampert 1971).

Lastly, Howitt (2001[1904]:402) reports that hollow sections of kangaroo bone were used as straws by young initiates in the Northeast region, stating that 'Wakelbura youth was not allowed to drink water out of a water-hole unless through a kangaroo bone'. In a similar fashion, Nind (1831:37) mentions that the women of King George Sound (Southwest region) would utilise 'a hollow rush, or the wing-bone of a bird (*nweil*), they suck the water, when it cannot conveniently be reached with their mouths'. He records that the name of the bird bone implement is knweel or nweil.

5. TOOLS

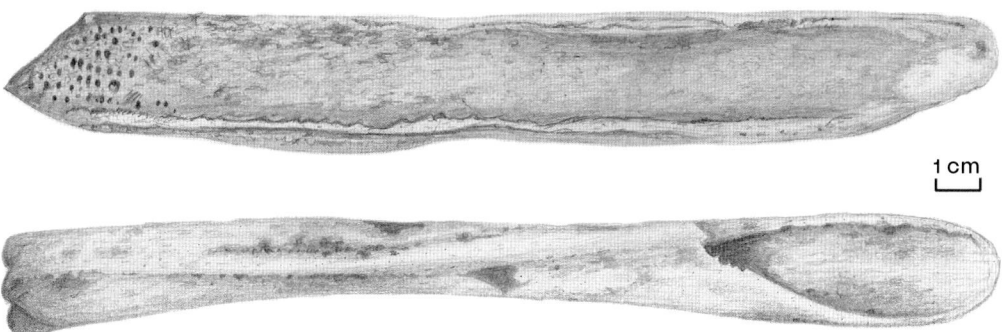

FIGURE 5.5. Two examples of spoons made on the long bones of macropods.

Fans and fly-flicks
Description
A fan or fly-flick is a handheld tool, shaped somewhat like a segment of a circle and is waved to create a breeze to cool an individual, disperse smoke or insects, fan a fire, and so on. Fans in Australia are typically made from bird feathers or whole sections of a wing.

Manufacture and use
Several early written accounts of northern Australia mention fans or fly-flicks, including Leichhardt (1847:502), who, while in the vicinity of the East Alligator River, mentions the people he encountered traded 'a great number of bunches of goose feathers, which the natives use to brush away the flies'. Similarly, further east, when he was passing through the countries of the Gulf region, he describes 'fans of emu feathers' observed at a campsite during 1845 near the River Robinson (Leichhardt 1847:410). Further east again, Roth in North Queensland states that:

> in most camps, during the hotter months, the wing of some comparatively large bird, such as the 'Native-companion' (*Grus australasianus*, Gld.) or 'Plain-Turkey' (*Eupodotis australis*, Gray) is often to be seen employed as a fly-flick, possibly as a fan. (Roth 1904:26)

This second type of fan—that which utilises an intact section of bird wing—is found in our museums, including an example where sectioned parts of magpie goose wings were placed one on top of the other and tied at the joint with string and resin to create the fan. On this particular example, the resin handle is painted over with red ochre and white dots and is simply stated as having come from the Northern Territory. A similar example was collected from the Arnhem region.

Fighting tools

Description

Fighting tools are objects specifically designed for inflicting bodily harm or physical damage in conflict. Two types of fighting weapons that include hard animal materials were identified: spears and the fighting knife. The spears include bone, self-barbed points, and spears tipped with stingray barbs, shark teeth, or bone flakes. The fighting knife features a series of tiger shark (*Galeocerdo cuvier*) or dusky shark (*Carcharhinus obscurus*) teeth attached to one side of a long hardwood ellipse, which is capped at the distal end with resin (see Figure 5.6). The proximal end terminates with the handle, which is made from twine being wound repeatedly around the end and covered over with resin. A loose loop of the twine enables the user to keep the knife attached to their wrist. On the edge of these knives, the shark teeth are set into a carved groove, with resin acting as the adhering agent.

Manufacture and use

Regarding the spears, an example of the self-barbed type was collected from Mapoon (West Cape region). This spear appears to follow the general form of fishing spears (see 'Spear points' below) but is accompanied by a note that it was only used in fighting. This single object might suggest that barbed spears were multipurpose (between fishing and fighting) or that spears of very similar form were made but used specifically for one purpose or the other.

Roth describes one of the other forms of fighting spear, those featuring stingray barbs. The spears he observed on the Pennefather River (West Cape region) were:

> armed with stingaree-barb fixed on to the tip—a few central ones surrounded by others in the form of a circlet. These spears, used for fighting, have all the general name of *lar-na-pe* (the Nggerikudi term for a stingaree-barb) applied to them. (Roth 1909b:191–2)

Roth also talks about the 'woomera-spear', a composite spear that can have stingray barbs attached and that was used on the Lower Tully River (Rainforest region). He states that when the barbs are present:

> the spear is called a *warra-katcha*, and its distal extremity covered with red and white rings, but if not present, this extremity is smeared with a uniform red. It is used for fighting purposes, and for spearing wallabies. (Roth 1909b:195)

He also mentions for the Brisbane area (Northeast region) that pi-lar fighting spears would sometimes be especially equipped with 'one or two stingaree barbs might be stuck on with beeswax and twine' for particular fights (Roth 1909b:197). The naturally strong, sharp, and barbed morphology of the stingray barb easily explains its popular use for battle weaponry.

An exceptional example of a war spear comes from Mer in the Torres Strait. This implement is a bamboo shaft about a metre long, with the top third covered in rows of shark teeth. Examination finds that the shark teeth have been attached in strips, the teeth still adhering to the membrane in which they grew within the shark's mouth. These

5. TOOLS

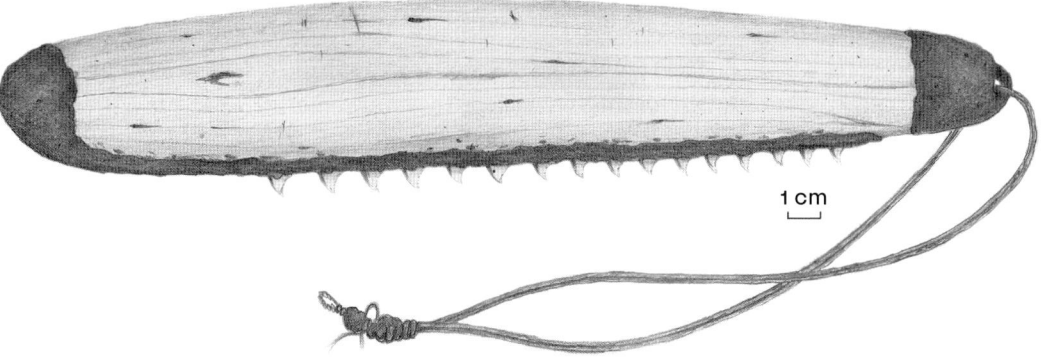

FIGURE 5.6. Shark-tooth fighting knives utilise the natural capacity of shark teeth to cause severe flesh wounds.

strips were removed in sections, whole, from the shark's mouth and then attached to the bamboo shaft using plant fibre ligatures. The result is tightly packed shark teeth surrounding the circumference of the pole and would surely have inflicted significant damage on an opponent.

Finally, there are those weapons that have been commonly termed 'death spears'. Early European observers noted that for these spears, the barbs were usually small quartzite flakes, although occasionally broken shell, fish teeth, and pieces of bone were also utilised for the barbs (Collins 1975[1798]:320; Flanagan 1888:80). An interesting example is illustrated by Charles-Alexander Leseur, who accompanied the Baudin Expedition (1800–1804) to Australia. This illustration shows a spearhead from a 'war spear', armed with small shark teeth, in the manner of the 'death spear'. Eleven teeth, probably those from the upper jaw of the common or black whaler *Carcharhinus obscurus*, are serially fixed with resin along the side of the wooden spear tip, and it appears to have been recorded for Port Jackson on the New South Wales coast (Bonnemains et al. 1988:89). Apart from these small tidbits, information regarding spears used specifically for fighting is sparse.

At the other end of the spectrum are the shark tooth fighting knives of northern Queensland, which are relatively well recorded. These weapons were restricted to fighting and were hidden from view by the warrior who either placed it under their armpit or hung it down behind their head, the twine loop resting on their forehead when heading into battle (Roth 1904:23). The knife was used to strike at an adversary's flank or buttocks (Roth 1904) and would cause deep cutting wounds. Roth (1904:23) specifies that these knives were 'used as a knife for the "hacking" purpose already described, and never for sawing meat'. These weapons have been collected from both East and West Cape York and the Torres Strait, as well as from the Batavia River in Western Australia. Sutton (1994:47) notes that the Wik-speaking peoples of central western Cape York used the wood of the milkwood tree (*Alstonia actinophylla*) as handles for these weapons, while McCarthy (1976) notes that ironwood was selected. Interestingly, a knife of this type but tipped with pieces of kangaroo bone was recorded at King George Sound (Southwest region) (Lockyer 1923), while Sutton (1994) mentions the use of sawfish (*Pristis* sp.) rostrum as a ready-made sword. Indeed, whole sawfish rostrums that are painted over with red ochre have been collected from Cape York and may represent these latter types of fighting knives. Thomson (1936:74) also notes that 'shark's teeth were used for ceremonial and fighting knives' in Cape York Peninsula.

Local names recorded for this tool include the following.

Stingray barb fighting spear:
- larna-pe (Nggerikudi, Pennefather River, West Cape region; Roth 1909b)
- pi-lar (Brisbane, Northeast region; Roth 1909b).

Shark tooth fighting knife:
- kulkong (Kundara (Gundara), Mitchell River, West Cape region; Roth 1904)
- alng-wa (Koko-Minni (Kuku Mini), Mitchell River, West Cape region; Roth 1904)
- kappatora (Gunanni (Gonaniin, West Cape region; Roth 1904).

Fishhooks

Description

Hard animal materials dominate the construction of fishhooks in Australia. While marine shell is most commonly used along the southeast coast, marine turtle shell and mammal bone are not infrequently utilised (Table 5.3). Turtle shell fishhooks are restricted to the Torres Strait and North Queensland (Banfield 1910; Roth 1904). The line is attached to the shank by being wound round the shank and tied off (see Figure 5.7).

One-piece bone fishhooks are also found in both the jabbing and rotating varieties, with the manufacturer utilising a bone wide enough to allow for the largely flat cross-section of a rotating hook or taking advantage of the natural cross-section of long bone to create the curvature required on a jabbing hook. Both types are attached to the plant fibre line, wrapped around the shank and tied off (see Figure 5.7).

Finally, the two-piece or composite fishhooks bring together two main components: (1) a shaft that can be of long bone or wood and (2) a bone bipoint to form the barb. These two parts are joined with the use of resin, and sometimes also ligatures, to create a jabbing fishhook. The plant fibre line is attached to the end of the shank by being repeatedly wound round and tied off (see Figure 5.7).

Manufacture and use

On the Australian continent, there is a general division of fishing labour between the genders that extends to the use of the fishing technologies themselves. Several authors note that women generally fished from their canoe using hook and line, with men utilising the multi-pronged fishing spear (described below in 'Spear points') from the shoreline (e.g. Bradley 1969[1786]; Collins 1975[1798]; Howitt 2001[1904]; Hunter 1963[1793]; Stockdale 1950[1789]; White 1962[1790]; Worgan 1978[1788]). Bowdler (1975:250), however, mentions that 'in the Edward River area there was a traditional composite hook of bone used by the men only', which is an interesting observation and challenges the simple 'women equals hook and line versus men equals fishing spear' narrative. Interestingly,

5. TOOLS

TABLE 5.3. Overview of (non-marine shell) fishhooks present across the Australian continent.

REGION	RAW MATERIAL	FORM	CONSTRUCTION
Kimberley			
Fitzmaurice	macropod bone	jabbing	composite
North	macropod bone	jabbing	one-piece
Arnhem	macropod bone	jabbing	one-piece
Desert	[none identified]		
Gulf	bone		composite
Torres Strait	turtle shell	jabbing; rotating	one-piece
West Cape	turtle shell; macropod bone	jabbing	one-piece; composite
East Cape	turtle shell; emu bone; brolga bone; dingo bone; macropod bone	jabbing	one-piece; composite
Rainforest	turtle shell	rotating	one-piece
Northeast	turtle shell	rotating	one-piece
Southeast	bird talon	jabbing	
Tasmania	bone		
Riverine	macropod bone; fishbone; macropod incisors	jabbing; rotating; gorge	One-piece; composite
Spencer	[none identified]		
Eyre	[none identified]		
Southwest	[none identified]		
Northwest	[none identified]		

despite Beveridge (2008[1889]:85–92) noting that Yaraldi women (for example) kept their fishhooks in their bags and therefore these tools were not highly visible to early Europeans except when in use, a comparatively huge amount of information about their construction and use is available.

To begin with the one-piece fishhooks, while marine shell usually dominates this form of fishhook (not covered here), in the Torres Strait and Northern Queensland as far south as the Keppel Islands, turtle shell is the prime material of choice. With marine turtles being plentiful along these coasts and the size and suitability of the shell they provide for material culture production, it is no wonder that communities made use of this resource for such important everyday tools. Roth (1904) notes a type of jabbing hook he terms 'bent-pin' made on the Batavia and Pennefather rivers (West Cape region). He described the manufacture of these hooks as follows:

> A more or less irregularly outlined length of shell is wedged out of the scutum, ground down on a piece of stone, and finally finished off with a shell-scraper, so as to produce a head-less pin about 2 to 2 1/2 inches long, tapering gradually from the blunt extremity to a fine point. This pointed end is now firmly inserted into a small hole (natural or

artificial) in a billet of wood which is placed vertically into the ground. Resting upon the projecting pin is next placed another piece of wood on the slant—the one end resting on the ground, the other free—and prevented from slipping off by being loosely tied to the vertical post with a loop or two of twine. A fire is then lighted, and, as the heat rises, the pin softens and, with the superincumbent weight of the slanting timber, becomes more and more bent into a gentle curve: it is then removed, alternatively dipped in water, heated at the fire, and bent with the fingers until the required shape is obtained . . . On the Palm Isles, where the bent-pin form of tortoise-shell hook has also been met with, Mr. Norris stated that he had seen them manufactured thus:—'a round pebble was heated in the fire, and a narrow strip of tortoise-shell bent across it, until the heat softened it, and the required curve was obtained'. (Roth 1904:33–4)

Examples of these fishhooks are present in museum collections and are a fine example of a supple jabbing hook.

The turtle shell fishhooks made on the Keppel Islands (Northeast region) are quite different, being a circular rotating hook and:

up to as much as an inch in its longer diameter, has the points very close together; it is attached to the line (*angkun*) by means of a connecting tea-tree twine (*ren*), the free extremity of which ties on the bait, usually a small soldier-crab (*ranga*)—none of these crescentic-shaped hooks ever transfixes the bait. (Roth 1901c:21)

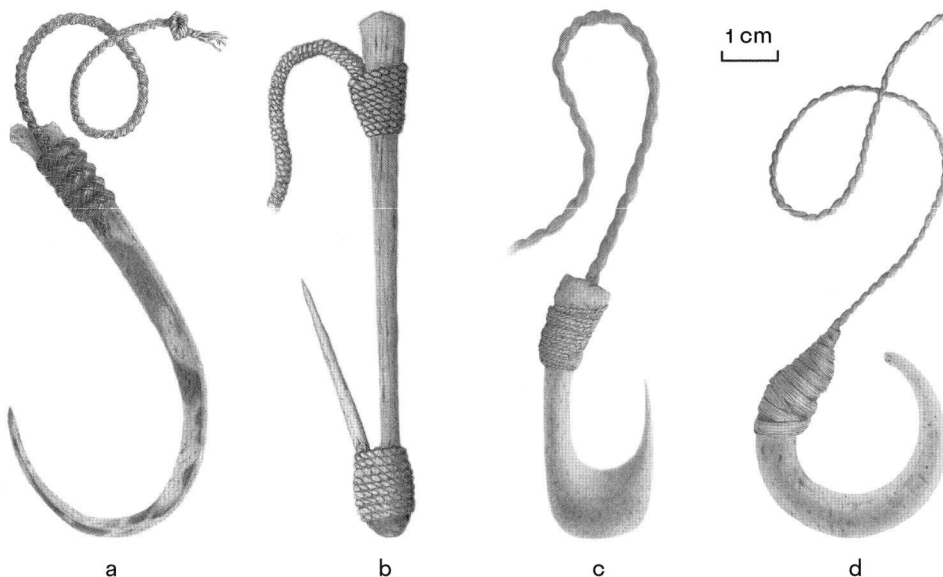

FIGURE 5.7. Most non-marine shell-based fishhooks are 'jabbing' hooks. In the Torres Strait, turtle shell was commonly used (a), while composite fishhooks featuring two main parts—(1) a wooden or bone shank and (2) a small bone bipoint connected using resin or wax—were used on the mainland (b). One-piece jabbing (c) and rotating (d) hooks were also made on terrestrial bone.

5. TOOLS

Roth (1901c) notes that Sub-Inspector Garraway observed similar turtle shell fishhooks on the Herbert River (Rainforest region) in 1883, while Brough Smyth (1972[1878]a:391) mentions their use at Rockingham Bay (Rainforest region). He illustrates a rotating hook and states that 'it is four inches in length, and about a quarter of an inch in width at the widest part. It is a very beautiful hook' (Brough Smyth 1972[1878]a:391).

Additionally, museums hold many examples of both rotating and jabbing one-piece turtle shell hooks from the Torres Strait. These Torres Strait hooks are often more elaborate in their style and can feature incised designs on their dorsal surface. The antiquity of this technology is at least 2500 years, as Barker (1991) has reported finding ground and cut turtle shell fishhook blanks at Nara Inlet on Hook Island (Whitsundays, Northeast region) dated up to this point in time.

Regarding the one-piece fishhooks made from bone, this technology was frequently observed along the southeast coast and into the interior of the continent. Macropod bone appears to be the most common choice for raw material where it is specified and the materials used to make the line was often also recorded. For example, Howitt (2001[1904]:761) notes that the fishing lines made and used by Kurnai people (Riverine region) were made of the inner bark of the Blackwood (*Acacia melanoxylon*). Descriptions of the hooks themselves often include crude sketches of their outline, giving us a broad idea of their appearance (jabbing versus rotating, etc.), with those used in Gippsland (Southeast region) being particularly well described. For example, Brough Smyth (1972[1878]a:391) details a rotating bone hook from Gippsland, adding that 'the women are expert anglers. They will sometimes secure as much as 60 lbs. weight of fish with the modern hook'. He further notes that for such hooks:

> I believe they found the bone-hook as good for fishing as the hooks supplied by Europeans, though no doubt it would be very troublesome to make it, as it had to be scraped out with flint and shells. (Brough Smyth 1972[1878]a:142)

These hooks are seen in Museum Victoria, with a beautiful example from Lake Tyers made on large (possibly kangaroo) bone and attached to a long length of plant fibre string (yowan) made from the inner bark of the blackwood (*Acacia melanoxylon*) tree particularly insightful. This koy-yun (fishhook) is almost a full circle, flat on the inferior surface and slightly convex on the upper superior surface. The string is attached to the hook by a tightly bound bark strip, which covers some 16 millimetres of the hook extremity (Massola 1956). Henry Haydon (1846:44) is recorded as talking about fishing in Gippsland, saying 'in the day the mode of fishing is with fish hooks made of bone', while George Augustus Robinson (quoted in Mackaness 1941, Clark 2000d:83) states that 'their mode of taking fishing is by net, spearing and line and hook, the latter ingeniously made from bone' (Augustus Robinson also illustrates bone rotating hooks from Gippsland in his 1844 journal).

Regarding records from further north and west, descriptions of similar rotating one-piece bone hooks were made for locations surrounding Sydney and into the interior of the Riverine region. Fraser (1892:78), for example, mentions 'fish hooks used by the natives were of bone and in the shape of a boar's tusk', while two archaeological examples of bone jabbing hooks were recovered from a burial site on Wallpolla Creek (Riverine region). These artefacts are described as being 'cut from bone and smoothed in the form of a U with uneven sides' (Gallus & Gill 1973:216). Similarly constructed hooks are also known on the other side of the continent, both in the Arnhem region—where Cole (1979:31) mentions 'fishing lines with bone hooks'—and the area surrounding Darwin (North region)—where Spencer and Gillen (1904:677) describe their use along the Daly River (Fitzmaurice region). Here, the jabbing hooks were made from kangaroo long bone (possibly femur) and feature a shank made a little wider at its extremity so that the string is unable to slip off. Examples of this type of fishhook have been collected from Darwin (North region), with Museum Victoria holding several examples from the Daly River with their lines still attached. Ongoing archaeological work in this region is also finding ancient examples, with several fragmented pieces of one-piece bone jabbing hooks recently identified from the Mirarr site of Madjedbebe (see Figure 3.5, colour section). These examples date to between the present and about 2000 years ago (Langley et al. 2023). Finally, they may also have seen use in the Gulf region, as Palmer (1884:284) reports that 'they know the use of hooks and lines for fishing, forming their hooks out of bone or hard wood', and Brough Smyth mentions that the Jardines saw at Maramie Creek:

> two parties of blacks fishing on the river ... They used reed-spears, pointed with four jagged spoons, and also hooks and line. Their hooks are made of wood, barbed with bone, and the lines of twisted *Currejong* bark. (Brough Smyth 1972[1878]a:388)

This quote suggests that fishhooks may also have been present in the West Cape.

Before moving on to the composite hooks, it is interesting to note that Brough Smyth cites the use of gorges in the Geelong district:

> for catching bream, a piece of hard wood or bone sharpened at both ends and attached to the line by a hitch-knot ... This cannot be called a hook. It was baited, however, and when seized by the fish and the line strained, the bone stuck in the jaws, and the prey was secured. This is a very simple but a very ingenuous contrivance for taking fish. (Brough Smyth 1972[1878]a:391)

The shown implement is a small bipoint attached across its midpoint in the same manner as experimented with by Justin Bradfield in a South African context (Bradfield 2019).

The composite fishhooks generally feature two main parts: a wooden or bone shank and a small bone bipoint, with these parts connected using resin or wax to create a large jabbing hook. Usually, the bone bipoint is half covered with the resin/wax, leaving just one end exposed to form the barb. The line is also held on using resin. Spencer and Gillen (1904:677) report that often the radius or fibula of a macropod was utilised to make these hooks in the Fitzmaurice area as well as the Gulf region, noting that the:

> swollen head serves to prevent the string from slipping off, and, as in the wooden one, the sharpened piece of bone which serves as hook is attached to the main shaft by a lump of resin. The attachment is rendered more secure either ... by twine which winds round and round the wax, or by tough strands stripped from the inner side of a bark and then wound round the wax ... The attachment of the line is rather ingenious. (Spencer & Gillen 1904:677–8)

They describe the method of attaching the string in detail:

5. TOOLS

> An ordinary piece of two-ply string, made out of tough inner bark, is placed by the side of the shaft, one or two ends of fibres being at first allowed to hang freely down from the end of the string of which they form the terminal part. A second piece is then taken. One end of it (c) is placed near to the head of the bone ... It is then wound round the line and bone. The end of the main line (a) is then turned upwards, making a loop with itself, and above the head of the bone it is intertwined with the two plies of the line for perhaps three to six inches. The end (b) of the second string is then wound round the two parts of the line which have thus been turned back on one another. Finally, the string is worn tightly round and round the proximal part of the line itself, the end (b) being then tied round the line or run down again for some little distance. (Spencer & Gillen 1904:678)

Berndt et al. (1993) also described a similar composite fishhook technology for the Lower Murray (Riverine region), stating that:

> the ordinary hook was made of the same material, kangaroo bone, and also termed 'werkurumi'. The shaft of an average hook was about three inches long, rounded at the top with a hole. The hole was made with a drill also of kangaroo bone: a small depression was first made with a quartzite flake and the drill twirled in the hands of the manufacturer. Aided by a little grit or charcoal in the incipient hole, the latter was soon deepened and a finer drill used to the penetrate the bone. A sharpened bone prong of one and a quarter inches in length was attached to the shaft by bound sinew and pine gum. Hooks we were told were of various sizes. The larger one noted here was used especially for cod, scallop, catfish and turtle; the smaller ones for freshwater perch. The flatted fibre 'ngempung' line was attached to the hook by a slipknot and during the summer months it was kept pliable in a piece of damp skin. (Berndt et al. 1993:96)

Examples of these hooks now residing in museums were collected from Princess Charlotte Bay (East Cape region) and were made with a main shaft on hardwood (*Erythrophlaeum laboucherii*), the hook made from emu bone, dingo bone, or kangaroo bone, and the line made from *Livistona australis* fibres. Roth (1901c:21) also mentions the use of brolga bone or 'one of the spines of the "cat-fish"'. The bone hook is a self-barbed bipoint, held on using ligature (usually kangaroo tail sinew) and resin (grevillea gum cement). Thomson also describes and collected examples of such composite fishhooks from Koko Tai'yuri (Koko Dhawa) people of the West Cape. He describes their manufacture as follows (see Figure 5.8):

> The haft of the hook is made from the wood of *Dodonaea hansenii—yukko meri' ata*—advantage being taken of the natural form of the side branches. A branch showing a suitable curve is selected and pulled downwards, leaving a long 'tongue' or 'shoe' of wood. The soft tissues down to the cambium are stripped off; the branchlet is scraped, and the 'tongue' is trimmed slightly, after which a straight piece of bone, generally from the fibula of a wallaby, circular in cross section, sharpened to a point at each end, and about two inches in length, closely resembling the bone rods called 'gorges' used by the Magdalenians and by the Eskimo, is cemented to the shoe. For this purpose the resin of either *Canarium australasicum* or *Erythrophloeum laboucherii* is employed. The

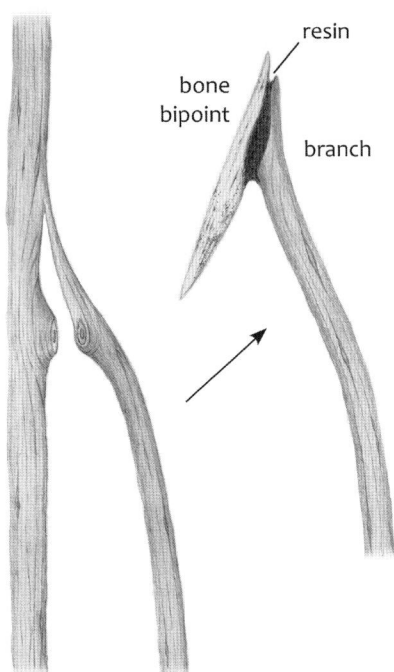

FIGURE 5.8. The construction of composite wood and bone bipoint jabbing hook. Redrawn after Thomson (1936).

hook is then firmly bound to the wood with sinews from the tail of the wallaby, *mina koton ta't*, and is finished with a final coating of resin . . . A typical hook measures eight inches overall, the bone portion being 1 3/4 inches in length and bound with wallaby sinew for a distance of nearly 3/4 inch. These fishhooks present one of the most perfect examples that I have seen of the adaptation of a natural form to a technological process. (Thomson 1936:73–4)

Spencer and Gillen (1904:677) describe the larger composite fishhooks as being used for taking large fish in the rivers and permanent waterholes near the Gulf, while Brough Smyth (1972[1878]a:204) provides some information regarding what fish were caught using both hook and spear technology in Gippsland, listing schnapper (local name: nerabogang), bream (kine), perch (tambun), trevalla (karie), sand mullet (krinyang), large flathead (bimbidng), flathead (brindat), and sea trout (billing) as having been caught with a bone fishhook, while flounder (pertpin), garfish (thacki), large flathead (bimbidng), flathead (brindat), and larger perch (wirrinbown) were speared.

Finally, it should be mentioned that—apart from marine shell—other hard animal materials were at least sometimes used as fishhooks. Massola (1956) recorded hooks not only of bone but also of bird talons and small mammal incisors. Indeed, the fisherwomen of the Sydney area were observed to sometimes use 'the talon of birds' as hooks (Barrington 1985:75; Hunter 1963[1793]:44), and a north Queensland fishhook was found to be made using the upper incisor of the black-footed tree rat (*Mesembromys gouldii*).

5. TOOLS

Along similar lines, a station owner at Lake Benanee (Riverine region) in the 1840s noted that 'the hook was a fish bone having a suitable barb, and with these rough appliances I have seen them catch fine fish' (Voss 1952:40), while James Kirby noted that people in the Murray Valley (also Riverine region) utilised a hook 'made of two teeth of a kangaroo tied in the form of a letter V' (Kirby 1894:34). Further, small mentions of 'pointed bone or sharpened shell' fishhooks in Tasmania should not be forgotten (Bonwick 1870:15).

Local names recorded for this tool include the following.

Rotating one-piece fishhook:
- ai-ya (Keppel Island, Northeast region; Roth 1901c)
- koy-yun (Lake Tyers, Southeast region, Item X001599 notes, Museum Victoria)
- bur-ra (Port Jackson area; Southeast region, Hunter 1963[1793]).

Composite fishhook:
- tarubal or tarwa (Princess Charlotte Bay, East Cape region; Roth 1902)
- werkurumi (Yarardi (Yaraldi), Lower Murray, Riverine region; Berndt et al. 1993).

Groovers/smoothing boards

Description

These multi-component tools are dominated by a hardwood board shaped somewhat like the end of a paddle some 15 centimetres long. Onto one end, a single macropod tooth is bound with ligature (usually sinew) onto a short stem that juts out of one short side. The tooth usually points back towards the board in a barb-like fashion and frequently has its tip broken off to provide a sharp cutting edge (see Figure 5.9).

Roth gives a good description of these artefacts:

> It is in the form of a flat leaf-and-stalk shaped piece of 'ironwood': one side of the 'leaf' is generally rough, either left so or made so with gum-cement, the other smooth,

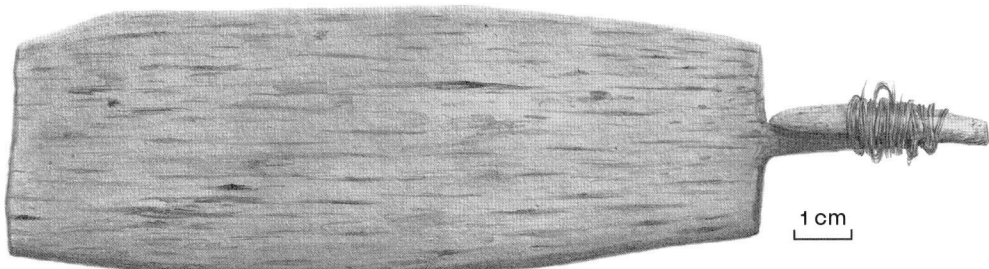

FIGURE 5.9. Smoothing boards or groovers are an essential maintenance tool used in Cape York.

> the tooth being attached to the 'stalk' on the latter side. The tooth (NGG. *mbau-u*), a kangaroo's lower incisor, is fixed with gut, or fibre-twine, and cement: its tip has been previously put into the due of a flame and broken off abruptly by well-directed and graduated pressure, so as to give a sharp cutting-edge to the enamel. (Roth 1904:21)

He also suggests that these implements may be 'fashioned after' the natural form of the kangaroo mandible engravers, described below.

These tools are recorded under a number of names, including 'putty knife', 'groover', 'smoother', 'smoothing board', and 'pallet'. Thick, dark resin traces are frequently clearly evident on the board surface.

Manufacture and use

These tools have been collected from both West and East Cape York, with Roth (1904:21) stating that they are found across 'practically the whole Northern Peninsula' of Queensland. The tool was held so that it worked towards the operator, and as Roth describes:

> the implement (NGG. *forma*) is employed for sharpening spear-tips, and, in some spears, for cutting the groove into which the barb is fixed . . . the blow of 'gum' usually found on the rough side helping to prevent its slipping along the palm. The chipping, or rather scraping, is, of course, made in a direction towards the operator. The smooth surface of the body or leaf of the implement, greased with face-perspiration, etc., is employed as a 'smoothing-board'. This use of it is . . . when the right hand is held fixed, the left one doing the twirling. (Roth 1904:21)

Local names recorded for this tool include:

- forma (Mapoon, West Cape region; Roth 1904).

Handles

Description

Handles—the part of a tool by which it is held, carried, or controlled—made in bone appear to be rare on the Australian continent.

Manufacture and use

Only one brief mention was located in the ethnographic literature regarding the use of bone as tool handles; instead, most examples were found in museum collections. The one brief mention was by Roth (1904:21), who states that for Rockhampton (Northeast region), a scraper was originally mounted onto a handle made from emu leg bone.

In the Australian Museum, a large gouge consisting of a stone flake hafted onto a near-whole macropod femur with resin is listed as a 'native chisel'. This object was collected from Renmark in South Australia (Riverine region). A very similar tool made in Broome, the Kimberley region, is part of the Buru collection (Western Australian Museum) and consists of a silcrete flake resin mounted to a kangaroo radius. It is stated to have been used for butchering game and whittling. Yet another museum example

5. TOOLS

has a stone adze mounted at both extremities, with this tool recorded as being made by Nyungatha Paddy for Kim Akerman in 1974 to demonstrate the type of adze used for the fine scraping needed in finishing off wooden technologies. The bone handle in this last case is the long bone from a very large bird. Another adze on a bone handle is found in the National Museum of Australia but is without specific provenance.

Smaller tools with bone handles were also found in the Australian Museum, with these objects noted as being used to haft glass splinters, which were used as 'prickers' in Katherine (Fitzmaurice region). It could be suggested that these prickers are similar to the bone unipoints used to draw blood on certain occasions or in medical procedures.

Local names recorded for this tool include:

- iram or kundolo (for the whole implement, Rockhampton, Northeast region; Roth 1904).

Harpoons
Description
Also from the far north are composite harpoons, consisting of a bone bipoint attached to a long wooden shaft, some about five times longer than the barb alone. It is mounted as a self-barbed point using plant fibre ligature covered with resin or wax. The proximal end of the harpoon is typically wider than the distal (barbed) extremity and is connected to the plant fibre line by being wrapped around that extremity repeatedly and tied off (see Figure 5.10). Essentially, these harpoons are just significantly larger versions (some examples reach beyond 20 centimetres) of the composite fishhooks found on the East and West Cape of Queensland.

Manufacture and use
The harpoons of Cape York (both East and West) are noted to have been used to catch turtle, shark, and dugong, as well as large fish (Roth 1901). As with the smaller composite fishhooks, kangaroo long bone, and wooden (*Acacia* sp.) components are joined with the use of plant fibre string and resin. The bone bipoint is almost entirely covered with resin so that only the very distal tip is visible. Roth (1904:32) notes that the people on the Batavia River (East Cape region) 'attached their bone barb (the only locality,

FIGURE 5.10. Harpoons made on the West Cape are used to take large fish as well as dugong.

apparently, where this material was used) in such position that the barb constituted the extreme tip of the implement'. In archaeology, Barker (1991) has reported finding parts of probable bone and wood dugong harpoons dated to <2500 BP at Nara Inlet in the Whitsundays (Northeast region).

Local names recorded for this tool include:

- tjalan (West Cape region; Roth 1901)
- nguma, omang, allukan (West Cape region; Roth 1901)
- ongar n'dambal perram-kaninag (Embley River, West Cape region; Roth 1901).

Housing

Description

Whole whalebones were used for the structural framing of huts and shelters.

Manufacture and use

Whalebones are briefly touched on in European writings and illustrations of coastal housing and include an 1842 painting by WA Cawthorne that depicts two whalebones used as part of a small shelter near Adelaide. Just two years later, Angas reworked this image to appear in his book *South Australia illustrated* (Angas 1967[1847])—this image is shown in Figure 5.11 (see colour section). In this painting, the large rib bones are anchored on one or both ends, their arches creating the structural frame over which nets and vegetation have been layered to create the walls and roof. Angas writes the following about this image:

> Natives of Encounter Bay. The view here given represents a part of the shore of Encounter Bay, with a native hut formed of the ribs of a whale. Numerous carcasses of whales being cast upon the shores adjoining the fisheries, most of the native huts are constructed with a frame-work of bones, the interstices being filled with boughs and dried grass. (Angas 1967[1847]:Plate LVI)

George Augustus Robinson mentions these huts in his 1846 journal, stating that 'some of the huts at the latter there I observed were constructed of whale bone' and were big enough to 'contain two or three families or more' (Clark 2000e:103).

Such use of whalebones for framing housing is also evident for the northwest coastline of Tasmania, where John F Jones observed whalebone structures eroding out of the sands and realised that the 'oblong dome' huts that 'might easily contain from 16 to 20 persons' observed by Jorgen Jorgenson (1829:48) in the late 1820s might not have been constructed using fire-hardened wood as that early European writing supposed but instead whalebone (see Memmott 2007 for discussion).

5. TOOLS

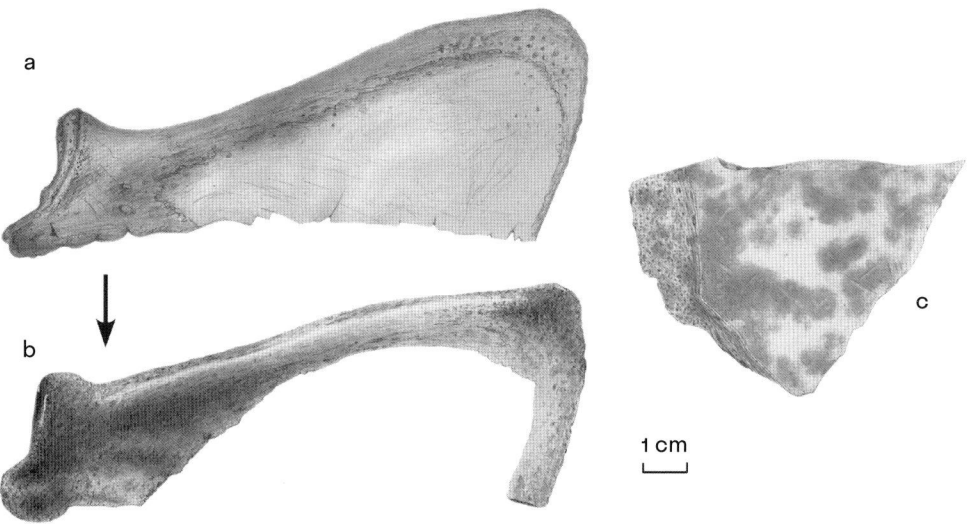

FIGURE 5.12. 'Yam knives' are made using the scapula of macropods, with use over time wearing the blade down (a and b). Flakes of turtle shell also provided a sharp organic knife in Arnhem (c).

Knives
Description
Knives are an eternally useful tool. The bone knives made on kangaroo or wallaby scapula and commonly referred to as 'yam knives' are the most well-known of the Australian variety. These tools consist of the glenoid fossa (which becomes the handle of the knife) and much of the blade. The rest of the scapula is removed, with the freshly snapped edge acting as the knife edge.

Also common in museum collections are turtle shell knives, which are roughly rectangular in shape with one long edge sporting a sharp, bevelled edge. Both are shown in Figure 5.12.

Manufacture and use
Macropod scapula knives have been collected from both the Desert and Arnhem regions and are usually connected to women (i.e. collected as 'women's tools'). Within museum collections, you find knives in varying states of reduction from use, the central section of the blade moving from a relatively straight edge to a more and more concave appearance as it moves through this reduction continuum. Several of these knives collected from Darbilla Creek (Central Arnhem Land) were hafted in dark resin (resin covering the glenoid fossa) to make them more comfortable in the hand. These knives are mentioned as being used to slice cycad seeds in the northeast of the Arnhem region (McCarthy 1976:32), and possible archaeological examples have been found at Currarong Shelter 1 on the southeast coast (Lampert 1971).

Turtle shell knives have also been collected from the Arnhem region, though details of their manufacture or use in early European writings are absent, and thus little is currently known about these tools despite their appearance in museums.

Finally, the National Museum of Australia curates a long, pointed knife made on camel bone that was collected by the Mawson expedition to Central Australia in 1914. No image was available to shed more light on this item, but it provides an interesting example of the uptake of new bone sources for technologies when desired.

Local names recorded for this tool include the following.

Macropod scapula knives:
- taraka wakala (Ooldea, Desert region; Item A27215 notes, South Australian Museum)
- bril'mil (Roper River, Arnhem region; Item DT002894 notes, Museum Victoria)
- kurwilli (North East Arnhem region; Item DT002902 notes, Museum Victoria)
- karritjambal gurrwilli djitamapoi (Howard Island, Eastern Arnhem region; Item DT002903 otes, Museum Victoria)
- kulipan nangarwan (Darbilla Creek, Eastern Arnhem region; Item DT002904 notes, Museum Victoria)
- gurrwilli nimburrwirri (Darbilla Creek, Eastern Arnhem region; Item DT002909 notes, Museum Victoria)
- kulipal (Mainoru, Eastern Arnhem region; Item DT007327 notes, Museum Victoria).

Medical or surgical tools

Description

Medical tools made on hard animal materials generally revolved around implements able to pierce or cut to treat an individual. Some items take advantage of naturally sharp materials (such as echidna quills), while others are worked to produce the required form.

Manufacture and use

An illustration of an Aboriginal doctor observed in southern Australia by William Blandowski during the late 1850s is curated within the Anthropology Library of the British Museum (Oc,B66.7). In this image, the doctor is shown seated within a shelter and surrounded by 10 medical objects including puncturing implements: a stingray barb object and several bone-tipped points. Some of these implements are found in museum collections. For example, from the Tanami Desert (Desert region), a bone 'pricker' made on a large fragment of (possible macropod long) bone sharpened into a blade is beautifully hafted within dark resin overlaid with plant fibre string. Red, white, and yellow painted designs overlay the resin and string. Other items curated as 'prickers' include another tool from the Tanami Desert—this one also hafted into a dark resin (but without string and paint additions) made on possible emu long bone. This particular object is ground to a very long and sharp point—and is similar to some of the Type 1 Awls

5. TOOLS

described above. It may be that some of these Type 1 Awls are actually medical instruments or at least sometimes utilised as such. Prickers are associated with blood-letting and have also been collected from the Eyre region, where Aiston (1928:128) states that 'to get blood for ceremonial purposes. Any sharp pointed flake or sharp bone that happened to be handy was used for this purpose'.

Bone points are also stated to have been used to lance the gums and for the knocking out of teeth (Collins 1975[1798]:481; Howitt 2001[1904]:569), while pieces of bone in different shapes were used in circumcisions and male subincisions (Basedow 1927:140; Howitt 2001[1904]:644). Bone points have also been noted for removing splinters in the Desert region, with an example made on fishbone (measuring some 10 centimetres long) collected as a 'scabies probe' from the Kimberley region. Brough Smyth talks about how, in Victoria:

> wounds, whether by accident or otherwise, are immediately attended to by their doctors . . . if little blood comes from the wound, they know all is not right, and will put the patient to pain by probing the wound with their lancet (a sharp bone). (Brough Smyth 1972[1878]a:264)

For swellings:

> when hard, they lotion the part well with decoction of wattle bark; when obstinate, they boil wild marshmallow, and poultice—if it softens and does not break, they apply their sharp bone-lancet. (Brough Smyth 1972[1878]a:264)

Similarly, Bennett mentions that a convict called George Clark lived with peoples in the interior for several years (unspecified location) and reported that smallpox was treated by:

> scorching the hair from the head, and piercing the pustules with a sharp-pointed fish bone, then squeezing out the fluid contained in them with the flat part of the instrument, was the next mode of cure adopted by the *kradjee* [medicine man]. (Bennett 1967[1834]:156)

He observed that those who got to this stage of the disease generally recovered.

Lastly, echidna quills are specifically mentioned as being used for removing splinters, bleeding the sick, and extracting thorns and lithic slivers (McCarthy 1976). Such quills have been collected as examples of medical tools from the Lake Eyre Basin, and Brough Smyth illustrates an unaltered echidna quill, stating that this figure:

> shows the lancet used by the natives. It is a spine taken from the hinder part of the porcupine (*Echidna hystrix*). It is strong, tough, and very sharp . . . They were used for bleeding and for extracting thorns, pieces of spear-points, and the like. (Brough Smyth 1972[1878]a:350)

Local names recorded for this tool include the following.

Pricker or other blood-letting tools:

- panji (Cooper Creek, Eyre region; Item A4304 notes, South Australian Museum).

Splinter (etc.) extraction tools:
- yertung (Kurnai, Riverine region; Howitt 2001[1904]:276).

Murder weapons
Description
Tools labelled specifically as 'murder weapons' are not found in the museum collections studied here, though the 'daggers' and 'stilettos' described above may very well have functioned as such, as they are consistent in form with murder weapons described in the literature below.

Manufacture and use
After reviewing the ethnographic literature, it is amazing just how frequently the use of a pointed bone tool is mentioned as being used as a murder weapon. This frequency probably reflects both the power that bone tools had in the Australian context and the preoccupation of early European writers with the topic of murder. Some specific details about bone murder weapons were included in McCarthy (1952), who cites a beautifully fashioned werpoo, a curved emu bone tapering from the condyle at one end and reaching some 36 centimetres long. He states that it was inserted downwards from the neck or upwards into the chest to the heart of the victim on the Adelaide Plains (Spencer region). Indeed, such a death was reported by Hassell (1966:24) in Adelaide in 1838. A Type 1 Awl ('stiletto') bone on emu fibula from Woonona Beach, Illawarra, is recorded as a 'weapon' or 'stabbing bone', while on the other side of the continent, Noongar-speaking informants told Bird and Beeck (1980) that a bone point was used as a murder weapon in their country, the point being inserted from between the ribs or behind the clavicle. A possible 4000-year-old archaeological example of the use of a macropod fibula point (Type 1 Awls) in this way is provided by Grave 45 at Roonka (Spencer region), where a man's rib cage 'has been transversely pierced by a bone point, causing the shattering and displacement of ribs' (Pretty 1977:311). Another example is also found at Roonka Grave 106 in which:

> most of the ribs of the left thorax were prised apart from the breast bone by a large pointed bone dagger. It was fashioned from a large fibula sharpened at one end. Its length is 29 cm. (Pretty 1977:317)

Another aspect of the use of bone points in murder is the addition of poison by inducing septicaemia in the victim. Accounts of Ngarrindjeri people (Riverine region) by Taplin (2009[1879]:30–1) talk of a weapon called the neilyeri. He states that:

> when a heathen native wants a method of revenge he takes either a spear-head, a piece of bone (often human), or else a piece of iron, sharpens it to a keen point, and cuts it a convenient length, generally about six or eight inches. He then sticks it into the fleshy part of a putrid corpse, and keeps it there for some weeks. He then takes

5. TOOLS

either a bunch of spun hair, or feathers, and soaks them in the fat of a corpse extracted for the purpose. In this he wraps up the point of the short dagger-like *neilyeri*, and thus possesses himself of a most deadly poisoned weapon. Let him only get near his enemy who he is asleep, and a single prick with the *neilyeri* will cause him to be inoculated with the virus of death, and he will be doomed to horrible agonies and probably death... And they are dreadfully afraid of it; the mere pointing of the *neilyeri* at them makes them feel ill. (Taplin 2009[1879]:30–1)

Taplin himself observed a victim of this weapon, reporting in 1879 that:

only a short time ago, upon examining a buried skeleton from which the sand had blown away, there was found, stuck fast between the ribs, the bone dagger with which the victim had been killed. (Taplin 2009[1879]:89)

Cameron similarly notes that:

there is a deadly practice of inflicting injury possessed by some of the tribes of the Murray River, but I have never heard of it in any of those east of the Darling River. A piece of bone is sharpened to a very fine point, and is inserted into a decaying corpse, being left there for some time, until it becomes thoroughly saturated with the poison. It is then wrapped up with some of the putrid matter and kept ready for use. A very slight stab with this is said to cause death. (Cameron 1885:362)

Another approach found across the Riverine region is described by Howitt when talking about Wurundjeri people, who talked about:

an instrument made of the sinews of a kangaroo's tail and the fibula of its leg (*ngyelling*), which had the same name. The sinew cord had a loop worked at one end, and the pointed bone was attached to the other... the cord was passed lightly round the sleeper's neck, and the bone being threaded through the loop, was pulled tight. Another *burring* was then passed round his feet and the victim carried off into the bush, where he was cut open and the fat extracted. (Howitt 2001[1904]:375)

Such a weapon is also mentioned for Victoria, where a bone point some 17 centimetres long was attached to a strangling cord and used against a sleeping victim (Brough Smyth 1972[1878]a). Brough Smyth (1972[1878]a:351) states that it was called nerum and:

consists of a needle about six inches and a half in length, made of the fibula of the kangaroo, and a rope two feet six inches in length. The cord is formed of twine of seven strands, which are five feet in length. The strands are doubled and stetted so as to form a loose rope of fortune strands. The end of the top is securely fastened to the head of the fibula by sinews (taken from the tail of the kangaroo), and the other end is made into a loop also securely bound by sinews. (Brough Smyth 1972[1878]a:351)

This same weapon is described by Davis (1972[1876]:313) for the Upper Murray.

Finally, ethnographic accounts from numerous early European sources report the power of simple bone fragments for sorcery. Bone fragments left over from someone's meal could be picked up and used against them (Howitt 2001[1904]), and it is for this reason that people were fastidious about cleaning up after their meals. Meyer provides an example of this behaviour at Encounter Bay (Spencer region):

> Enemies watch each other, and search diligently for places where they have eaten ducks, parrots, cockatoos, a kind of sign called bone, &c. If any one who has eaten of either of these animals, and neglected to burn all the bone, his enemy picks them up. But if the other has been too careful to enable him to do this, he takes one of these animals and cooks it, and offers it in a friendly manner to his intended victim—having previously taken from it a piece of bone. This he keeps carefully, and fixes with grass-tree resin upon the end of a small needle-shaped piece of kangaroo bone about three inches long. This is the *ngadungge*, which he places next to fire, in order to produce illness and death. (Meyer 1846:8–9)

Local names recorded for this tool include the following.

Bone daggers:
- werpoo (Adelaide Plains, Spencer region; McCarthy 1952)
- neilyeri (Narrinyeri (Ngarrindjeri), Riverine region; Taplin 2009[1879]).

Bone point with cord:
- burring (Wurundjeri, Riverine region; Howitt 2001[1904]:375)
- nerum (Victoria, Riverine region; Brough Smyth 1972[1878]a).

Musical instruments
Description
Bone objects used to produce musical sounds appear in three forms, as far as museum collections record: (1) clap sticks, (2) pipes, and (3) bull roarers.

Manufacture and use
Clap sticks are most common in museum collections, being made on pairs of macropod clavicles or fibulae. Examples in museums display polish on their extremities—consistent with wear from handling—and some feature small knobs of resin at each end. Such clap sticks have been collected from the Kimberley and Desert regions and are stated to have been used in both ceremonies and secular dance performances.

The Australian Museum curates a 'bone whistle (or pan pipe)' made on hollow bird bone collected from Normanton in the Gulf region. This instrument is some 10 centimetres long and 1.9 centimetres in diameter, being straight cut across one extremity, the other end covered with resin. Roth (1902:24) comments that this type of artefact is made on—'hollow bones ... with ends cut off abrupt, and blown across their tops—something after the manner of the units composing a pan-pipes'—at Normanton and Cape Grafton. He records that such an instrument was known as a yiki-yiki at Cape Grafton (Rainforest region).

Finally, the Australian Museum also curates a bull roarer made on bone from Cape York. Bull roarers are strongly connected to ceremonies and are stated to produce the

5. TOOLS

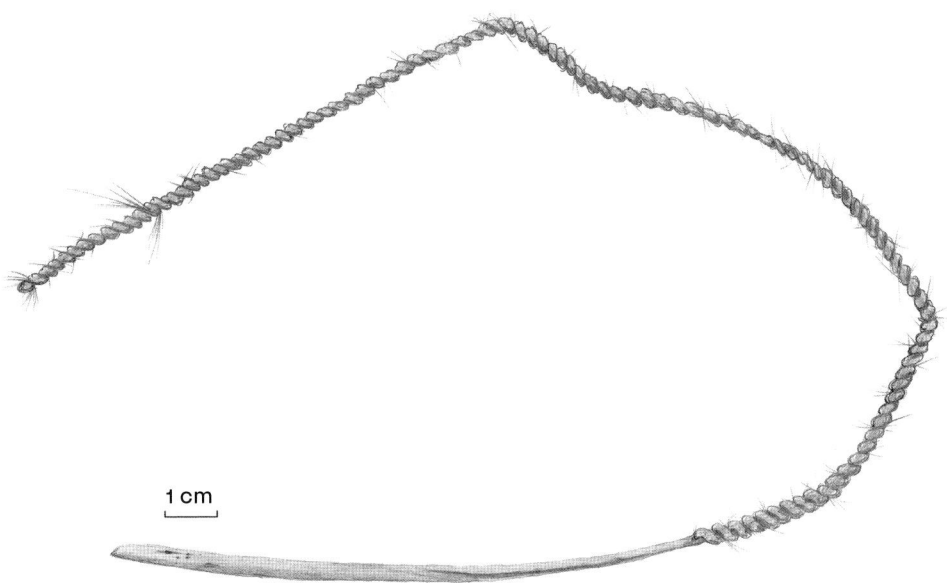

FIGURE 5.13. The eyed needle made on a large feather quill known as a tatti.

sounds of spiritual beings (Van Baal 1963). As such, bull roarers are commonly not suitable to be viewed by women and children (Van Baal 1963).

Needles
Description
Very fine points—many with drilled eyes for carrying thread—are also made from hard animal materials in Australia. These needles generally come in two forms: (1) those made on long feather quills and (2) those made on bone.

Manufacture and use
The Australian Museum holds two needles made on the quill of a long bird feather (often wing feathers) about 10–11 centimetres long. The feather barbs have been stripped, leaving only the central calamus, and a hole is drilled through one end for twisted-hair twine to pass through (see Figure 5.13). Roth notes that:

> in the Boulia district, and beyond it on the Georgina, the needle was employed in weaving the pituri-bags and other such netting-stitch bags was formerly made from the mid-rib of a Plain-Turkey's wing-feather, with a piece of twine attached to its proximal extremity. (Roth 1904:26)

From Victoria comes a group of small, bone, eyed needles that still have vegetable fibre twine threaded (curated in Museum Victoria). No further information is recorded in the museum notes for these particular tools, though McCarthy (1976:86) mentions that 'netting needles made from the mid-rib of a plains turkey wing were used in the western Queensland and central Australian region' (presumably referring to Roth's firsthand report) and cites these particular objects for eastern Australia.

An interesting account of the use of weaving needles is given for the Channel Country (Eyre region) in South West Queensland. Duncan-Kemp writes that:

> taking the loom on her knees the [woman], with a small bone or wooden netting needle passed the thread (string) through with an over-and-under motion, working perpendicularly backwards and forwards until the piece was '*koomi-pa*' or woven... Next to her dog and yam stick, the loom and the spindle are two of the [woman]'s most cherished possessions. (Duncan-Kemp 1964:155)

She states that these needles were about seven to eight inches long and that 'no man may use a netting needle' (Duncan-Kemp 1964).

Local names recorded for this tool include the following.

Long feather needle:
- tatti (Glenorminston, Riverine region; Roth 1904).

Bone or wooden netting needle:
- koonupa (South West Queensland, Eyre region; Duncan-Kemp 1964).

Pins or fasteners
Description
Pins are here defined as thin pieces of bone (etc.) with at least one sharp point used for fastening pieces of cloth (etc.) together.

Manufacture and use
Type 2 Awls were also utilised as 'cloak pins' or 'fasteners'. They are often seen pinning possum or kangaroo skin cloaks at the shoulder in early photographs. Brough Smyth (1972[1878]a:271) described seeing waller-wal-lert (possum skin rug) in Victoria being used by the living: 'hung loosely about the body, had a knot at each upper corner, and was fastened by a small stick thrust through holes made by the bone-needle—*Min-der-min*'.

Most references to the use of pins come linked to cloaks. The manufacturing process of cloak pins (also called 'fasteners') is the same as that described above for awls, often because these 'cloak pins' were actually the multifunctional Type 2 Awl. Howitt (2001[1904]:740–41) gives one example of this multifunctionality when he cites how Port Stephens (Southeast region) people would use a bone point to 'pin their blankets across their chests with the bone nose-peg. When not in use it was kept in the nose'. Similarly, Bird and Beeck (1980) mention that babies were carried in skin bags fastened to the mother's shoulders using the bone pin (Bird & Beeck 1980).

Bone pins are also found to fasten the ends of bark containers. 'Pleat type' containers are made from an oblong sheet of bark (*Eucalyptus corymbosa*, *Eucalyptus tetradonta*, or *Tristania suaveolens*) folded into pleats at each extremity to create a roughly rectangular container. The two extremities of bark were prepared for pleating by thinning and paring them down with a 'bone stiletto' (Type 1 Awl?) before they were pinned with a single small bone bipoint. Such containers have been collected from Bloomfield River (East Cape region) and are stated in museum archives as having been used to transport honey, as a utensil in food preparation and for carrying infants and small objects across creeks. These containers have been collected from both the East and West Cape regions of northern Queensland, while a folded bark container from the Arnhem region features a small bone pin that holds shut the side (curated in National Museum of Australia).

Containers were also made from a whole animal skin, including from kangaroo, pademelon, possum, and occasionally dingo. In each case, the skin was cut all the way round, high up in the neck, with the front paws and tail removed. The front paw and tail openings, together with those of the natural passages, are closed with a bone or wooden peg pierced through opposite edges, below which some strong twine or tendon is wound. Tears may also be mended with pins. Finally, the two hind legs are tied together to act as a strap so that the container may be slung over a shoulder or carried in the hand. Occasionally for transport, if a large skin, the two front paws may be left and tied to the mouth of the bag. Then a pole resting on the bearer's shoulder is passed through both sets of limbs and allows for easy carrying of the bag (Roth 1904:29). An example of a macropod skin bag—known as a nappayeonga—collected from Wonkonguru (Wangkangurru) people (east of Lake Eyre) features openings pinned shut with bone pins and string. In all, pins saw widespread use across the continent (Hammond 1933; Stormon 1977).

Archaeologically, Laila Haglund discovered several macropod fibula unipoints with acute tips among the burials excavated from the Broadbeach burial ground and thought that they represented pins used to keep the burial wrappings closed (Haglund 1976:83). Similarly, at the burial ground uncovered at Roonka (Spencer region), macropod fibula awls were discovered in positions indicating they held cloaks closed around the body in several 4000- to 5000-year-old burials (Pretty 1977).

Local names recorded for this tool include the following.

Cloak pin:
- min-der-min (Yarra River, Southeast region; Brough Smyth 1972[1878]a).

Pleat type bark container with bone pins:
- tu-bal (Koko-Yellanji, Bloomfield River, East Cape region; Roth 1904)
- jo-ára (Koko-Minni (Kuku Mini), Middle Palmer River, East Cape region; Roth 1904)
- gurlnggo (Koko-Yimidir (Gugu Yimithirr), Cape Bedford, East Cape region; Roth 1904)
- an-dú (Koko-Rarmul (Gugu Rarmul), Hinterland and coast of Princess Charlotte Bay, East Cape region; Roth 1904)
- kor (Koko-Warra (Kuku-Warra), Hinterland and coast of Princess Charlotte Bay, East Cape region; Roth 1904)
- anó-a (Nggerikudi, Pennefather and Batavia rivers, West Cape region; Roth 1904)
- bo-ata (Gunanni (Gonaniin), West Cape region; Roth 1904)
- wor-de (Mornington Island, Gulf region; Roth 1904).

Skin bag with bone pins:

- nappayeonga (Wonkonguru (Wangkangurru), Eyre region; Item X084131 notes, Museum Victoria)
- nilpa (Boulia, Eyre region; Roth 1904)
- aggara (Glenormiston, Eyre region; Roth 1904)
- norlo (Kalkadun (Kalkatungu), Gulf region; Roth 1904).

Skin-working tools
Description
At the beginning of this chapter, it was outlined how Type 2 Awls were used in both piercing and pegging out fresh skins for stretching and drying. Skin-working is now revisited to provide further information on piercing tools as well as another skin-working tool, a tool that may be called a flying knife. This knife consists of a macropod tooth hafted to a wooden shaft, its construction sounding similar to that of the macropod tooth drills of Cape York described above (see Figure 5.4).

Manufacture and use
A multipurpose tool, the flaying knife is made from one or two macropod incisors hafted to a wooden shaft. Hassell and Davidson (1936:691) reported for Wheelman (Wiilman) and surrounding peoples of southwestern Australia that this implement:

> differed from the men's instrument. It consisted of a stick with a kangaroo tooth embedded in gum at one end. It was used in scraping skins, cutting away sinews, and for skinning. The women were able to skin a kangaroo with it as rapidly as a man with a European knife. (Hassell & Davidson 1936:691)

Bates (1985:278) provides the Bibulman name tangul for this tool and indicates that the tooth was split to create a sharp edge before being hafted. Similarly, Aiston (1928:13) notes that:

> when the rug was completed, it was scored across diagonally in opposite directions—so that it made a diamond pattern—with an opossum or rabbit's tooth set in grass-tree gum.

Brough Smyth (1972[1878]a:271) also mentions their ornamentation in Victoria, stating that:

> the rug was usually ornamented on the inside. Lines straight, of herring-bone pattern, or sometimes representing men and animals, were drawn with a sharp bone-needle, and filled in with colours.

Other tools briefly mentioned as being used in skin-working include 'a thin painted bone' mentioned as being used to pierce holes for sewing the furs of macropods or possum furs at Port Lincoln (Spencer region) (Schürmann 2009[1879]:210), while Nind (1831:37) reports that the women of King George Sound (Southwest region) utilised 'the

5. TOOLS

claw of a kangaroo ... for a needle'. In Brisbane (Northeast region), Petrie (1904:82) recalled that when echidnas were caught, 'sometimes these prickles [were] kept for piercing 'possum rugs sewn by the women and old men'. Mulvaney (1960:66) may have found just such an artefact at Fromms Landing on the Lower Murray River, where in Level 6, dated to about 3500 years ago, 'a porcupine quill which is burnished and may have been utilised' was recovered. Schrire (1982:128) also reports 'unipoints ... two on a quill and one on a fish bone' found at Nawamoyn.

Another archaeological find worth mentioning is a Pleistocene-aged small unipoint made on the end of a bird fibula found in Devils Lair, Western Australia (Dortch & Merrilees 1973). This tiny artefact is only 14 millimetres long and features a sharp point and polish on its distal half, suggesting use in skin- or plant-working (Dortch & Merrilees 1973). Another similarly sized bone fragment with a perforation at one extremity is also suggested to have functioned similarly, though Dortch and Merrilees (1973:110) state that it could also have been part of an ornamental piece.

Local names recorded for this tool include the following.

Macropod tooth flaying knife:
- tangul (Bibulman, Southwest; Bates 1985).

Bone peg/awl:
- min-der-min or min-dah-min (Victoria; Brough Smyth 1972[1878]a).

Smoking pipes
Description
Smoking pipes have been made using the very tip of crab claws (as a shellfish, not included here) and hollow long bones from large birds.

Manufacture and use
Not many examples of bone smoking pipes have found their way into museum collections, though Donald Thomson brought back two examples made on brolga long bones from East Arnhem. The ends of these implements are chipped roughly and not finished off in any particular way. The local name for these pipes is recorded in Museum Victoria as kurdurkur ngarraka pamatuka.

Spear points
Description
A number of authors make generalised statements regarding Australian spear technology and the fact that they are 'tipped or barbed with sharp points made from stone, wood, bone, or stingray spine' (Mulvaney & Kamminga 1999:89) (also see Bonwick 1870). Below, a more nuanced description is attempted, with Table 5.4 providing an overview of ethnographies and museum collections. The vast majority of spears held in museum collections are multi-pronged fishing spears collected from Cape York, a bias that needs to be kept in mind when assessing the currently available information.

TABLE 5.4. Characteristics of spears pointed with hard animal materials from ethnographic reports and museum collections. These spears have bone tips unless specified otherwise. Archaeological examples of small bone bipoints that may have tipped such spears are discussed only in the text.

REGION	SINGLE-POINT SPEAR	SINGLE-POINT WITH BARB	MULTI-PRONGED SPEAR	RAW MATERIAL UTILISED	EVIDENCE FOR HAFTING
Kimberley	single stingray barb point; single bone blade spear			stingray barb; bone	resin; resin and sinew
Fitzmaurice	[none identified]				
North	single-point spear			bone	
Arnhem	single-point spear; single stingray barb point		4-pronged kangaroo claws; many-pronged stingray cluster	bone; kangaroo claw; stingray barb	resin; ochre; plant fibre and resin
Desert	[none identified]				
Gulf	single-point spear		4-pronged, small bipoint, self-barbed; 5-pronged stingray barb	echidna quill; stingray barb; bone	plant fibre string coated with resin
Torres Strait		single-point with barb	4-pronged; 8-pronged	bone	plant fibre string covered with skin band; plant fibre string coated with resin; red ochre
West Cape		single-point with barb	4-pronged, small bipoint, self-barbed; 3-pronged, small bipoint, self-barbed	bone	plant fibre string coated with resin; white ochre; possible sinew and resin
East Cape		single-point with barb	3-pronged, small bipoint, self-barbed; many-pronged stingray cluster	bone; stingray barb	plant fibre string coated with resin; white ochre
Rainforest			many-pronged stingray cluster	stingray barb; bone	plant fibre and resin; red and white ochre
Northeast	single-point spear		3-pronged, small bipoint, self-barbed; many-pronged stingray cluster	stingray barb; bone	resin; fibre and resin; red ochre
Southeast		single-point with barb	4-pronged	bone	resin
Tasmania	[none identified]				

5. TOOLS

REGION	SINGLE-POINT SPEAR	SINGLE-POINT WITH BARB	MULTI-PRONGED SPEAR	RAW MATERIAL UTILISED	EVIDENCE FOR HAFTING
Riverine	single-point spear	single-point with barb	3-pronged, small bipoint, self-barbed	emu bone; bone	plant fibre and resin
Spencer	single-point spear				
Eyre	[none identified]				
Southwest	[none identified]				
Northwest	[none identified]				

Spears tipped with bone or stingray barbs make up a large proportion of the hard animal material artefacts collected from across the Australian continent. Spears tipped with a single-point spear or a single-point spear with a barb, as well as multi-pronged spears, are found (see Figure 5.14). Multi-pronged spears have at least two prongs, though most have three or four. Also included below are several rare examples of spears that are different from these more commonly seen forms, including examples with layers of echidna quills. While all these weapons function in very similar ways, their overall designs are diverse.

Manufacture and use

Regarding the single-point spears, examples have been either mentioned in accounts or collected for museums across a large swathe of the north (Table 5.4). Jardine noted for Somerset on the tip of Cape York (East Cape region) that:

> four sorts of spears, made from the suckers of a very light wood tree with large pith, headed with hardwood and generally topped with bone so as to form a point or barb, are most common. The end of the tail of a soft ray-fish is sometimes used as a point. It is serrated and brittle, and on entering any object breaks short off. It is said to be poisonous, but I do not believe such to be the case, as one of the marines stationed here was speared in the shoulder with one of these spears, and no poisonous effect was produced. The point, which broke short off, however, remained in the wound and could not be extracted for many months. (Jardine 1866:81)

A particularly interesting example was collected from Normanton in the Gulf region (curated in the Australian Museum) and is tipped with a single echidna quill tied on by plant fibre string coated over with resin. The only other spear located that utilised echidna quills was also collected from 'Northern Queensland, pre-1902' (Item X010109 notes, Museum Victoria). This second spear features several rows of echidna quills that have been laid down side by side in bands that circle the shaft. The quills are positioned so that their sharp tips point slightly out and away from the shaft and are held in place with resin. The spear is further decorated with red and white paint and has the local name ungine. While it is tempting to suggest that this spear was a ceremonial item rather than a hunting or fighting weapon, the sharpness and resiliency of echidna quills make this spear a very effective tool in all circumstances.

A RECORD IN BONE

Most single-point spears are tipped with bone. Schrire (1982:36) reports that her informants at Gunbulunya (Arnhem region) 'said that bone bipoints were used as nose bones and could also serve as spear points'. Spencer (1914:357–9) also recorded both single- and multi-pronged bone-tipped spears made at Gunbulunya in 1912, while White (1967) states that 'Kakadu people' had two types of wooden spears made from bamboo (reed?) foreshafts, which featured bone points stuck in resin at the tip. Similar-sounding spears are described by Bassett-Smith (1894) for Port Darwin (North region): 'short spears either partially of bamboo or wholly of hard wood; they were not barbed, but occasionally pointed with bone; these latter are mostly used for kangaroo hunting'.

Regarding spear points further south to Sydney, 'short spears pointed with the leg bone of the kangaroo, which were supposed to be designed for stabbing the calves when caught' were described by Collins (1975[1802]) as part of his observation of Indigenous hunting of livestock in 1798. The following year, Collins described a similar-sounding spear observed on Curlew Island near Hervey Bay (Northeast region):

> the spears were of solid wood, of twelve feet in length, and could not have been used with a throwing-stick. One of them was barbed with a small piece of some animal's bone. (Collins 1975[1802]:185)

Along the Murray (Riverine region), bone-tipped spears were also observed. Angas (1967[1847]:54), speaking about canoes at Lake Alexandrina, stated that 'they are paddled by means of a long spear, having a sharpened kangaroo-bone fixed at one end, for spearing fish'. While travelling the Murray River in 1836, Mitchell (1965[1839]b:144) mentions that on 21 June, during a hostile interaction between his guide, Piper, and local men, 'the spears used on this occasion were made of reed, and pointed with bones of the emu'. Speaking about the broader Victorian region, Brough Smyth states that he knew of:

> two forms of spear . . . [on one] the head and barb are formed wholly of bone which is firmly attached to the shaft of wood by sinews and gum. [On the other] the head and shaft are of wood, and the barb is a piece of bone, which is fixed by sinews and gum to the side. These are used principally for spearing fish. Dr Gummow, of Swan Hill, who is well acquainted with all the weapons and implements of the natives, states that these are used also in war. The name of the spear is *Koanie*; the spike of bone is called *Kulkie*, the barb *Tilloo*, and the shaft of the spear *Marrongie*. (Brough Smyth 1972[1878]a: 306)

Finally, the peoples of the Glenelg River (Spencer region) were seen to use 'a spear with a bone point used for killing rats called *wil.long*' in 1841 (Augustus Robinson in Clark 2000b:268).

Next are those spears that include the addition of a single barb separated from the distal point. Such spears from Archer River on the West Cape feature a single bone barb situated down from a much larger bone distal extremity. These spears are recorded in the museum archives as having been used for wallaby, emu, and other similarly sized game, while others (of the same form) were used as fighting spears. McCarthy (1939:419) mentions that 'the middle Palmer River natives make the proximal portion of bamboo,

5. TOOLS

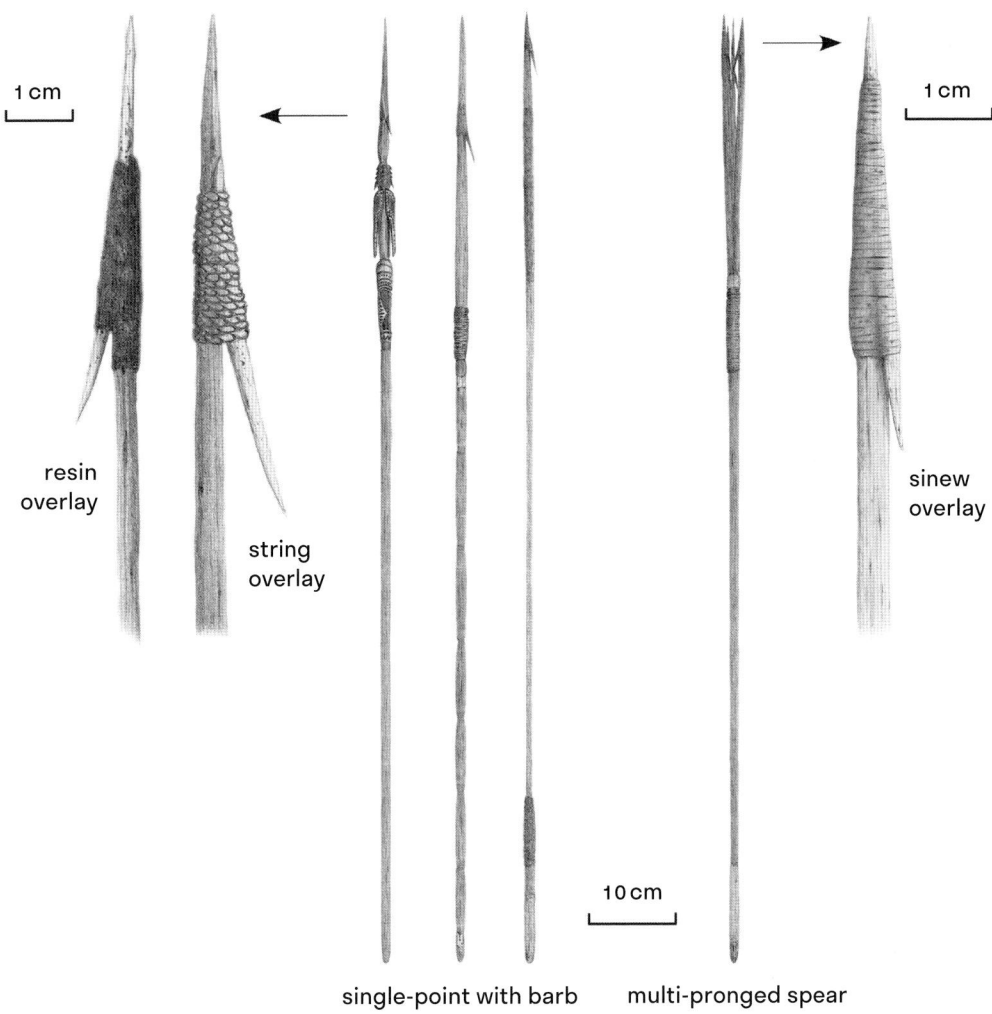

FIGURE 5.14. Bipoints are used to create the bone-tipped spears. These could be hafted at the distal end of the spear (a self-barbed point, as on the multi-pronged spear) or down from the distal edge to act solely as a barb (as on the single-point with barb spears).

which is bartered from the Princess Charlotte Bay blacks, and use bone-barbs', which may be these same weapons. Multiple examples of such spears were collected from Mer, Torres Strait (in particular), with the examination of photographs revealing that the point is made from a large bone rather than the sometimes ascribed hardwood and a smaller bone barb attached. The distal extremity is often ground into a large bipoint, which is then covered with a tight leather wrap so that the bone point itself is barely visible. This type of spear may have been described by Lumholtz, who states that:

> in Northern Queensland I have occasionally seen the point of the spear furnished with a barb of fish bones for a length of one or two feet up the spear. Such javelins were

thicker and shorter than the common ones and are used only for fishing. (Lumholtz 1889:93)

On the other side of the continent, a similarly designed weapon may have been present, as Threlkeld (1855:110) describes spears terminating with a length of hardwood sharpened to a point, to which 'in some instances a bone barb is fastened' at Lake Macquarie (Southeast region). Threlkeld (1855:229–30) noted that these spears were used in hunting terrestrial fauna and were made only by coastal people but sometimes traded inland. Finally, spears with bone barbs have also been noted to have been used in fishing on the Lower Darling River (Riverine region). Worth mentioning here is an ornately carved, one-piece, bilaterally barbed point of hardwood that was mended with small bone points—the bone points replacing broken hardwood originals. The importance of mending broken barbs on unilaterally and bilaterally barbed spear points has been demonstrated by osseous projectile points from Magdalenian contexts of Western Europe (Langley 2015). This extraordinary example was collected from Condah (Riverine region) and is currently curated in Museum Victoria.

Multi-pronged fishing spears were such a common sight on European arrival that both good written descriptions and illustrations of the technology along the Southeast coast are available. Hunter describes these spears in the following manner:

> the fish-gig is in length something more than the war lance, but they can, according to the depth of water, increase its length, by a variety of joints; some have one, some two, three, or four prongs, pointed and barbed with a fish, or other animal's bone. (Hunter 1963[1793]:41)

He also states that the fishermen were very dextrous with these fishing spears:

> we have sometimes, in fine weather, seen a man lying across a canoe, with his face in the water, and his fish-gig immersed, ready for darting: in this manner he lies motionless, and by his face being a little under the surface, he can see the fish distinctly; but were his eye above, the tremulous motion of the surface, occasioned by every light air of wind, would prevent his sight: in this manner they strike at the fish with so much certainty, that they seldom miss their aim. (Hunter 1963[1793]:44)

Collins similarly described the fishing spears and their users, stating that around Sydney:

> fish is their chief support. Men, women, and children are employed in procuring them; but the means used are different according to the sex; the males always killing them with the fiz-gig, while the females use the hook and line. The fiz-gig is made of the wattle; has a joint in it, fastened by gum; is from fifteen to twenty feet in length, and armed with four barbed prongs; the barb being a piece of bone secured by gum. To each of these prongs they give a particular name; but I never could discover any sensible reason for the distinction. (Collins 1975[1798]:461)

Reports regarding the specific material used to tip the prongs slightly differ among sources, with some stating that what was used to tip these spears in the Sydney region were 'fish teeth' (White 1962[1790]:189, 293), fishbone (Hunter 1963[1793]:62–3), or more simply just 'bone' (Bradley 1969[1786]:92, 69; Hunter 1963[1793]:62–3; Threlkeld 1855:229).

Still regarding spear points in the south, Taplin describes how Narrinyeri (Ngarrindjeri) people (Riverine region) fished using:

> the three-pronged fishing spear. This weapon is a slender pole, about fourteen feet long, with three points of sharp bone lashed to its top with twine. Every native carries one in his canoe. The men are very expert in the use of them. They are used in much the same way as our eel spear. A man will stand in a canoe silently watching with uplifted spear until a fish comes beneath, when the weapon is darted down on its back, and it is lifted transfixed from the water. (Taplin 2009[1879]:42)

He later describes how these spears were sometimes used to intimidate unwanted visitors:

> When I got there I saw all the Lower Murray tribe—about sixty men—drawn up in rank about 200 yards off with their fishing spears (ugly three-pronged weapons) in their hands, and trying to look as fierce and angry as they could. (Taplin 2009[1879]:106)

Chauncy, also discussing spear points used along the Murray River, also describes:

> spears for fishing made of the reed which grows in vast beds from Swan Hill downwards for thirty miles, and also at Lake Moira above the confluence of the Goulburn River. These spears are pointed with bones of the emu, or such substitute as they may be able to procure. (Chauncy 1972[1876]:249)

Further south in Gippsland (Southeast region), Augustus Robinson talks about local fishing practices observed in 1844, when trout, perch, and herring were caught using a four-pronged spear (Clark 2000d:166; 2000c:118).

As mentioned above, the three- or four-pronged fishing spears were collected in great numbers from Cape York Peninsula and now make up much of the bone spear assemblages held in Australian museums. Their striking appearance no doubt led to these items having a certain 'collectable' quality about them for Europeans. Three- and four-pronged spears from the West Cape are about equally numerous in the studied collections, with small bone bipoints mounted on each prong oriented inwards to act as self-barbed points.

Roth (1910a:10) states that 'four-pronged fish-spears' were made and traded from 'Mulgrave and Upper Russell Rivers, Johnston River, Clump Point, etc'. In another report, Roth states that on the Pennefather River (West Cape region), the multi-pronged spears are made with:

> the barb, except in the stingaree-tail spears, is of a kangaroo-bone pencil (nowadays oft replaced by thick iron wire) tied into a longitudinal groove, cut with a tooth-scraper, into the spear tip beyond which it projects; it is bound round and round with twine, the cording finally giving place to a plain looping, the whole of which is ultimately covered with cement substance. (Roth 1909b:191)

Roth mentions that at Princess Charlotte Bay (East Cape region), multi-pronged fishing spears are made with barbs of hardwood or bone and that people would:

> throw these spears either at fish *in situ*, or else, as I have often watched them do in a muddy water-hole, aim here and there in the water on the chance of hitting one. (Roth 1909b:193–4)

These spears are also noted to have been used in hunting emu, jabiru, ducks, and similar, with one West Cape spear curated in the South Australia Museum stated to have been used for fish, birds, goanna, and koala. Three-pronged spears barbed with bone appear to also have been present as far south as Rockhampton (Northeast region), with Bird (1904:407) reporting an incident where two people 'were disturbed fishing by puddling the water in the holes. They had jagged tipped spears tipped with flint, fish bones, and iron'. Regarding spear points used to the west, Bennett (1927:409) mentions that Dalleburra (Dalla) people of north Central Queensland fished using 'another spear, with prongs of bone fastened to the shaft below the point'. In West Arnhem Land, single-pronged and multi-pronged spears tipped with bone points were used to hunt fish, tortoise, and water snakes (Spencer 1914:357), while they are recorded as fishing spears in the Torres Strait.

As the resin that hafts the small bone points to the tips of multi-pronged spears covers most of the point, researchers have resorted to taking X-rays of the spears to learn more about their manufacture. X-rays of multi-pronged fishing spears held in the Spencer Collection of Museum Victoria but collected from the Alligator rivers region of Arnhem Land discovered that the pointed bone tips were actually bipoints (Brockwell & Akerman 2007; Schrire 1982). Schrire similarly X-rayed the prongs of three fishing spears, finding that:

> the tips are clearly bone bipoints which have been pushed into the wooden prong and then backed round with resin. There are thin cracks in them well below the tip of the bone points, suggesting that considerable force was used to force the point home. The position of the retaining resin suggests that broken bipoints might or might not retain the characteristic bulge [in the midsection]. (Schrire 1982:36)

Archaeological examples of these fishing spear tips have recently been recovered in great number from the Mirarr site of Madjedbebe, dating back over the past 7000 years (Langley et al. 2023), with very similar examples found in the Arnhem region, such as at Arguluk Hill (McCarthy & Setzler 1960), Burial Cave (Kamminga & Allen 1973), and Ngarradj Warde Jobkeng (Kamminga & Allen 1973). Quite a number of sites in the Southeast region have also produced small bone bipoints argued to be connected to fishing spears, with these sites including Bass Point (Bowdler 1979), Currarong (Lampert 1971), Curracurrang Shelter (Lampert 1971), Durras North (Langley et al. 2021b), and of course, Ngaut Ngaut (Hale & Tindale 1930). John Mulvaney recovered a number of small bone unipoints and bipoints in Levels 5 and 6 at Fromms Landing dating to about 3500 years old (Mulvaney 1960), as well as at Aire River Shelter II, where most of the deposit dates to less than about 370 years ago (Mulvaney 1962). From the illustrations provided, several of the recovered bone points appear to be consistent with those that tipped fishing spears, though Mulvaney appears to have favoured their use as fishing gorges (Mulvaney 1960, 1962).

5. TOOLS

Also fairly common within photographs and museum collections are striking spears tipped with clusters of stingray spines. These spears were noted by Thomson (1936:74) for Cape York Peninsula, stating that 'the serrated spines of the stingray were used for ceremonial and fighting spears'. These barbs are backed together to form a tightly gathered bunch, with one example from Elcho Island (Arnhem region) recorded as a warungul. It also features a decorative feather tassel. The accompanying museum note states that 'only a few old men are permitted to make these, an unauthorised man who attempted to make one was speared. Psychological effect of possession very great; highly treasured' (Item A16299 notes, South Australian Museum). Petrie for South East Queensland (Northeast region) states that:

> sometimes these spears were notched almost through at the point, and then thrown at a special enemy with the hope that they would hit and break off, leaving the end stuck in the wound. Again, the sharp barb from the butt of a stringaree's tail might be used for the point of a spear. It was fastened on with bees' wax and string. Spears were thrown with the hand only, no woomera was used. (Petrie 1904:102)

Roth (1910a:17) mentions that on the Bloomfield River (East Cape region), people would barter for 'stingaree-spears', among other items of interest, while at Princess Charlotte Bay (also East Cape region):

> the Koko-rarmul of the Morehad River give the Koko-warra (whose 'country' extends along the course of the Normanby and Deighton Rivers) reed-spears, iron scraps, European tomahawks, etc. getting in return Melo shell, grass-reed-spears, nautilus-shell necklaces, stingaree spears and fishing-nets. (Roth 1910a:18)

He also notes that 'the Mapoon, obtain from the Northern shores of Port Musgrave the "ombo" spears, for these they give bamboo and stingaree-spears, which they have obtained from the Pennefather River men' (Roth 1910a:18). More detail regarding stingray barb spears from Princess Charlotte Bay, Cape Bedford, and Bloomfield and Middle Palmer rivers is given in his earlier monograph:

> (a) Stingaree-barbed, single or multiple with the barb or barbs pointing forwards, long proximal end of bamboo or reed and short distal end of *Acacia holocarpa*, or *Drymophloeus normanbyi* . . . (b) Stingaree-barbed, multiple, with the barbs placed one behind the other, pointing backwards; long proximal end of reed, short distal portion of black-palm or hardwood, and known as *dekara*. (Roth 1909b:192–3)

These spears appear to have been used as far south as the Lower Tully River, where Roth (1909b:195) talks about the 'woomera-spear', a composite spear that may have stingray barbs attached. He states that when the barbs are present:

> the spear is called a *warra-katcha*, and its distal extremity is covered with red and white rings, but if not present, this extremity is smeared with a uniform red. It is used for fighting purposes, and for spearing wallabies. (Roth 1909b:195)

Regarding spear points used to the west into the Gulf region, Palmer reported that:

one spear found in the Normanby River had eight jags laid on one after another, flat and close to the shaft; these were all of the end the sting-ray's tail, fastened very neatly to a shaft made out of the cabbage-tree (*Corypha australis*). (Palmer 1884:286–7)

Finally, a brief mention by Nind (1831:33) suggests that the use of stingray barbs may have been much further spread (or traded), as he saw their use on King George Sound (Southwest region).

'Death spears' have a fearsome reputation for not only looking threatening but also being very effective interpersonal weapons. Described early on as 'a barbed spear, for close fighting' (Hunter 1963[1793]:272), the Goon-gan people were:

> generally . . . armed for seven or eight inches from the point with small bits of sharp stone, bone, or shells; and, since our settling amongst them, bits of glass bottle: these are fixed on with the yellow gum, which is softened by fire and afterwards grows hard and firm, making a very good cement. (Hunter 1968[1793]:329)

A final interesting example worth mentioning is a particularly unusual four-pronged spear from Gunbalanya (Arnhem region) found tipped with kangaroo claws in Museum Victoria. Though little information is available regarding this item, it suggests that animal claws may have seen use in tipping spears in some areas or in some circumstances.

Local names recorded for this tool include the following.

Single-point spear:
- ri-angapa (stingray barb tipped, Koko-Warra (Kuku-Warra), Gulf region; Roth 1909b)
- opop (Mer, Torres Strait region; Item E017248 notes, Australian Museum)
- le op (Mer, Torres Strait region; Item E017248 notes, Australian Museum)
- day-ro (Mapoon, West Cape region; Item E005243 notes, Australian Museum)
- alahu (Mapoon, West Cape region; E011752 notes, Australian Museum)
- to-ono (Mapoon, West Cape region; Item E015073 notes, Australian Museum)
- sya matangganna (Mapoon, West Cape region; Item DT004010 notes, Museum Victoria)
- kek pinta (West Cape region; Item DT003976 notes, Museum Victoria)
- kek sandal (Aurukun, West Cape region; Item X083652 notes, Museum Victoria)
- ta-chal (stingray barb tipped, Bloomfield River, East Cape region; Roth 1909b)
- ri-ang-pal (stingray barb tipped, Koko-Rarmul (Gugu-Rarmul), East Cape region; Roth 1909b).

Multi-pronged spear:
- ekolpen (East Alligator River, Fitzmaurice region; Leichhardt 1847)
- takul (Torres Strait region; Item E008193 notes, Australian Museum)
- dagulal (Torres Strait region; Item E021011 notes, Australian Museum)

5. TOOLS

- kek wan'k'n (West Cape region; Item DT003969 notes, Museum Victoria)
- kek paint'n tjimpa (West Cape region; Item DT003972 notes, Museum Victoria)
- kaka itjingot (West Cape region; Item DT003973 notes, Museum Victoria)
- kek yikan (West Cape region; Item DT003974 notes, Museum Victoria)
- kek kangarin (Archer River, West Cape region; Item DT003971 notes, Museum Victoria)
- sya n'diuru twarra (Mapoon, West Cape region; Item DT004078 notes, Museum Victoria)
- kek anchtan (Aurukun, West Cape region; Item X083653 notes, Museum Victoria)
- ché-a (Pennefather River, West Cape region; Roth 1909b)
- yirmba (Bloomfield, East Cape region; Item E015129 notes, Australian Museum)
- mu-lon (Cape Bedford, East Cape region; Roth 1909b)
- lu-yu, gurrpan, larwa, karana, or pur-ta (Princess Charlotte Bay, East Cape region; Roth 1909b)
- urr-ché-ra (Middle Palmer River, East Cape region; Roth 1909b)
- ca-la-ra (Port Jackson/Sydney area, Southeast region; Hunter 1963[1793])
- cal-larr (Port Jackson/Sydney area, Southeast region; Collins 1975[1798])
- moo-tang (Port Jackson/Sydney area, Southeast region; Hunter 1963[1793])
- mugaroo (Lower Murray, Riverine region; Angas 1967[1847]).

Multi-pronged stingray barb spear:
- warungul (Elcho Island, Arnhem region; Item A16300 notes, South Australian Museum)
- ché-a (Pennefather River, West Cape region; Roth 1909b)
- larnape (Nggerikudi, West Cape region; Roth 1903b)
- mu-lon (Cape Bedford, East Cape region; Roth 1909b)
- tikara (Middle Palmer River, East Cape region; Roth 1909b)
- challawang (Koko-Rarmul (Gugu Rarmul), East Cape region; Roth 1909b)
- gulaba (Koko-Rarmul (Gugu Rarmul), East Cape region; Roth 1909b)
- dekara (Princess Charlotte Bay, East Cape region; Roth 1909b)
- warra-katcha (Lower Tully River, Rainforest region; Roth 1909b).

Spearthrower pegs
Description
Spearthrowers—often called 'woomera' or 'throwing sticks' in Australia—are tools that utilise leverage to achieve greater velocity in the spear being thrown. Using a spearthrower allows a hunter to launch their spear over much greater distances than those that are achievable by hand alone. These tools include either a cup or spur at one end that supports the butt of the spear. This spur is usually called a 'peg'. While the main part of the spearthrower is made from hardwood (themselves coming in a variety

of forms reflecting their country of origin), the small, pointed peg is often made from an osseous material: usually a bone point or macropod incisor. These pegs are held on with sinew or plant fibre ligatures covered with dark resins so that only the very tip (about one centimetre) is visible.

Manufacture and use

As only the very tip of the peg is exposed, it is sometimes hard to determine if the peg is bone or tooth. Museum-curated spearthrowers utilising macropod incisors have been collected from Binnum Binnum, South Australia (Riverine region); the Murray River (Riverine region); Lower Murray River, South Australia (Southeast region); and Alice Springs (Desert region). On this last example, curated in the South Australian Museum, the tooth is arranged so that the more cylindrical root section acts as the peg rather than the crown. Bone is found on examples collected from Coorong, Younghusband Peninsula, and Adelaide, both in South Australia (Spencer region); Mount Gambier, South Australia (Riverine region); Cape Otway, Victoria (Southeast region); and the Lower Murray (Riverine region). On the example from Adelaide, the resin is recorded as yacka (*Xanthorrhoea*) gum.

Ethnographic accounts of bone- or tooth-based spearthrower pegs include Eyre's general description of the spearthrower as follows:

> the *ngā-wǎ-ōnk*, or throwing stick is from twenty to twenty-six inches in length, and is of a very similar character throughout the continent, varying a little in width or shape according to the fashion of particular districts. It consists of a piece of hard wood, broad about the middle, flattened and sometimes hollowed on the inside, and tapering to either extremity; at the point the tooth of a kangaroo is tied and gummed on, turning downwards like a hook; the opposite end has a lump of pitch with a fine set in it, moulded round so as to form a knob, which prevents the hand from slipping whilst it is being used, or it is wound round with string made of the fur of the opossum for the same purpose . . . the head of the spear, in which is a small hole, is fitted to the kangaroo tooth. (Eyre 1845:306–7)

For Port Leschenault in the Koombana Bay area (Southwest region), spearthrower pegs are reported to be a kangaroo tooth fixed with gum (Roth 1902), though Balme (1979) notes that other accounts for the same region described the function of this kangaroo tooth as a knife or scraper rather than as a peg. In particular, the tooth being mounted on the distal (handle) end rather than the proximal end appears to support these latter functions, and Moore (1842) reports that it was used for a variety of purposes, including scraping the points of spears. Similarly, Hassell and Davidson comment that for Bremer Bay:

> spears were usually thrown with the aid of a *Meera* or spearthrower, generally made of 'raspberry jam' wood . . . the peg was a small wooden pin about one half inch long fastened to one end with gum and kangaroo sinew. The other end of the *Meera* had a piece of gum for a handle. A kangaroo tooth was often embedded in the gum for use as a knife. (Hassell & Davidson 1936:691)

5. TOOLS

Such an example of a spearthrower with a gum handle retaining a kangaroo incisor is curated in the Western Australian Museum (Item WAM361).

Regarding spearthrowers used in the southeast of the continent, Augustus Robinson noted in 1841, while in the Port Fairy region, that 'I observe that the point of the *leree* or *wongin* of the natives is a kangaroo tooth and not wood' (Clark 2000b:157), while Brough Smyth describes the spearthrower used along the Yarra as the '*Kur-ruk* or *Gur-reck*' and that:

> when a *Kur-ruk* is broken, either by accident in the chase or in battle, the body is kept, and a new hook fitted to it. Sinews of the tail of the kangaroo and *Pid-jer-ong* enable the black to effect the repairs with ease. It will be seen that in some of the weapons a tooth is fitted not the wood at the upper end. These have either been repaired in the manner above described or, for greater convince, originally so fashioned. (Brough Smyth 1972[1878]a:309–10)

Stone-working tools
Description
Soft hammers and organic pressure-flaking instruments are not uncommon in museum collections, though specific descriptions of their use are rather rare (see Martellotta et al. 2021). These tools are minimally altered for their purpose, though those used in pressure-flaking usually had a point ground into a spatulate form to act as the active edge of the tool. Frequently, these pressure-flaking tools are referred to as 'denticulators', 'denticulating tools', or 'bone indentors' in the literature.

Manufacture and use
Denticulating tools appear to have been most frequently made on macropod ulnas, the size and shape of which are a comfortable fit in the hand. Many such examples have been collected from the Kimberley region (including from Port George IV and Broome Bay, but very frequently just stated as having come from the 'Kimberley'), probably owing to the popular trade in 'Kimberley points' and the fascination with how these beautiful stone artefacts were made. Indeed, whole 'spear point making kits' were collected and placed in museums. One such example from Kunmunya (the Kimberley) in Museum Victoria includes a bone implement made on 'leg bone, dingo'.

Another interesting example is also not made on macropod ulna but instead on half of a freshwater crocodile jaw with the teeth removed (from Mowanjum, the Kimberley). This tool is stated to have been used to 'pressure-flake stone and glass spearpoints' in the museum register, and Mathews (1901:84) mentions the use of freshwater crocodile mandible being used in this fashion. Macropod fibula (rather than ulna) used for this purpose are also not infrequently found, and there is also mention of dugong ribs being used on occasion (Akerman et al. 2002).

Some of these pressure-flakers may have been hafted with resin to create a comfortable handhold, with a sole tool collected from Hanover Bay, Western Australia (Southwest region) providing a curated example.

Local names recorded for this tool include the following.

Macropod ulna pressure-flaker:
- joomba (Port George IV, Kimberley region; Item X025251 notes, Museum Victoria)
- jumba (Worora/Wunambal (Worrorra/Wunambal), Kalumburu, Kimberley region; Item 115 notes, Western Australian Museum).

Macropod fibula pressure-flaker:
- tingkalya (Worora/Wunambal (Worrorra/Wunambal), Kalumburu, Kimberley region; Item 277 notes, Western Australian Museum).

Toys
Description
Children's playthings—or toys—do not feature in early European accounts of Indigenous Australia. As such, there are not a lot of data surrounding the material culture of children on this continent (but see Haagen 1994).

Manufacture and use
The only possible toy made using bone that was found during this study is a perfectly round ball made from bullock bone, gypsum dung, and ochre purchased in 1889 from Kalkadoon (Kalkatungu) people, Queensland (Eyre region) (curated in the Australian Museum). This ball is about five centimetres in diameter and may be a spinning ball that was used primarily by children, as observed for the Lake Eyre District and parts of Queensland. Thomas observed that:

> other ball games are more like top-spinning, which is also found in parts of Queensland, the top being a gourd or plate of beeswax. A round ball is made of lime, ashes, clay, or some similar material, and spun between the fore and middle fingers, the object of the game being to keep it up as long as possible. (Thomas 1906:139)

Adults also used similar balls, which could be of a size similar to, or larger than, that of the Australian Museum example. Haagen (1994) reports that men of the Lake Eyre region of South Australia and the Warrina region of Victoria played a 'target-ball' game similar to the French *jeu de boules*.

Many of the children's toys surveyed in Haagen's (1994) book *Bush toys* are made from marine shells or plant-based materials, with almost no mention of bone examples. This lack of bone-based toys does not reflect that this raw material was not used by children or in the making of toys for children by adults but rather the lack of observation of what children were playing with in the early days of invasion. A child's toy 'rainbow snake' made from the rib bone of a dugong collected from Maningrida in the Northern Territory by Kim Akerman supports this idea (Akerman 2018).

5. TOOLS

Woodworking tools
Description
There are four main types of woodworking tools: (1) chisels, (2) gouges, (3) tooth-based engravers, and (4) rasps (Table 5.5). Chisels are a large tool with a wider, bevelled cutting edge, while gouges are usually of a similar size but with a concave active edge. Engravers, primarily consisting of a whole marsupial jaw with the incisors intact, provide a smaller cutting edge for more detailed work. Rasps essentially act as sandpaper does today—to smooth over a surface—and usually take advantage of naturally rough surfaces.

Manufacture and use
Most chisels and gouges are made from a piece of long bone split in half lengthways and with at least one of its extremities shaped into a spatulate form. Chisels and gouges

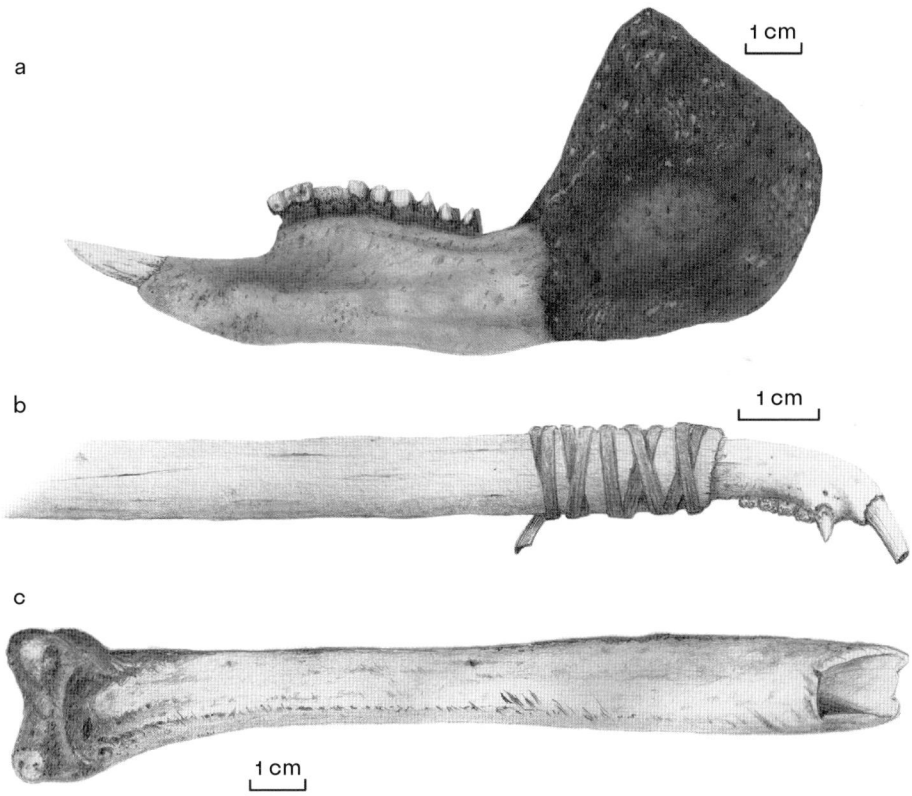

FIGURE 5.15. Whole macropod mandibles, sometimes with their processes covered in resin haft, are used for a range of woodworking (a). Possum mandibles were hafted onto wooden shafts and used for fine wood engraving (b), while sections of large mammal long bones were used as heavy gouges (c).

collected from the centre of the continent appear to have been primarily made on emu long bone, though macropod is a possibility in some cases. One such example from Barrow Creek (Desert region) features a heavily rounded and smoothed working edge and, interestingly, a wide band of dark residue just above the end of the bevel. This same thick, dark brown and red residue was also noticed on a tool from the Frew River (Northern Territory) and may stem from the practice of using wax and/or red ochre in treating wooden implements for longevity (Eyre 1845; Roth 1904). Indeed, a bright red ochre staining is clearly visible on several woodworking implements collected from different regions in museum collections.

In North Queensland, too, emu bone was a preferred raw material for gouges. Museum Victoria curates a number from West Cape York, with these examples having been made using a different design from those from the interior. Instead of splitting the long bone in half lengthways, only about four to six centimetres at one end of a whole long bone is flaked or cut away to create a concave working edge (see Figure 5.15). The condyle at the opposite end then acts as a handhold when present, though several examples have this section removed. Dark staining at this extremity may indicate that resin often covered the proximal extremity (either an intact condyle or modified extremity), creating a comfortable handhold. This suggestion is supported by an artefact collected by Donald Thomson in West Cape York, which still retains part of its resin handle. On this particular item (curated in Museum Victoria, Item DT3917), it can be seen that the resin coated much of the tool—only leaving the working edge and about five millimetres above clear.

Regarding woodworking tools used in Queensland, Roth (1907) saw these gouges used for scooping out the core of spear shafts to prepare the socket for the spearhead, and Thomson witnessed the hollowing out of large softwood water troughs and shaping of the ends of dugout canoes:

> wooden, trough-like vessels called *tawat*, hollow out of the soft wood of the tree *Gryocarpus jacquini*, called *yukko karln'tun*, are employed by the Koko Tai'yuri for carrying water and for the preparation of *maj dantj*. For the manufacture of these *tawat*, bone gouges are made from the tibiae of the emu and kangaroo. These bone gouges, many of them very old and exhibiting unmissable evidence of long service, were in use on the Edward River. They are known generally as *nampi* (emu), or, more specifically, by the name of the principal bone from which they are made—*yan'ka nampi* (*nampi*, emu, *yan'ka*, tibia), or *min nampi kummandonon*. The medullary cavity of the bone is generally filled with a plug of bark or wood to prevent entry of chips and splinters. A typical example is twelve and a half inches in length. The shaft is cut away for a distance of nearly two and a half inches and is sharpened to a chisel edge. (Thomson 1936:73)

A similar implement was used at Princess Charlotte Bay (East Cape region) for stripping pandanus fibre (Hale & Tindale 1933), while yet another was reportedly 'used to split the end of spear shafts and to clean the centre out to take the hardwood point. This tool is used as an alternative to the heel drill' (Item QE11320 notes, Queensland Museum). It was collected from the West Cape, is referred to as a 'splitting tool' and is hafted in resin.

Such tools were also observed in the south, where Augustus Robinson described the work of a man near Lake Elingermite (Riverine region) in 1841, stating he:

5. TOOLS

> saw a man making a marl or mulgar. The hole for putting the fingers through about five inches by 1 1/2 or two inches through. He morticed with the gouge made from the leg bone of a kangaroo and which was made of a similar pattern to an iron gouge. (Clark 2000c:137)

A similar observation was made by Schürmann at Port Lincoln (Spencer region) for the construction of spears:

> The root end, which is about as thick as a man's thumb, is poised, being previously hardened in the fire, and at the taper end a small hole is bored by means of a sharp kangaroo bone, into which the catch of the wommera is hooked in throwing the spear. (Schürmann 2009[1879]:213)

Items classified as 'gouges' (which are sometimes actually chisels) are also represented in museum collections from the Southeast and Arnhem regions. A possible split long bone example from the Arnhem region is held in the National Museum of Australia, though this item is very clean, so it might instead be a 'poison bone' (see 'Use of human bone' below). Kim Akerman collected a small edge-ground piece of tooth enamel or thin dense bone that he suggests was possibly a small gouge or engraving tool from the Kimberley.

In other cases, woodworkers took advantage of the sharp and spatulate edges naturally provided by dugong incisors. When utilised as a chisel, the crown edge is reduced through the development of chipping and rounding. This anthropogenic use wear is far more significant than that accrued by the animal throughout its lifetime. Another indicator that one of these teeth was utilised as a woodworking tool is the presence of plant fibre residues gathering at the top of the tooth crown, appearing as a band of dark residue. Examples collected from the Kimberley by Kim Akerman are stated to have been used to work softwoods such as *Gyrocarpus americanus*. Dugong chisels are also known to have been used on Stradbroke Island (Northeast region) (Colliver & Woolston 1975:93) and on the Dampier Peninsula of Western Australia by Bardi- and Draw-speaking peoples (Kimberley region) (Akerman 2010). Other museum-curated specimens include one each from Crocodile Island and Groote Eylandt (both in the Arnhem region), one from Sunday Island (Kimberley region), and one from 'Queensland' (no further provenance provided). While this ethnographic and museum collection only includes a few examples, their geographical distribution indicates that dugong teeth were widely utilised as woodworking chisels where the raw material was available.

A singular artefact that might be a type of gouge consists of a distal fragment of a large tool made on macropod tibia recovered from the Holocene levels of Riwi (Kimberley region). This artefact was deliberately altered to create a bevelled and concave distal extremity and has accrued significant use wear in the form of rounding and polish. Also observed was possible spinifex resin residue (Langley et al. 2021a). These features, along with insights provided by Gooniyandi Elders regarding the collection of resin lumps created by the spinifex ant for tool manufacture, suggested that the artefact may have been used in breaking up larger lumps.

Engraving tools made from unaltered or minimally altered jaws of macropods and possums (but also sometimes bandicoots and other marsupials) are common across the continent (see Figure 5.15). When the jaws are altered, this change involves the snapping off the very edge of the incisor after heating to create a sharp edge (Roth 1904).

Indeed, at Princess Charlotte Bay (East Cape region), woodworkers were observed to re-edge the incisor by biting off the blunt end with their own teeth (Hale & Tindale 1933). Roth (1904:21) states that mandible engravers formed a 'staple article of barter' and that when a kangaroo was cooked whole on the Pennefather River (West Cape region), 'the tongue is next drawn out and skewered with a wooden splinter over the incisors (required for spoke-shaves) to prevent them being too much damaged by the heat' of the fire (Roth 1901:8). In addition to the edging of the tooth (which is the active edge of the implement), these tools were sometimes hafted in resin to create a comfortable handhold. Evidence for resin handles has been observed on curated West Cape region examples as well as on one in the National Museum of Australia from the Central Desert. On this last tool, the resin handle is almost completely intact, showing that the whole of the condyle was covered with a thick layer of dark resin. Porteus (1931:Plate 16) also illustrates a resin-mounted mandible engraver from Central Australia, attributing the jaw to a 'rabbit eared bandicoot'. Examination of the plate, however, suggests that it originally came from a small macropod (Akerman 2010).

These jaw tools are reported to have been used for engraving linear and other designs on boomerangs, shields, clubs, and spearthrowers, for cutting hand-holes in shields, for sharpening spear tips, and for cutting grooves into barbs (Dawson 1981[1881]; Roth 1904). They were also seen to be used in incising and perforation stone and wooden tjurunga in Central Australia (Spencer 1922). Specific descriptions of their use are provided by Brough Smyth (1972[1878]a:339), who described wooden shields from Victoria as being 'rough-hewn with a stone-chisel, and carved and finished with the teeth of the opossum or kangaroo-rat'. He further adds that 'all the shields from West Australia are ornamented in the same manner' (Brough Smyth 1972[1878]a:339). Bennett (1967[1834]:275) similarly mentions that at Bogong Mountain (Southeast region), 'weapons are clubs, spears, and the boomerang, and shields, which latter have rude ornaments carved with the incisor tooth of a kangaroo upon them'.

Whole jaws could also be hafted to a wooden handle for use, as was the case for a possum mandible implement from Charters Towers (Northeast region). The tooth is again snapped to create a sharp edge, and tendons have been used to attach it to the wooden shaft. These hafted mandibles are known to have been used not only in the Northeast (Roth 1904:21) but also in the Southeast (Akerman 2010) and Eyre regions (Roth 1904:21). In addition, an illustration provided by Brough Smyth (1972[1878]a:349) shows this same implement for the Yarra near Melbourne (Riverine region). Roth (1904:21) reports that these possum-tooth engravers were mainly 'for the graving of the boomerangs, and occasionally for the special and fine fluting met with on extra good spears or nullas: in its manipulation, the movement is always towards the operator'.

A variation on macropod incisor engraving tools includes a single incisor (removed from the jaw) and hafted to a wooden handle. Such tools are recorded in museum collections from the Kimberley, from 'Queensland', and from Newcastle Waters and Alice Springs in the Desert region, with this last object being recorded as an 'adze, stone, hafted, kangaroo tooth engraver mounted at the opposite end'. Akerman (2011:135) notes that in western Cape York, mounted scrapers with edged incisors were used to fashion the fusiform bone points required to arm composite fishhooks, while in the Great Sandy Desert areas of Western Australia, an engraving tool was made by hafting the lower incisor of a kangaroo to a curved stick handle with resin and tendon. Here again, it is noted that in most instances, the working edge of the tooth was prepared and resharpened by pressure, often applied by the jaws of the artisan (McCarthy 1976:88). Again, it is noted that the immediate tooth tip was heated prior to snapping, the produced edge being a small curved gouge of dentine, eminently suitable for the engraving of hardwoods, bone, soft schist stone and pearl shell.

In the south, Brough Smyth describes this tool as the leange-walert:

> the lower-jaw of the opossum is firmly attached to a piece of wood (which serves as a handle) by twine made of the fibre of the bark of *Eucalyptus obliqua* and gum. This tool, simple as it is, enables the black to carve patterns in the hard, tough woods of which his weapons are made with ease and rapidity. The front tooth is like a gouge or chisel, and with it he scopes or cuts out the wood with great facility. The old weapons are easily known by the marks made by the tooth; those fabricated since the introduction of knives and other European tools are altogether different in the surfaces which they present, though patterns may be the same. (Brough Smyth 1972[1878]a:349)

Unhafted single incisors were also observed in woodworking. Hassell and Davidson (1936:692) report for the Wheelman (Wiilman) and surrounding peoples of the Southwest region that in carving wooden letter sticks, 'the carving was done with a sharp piece of stone or the front tooth of a kangaroo'. In southwestern Australia, Akerman (2011) notes that rather than producing a working edge transverse to the axis of the incisor, it was formed by carefully flaking one lateral margin of the occlusal surface, an approach witnessed by Bates (1985:276), who stated that the tooth was split along its length. The split or flaked tooth, with the root area reduced or removed completely, was then hafted by embedding it in resin on the proximal end of a spearthrower with the featured edge exposed. The axis of the cutting edge of the adze was set at an oblique angle to the major axis of the spearthrower and in the same place as the body of that tool. The tooth was known as kambar (Moore 1884:39). This small adze was probably used to repair damaged spear tips (Davidson & McCarthy 1957:452–3; Balme 1979:238–41). Another observation of the use of individual incisors was recorded by Nind (1831:30), who noted that peoples in the Southwest region would first extract the lower incisors of a caught kangaroo for use in sharpening their spear points during butchery practices.

One's own teeth can be considered woodworking tools. Akerman (2011:135) summarised this idea, stating that:

> first and foremost one must take into consideration the many uses to which Aboriginal people across the continent utilised their own jaws and teeth in daily life. Spears were straightened after warming the warped section by using the jaws as a vice and gently manipulating the flexible shaft with the hands. The teeth were used to strip barks from setons of wood intended for use as spears, clubs or tool shafts. In the Western Desert regions the teeth were used to trim stone tools or prepare the edges of engraving tools made from the lower incisors of possums, kangaroos or other macropods. Bonwick also notes that piercing of shells for stringing, was also done with 'an eyetooth' or by cracking the apices off with the teeth' (Bonwick 1870:26). (Akerman 2011:135)

TABLE 5.5. Woodworking tools identified in museum collections and ethnographies. *Italics* = ethnography indicated only.

REGION	CHISEL	GOUGE	ENGRAVER	RASP
Kimberley	dugong incisor	split long bone (?)	whole macropod jaw; single or pair of macropod incisor hafted	Stingray tooth plates; large fish pharyngeal plate
Fitzmaurice	[none identified]			
North	[none identified]			
Arnhem	dugong incisor	split long bone		
Desert		emu (?) split long bone	whole macropod jaw with resin handle; whole possum jaw; single or pair of macropod incisor hafted	
Gulf	[none identified]			
Torres Strait	[none identified]			
West Cape		emu long bone with resin handles; *macropod long bone*	whole macropod jaw with resin handle; single or pair of macropod incisor hafted	
East Cape		*split long bone*	*whole macropod jaw*	
Rainforest	[none identified]			
Northeast	dugong incisor		*hafted whole possum jaw*	*one's own teeth*
Southeast		bone	*hafted whole possum jaw*	
Tasmania	[none identified]			
Riverine		*macropod long bone*	*hafted whole possum jaw*	
Spencer		emu (?) split long bone		
Eyre		split long bone	*hafted whole possum jaw*	
Southwest			single or pair of macropod incisors (?)	
Northwest	[none identified]			

FIGURE 2.2. Along with macropod incisors, keratin-based claws, stingray barbs, and the cassowary casque are used in creating tools and ornaments. (Photographs of the cassowary casque kindly provided by D Naish and R Perron.)

FIGURE 2.4. Examples of chop marks, cut marks, saw marks, and scrape marks.

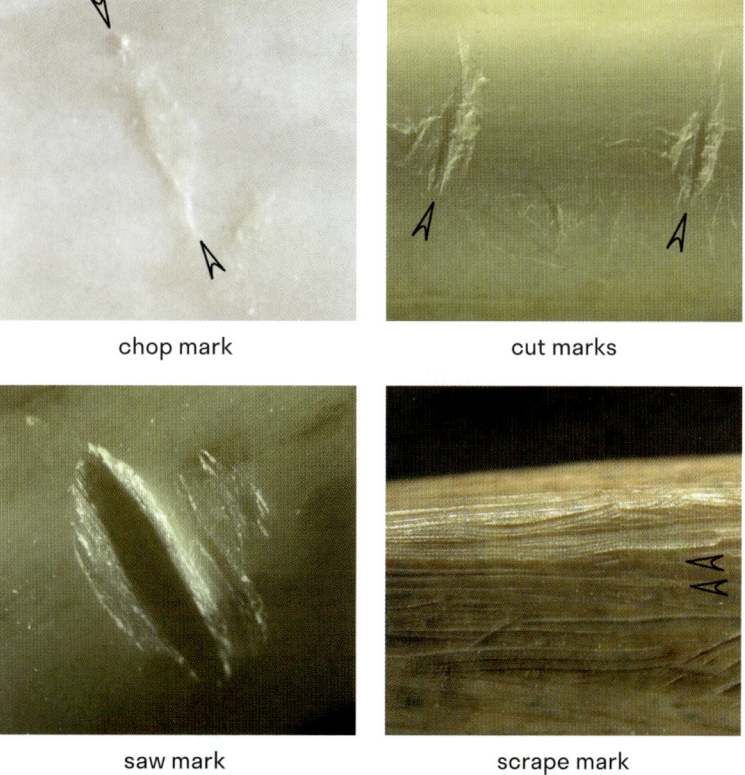

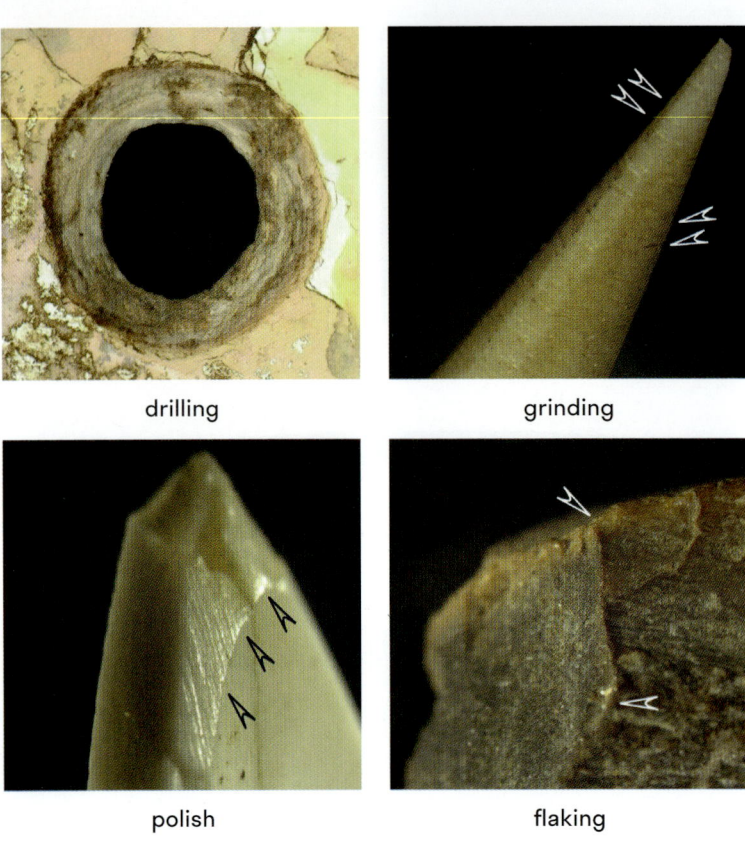

FIGURE 2.5. Examples of drilling, grinding, polish, and flaking.

FIGURE 2.6. This large unipoint found at Riwi Cave on Mimbi Country in south-central Kimberley was created on a macropod tibia some 35,000 years ago. The numerous flake scars may have occurred during butchery or to deliberately shape the tool; nevertheless, it displays traces of use on both its distal and proximal extremities. Included with permission of the Mimbi community.

FIGURE 2.7. Examples of use wear developed from cutting, digging, handling, and hafting.

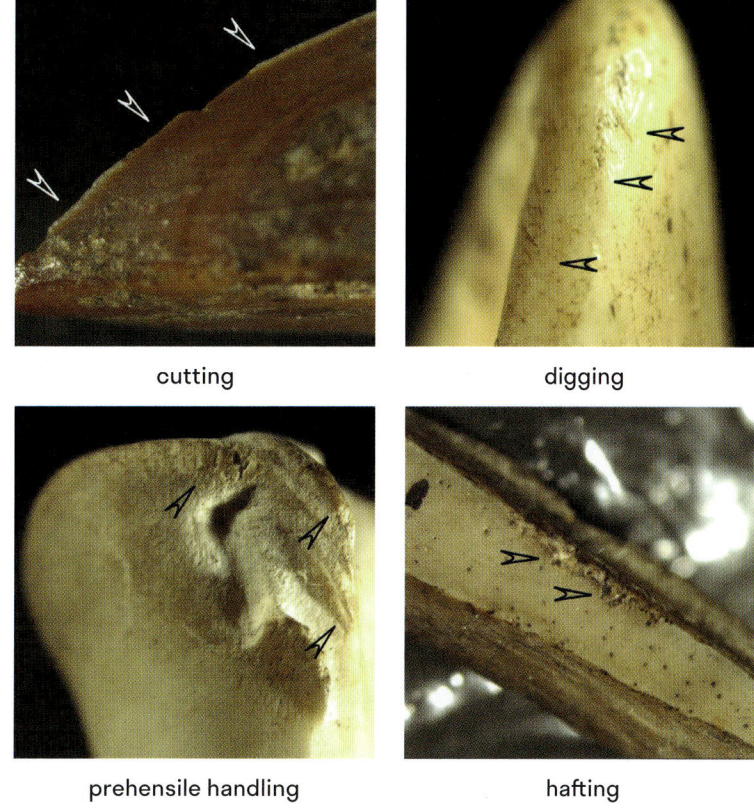

FIGURE 2.8. Examples of use wear developed from projectile impact and repetitive piercing activities.

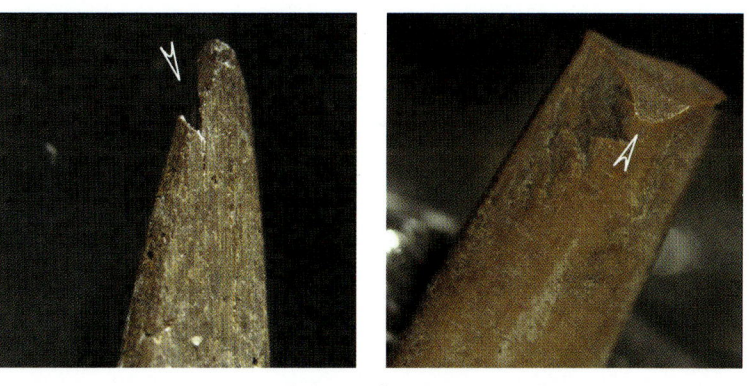

FIGURE 2.9. Examples of abrasion, digestion, gnawing, and tooth marks.

FIGURE 2.10. Example of a fracture from trampling, marks from root etching, and manganese staining.

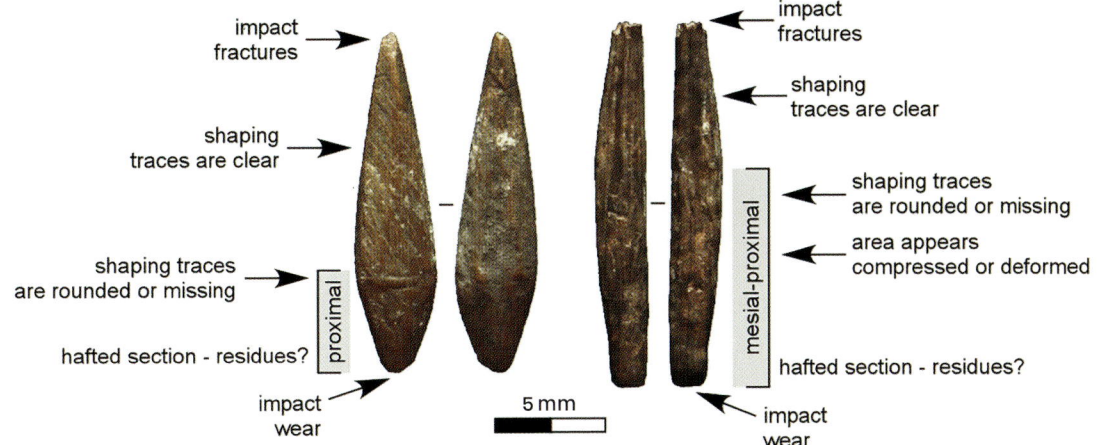

FIGURE 3.2. Determining the distal (active) and proximal extremities on projectile points can sometimes be tricky. For these two examples from Madjedbebe, located on Mirarr Country, identifying the distal tip relies on the presence of impact fractures. Conversely, the proximal edge displays crushing and rounding from contact with the shaft. Traces of manufacture will be partially or fully erased by the haft, allowing us to identify how much of the point was covered. Included with permission of the Gundjeihmi Aboriginal Corporation.

FIGURE 3.5. This 1000-year-old bone jabbing fishhook from Madjedbebe was made using a combination of flaking, gouging, and grinding. Different directions of grinding are evident, as are notches from the attachment of a ligature (the fishing line). Included with permission of the Gundjeihmi Aboriginal Corporation.

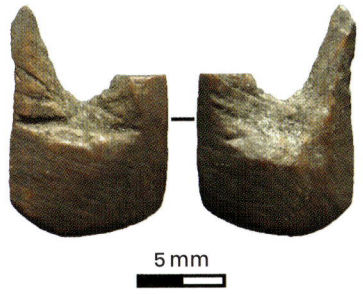

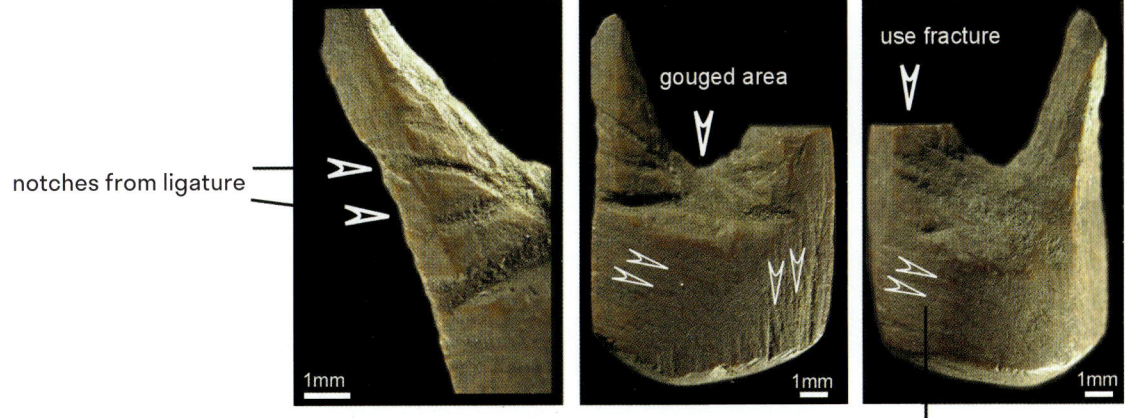

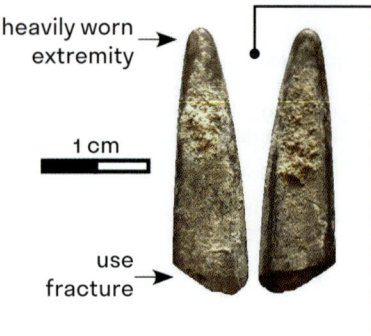

FIGURE 3.6. Skin- and plant-working tools are most clearly identified by their heavily rounded and polished active edge. This distal extremity of a plant- or skin-working tool fractured during use some 4000 years ago at Madjedbebe on Mirarr Country. Included with permission of the Mirarr community.

FIGURE 4.2. An example of a 'point of attack' (left) and keyholing (right), both indicated by an arrow.

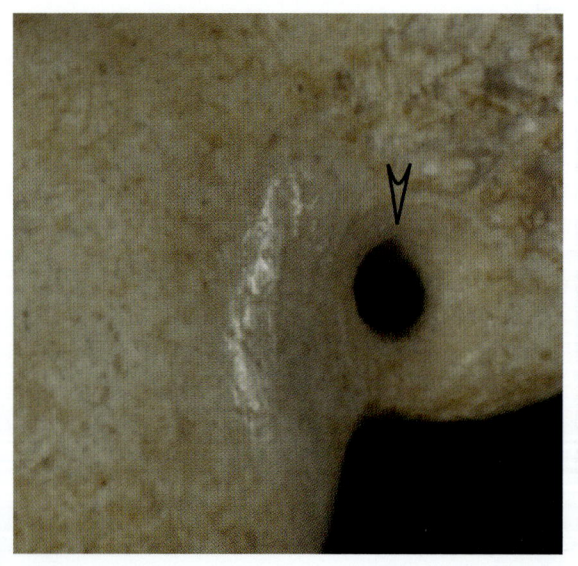 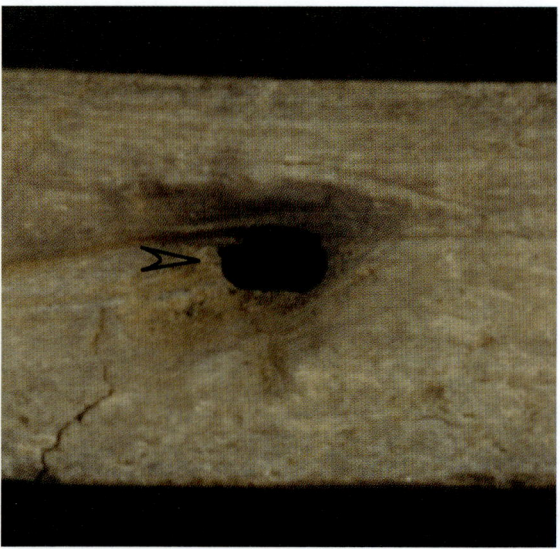

FIGURE 5.11. Whalebone houses were observed in Encounter Bay, South Australia. This illustration, by GF Angas (AA8/14/2, South Australian Museum Library), was a copy of that painted by WA Cawthorne in 1842.

FIGURE 5.16. Portrait of Tasmanian man, Malapuwinarana, painted by Thomas Bock (Oc2006,Drg.70, the British Museum).

5. TOOLS

Chauncy (1972[1876]:250) similarly noted that in Western Australia, 'they also stick the splinters of quartz, broken with their teeth, in a row like teeth to the side of a short stick, to serve as a saw'.

Moving onto rasps, Roth (1904:9) reports that in regard to smoothing down wooden items, 'on Keppel Island I have seen the same effects produced by rubbing the article across the front teeth'. Also reported is the use of various pharyngeal plates from large fish:

> on the Dampierland Peninsula pharyngeal plates of a large parrotfish (either *Scarus gibbus* or *Bolbometopon muricatus*) and the broad tooth row of the eagle ray (*Aetobatus narinari*), were used as wood rasps and burnishers respectively. The skins of ray and sharks, studded with small sharp enamel denticles, was often used as fine abrasives when smoothing and polishing wooden artefacts, by Aboriginal artisans living on the tropical coast. (Akerman 2011:136)

Both whole mandibles and single incisors from macropods, possums, and even seals that bear traces of having been used as tools have been recovered from archaeological contexts across the country. For example, kangaroo and wallaby incisors were found at Paribari (Padypady) in Arnhem Land in a deposit dated to from about 3000 years ago to the present (White 1967), as well as in the upper levels at Malangangerr (Schrire 1982). Here, single wallaby (*Wallabia agilis*) incisors found with visible signs of use were reported by Schrire:

> the first has a very high gloss on one lingual surface. The other has a broken tip and side and was ground on that side and on the lingual surfaces. All the ground surfaces are covered with a high gloss. (Schrire 1982:94)

On the other side of the country, macropod incisors, as well as a complete seal mandible, were found to display use-related damage at Durras North on the southeast coast (Lampert 1966; Langley et al. 2021b), while Balme (1979) used the marked absence of lower macropod incisors in the Devils Lair deposit to suggest that they were being taken for tool or ornament manufacture. Dortch and Merrilees (1973:111) did find a Pleistocene-aged macropod incisor 'which has been worked on the proximal end, perhaps to facilitate its being hafted' at Devils Lair, suggesting their use in a hafted tool form. Finally, Jones (1971) suggested the use of wallaby incisors as tools—both retained in the mandible and taken out—at Rocky Cape on the North West coast of Tasmania.

Local names recorded for this tool include the following.

Chisels:
- joomba (Port George IV, Kimberley region; Item X025251 notes, Museum Victoria)
- jarungku (Bardi word for dugong chisel, Kimberley region; Item 206 notes, Western Australian Museum).

Gouges:
- nampi (Edward River, West Cape region; Thomson 1936).

Engravers:
- watra-kukatja (whole macropod jaw, Balgo Hills, Kimberley region; Item 472 notes, Western Australian Museum)
- no-ana (whole macropod jaw, Pennefather River, West Cape region; Roth 1904)
- mina ken (whole macropod jaw, West Cape region; Item DT003933 notes, Museum Victoria)
- wall' mant' kanji pank (whole macropod jaw, Archer River, West Cape region; Item DT003937 notes, Museum Victoria)
- leange-walert (Riverine region [?]; Brough Smyth 1972[1878]a)
- kambar (southwestern Australia; Moore 1884).

Material culture made on human bone*

*Readers should be aware that the following section describes material culture made on human skeletal remains.

As elsewhere in the world, human bone saw common use for the manufacture of tools and ornaments on the Australian continent. Also as elsewhere, human bone was frequently (but not always) viewed to holding special qualities that required it to be reserved for sacred or particularly powerful purposes. In the Australian context, ethnographies universally talk about how it is only particular bones that are saved for use, these bones mostly being the fibula or skull. Below, previously published information has been grouped together into common uses.

Containers

In the southern regions of Australia, early observers frequently noted that drinking vessels made from human skulls were present. While Bonwick (1870:42) notes that 'the Tasmanians did not, as the South Australians and others, use skulls for drinking vessels', a collection brought together by Archibald Meston includes just such a vessel, suggesting that this tradition may have been present in Tasmania also. Meston (1956:191) reports that this particular example was found on 20 June 1929 'on a midden close to a spring of sweet water at Port Sorell, north coast of Tasmania'. He discusses in this manuscript how Allan Cunningham, who visited Macquarie Harbour in 1819, talked about meeting Tasmanian peoples who 'greatly prized bottles', as they used shells (though these were generally quite small, with large shells like baler used in the north not being available in this southern environment) and seaweed vessels and called water vessels moka. He suggests that this skull vessel was also termed a moka.

Similarly, Lumholtz (1889:301) states that 'in South Australia and in Victoria the head is not buried with the body, for the skull is preserved and used as a drinking-cup' (this practice is also mentioned in Eyre 1845:345). Indeed, Augustus Robinson (cited in Clark 2000e:102) states in his 1846 journal that 'the customs of the Adelaide and Encounter Bay natives is more dissimilar than any other I have met with ... with these people, the human skull is used as a drinking vessel'. He again mentions these vessels on the following page, stating that at Port Lincoln, he 'saw several cranium used as drinking cups'. These skull vessels from the Southeast region and southern end of the Riverine regions are described as being 'used solely as water-vessels. Gum was smeared over the sutures. The upper jaw and malar bones have been broken off many specimens' (Davidson 1937:184). Taplin (2009[1879]:42) also notes that the Narrinyeri (Ngarrindjeri) used 'a resinous gum called pitching' for stopping up the sutures in the human skull vessels.

Observers often commented that these cups were used by close family and friends of the deceased (Eyre 1845; Massola 1961; Tindale 1938), with Brough Smyth quoting Wood, saying that the vessel was:

> slung on cords and carried by them, and the owner takes it wherever he or she goes. These ghastly utensils are made from the skulls of the nearest and dearest relatives; and when an Australian mother dies, it is thought right that her daughter should turn the skull of her mother into a drinking vessel. The preparation is simple enough. The lower-jaw is removed, the brains are extracted, and the whole of the skull thoroughly cleaned. A rope handle, made of bulrush fibre is then attached to it, and it is considered fit for use. It is filled with water through the vertebra. (Brough Smyth 1972[1878]a:348)

Following this observation, Angas (1967[1847]:136) describes coming across a girl of about 10 years of age on the Lower Murray (Riverine region) who 'carried a human skull in her hand: it was her mother's skull, and from it she drank her daily draught of water'. He also states that:

> the natives around Lake Albert and the adjoining portions of the Coorong use the skulls of their friends as drinking vessels. After detaching the lower jaw, they fasten a handle of bulrush fibre to them, and carry them, whenever they travel, filled with water, always putting in a twist of dry grass to prevent the contents from upsetting. (Angas 1967[1847]:68)

In terms of their curation, McCarthy (1976:90) reports that 'only eleven examples exist, of which six are in Australian, two in English and three in Italian museums'.

Interpersonal weapons

Two forms of interpersonal weapons are recognised. The first form is known as 'poison bones', with examples curated in the British Museum and collected from 'Aranda' (Arrernte) people of the central Desert region by Spencer and Gillen. These items are made on pieces of human bone split in half lengthways, with at least one of their extremities made into a spatulate and concave form. One of these examples is about 20 centimetres long and shows a high degree of polish. The British Museum has a second example that appears to be shorter but otherwise very similar, though red ochre traces are clearly visible in the provided photograph. The note accompanying this second example reads, 'brought from rangers on border of south & west Australia; said to be from a killed and eat man [sic]; given to collector by Kallagiri (killed by a train)'.

The other type of interpersonal weapon is described by Bonney for the Darling River (Riverine region):

> The *Yountoo* is made of a small bone taken from a leg of the dead body of a friend either before or after burial; it is wrapped up with a small piece of sun-dried flesh, cut from

the body of another deceased friend; string made with the hair from the head of a third friend generally serves as a tie. When this charm is required to be used it is taken to the camp where the enemy sleeps and placed in the hot ashes of a fire, with a piece of string tied to it, where it is warmed and then pointed at the person to be killed, a small piece of the bone being chipped off and thrown at the sleeping enemy. The *Yountoo* is taken away, and in about five weeks amid under the surface of the ground, and a fire lit over it which burns it gradually. (Bonney 1884:130)

Roth (1903a:32–3) describes the use of bone unipoints as 'charms' utilised in making another person sick. One such charm he describes as:

a long, thin, pointed pencil, cut from a young man's shin-bone, the most potent material, or from a kangaroo, or native-companion bone: it is from 3 to 6 inches long, the blunt end being covered with gum-cement.

He states that the 'generic term for any such bone-charm is *mó-kad* (KMI): each being further specialised, a *mar-* (a young man's), *ngan-dá* (a kangaroo's), and *ka-va-* (a native companion's) *mó-kad*'. Another form he describes from Princess Charlotte Bay (East Cape region) is a:

pointed piece of human fibula stuck with wax on to a reed spear. It is believed that when the spear is thrown in the direction of the intended victim, the shaft remains in the hands of the thrower, while the bone splinter travels across the intervening space, becomes lodged in the victim's body—the wound immediately closing without leaving a scar—and so causes sickness or disease. (Roth 1903a:33)

Medicines and medical tools

Human bones—either whole or ground into powder—were a powerful drug used to cure a number of ailments. Statements such as 'when a man died . . . His father, own or tribal, made magic of the fibula bones of the legs' (Howitt 2001[1904]:453) are common across much of the continent. Indeed, medicine men were often reported to utilise human bones in their work, with Bonwick (1870:176), for example, reporting that in Tasmania, 'the doctors . . . used the formidable rattle of dead men's bones', while Duncan-Kemp (1964:140) for Queensland Channel Country stated that a medicine man carried in a small bag 'two small bones from a human arm. These were "sung" spirit bones, that is, they have been charmed and were dangerous to anyone except medicine-men'.

In application to an individual seeking medical help, Backhouse (1967[1843]:84) recorded that on Flinders Island in Bass Strait, 'a man who had a head-ache to-day, had three leg bones fixed on his head, in the form of a triangle for a charm'. And on mainland Tasmania, a very similar observation was made:

human bones were attached to the part affected as a certain alleviate. Mr. Woodward saw a big fellow with three leg bones about his head, he being sick with a severe headache. A child's skull hung round the neck was considered of great virtue. (Bonwick 1870:89)

5. TOOLS

Brough Smith provides similar details for the peoples of Tasmania, citing information from Davies, Dove, and Hull printed in the *Tasmanian Journal* in 1842:

> an anxiety to possess themselves of a bone from the skull or the arms of their deceased relatives, which, sewed up in a piece of skin, they wear round their necks, confessedly as a charm against scenes or premature death ... Davies states that the bones he has seen carried by them were most commonly the jaw-bone, or the bone of the thigh; as also the skulls of children the latter wrapped up in a skin ... These bones are worn by people in perfect health, most probably as mementoes of deceased relations; but, if so, they lend them to others of their own tribe when ill, who wear them as charms round the neck. (Brough Smyth 1972[1878]b:398–9)

Mementos of loved ones

The above-mentioned human bones—particularly those of a child—being utilised to help alleviate headaches and other maladies crosses over heavily (or even completely) with the widespread tradition of keeping several bones from loved ones that have passed. Perhaps some of the most heart-rending examples come from Tasmania (see Figure 5.16, colour section), where Bonwick (1870:179) recorded that the great leader:

> Manalagana [sic] carried the jawbone of his friend against his breast. Such a treasured memorial of past affection could often soothe the sufferer if laid upon the part then in danger.

In another account, Bonwick records that:

> A bone suspended in a bag from the neck, as it hung again the breast, reminded the wearer of a former love. So many skulls and limb bones were taken by the poor natives ... Manalaganna [sic], who was out with Mr Robinson, was never once known to speak harshly to Taulbeboyer, his wife. He had the jawbone of a friend covered over with native string, and hung upon his chest. (Bonwick 1870:10)

In another heartbreaking story, Backhouse (1967[1843]:84) relates the story of a Flinders Island couple 'who lost their only child in infancy, and its skull is generally to be seen suspended on the bust of either its father or its mother'. The carrying of the bones of a lost child by their mother appears to be connected to the belief that the spirit of that child will return to their mother to be reborn, and so they are kept close—a belief held both in the south and as far north as West Arnhem Land (Berndt & Berndt 1977:466; Duncan-Kemp 1964). Indeed, Fison and Howitt (1991[1880]:244) note for Kurnai people of Gippsland (Southeast region) that 'sometimes the father or mother carried the lower jaw of the deceased as a memento', a story echoed by Brough Smyth (1972[1878]a:111), who states that 'the mother sometimes secur[es] the small bones of the legs, to wear round her neck as a memorial'. George Augustus Robinson's journals for Port Phillip and surrounds also mention this practice as being widespread in the region (Clark 2000e:171; Plomley 2008:301, 349, 395, 586, 921).

William Buckley observed this practice firsthand when he lived west of Port Phillip, stating that these practices are carried out to show:

> respect for the deceased, the cap bones of whose knees, in this instance, after being carefully cleaned, were tied up in a sort of net of hair and twisted bark. Under such circumstances, these relics are carried by the mothers, tied round their neck by day, and placed under their heads by nights, as affectionate remembrances of the dead. (Flannery 2009:117)

Finger bones, being small and light, are most frequently mentioned as the bones carried long term. These bones were kept in a bag and 'especially if the deceased was a great fighting-man, or had any special virtues' (Howitt 2001[1904]:474). Roth reports that:

> on the Proserpine River [Rainforest] the hunter would, while warming various of his knick-knacks in his hand over the first, talk to them, and tell them to get him fish or game, etc.: these curios, carried in a little dilly-bag under the left arm-pit, consisted of knuckle-bones, knee-caps. (Roth 1903a:27)

The only mention of such use of the human skull in a northern area comes from Carnegie (1898:281–2), who states that near Mount Webb in the Gibson Desert, they collect 'a "sporran" [pubic cover] consisting of a pearl oyster-shell or large crunch shell, also one formed from the top portion of a human skull'.

An exceptional example of the power these mementos held is reported by Howitt, who states the following:

> The most remarkable connection with the dead was that of the 'bret' or hand. The Kurnai cut off one hand of the corpse, or both hands, soon after death, which they wrapped in grass and dried. A string of twisted opossum fur was attached to it, so that it could be hung round the neck and worn in contact with the skin under the left arm. It was carried by the parent, child, brother, or sister. The belief of the Kurnai was that at the approach of an enemy the hand would push or pinch the wearer. Such a signal being experienced, the hand would be taken from the neck and suspended in front of the face, the string being held between the finger and thumb. The person would then say, 'which way are they coming?' If the hand remained at rest, the question would be again put, but now facing another way, and on. The response being that the hand vibrated in some direction, and it was thence that the danger was coming. (Howitt 2001[1904]:460)

In some countries, one or both of the front teeth were removed as part of the transition to adulthood. For the Yuin nation, Howitt relates that:

> The limits of the district within which wives were thus obtained by exchange of sisters is indicated by the round which the boy's tooth, which is knocked out at the initiation ceremonies, is carried, the tooth being passed on from one headman to another. (Howitt 2001[1904]:262)

He continues with the statement that the tooth 'conveys its message, which is that so-and-so has been made a man' (Howitt 2001[1904]:561) and that after the ceremonies were completed, the teeth were gummed to fibre with grass tree resin and worn by the initiate as an ornament. Roth (1907:389) reports for North Queensland that 'female relatives, generally the nieces of either side, look out for the teeth and wear them after the manner of a forehead ring, each tooth attached by a blob of wax to tufts of the frontal hair'. Similarly, Collins (1975[1798]:483), for those around Sydney at English arrival, talks about how the front tooth, removed from boys in their coming of age ceremony, was collected by the women who 'fastened them to pieces of small line, and were wearing them round their necks'. He later reports (p. 485) that 'Bennillog at other times told us, that his own tooth was *bour-bil-liey-pe-mul*, buried in the earth, and that others were thrown into the sea'.

While anyone could carry bones from deceased relatives around their necks or in their bags, most frequently it was the burden of a female relative (e.g. Clark 2000d, Backhouse 1967[1843]:84; Berndt & Berndt 1977; Bonwick 1870:27; Duncan-Kemp 1964:298; Petrie 1904:32, 34; Plomley 2008:451; Roth 1904, 1907; Wyatt 2009[1879]:165). It is most often reported that wives carried the skeleton of a deceased husband for a period of several months to two years (e.g. Howitt 2001[1904]:456) and often a child for an extended period (Angas 1967[1847]:75; Plomley 2008:623–4; Clark 2000a:84; Bennett 1967[1834]:125; Brough Smyth 1972[1876]a; Flannery 2009:117; Howitt 2001[1904]:459; Lumholtz 1889:278; Meyer 1846:198; Palmer 1884; Roth 1907:398; Wyatt 2009[1879]:165).

Stone- and organic-working tools

Utilitarian tools made on human bone are quite rare in the Australian context, though not unheard of. For example, Akerman et al. (2002:19) describe the use of bone indentors in the Kimberley, which may be made on large splinters of human bone taken from the distal tibia, while an 'awl' (as described in the Tasmanian Museum and Art Gallery's notes for Item M6865) made on human fibula was collected from Point Cook, Victoria. In addition, the South Australian Museum holds a 'human bone implement for stripping pandanus fibre in floor debris of Walaeimini Shelter, Bathurst Head' (Item A13856 nots, South Australian Museum).

Toys

The only mention of the use of human bone in games is provided by Roth, who describes a game called 'pit-throwing' played by the 'Kalkadun' (Kalkatungu) (Gulf region):

> any fairly-sized bone, often a human shin, is slung by means of an attached twine over an emu net into a pit or hole excavated on its further side. Considering the great distance often intervening between the thrower and the excavation, great skill is apparently necessary in making the bone fall into the hole without the touching the net. (Roth 1902:19)

Weapons

Only two reports of the explicit use of human bone to tip spears were noted. The first comes from Durrand (1940:402), who states that for arrows made in the Torres Strait, the tips were pieces of human bone 'about ten inches long, tapering to a very sharp point. The arrows were not poisoned, but bows were charmed to make them more deadly in their aim'. At the other end of the continent, Bonwick (1870:97) observed in Tasmania 'a grave, and in the middle of it was deposited a spear, pointed to the depth of two feet, and the upper end of it pointed with a human bone'.

Other brief mentions include Roth (1903a:27), who reports that 'the Olkulo blacks, on the northern extremity of Princess Charlotte Bay, will fix a piece of human bone to the spear-thrower for luck when after kangaroo and emu'.

SUMMARY

- Great diversity is evident in the use of hard animal materials to create tools across the Australian continent.

- Some raw materials, particularly macropod and emu long bones, along with macropod incisors, have seen extensive use across the continent, while other raw materials were more restricted in their use either regionally or owing to the cultural traditions of different communities.

- This summary is far from comprehensive—from the tables provided, it is clear that great gaps in our knowledge of who made and used what kinds of technologies in the past are present.

CHAPTER 6
ORNAMENTS

Introduction

This chapter explores the variety of ornaments used to decorate the human body in Indigenous Australia. These ornaments are discussed in relation to what part of the body they were worn on to highlight similarities and differences across the continent. While this format helps organise this discussion, it should be remembered that many subtleties that were not necessarily recorded in European writing were (and are) present in their use. This complexity was neatly summarised by Roth, who said:

> A necklet may be worn as a waist-belt; an article donned by a male may be forbidden to a member of the opposite sex, and vice versa; an ornament worn throughout one district with a special signification attached to it may have no meaning whatsoever in others; certain ornaments according to their materials of construction are found only in certain areas; a decoration donned on different parts of the body will convey different meaning, an article of dress essential to early life may be discarded with adolescence; and often nothing at all may be worn in contradistinction to a complete costume indicative of rank, vicinity, grief, fight, etc. (Roth 1910b:21)

In the following sections, each ornament type is marked as 'present' or 'absent' for each region. This presence or absence is based on what materials are curated in the studied museum collections and the available ethnographic (including photographic) records (see Figure 6.1). In many cases, the available photographs of ornamented people do not provide enough detail (being too grainy or too far away from the person/people of interest) for a positive identification to be made. As such, the tables presented below should be treated as an early starting point that will change as research into Indigenous Australian ornament traditions continues.

The chapter first describes ornaments worn at the top of the head and works down the body towards the feet. At this stage, no ornaments worn on the legs, ankles, or feet that incorporate hard animal materials have been identified.

Ornaments worn on the head

Ornaments used to decorate the head are most numerous in museum collections, early photographs, and European descriptions of Australian Indigenous peoples, reflecting a focus on adorning one's head both on a day-to-day and 'for a special occasion' basis. Of these decorations, six main forms are evident: (1) hair pins, (2) circlets, (3) headbands, (4) forehead pendants, (5) sidelock pendants, and (6) nose bones (see Figure 6.2 and Table 6.1).

A RECORD IN BONE

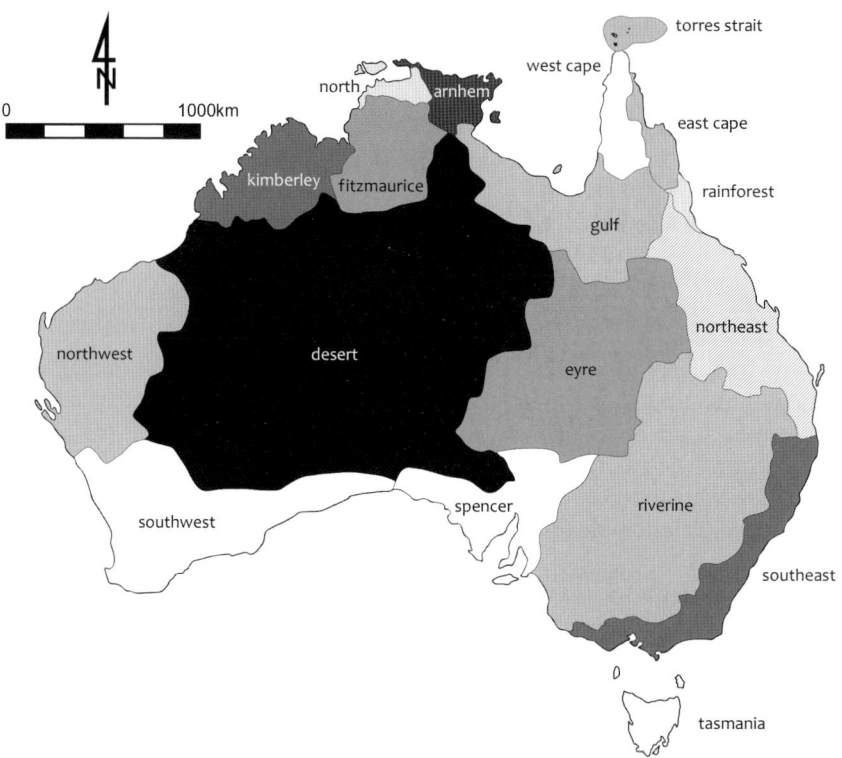

FIGURE 6.1. Some regions are better represented (more pieces of ornamentation have been collected) in Australian museums than others. On this map, the darker colours indicate better representation, and the lighter colours indicate the least represented areas.

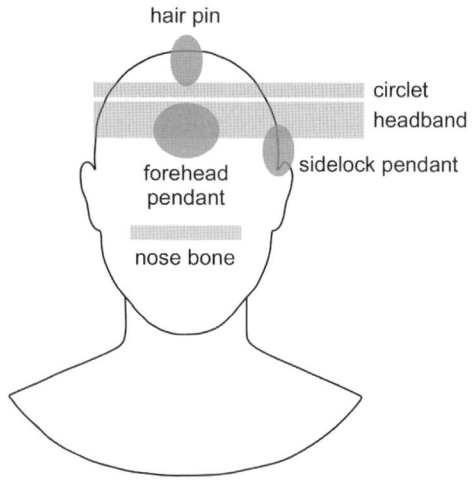

FIGURE 6.2. Broad forms of ornamentation worn on the head in Indigenous Australia.

6. ORNAMENTS

TABLE 6.1. Presence of head ornaments recorded in museum collections. **Bold** = museum presence; *italics* = ethnography indicated only.

REGION	HAIR PINS	CIRCLET	HEADBAND	FOREHEAD PENDANT	SIDELOCK PENDANT	NOSE BONE
Kimberley	**present**	**present**; *present*	**present**	**present**		**present**
Fitzmaurice		**present**	**present**	**present**		**present**
North	**present**; *present*	**present**	**present**; *present*	**present**; *present*		*present*
Arnhem	**present**; *present*	**present**; *present*	**present**	**present**; *present*	**present**	**present**
Desert	**present**; *present*	**present**; *present*	**present**; *present*	**present**; *present*	**present**	**present**; *present*
Gulf	**present**	**present**	**present**	**present**; *present*	**present**; *present*	**present**
Torres Strait	[none identified]					
West Cape	*present*		*present*			*present*
East Cape	*present*					**present**; *present*
Rainforest	*present*	**present**		*present*	**present**	**present**; *present*
Northeast	*present*		**present**; *present*			*present*
Southeast			*present*		*present*	**present**; *present*
Tasmania						*present*
Riverine		*present*		*present*	**present**; *present*	**present**
Spencer		*present*		**present**	*present*	
Eyre		*present* (?)		**present**	**present**	**present**
Southwest		*present* (?)				**present**; *present*
Northwest	**present**; *present*					**present**

Hair pins
Description
Hair pins consist of a pin a few centimetres long made on macropod bone, emu bone, or echidna quill, onto which a plume of usually light- or bright-coloured feathers is attached. Resin, wax, sinew, and/or plant fibre or human hair string is used to attach the pin to the feather plume.

Manufacture and use

This headpiece is a noticeable accoutrement worn principally by men across much of the north and centre of the continent (Tables 6.1 and 6.2). Numerous photographs taken during the 1800s and early 1900s show individuals wearing a mass of feathers just behind a fabric or woven plant fibre headband. In some of these photographs, it would appear that the pin is placed under the headband so that the feathers sit up and out against the crown. This placement creates a striking profile (see Figure 6.4). Photographs also show this type of ornament worn towards the back of the head (but still on top of the crown) in the North region as well as in Far North Queensland (Rainforest and Cape York regions).

Roth (1910b:24) refers to this ornament as 'feather-tufts' or 'aigrettes', stating that:

> amongst birds thus utilised are the emu, white cockatoo, eagle-hawk, pelican, turkey, etc., but on the Upper Georgina River [Desert] I have seen feather-tufts replaced by the tails of the *Peragalea lagotis*.

He further states that:

> the white cockatoo feather-tuft is met with almost throughout Northern Queensland, but is very common indeed in the eastern half of the state, and is used by males only, either at corrobborees, for decorative purposes generally, on fighting expeditions often. At Headingley (Upper Georgina River) it is stuck into the forehead-band (or armlet); between the Mitchell and Staaten Rivers, the Gunanni fix it upright on the top of the head and call it *workai-a*. The Middle Palmer River Blacks obtain the ornament (KMI *kwa-chil*) by trade and barter from the Musgrave and Saltwater River Natives of the eastern coast. (Roth 1910b:24)

Roth (1910b:19) notes that 'cockatoo top-knot head-dresses' were made and traded from the Barron River and Port Douglas (Rainforest region) for the 'Cape Grafton northern trade'. Additionally, Roth (1909a:211) describes how, on the Bloomfield River (East Cape region), when inter-clan battle was to occur:

> one individual, not necessarily the oldest, who took the lead and planned out the whole mode of attack; this leader wore the cockatoo top-knot feather-tuft head ornament, which rendered him sufficiently conspicuous.

In a very different context, Roth (1909a:170) mentions that during certain initiation ceremonies, performers will decorate themselves with 'the cockatoo-top-knot feather head-dress', and at Princess Charlotte Bay (East Cape region), the young initiates will be decorated with this same headdress and ochre (Roth 1909a:179).

Little is published regarding the use of these ornaments in the North region—only a brief mention by Daly (1887:71–2) regarding Larrakia men at Port Darwin which states that they would 'wear crowns of feathers, which stand upright in a true barbaric fashion' for corroborees. Much more information is available for the next region over, with Donald Thomson recording that for East Arnhem, these adornments are known as kut'kut or manjotji woi (for 'making eyes'—that is, attracting the eyes of women) (Item 477 notes, Museum Victoria). He also notes that these ornaments are worn during

6. ORNAMENTS

FIGURE 6.3. Two broad forms of hair pins have been found. The hair pin on the left was usually worn against the crown like the man in Figure 6.4, and those on the right were worn towards the back of the head.

FIGURE 6.4. Portrait of an unnamed man at Ooldea, South Australia, c. 1919 (photograph by AG Bolam, B45287/47 SLSA).

TABLE 6.2. Presence of hair pins recorded in museum collections. **Bold** = museum presence; *italics* = ethnography indicated only.

REGION	HAIR PINS	RAW MATERIALS UTILISED
Kimberley	**present**	macropod bone; emu bone
		feathers: emu
Fitzmaurice	[none identified]	
North	**present**; *present*	macropod bone
Arnhem	**present**; *present*	macropod bone
		feathers: emu, brolga, white cockatoo, small parrots
Desert	**present**; *present*	macropod bone; emu bone
		feathers: Major Mitchell's cockatoo
Gulf	**present**	feathers: unidentified—large white
Torres Strait	[none identified]	
West Cape	*present*	feathers: emu, white cockatoo
East Cape	*present*	feathers: emu, white cockatoo
Rainforest	*present*	feathers: emu
Northeast	*present*	macropod bone
		feathers: white cockatoo
Southeast	[none identified]	
Tasmania	[none identified]	
Riverine	*present*	feathers: emu
Spencer	*present*	
Eyre	*present* (?)	feathers: white cockatoo
Southwest	*present* (?)	feathers: white cockatoo, black cockatoo
Northwest	**present**; *present*	macropod bone
		feathers: Major Mitchell's cockatoo

ceremony. Another example, this time made with emu feathers and collected from Milingimbi, is recorded as being called wai-i-wai-i (Item X037716 notes, Museum Victoria). Smaller, thinner examples of feathered hair pins are also found in museum collections and photographs (see Figure 6.3). A photograph by Thomson taken in East Arnhem Land shows an older man wearing this ornament at the back of his head. One example matching this photograph is curated in the Australian Museum and features long white feathers along with a strand made up of small, bright orange parrot feathers.

Moving to modern Western Australia, an example from Northampton in the Northwest region is recorded as a jinkarra—an ornament worn by men when dancing—while Chauncy (1972[1876]:251) noted that in the vicinity of the Swan River Colony (Perth; Southwest region), men would wear 'bunches of beautiful long feathers of the large black cockatoo or of the white cockatoo on the top of the head'. Across at Cooper Creek (Eyre region), Howitt (1972[1876]:302) briefly noted that 'a bunch of feathers is tied on the top of the head' for decoration in this location.

6. ORNAMENTS

For Quandamooka's Minjerribah (Stradbroke Island) in Queensland (Northeast region), Backhouse (1967[1843]:370) states that men would wear their hair 'tied up, often forming a knot at the top of the head, and decorated with feathers. In this knot, they stick their bone skewers, and other implements', which might refer to this type of ornament. A similar statement was given by Tom Petrie, who noted that:

> some of the great men had their hair tied up in a knob on the top of the head, and when such was the case they wore in this knob little sticks ornamented with yellow feathers from the cockatoo's top knot. The feathers were fastened to the ends of the sticks with bee's wax, and these sticks were stuck there in the knob of hair, as Japanese places little fans; and they looked quite nice. (Petrie 1904:20–1)

The Queensland Museum holds a number of feather bundles described as 'headdresses', which are made up of white and yellow cockatoo feathers, and while these examples collected are from much further north at Cardwell (Rainforest region), they could be something similar to what Petrie was here describing for the Moreton Bay area.

Authors also note feather plumes being worn in the south. Curry (1965[1883]:117), commenting on Bangerang people (Riverine region), speaks of how young men after the age of 16 'now affected the use of red ochre, adorned [their] head with plumes, and made [themself] an opossum-rug, which [they] scored and coloured in the approved way'. Along the Darling River (Riverine region), such an ornament was noticed:

> his [man of the 'bogan tribe'] costume was rather imposing, consisting of a net-work, which confined his hair into the form of a round cap, having in the front, a plume of white, light feathers. (Mitchell 1965[1839]a:322)

In this volume, Mitchell (1965[1839]a:218, Plate 19) includes an illustration of 'Tánambé—A young native of the bogan tribe' with feathers on the forehead, which could be this ornament.

Further west in Spencer, Meyer (1846:13) noted that 'the young men are ornamented, after their fashion, with a tuft of emu feathers in the hair' at Encounter Bay for corroboree, while Schürmann (2009[1879]:211) describes the fur yarn cord wrapped round the forehead on men at Port Lincoln and that 'those who wish to appear very smart embellish this ornament still further by placing a bunch of emu feathers in it, above the forehead'.

It is possible that this form of ornamentation was more widespread and that the frequent mentions of individuals who 'adorned [their] head with plumes' (Curr 1883:117) refer to such an ornament that was not seen close enough or not of interest for further description by the writer. Also, it should be noted that while all the information about these feathered headpieces has been connected to men up to this point, it is possible that women also wore such ornaments. A single example curated in the Australian Museum made of Major Mitchell's cockatoo (*Lophochroa leadbeateri*) feathers is recorded as a women's ceremonial head decoration made in the Warlpiri community (Desert region), and ethnographies sometimes refer to women wearing their husband's ornaments in certain circumstances (Roth 1907).

Macropod bone appears to have been used to manufacture the pin in most regions (Arnhem, Desert, Eyre, the Kimberley, North, Northwest, Rainforest), though emu bone examples are also known for the Desert and the Kimberley regions. Examples from the Arnhem region utilise resin or wax along with plant fibre string to attach the feathers to the pin, these feathers drawn from emus, brolga, cockatoos, and smaller more colourful parrots. Emu feathers were also selected in the Kimberley and northern Queensland regions, while Major Mitchell's cockatoo feathers are found on several examples from the Northwest region. On these last examples, sinews from kangaroo tail (rather than string) were used to attach the feathers to the macropod (fibula) bone pin. Whether the pins are pointed under the attachment media—making them bipoints—is currently unknown. Sometimes, a short length of plant fibre or human hair string is attached to the ornament, though it is unclear if the string assists with the attachment to the head or is for another purpose. Examples of feathered hair pins have also been collected from the Gulf region, though little information regarding these examples is currently available.

Local names recorded for this ornament include:

- kut'kut (Djinang, East Arnhem, Arnhem region; Item DT481 notes, Museum Victoria)
- manjotji woi (Rirratjingu, East Arnhem, Arnhem region; Item 477 notes, Museum Victoria)
- wai-i-wai-i (Milingimbi, Arnhem region; Item X037716 notes, Museum Victoria)
- workai-a (Gunanni (Gonaniin), between Mitchell and Staaten rivers, West Cape region; Roth 1910b)
- kwa-chil (Koko-Minni (Kuku Mini), Middle Palmer River, East Cape region; Roth 1910b)
- arrirgurr (Koko-Wara (Kuku-Warra), hinterland and the coast at Princess Charlotte Bay, East Cape region; Roth 1910b)
- merrimbal (Cape Bedford, East Cape region; Roth 1909a, 1910b)
- tchura (Mallanpora, Lower Tully River, Rainforest region; Roth 1910b)
- ter-ral (Pork Jackson, Southeast region; Hunter 1963[1793])
- jinkarra, wanardy, or yowarda (Northampton, Northwest region; Item X000859 notes, Museum Victoria).

Circlets

Description

Circlets are worn atop the crown or forehead (see Figure 6.2). Typically, the circular crown itself is constructed using multiple strands of string wound together to make a band. Attached to this band are singular or paired teeth or small bones set into resin or perforated and tied with short lengths of string to the main band at intervals so that the teeth hang about the face and shoulders (see Figure 6.5). The strings are recorded as having been made from human hair, possum fur, kangaroo fur, or plant fibres, with teeth from kangaroos and crocodiles the most common pendants, though small animal bones are also frequently used. These headdresses create a tinkling sound as the small bones and teeth clink together as the wearer moves.

6. ORNAMENTS

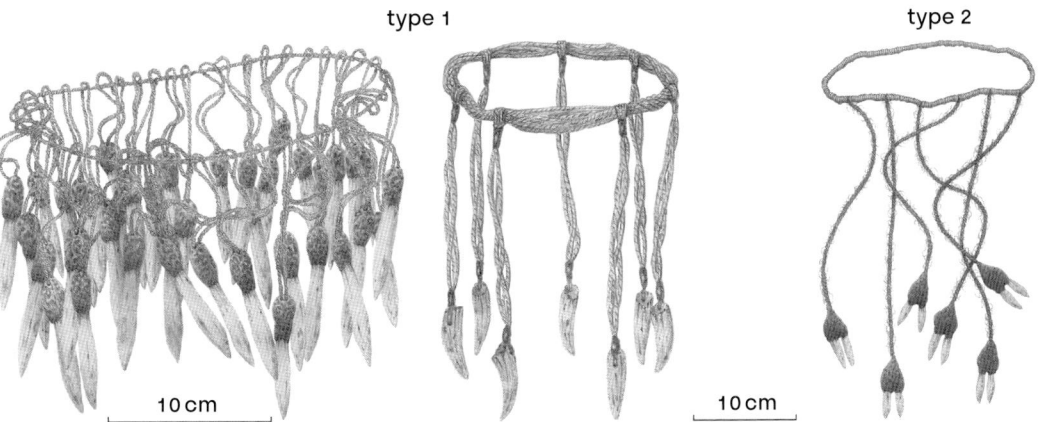

FIGURE 6.5. Circlets could incorporate any number of teeth or small animal bones, though macropod incisors remain a favourite material. Type 1 Circlets feature equidistant pendants, while Type 2 Circlets feature pendants concentrated at the front of the piece.

Manufacture and use

These ornaments have been collected from many of the northern regions and incorporate the teeth of several different animals, including humans (Table 6.3). Some variation appears to be present within the design of these adornments, with Type 1 spacing the bone or tooth pendants equidistant around the entire band and Type 2 having the pendants gathered at the front so that they fall only across the face (see Figure 6.5).

Most have attached the tooth/small bone individually to the band, though a few Type 2 Circlets examples from the Kimberley region have attached macropod incisors in pairs. These pendants with paired teeth could be misidentified as a form of sidelock pendant (see 'Sidelock pendants' below) if found separated from their band. The only other circlet examples in which the components have been set into resin in pairs are the Type 1 eel cheekbone examples from the Rainforest region of Queensland. On these circlets, the eel cheekbones are oriented so that they oppose each other, making rough diamond shapes. Roth states that:

> The eel-bone ornament (MAL. *wakai*) of the Tully River and neighbourhood is formed of two such bones attached, with their concavities inwards; into a blob of beeswax. Several of such units may be attached to a length of fibre-twine, and tied across the forehead at the back of the head; sometimes, it may be fixed and used as a necklace, while on occasion a unit by itself may be seen attached to the fore-lock. (Roth 1910b:27)

Notes accompanying those circlets collected from the Arnhem region record that the ornaments were worn by women. Indeed, such an ornament, recorded as a lindirri liapoi, is featured in one of Donald Thomson's most republished photographs—a portrait of a young woman from Caledon Bay, Arnhem Land (1948). This particular example is made from possum fur string and has seven crocodile teeth evenly spaced around the circumference. Each tooth is attached with a single perforation through which possum

TABLE 6.3. Presence of circlets recorded in museum collections. **Bold** = museum presence; *italics* = ethnography indicated only.

REGION	CIRCLETS PRESENT	TOOTH/BONES UTILISED
Kimberley	**Type 2**; *Type 2*	macropod incisors; bandicoot tails; small animal long bones
Fitzmaurice	**Type 2**	macropod incisors
North	**present**	beak
Arnhem	**Type 1**	macropod incisors; crocodile teeth; human teeth; swordfish teeth; emu claws
Desert	**Type 2**; *Type 2*	small animal long bones and jaws
Gulf	**Type 1**	macropod incisors
West Cape	[none identified]	
Torres Strait	[none identified]	
East Cape	[none identified]	
Rainforest	**Type 1**	eel rays
Northeast	[none identified]	
Southeast	[none identified]	
Tasmania	[none identified]	
Riverine	[none identified]	
Spencer	[none identified]	
Eyre	[none identified]	
Southwest	[none identified]	
Northwest	[none identified]	

fur string is threaded. Resin or wax seals the connections. Of note are two other Type 1 Circlet examples, also collected by Thomson from East Arnhem in 1935 that incorporate human teeth: one with four teeth and the other nine. Both sets are attached to plant fibre string by using resin or wax into which each tooth is set. Additionally, a unique circlet was collected by Thomson from 'Wullaki' (Wurlaki) people of East Arnhem Land and utilises emu claws. Each of the 12 claws is individually attached to the plant fibre string (Type 1 Circlet) utilising the usual resin method, and the name of this ornament is recorded as tjilprinin.

Circlets are also found in the Gulf region. Both examples found in museum collections utilised macropod incisors but in much greater number than the Arnhem region examples (between 32 and 35 teeth each). The effect appears as a fringe of teeth.

In the Kimberley region, the circlets are made with human hair string and wallaby incisors that are paired together into a mass of resin. Five or six of these teeth pairs are tied to the front of the circlet so that they fall over the face (Type 2 Circlet). Kim Akerman describes such ornaments as follows:

6. ORNAMENTS

> Walmajarri and Mangala women of the northern Great Sandy Desert and south Kimberley make and wear a hair string head ring, known as a *marrni*, from which a dozen or so pendants made from paired agile wallaby (*Macropus agilis*), lower incisors hang to conceal the face. (Akerman 2011:134)

Museum Victoria notes (Item DT106 notes) state that they were worn by the women while dancing.

In the Desert region, Type 2 Circlets incorporating numerous bones (long bones and mandibles) of small mammals are found. These circlets are recorded as 'mourning chaplets' worn by the widow of a dead man or mother of a dead child during ceremonies. The various bones (and sometimes also seeds) are connected to human hair string using resin. The mandibles in the Museum Victoria example are attached via the incisors so that the widest part of the mandible points down when worn. Such an ornament is described by Berndt and Berndt citing observations of Spencer and Gillen:

> In many cases a widow's hair is cut and she wears a chaplet. Among the Aranda such a chaplet is specially prepared from animal bones and locks of hair of certain relatives of the deceased; it is used in the final rites and eventually torn to pieces and put in the grave. (Berndt & Berndt 1977:457)

Edge-Partington (1969[1890–1898]:116) describes a type of circlet with many small animal bones attached using resin as being worn by Arrernte men during the final mourning ceremony. This ornament was also smashed and included in burial. A possible archaeological example of such a circlet may be found in a lizard mandible with one end embedded in resin discovered at Currarong Shelter 1 (Southeast region) (Lampert 1971), though it could equally also constitute a pendant from another type of head or neck piece.

Finally, a particularly interesting example from the Alligator River is curated in the South Australian Museum and is stated to be a 'head-ring' made from plant fibre string and decorated with a beak surrounded by feathers of a rainbow lorikeet (*Trichoglossus moluccanus*).

Local names recorded for this ornament include:

- marrni (Kimberley region; Akerman 2010)
- lindirri liapoi (Caledon Bay, East Arnhem, Arnhem region; Item DT106 notes, Museum Victoria)
- mitpurkula (East Arnhem, Arnhem region; Item DT001042 notes, Museum Victoria)
- tjanankara or tjimburkna (Desert region; Item A14738 notes, South Australian Museum)
- chimurilia (Warlpiri, Desert region, Item X005387 notes, Museum Victoria)
- wakai (Tully River, Rainforest region; Item E014547 notes, Australian Museum).

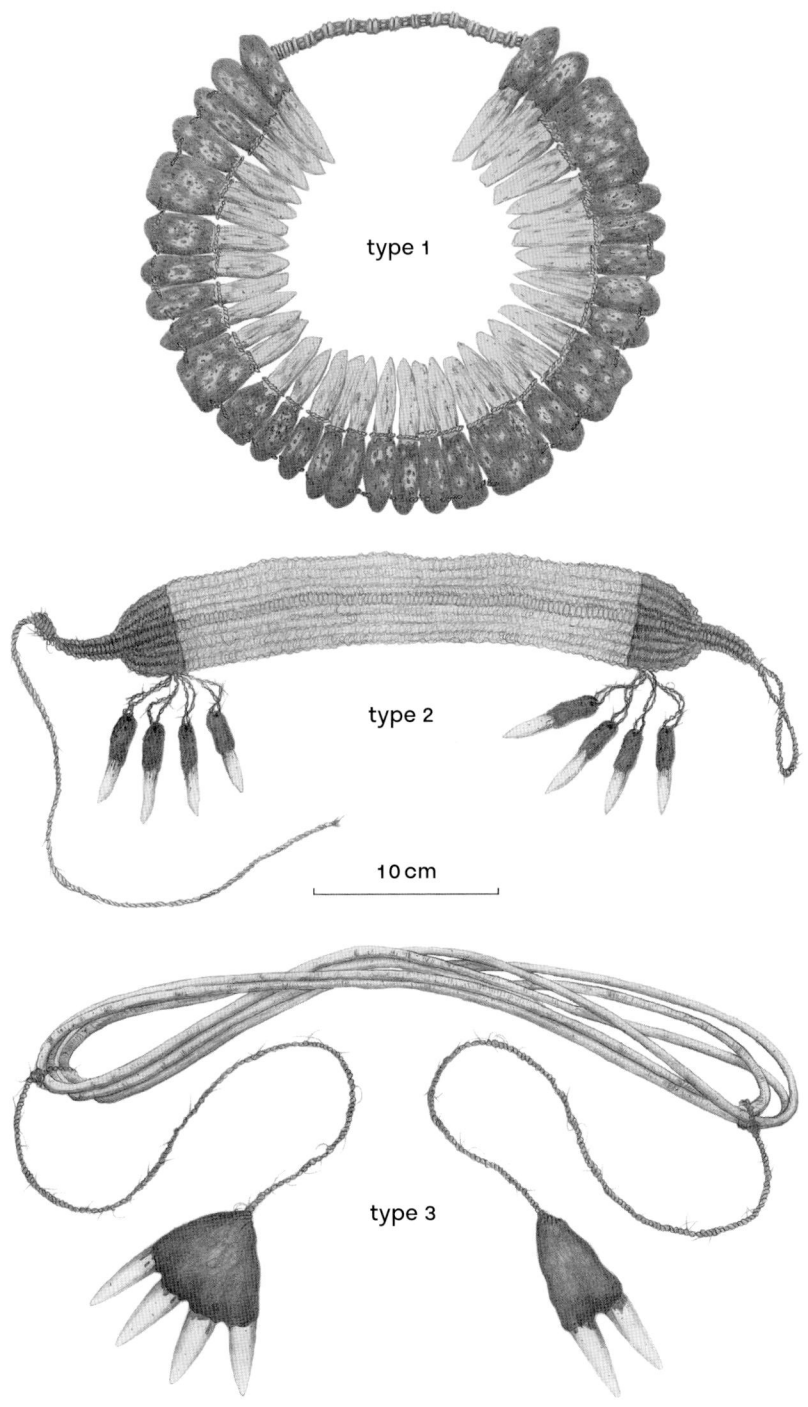

FIGURE 6.6. The three broad types of headbands that incorporate hard animal materials.

6. ORNAMENTS

Headbands
Description

Headbands that include an osseous component come in three main forms: (1) those on which the band is composed of kangaroo incisors placed tightly side by side (Type 1 Headband), (2) those on which the band is made from woven fibres and feature a few teeth attached at each extremity (Type 2 Headband), and (3) those that have a band made from thick string and feature a resin/wax and tooth pendant at one or both extremities (Type 3 Headband) (see Figure 6.6 and Table 6.4). In ethnographies, these accoutrements are sometimes referred to as 'fillets' (e.g. Lumholtz 1889; Roth 1910b).

Manufacture and use

Type 1 Headbands have been captured in film by several early European observers who made photograph portraits of warriors in Darwin (North region) and, in one case, a young warrior from Gubbi Gubbi Country in South East Queensland (Northeast region). Each warrior wears the headband across his forehead so that the teeth point down towards his eyes. An example recorded only as coming from the 'Northern Territory' is accompanied by a note stating that it was worn by men, as is indicated by early photographs, and a brief comment by Breton (1834:184), who noted the use of headbands by men in Australia, stating 'the only ornament that I procured was a string of kangaroo teeth worn round the head'. Another photograph by P Foelsche, dated to c. 1883, shows a woman from the Northern Territory wearing this type of headband, perhaps indicating that women also wore this form of ornamentation or that they were dressed as such specifically for photography. Interestingly, Roth (1907:367) provides one scenario regarding women wearing usually male headbands in North Queensland, stating that a widow 'may be found now and again even after her re-marriage wearing her late husband's necklet, forehead band, etc.'.

Around 30 to 35 macropod incisors are utilised to construct the piece, with each tooth bound first by string (both plant and fur string are found) around the top and bottom of the tooth root before being encased in a thick layer of resin (see Figure 6.6). The teeth are not perforated for stringing and are often painted over with red or white ochre. The resin creates a thick band across the top half of the headband and is frequently seen to be coloured with red pigment. Some examples from the North region have string wound repeatedly around the back part of the band (that which rests against the back of the head), while others have the various strands uncovered (Arnhem region). One particular example curated in the National Museum of Australia and collected from the Arnhem region has the string overlaying (instead of underneath) the resin, which might suggest how these headbands were sometimes repaired.

Type 1 Headbands are sometimes misidentified as a macropod incisor necklace (see 'Ornaments worn around the neck' below) but can be differentiated by length (which is often shorter than a necklace), close binding of the teeth so that they sit directly and entirely next to each other, and a thick band of resin across their roots.

Type 2 Headbands are woven with plant fibres in a close-knit weave. The outer surface is commonly covered in ochre—with around 80 per cent (the middle section) covered in white pigment, while the extremities are in a dark red or mulberry pigment. To each end are attached a few kangaroo incisors, each individually set into resin, and the

TABLE 6.4. Presence of headbands recorded in museum collections. **Bold** = museum presence; *italics* = ethnography indicated only.

REGION	HEADBAND TYPES PRESENT IN MUSEUM COLLECTIONS
Kimberley	**Type 1; Type 3**
Fitzmaurice	**Type 1**
North	**Type 1**; *Type 1*
Arnhem	**Type 1**
Desert	**Type 1; Type 2; Type 3**; *Type 3*
Gulf	**Type 2**
Torres Strait	[none identified]
West Cape	*Type 1*
East Cape	[none identified]
Rainforest	[none identified]
Northeast	**Type 1**; *Type 1*
Southeast	*Type 2*
Tasmania	[none identified]
Riverine	*Type 2*
Spencer	[none identified]
Eyre	[none identified]
Southwest	[none identified]
Northwest	[none identified]

same plant fibre string connecting them to the main band (see Figure 6.6). Most examples of Type 2 Headbands appear to have only two or three macropod incisors attached to each side, though an example collected from Mornington Island (Gulf region; in the National Museum of Australia) has five on each side. Photographs of individuals wearing this type of headband are few and hard to identify given that the characteristic suspended teeth hang near the back of the head, making them largely invisible in images.

Museums record that Type 2 Headbands have been collected from the Gulf region (specifically Mornington Island), the Desert region, and Cape York Peninsula. Of the examples from the Desert region, one collected by Gillen in 1899 from Kaytetye people in Central Australia is noted to have been 'worn by women of the Kaitish, Warramunga, and the northern Central Australian groups' (Item X005365 notes, Museum Victoria), whereas those from the Gulf are accompanied by a note stating that they were 'worn in ceremonial ritual' (Item X097047 notes, Museum Victoria. Best (2012:9) notes that for the Wellesley Islands (Gulf region):

> Headbands . . . are signifiers of final initiation. Materials include opossum hair, vegetable fibre and red or white pigment. An example from Mornington Island is further decorated with macropod teeth pendants.

6. ORNAMENTS

Finally, an example collected from 'Victoria' is said to be worn by both men and women and includes two pairs of incisors strung together using kangaroo sinew and then attached as pendants (which are known as liangerra) to the woven headband made from plant fibre. The local name for this item is murloug-nird and it was worn across the forehead. For the Lower Murray (Riverine region), Brough Smyth (1972[1876]a:276) noted that 'a closely woven forehead band with kangaroo teeth pendants attached with sinew was worn by both men and women'. Similarly, for the Gippsland District, it is reported by Brough Smyth (1972[1876]a:274) that 'men, and sometimes, women wore a headband to which was attached an ornament made of kangaroo teeth, the teeth hung onto each temple'.

Petrie also observed that in South East Queensland (Northeast region):

> in addition to his everyday dress, during a corroboree a black fellow would wear round his forehead a band made from root fibre, very nicely plaited, and painted white with clay; also the skin of a native dog's tail (cured with charcoal and dried in the sun), or, rather, a part of one, for one tail made three headdresses when cut up the middle. This piece of tail stuck round the head like a beautiful yellow brush—the natives Called it '*jilla*', and the forehead band '*tinggil*'. (Petrie 1904:20–1)

Headbands made from dingo tail are seen in several studio portraits of both men and women and have been described by Roth:

> In the Boulia District, a Dingo-tail may sometimes be worn over the forehead like a fillet and tied by strings at the back ... The Dingo-tail was also worn by the Brisbane males, who called it *gilla*; used at corrobborees, fights, and first put on at the invitation ceremony. (Roth 1910b:27)

Nind (1831:25) similarly describes that the single men living at King George Sound (Southwest region) would 'ornament their heads with feathers, dogs' tails, and other similar articles', with Wheelman (Wiilman) wearing a tyre, a head ornament worn in front of the barlkey (headdress of woven possum fur), with the:

> *twert-tyre* ... made from two or three tails of the wild dog, and two pieces of skin from the inside of the hind leg fastened around a small stick with blackboy gum ... The headdresses for the dances were striking. Some consisted of a row of dog tails across the head and strips of fur down each cheek tied under the chin. (Hassell & Davidson 1936:695).

Chauncy also mentioned such ornaments, noting that in the vicinity of the Swan River Colony (Perth; Southwest region):

> The natives use a number of different kinds of ornaments, especially the men, who ... wear bunches of emu fathers on the arms, a wild dog's tail round the head just over the brow, and bunches of beautiful long feathers of the large black cockatoo or of the white cockatoo on the top of the head. The young men wear the small bone of the leg of the kangaroo through the cartilage of the nose as a sign of their having attained the age of puberty. (Chauncy 1972[1876]:251)

A RECORD IN BONE

Dingo is again mentioned for the Kurnai of Gippsland, with Fison and Howitt (1991-[1880]:195) describing that girls, when being initiated, were ornamented with 'the ears of the native bear (*Phascolarctos kouala*) tied above their own and the tails of the native dingo hanging down their back'. Another use of dingo is mentioned by Brough Smyth, who states that in Victoria, a 'hunger-belt' was used:

> The native used occasionally a belt, made of the skin of the native dog (*Wer-ren-Willum*), which was worn round the waist, and so arranged as to admit to its being tightened when required. The fur of the animal was outside, and the skin pressed against the body, this belt was called *Ber-buk*, and it was used chiefly when travelling rapidly, or on some expedition requiring secrecy in the course of which the native might have difficulty in procuring food or water. (Brough Smyth 1972[1876]a:272)

Finally, dog tail again appears in the Spencer region, with Schürmann (2009[1879]:211) stating that at Port Lincoln:

> The tip of the tail of a wild dog or wallaby is often attached to the taper end of the beard, and the whole tail of a wild dog tied round the head, is considered very ornamental'.

Interestingly, Brough Smyth brings together the use of the Type 2 Headband with dingo and koala ornaments, citing observations made by Reverend Bulmer:

> The Rev. Mr. Bulmer has given me a description of the ornaments which were worn by the natives of Gippsland in the olden times... Round the forehead (*Nern*) the males wore a piece of network, made of the fibre obtained from the bark of a small shrub which grows plentifully near Lake Tyers. The length of the band was from nine inches to one foot, and the breadth about two inches. It was called *Jimbirn*. It was worn sometimes by females, but very seldom; and was always regarded as belonging to men. The *Jimbirn* was useful as well as ornamental, as it kept the hair from falling over the eyes. To the *Jimbirn* was attached an ornament, made of the teeth of the kangaroo—*Nerndoa jirrah* (*Nerndoa*, teeth; *jirrah*, kangaroo)—and string formed of the wool of the opossum, which was so arranged as to cause the teeth to hang on each temple. At the back of the head was suspended from the string which fastened the *Jimbirn* a wild dog's tail—*Wreka baanda* (*wreka*, tail; *baanda*, dog)... Over the ears and pointing to the front was placed the fur of the tips of the ears of a native bear (*Koola*), called by the natives *Kinanga Koola*. Over the forehead was worn sometimes the feather of the eagle, a tuft of emu feathers, or the crest of a cockatoo. (Brough Smyth 1972[1876]a:273-4)

Before moving on to the last type of headband, the writings of Bennett, who spent most of his time around the Yass and Murrumbidgee rivers (Riverine region), describe how tendons were used to make the string of the Type 2 Headband in this area. In particular, for the Goulburn River Plains, he states that the women:

> are conspicuous principally for their head gear; glowing in grease and red ochre, the ringlets of these 'dark angels' were decorated with opossum tails, the extremities of other animals, and the incisor teeth of the kangaroo; some had the '*Cambun*'

6. ORNAMENTS

('*Bolombine*' of the Tumat country), or fillet daubed with pipe-clay bound round the forehead: this ornament is sometimes made from the stringy bark tree, as well as from the tendons of the kangaroo's tail. (Bennett 1967[1834]:325)

He also provides a firsthand description of how they were manufactured:

> the tendons of the muscles out the tail of the kangaroo, and those of the legs of emu, are converted into thread by the native, who manufacture from it a neat net ornament, called '*Bollombine*'. One of these ornaments, made for me by a native female, of the tendons proved from the kangaroo, was executed in the following manner:—The longest tendons selected from the tail were laid in an extended position to dry in the sun; they were afterwards divided into threads; (when dry they are capable of producing threads of considerable fineness) the cord intended for this ornament was made by two of these threads being rolled upon the thigh, additions being made until a sufficient length was obtained for the purpose required, usually extending to several yards. The netting process is executed in a manner somewhat similar to our own; the ornament, one inch and a-half in breadth, extends like a fillet around the front part of the head, being tied behind by strings of the same material: it is worn by males and females, and coloured with red ochre or pipe-clay, according to the taste of the wearer. (Bennett 1967[1834]:288)

The last type of headband considered here (Type 3)—or those that have a band made from thick string and features a resin and tooth pendant at one or both extremities (see Figure 6.6)—is rare in museum collections. McCarthy (1953:97) reports for Groote Eylandt (Arnhem region) at circumcision ceremonies in 1948: 'a head circlet of cuddled possum cord on each end of which is suspended up to five wallaby incisor teeth in one set and a number of shell-valves in the other set', which sounds like one of these ornaments. In terms of those currently curated within museum collections, an example of a Type 3 Headband was collected from Arrernte people (Desert region) in 1889 and consists of a single length of string coated in resin, which was wound round the head several times before being secured with human hair string. To this string, tassels of bilby tail tips and two small animal bones are attached. This item is curated as a neck ornament, but multiple drawings and photographs of both men and women (though mostly women) wearing such an ornament—or extremely similar ornaments—around their crown are available. Indeed, Spencer and Gillen (1927:435) include a drawing of this same type of ornament, noting that Arrernte widows wore headbands with jaws of animals attached with spinifex resin. Spencer and Gillen also mention that:

> the commonest form of neck-band in the Arunta tribe consists of a single thick strand of fur-string profusely coated with grease and red ochre so as to have a smooth surface. It is closely similar to the ordinary woman's headband. A second form frequently met with amongst the tribes consists of four or five strands united together at either end. Sometimes they form a flat, band-like structure, but more often, as in Fig. 262, the strands are coiled upon one another. From each end passes off a string which serves to tie the band round the neck. Very often the ends of the strings are ornamented with tassels of feathers, birds' down, dingo or rabbit bandicoot tail-tips attached to a central stick ... Neck-bands of this form are worn by both men and women, but the

ornamented ones are more frequently seen on the former than on the latter. (Spencer & Gillen 1904:690)

Similarly, Gillen photographed a young Central Australian woman wearing one of these Type 3 Headbands, at the end of which are paired eagle talons.

Of note is that headbands are cited as having been an item of trade in some regions, specifically on Cape York, where Roth described the trade at Cape Bedford as sending:

> out or export[ing] iron tomahawks, iron digging-sticks, nautilus-shell, different kinds of dilly-bag, pearl-shell chest ornaments and Melo-shells. In return, they obtain forehead-bands . . . They travel in barter along the Northern Coast-line as far as, very probably, the Flinders River. (Roth 1910a:18)

In an archaeological context, the burial of an adult male (Grave 108) was found wearing a headband composed of a double strand of notched marsupial upper incisors at Roonka (Spencer region), dating to about 5000 BP. A probable second headband of the same type was found stretched out across the man's left arm (Pretty 1977). These headbands have no more recent equivalents in archaeological contexts.

Local names recorded for this ornament include the following.

Headband (unspecified):
- tinggil (Brisbane area, Northeast region; Petrie 1904)
- barlkey (Wheelman (Wiilman), Southeast region; Hassell & Davidson 1936)
- bollombine (Riverine region; Bennett 1967[1834])
- cambun (Riverine region; Bennett 1967[1834]).

Type 2 Headband:
- murloug-nird (Victoria; Item X001576 notes, Museum Victoria)
- jimbirn (Gippsland, Riverine region; Brough Smyth 1972[1876]a)
- barmarr (Lardil, Gulf region; Item QE1100 notes, Queensland Museum).

Forehead pendants
Description

Ornaments that feature a large pendant that rests on the middle of the forehead appear to have been extremely common across the north and centre of the Australian continent, being both widely collected and common in photographs (Table 6.5). These ornaments show great variety in style and are here divided into eight types for discussion (see Figure 6.7). These types are:

> *Type 1*   A bar of resin around 10 centimetres long into which teeth are set along the bottom edge
>
> *Type 2*   A much longer (several centimetres longer than Type 1) bar of resin into which teeth are set along the bottom edge
>
> *Type 3*   Wide ellipse, quarter circle or almost full circle of resin with around seven to 13 teeth set into the bottom edge and continuing up around to the sides

6. ORNAMENTS

Type 4   A circle of resin with teeth set into most of the circumference, though not the very top

Type 5   A quarter circle of resin with four to six teeth set into the bottom. This type resembles a kangaroo paw

Type 6   A ball of resin with teeth set into the bottom surface to form a mass of downward-pointing teeth

Type 7   Other examples made from resin and teeth that do not fit with previous ones

Type 8   A largely flat, tear-shaped piece of bone

Manufacture and use

With the exception of Type 8 Forehead Pendants, each of these ornaments is made from macropod incisors inserted into a body of resin, with this body of resin attached to string for fixing to the front of the head. Without the use of X-ray or other non-destructive technologies, it is impossible to determine whether the teeth were perforated before being encased in the resin, though one item curated in the South Australian Museum offers some insight. This object shows that the teeth were first joined together using string, with the string wound around their roots and to their neighbours, but not perforated before being encased in resin. As with the macropod incisor headbands described above in 'Headbands' (and necklaces below in 'Ornaments worn around the neck'), perforation of the tooth for attachment was not necessary.

Looking at the examples held in museum collections, it quickly becomes evident that these ornaments frequently have the outward-facing side painted with designs in red, white, or yellow pigment—an aspect of these ornaments that is almost invisible in early photographs. Similarly, some ornaments have (usually red) seeds fixed into their face as part of the composition, which are also not always visible in images. As such, the beauty and complexity of these ornaments have been largely hidden from view.

Type 1 Forehead Ornaments feature a 10-centimetre (or thereabouts) bar of resin, which may or may not be decorated with painted lines or dots on the outward face. Between about 10 and 17 macropod incisors or between seven and 11 crocodile teeth fit along the bottom edge, sitting directly next to each other, sometimes slightly overlapping. Occasionally, the teeth themselves are painted over with white ochre. The strings come out from each end of the bar.

In the Arnhem region, the bar typically incorporates 11 macropod incisors, though they range between seven and 13 kangaroo incisors. Museum notes kept with Type 1 Forehead Ornaments state that this type of adornment was worn by men of war and was called kiamur' at the Kaparlgoo Mission in the Arnhem region, while Donald Thomson recorded the name karritjambal dirrpal bim'ere at Darbilla Creek (Arnhem region), and ngubukula at Katji Lagoons (Arnhem region). A macropod tooth example collected opposite Elcho Island is noted to have been worn by men at ceremonies and to be called jiltpaning.

Two other Type 1 examples collected by Thomson at Cape Stewart (Arnhem region) are made with crocodile teeth and possum fur string and are noted to have been called r'erri marntjilla. Other crocodile tooth examples have been collected from the Alligator River (North region) and Elcho Island (Arnhem region). Both macropod incisor and crocodile tooth versions appear in the same locations (for example, both kinds have been collected from Elcho Island, Arnhem region). For the crocodile examples,

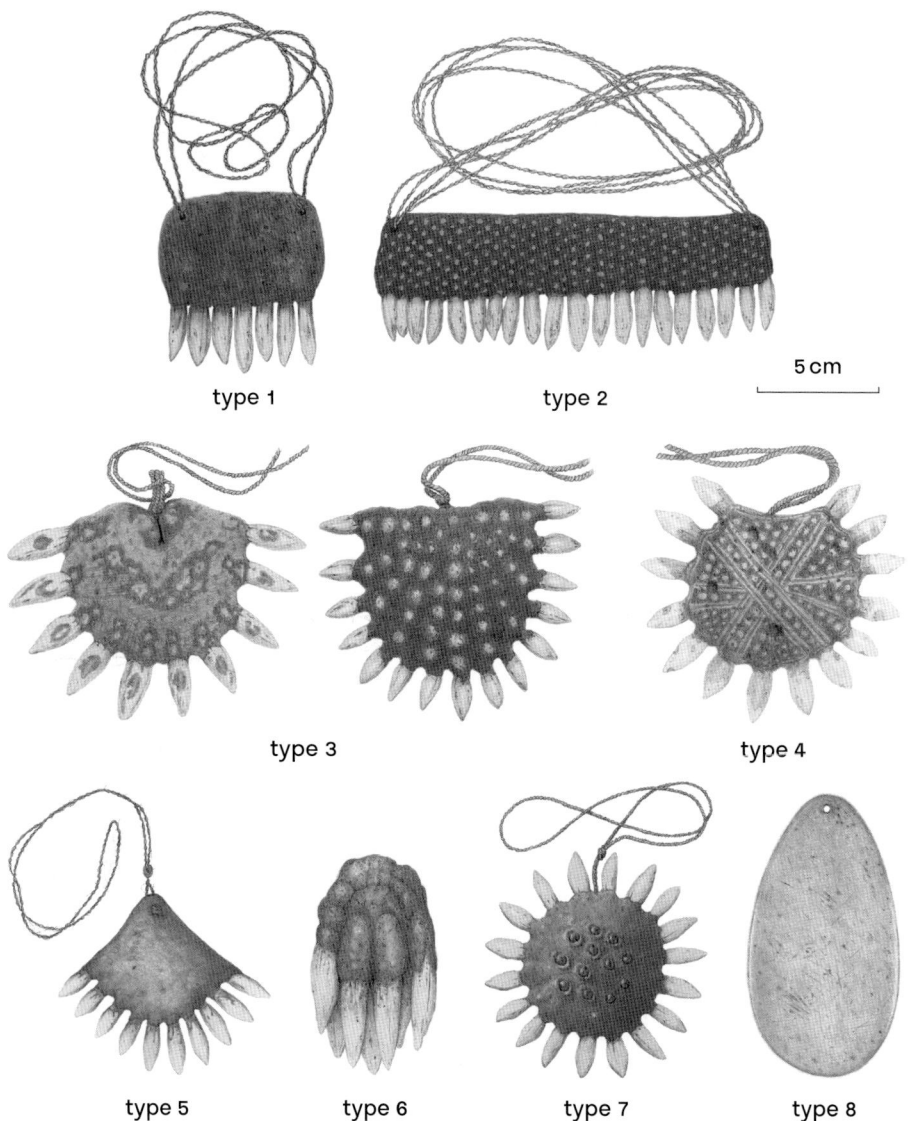

FIGURE 6.7. Types of forehead pendant. Most incorporate a number of macropod or crocodile incisors, though the teeth of other animals, echidna quills, and large pieces of bone also appear. Often, pendants also feature designs pressed into the resin, painted designs, or colourful seeds.

only bar versions (Type 1 or Type 2 Forehead Ornaments) are thus far known, and they incorporate between three and 15 teeth. Given that crocodile teeth are significantly larger and wider than kangaroo incisors, it could be that the raw material dictates the best form of head ornament these teeth can be incorporated into.

Type 2 Forehead Ornaments are characterised by a longer bar of resin (longer than 10 centimetres) and feature either around 12 crocodile teeth set side by side or around

6. ORNAMENTS

TABLE 6.5. Presence of forehead pendants recorded in museum collections. **Bold** = museum presence; *italics* = ethnography indicated only.

REGION	FOREHEAD PENDANT TYPES RECORDED	OSSEOUS COMPONENT UTILISED
Kimberley	**Type 3; Type 4; Type 8**	macropod incisor; crocodile teeth
Fitzmaurice	**Type 1; Type 3; Type 5; Type 6**	macropod incisor
North	**Type 1; Type 2; Type 3; Type 5**; *Type 4*	macropod incisor; crocodile teeth
Arnhem	**Type 1; Type 2; Type 3; Type 4; Type 5; Type ?**; *Type 2*	macropod incisor; crocodile teeth; cassowary crest
Desert	**Type 2; Type 3; Type 5; Type 6; Type 7**; *Type 3; Type 5; Type 7*	macropod incisor; echidna quills (?)
Gulf	**Type 6**; **Type 7**	macropod incisor; porpoise or dolphin teeth
Torres Strait	[none identified]	
West Cape	[none identified]	
East Cape	[none identified]	
Rainforest	*Type 3*	macropod incisor
Northeast	[none identified]	
Southeast	[none identified]	
Tasmania	[none identified]	
Riverine	[none identified]	
Spencer	**Type 3; Type 5**	macropod incisor
Eyre	**Type 5; Type 7**	macropod incisor
Southwest	[none identified]	
Northwest	[none identified]	

20 macropod incisors. The strings on these examples are typically attached between the last two teeth on each side and across the bar of resin so that it hangs from the top. Examples of these ornaments have been collected from Central and East Arnhem Land. An example collected by Donald Thomson made with crocodile teeth is noted to have been called lirra baru and to have been used by women, while examples made with kangaroo or crocodile teeth are recorded as being called lindiri. Strings of both plant and human hair are found on Type 2 Forehead Ornaments, including one from East Arnhem made from kurrajong fibre.

Type 3 is the first of the more circular designs (see Figure 6.7). Type 3 Forehead Ornaments feature a resin body, which can be a quarter circle, almost a full circle or a wide ellipse pressed flat on both sides and into which the seven to 13 teeth are inserted around the bottom edge and up the sides. The teeth can cover up to about 250 degrees of the circumference. The strings—made from plant fibres or human hair string—attach to the top centre of the ornament. These ornaments are commonly painted on the outward-facing surface with line or dot designs. The teeth can also be painted, and seeds commonly appear. Some examples feature incised or stamped resin bodies, the designs carefully pressed into their surface. A great example from the Kimberley is kept in the Australian Museum. It is sub-circular with 10 kangaroo incisors pressed into 75 per cent of the circumference so that they fan outwards. The wax has been painted with yellow and red bands, with dots in alternating colour over the top. A single red dot has been added to the top of each tooth.

There may be some nuanced differences in the designs of Type 3 Forehead Ornaments utilised or preferred between the regions (and Countries therein), as the Arnhem region examples are more half circle or elliptical in shape than those from elsewhere. However, the sample is currently not large enough to delve further into this possible stylistic patterning. Museum notes state that this form of ornament, particularly one that is a quarter circle in body and has teeth fanned out along the bottom curved edge, was worn by women of the Kaitish (Kaytetye), Warramunga (Warumungu), and other northern Central Australian groups in the Desert region of Central Australia.

Skipping forward to Type 5 Forehead Ornaments, these items are generally smaller overall than the other forms of this adornment. The number of macropod incisors seen on these examples range between four and nine teeth, and the string utilised can be human hair, plant fibre, or fur string. They are noted to have been worn by women of Kaitish (Kaytetye), Warramunga (Warumungu), and other northern Central Australian Aboriginal people.

A particularly unique example of a Type 5 Forehead Ornament has been collected from the Arnhem region and is a symmetrical oval of resin with three macropod teeth set into the bottom. Red seeds are embedded in the front surface, and a yellow painted design has been added. The overall appearance of this ornament is reminiscent of a kangaroo paw—which may or may not be an intentional part of the design.

Type 4 Forehead Ornaments are rarer than the preceding four types and might be considered a more 'extreme' version of Type 3 ornaments—the teeth are set almost the whole way around the circumference of the piece. Their construction and decoration are the same as for the previous four, including the addition of painted elements.

Type 6 Forehead Ornaments, on the other hand, employ a somewhat different approach. Instead of a rod or flattened shape as the resin base, teeth are brought together into a tight bunch and then embedded into the resin as one mass. Between six and eight teeth have been observed to be included on Type 6 Forehead Ornaments. Interestingly, an example from the Fitzmaurice region (Willeroo Station) might also be classified as a Type 6 Forehead Ornament, though the teeth seem to be individually (instead as put in as one) encased in resin. Seven macropod incisors are included, yellow ochre covers the resin, and the teeth are painted over with white ochre. In a similar case, an artefact from the Desert region (curated in the National Museum of Australia) features some 20 echidna quills. It is unclear if it is a forehead pendant or another type of ornament.

Type 7 Forehead Ornaments include all those examples which do not readily fall into one of the preceding categories. For example, a single item from the Kimberley region is perfectly round with 18 macropod incisors around the perimeter and red seeds in the middle, and it is threaded on plant fibre string.

6. ORNAMENTS

Type 8 is a forehead ornament worn in the same fashion as those made from wax and tooth but is made on one piece of bone. Specifically, they are made from kangaroo scapula, are shaped into an oblong, and are highly symmetrical. The South Australian Museum records that one of their examples from Cooper Creek (Eyre region) is called a kuripkin and was worn on the necks of male youths to be initiated. These same ornaments are seen in photographs, worn in the middle of the head in the north. For example, a Samuel Nixon photograph of a group of people 'of the Bogan River area, NSW, circa. 1870' shows both men and women wearing these bone forehead ornaments.

A final, extraordinary ornament that should be highlighted is a unique adornment collected in 1935 from Milingimbi (Arnhem region). It is a cassowary casque, with the pendulous part worn over the forehead, as with the previous examples. Both sides of the casque are painted with red, orange, and yellow pigment, and plant fibre string attaches the piece from its pointed corner through a single perforation. Given that cassowary do not live close to Milingimbi, this item must have been collected or traded from North Queensland.

Within the ethnographic literature, these forehead adornments see only a few mentions. Edge-Partington (1969[1890–98]:132, Nos. 14–16) illustrates a number of forehead ornaments that are reminiscent of those found in the museum collections, including one made from:

> a Queensland bean (*Castanospersum australe*), either carved or painted with a somewhat owl-like, or possibly anthropomorphic design, and into which four porpoise or dolphin teeth have been inserted so that they appear to represent four limbs. (Akerman 2011:134)

Spencer and Gillen, in reference to the MacDonnell Ranges (Desert region), describe these types of ornaments, stating that:

> [in] the Kaitish and Warramunga tribes especially, the women wear as ornament on the forehead a small mass of porcupine-grass resin, into which from six to twelve incisor teeth of a kangaroo are fastened in a radiating manner along the lower edge. A strand of human hair-string fastened into the resin, serves to attach it to the hair of the wearer, over whose forehead it hangs down. (Spencer & Gillen 1899:574)

In a later work, these same authors state that:

> often by way of ornament ... made of a lump of resin with kangaroo teeth fixed. These ornaments are worn hanging down over the forehead, and they are met with amongst all tribes. (Spencer & Gillen 1904:687–8)

They further note that:

> the simplest form of head-band met with amongst all the tribes is a smooth, red-ochred band similar to the common neck- or arm-band. This is worn, as a general rule, exclusively by women, though on rare occasions a man may wear one of his wife's as a remedy for headache. Often by way of ornament, tufts of alpita are attached to these rings ... or an ornament made of a lump of resin with kangaroo teeth fixed into it. (Spencer & Gillen 1904:687–8)

A RECORD IN BONE

Again for the Desert, Chewings describes how the Arrernte:

> women, with much shouting from camp to camp and calling for dogs, follow, laden with water, yam-sticks, nulla-nullas, pittis (in which are hair- and bark-string, bound up *tjurunga*, stone knives, ochre, personal adornments such as necklaces of string or beans, headbands, kangaroo teeth set in spinifex gum or what not) children and dogs that cannot or will not follow. (Chewings 1936:40)

Local names recorded for this ornament include the following.

Type 1 Forehead Ornaments:
- kiamurk (Kaparlgoo Mission, Arnhem region; Item E010332 notes, Australian Museum)
- karritjambal dirrpal bim'ere (Darbilla Creek, Arnhem region; Item DT001047 notes, Museum Victoria)
- ngubukula (Katji Lagoons, Arnhem region; Item DT001051 notes, Museum Victoria)
- r'erri marntjilla (Cape Stuart; Item DT001053 notes, Museum Victoria)
- jiltpaning (Elcho Island, Arnhem region; Item A16370 notes, South Australian Museum)
- lindaree (Port Essington, Arnhem region; Item A3262 notes, South Australian Museum).

Type 2 Forehead Ornaments:
- lirra baru djilpin'in (Cape Stewart, Arnhem region; Item DT007702 notes, Museum Victoria)
- lindiri (Marrangu, Arnhem region; Item DT7767 notes, Museum Victoria)
- balirr (eastern Arnhem, Arnhem region; Item X90086 notes, Museum Victoria).

Type 3 Forehead Ornaments:
- majimbo (Alligator River, Arnhem region; Item X100435 notes, Museum Victoria)
- lindaree (Port Essington, Arnhem region; Donald Thomson notes in Museum Victoria)
- narurjia (Fitzmaurice region; Donald Thomson notes in Museum Victoria).

Type 4 Forehead Ornaments:
- lindaree (Port Essington, Arnhem region; Item A3260 notes, Museum Victoria).

Type 5 Forehead Ornaments:
- clora clinia (Desert region; Item A3276 notes, South Australian Museum)
- lartcheena (Desert region; Item A3282 notes, South Australian Museum)
- tamburalgee (Northern Territory; Item A32777 notes, South Australian Museum).

6. ORNAMENTS

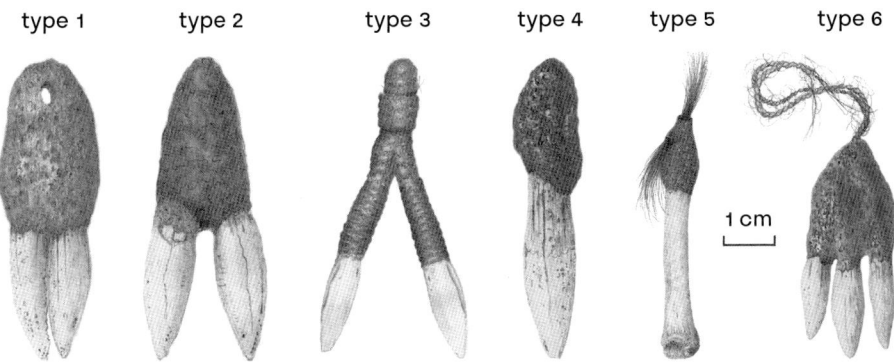

FIGURE 6.8. Sidelock pendants are attached to a lock of hair so they fall just in front of the ear. A range of types are evident in museum and photographic archives.

Type 8 Forehead Ornaments:
- kuripkin (Cooper Creek, Eyre region; Item A9511 notes, South Australian Museum).

Sidelock pendants
Description
Sidelock pendants were attached to a lock of hair above the ear so that the pendent fell just in front of the ear. Each of these ornament types is threaded with human hair or plant fibre string and consists of between one and three macropod incisors or small animal long bones embedded into a resin mount. Variations in these hair decorations were noted and are here split into six types for discussion (see Figure 6.8):

Type 1	Paired kangaroo incisors set into resin/wax—the incisors are pressed together to form a single downward-facing point.
Type 2	Two kangaroo incisors set into resin/wax, but set apart
Type 3	Two kangaroo incisors attached to sinew or string and then resin—the teeth are set apart.
Type 4	Single tooth set into resin/wax
Type 5	Single small bone set into resin/wax
Type 6	Three kangaroo incisors sct into resin/wax.

Manufacture and use
This form of decoration appears to be more restricted in its use, with museum collections and ethnographies finding them primarily in the interior, though ethnographies suggest their presence on the southeast coast, as well as some parts of the northeastern coastline (Table 6.6). Photographs help us with determining the use of these ornaments. From these images, it is evident that they were worn attached to the sidelock, with those images from Central Australia showing that it was usually the

right side on both men and women. The ornament sits just in front of the ear, where it is highly visible.

Unfortunately, most ethnographic reports of these ornaments are too vague to provide insight into the different designs attested to in the museum collections, though who wore them is shown. In western Victoria, 'chiefs' are stated to have 'in the hair . . . fastened several incisor teeth of the large kangaroo' (Dawson 1981[1881]:81), while Angas also describes how men would wear this type of ornament (and perhaps another similar form but worn from forelocks) along the Lower Murray River and near Lake Alexandrina (Riverine region): 'and his hair was ornamented with kangaroo teeth, fastened into it with clay, which hung down over his forehead' (Angas 1967[1847]:58); 'their chief ornaments are kangaroo-teeth fastened into their hair; a bone through the cartilage of the nose' (Angas 1967[1847]:92); and 'the lads thus initiated are entitled to wear two kangaroo teeth, and bunch of emu feathers in their hair' (Angas 1967[1847]:98). This last mention may refer to any of the first four types of sidelock pendant, though only Type 3 is found in museum collections from this region. Further, Augustus Robinson noted in his journal for June 1841 that in the Port Phillip area, 'kangaroo teeth I find are worn as ornaments among nearly all the tribes I have visited. They are bound in Paris, and form angles thus' (Clark 2000b:245). The accompanying sketch appears to be showing multiple examples of Type 3 Sidelock Pendants, with a number of these tied to the forelocks so they fall across the forehead.

An interesting and important side note is highlighted by Augustus Robinson, whose Port Phillip journals note on several occasions that when family or friends (who did not usually live together) would meet, they would swap the ornaments that they were wearing with their loved one of the other group. For example, in June of 1841, Augustus Robinson observed how:

> She [Mar.ke] recognised an old acquaintance and, without ceremony, took the kangaroo teeth ornaments that adorned his hair and reed necklace that adorned his neck and decorated her child therewith. This I observed to be the custom of the natives when meeting with friends. (Clark 2000b:246)

Such friendly trading of ornamentation will have implications for their movement across the landscape and needs to be kept in mind in future studies.

Staying in the Riverine area, Bennett (1967[1834]:275) described how 'many of the females wore the front teeth of the kangaroo as ornaments attached to their hair, and esteemed them for that purpose' when he visited 'Bugong Mountain' (presumably Mt Bogong). Eyre (1845:Plate I) similarly includes a brief mention and illustration of a group of five kangaroo teeth, each found and clustered together as a Type 3 example. They are stated as having been 'tied to the hair of young males and females after the ceremonies of initiation' in the Riverine region. Finally, when travelling along the Murray River in 1836, Mitchell (1965[1839]b:142) mentions that on 21 June, 'Piper found in their huts some fragments of blue earthernware, nicely attached with gum to threads, by which it would appear, that the gins wore them in their hair as ornaments'. This note provides an interesting example of how recently introduced light-coloured materials were being incorporated into traditional ornament forms.

Moving to the southeast coast, a number of firsthand observations by the English administrators and surveyors who arrived from the First Fleet onwards are provided.

6. ORNAMENTS

Governor Arthur Phillip noted that the people living around Sydney Cove (Southeast region):

> sometimes had in their hair the teeth of dogs, and other animals, the claws of lobsters, and feral small bones, which they fasten there by means of gum; but such ornaments have never been seen upon the women. (Phillip 1789:137)

Collins made similar observations, stating that:

> to their hair, by means of the yellow gum, they fasten the front teeth of the kangaroo, and the jaw-bones of large fish, human teeth, pieces of wood, feathers of birds, the tail of the dog, and certain bones taken out of the head of a fish, not unlike human teeth. (Collins 1975[1798]:457)

He also noted that this ornamentation began early in life:

> the parents begin early to decorate them [children] after the custom of the country. As soon as the hair of the head can be taken hold of, fish-bones and the teeth of animals are fastened to it with gum. (Collins 1975[1798]:465)

Hunter too noticed these ornaments, stating that the young man Bu-ro-wan of the 'Bu-ru-be-ron-gal' had his hair 'ornamented with the tails of several small animals' (Hunter 1963[1793]:41). Somewhat later, first Mitchell (1965[1839]a:49) noted 'around her brow she had kangaroo teeth fastened to the few remaining hairs, and a knot of brown feathers decorated her right temple', describing an elderly woman near Maule's Creek, and then Brough Smyth (1972[1876]a:72) made similar notes of this continuing tradition: 'the hair is usually matted with gum, and decorated with dogs' tails and teeth' on the Macleay and Nambucca rivers. Moving further south again, Bonwick illustrates sidelock ornaments for Tasmania (Bonwick 1870:37), stating that 'the men would stick a few kangaroo teeth or cockatoo feathers in their hair' (Bonwick 1870:27). From the drawing, these ornaments appear to be of the Type 3 Sidelock Pendant variety.

In the Eyre region, several observers provide comment. Roth states that:

> knuckle and similar bones from the kangaroo or dingo, and up to about two and a half inches in length, are fixed with cement by string to the tuft of hair over the temporal region, whence they dangle on each side in front of the ears, in the Boulia and Upper Georgina Districts. (Roth 1910b:25)

He also provides a good description of ornament morphology, including what sounds like a Type 1 Sidelock Pendant:

> the double tooth-ornament is formed of an oval-shaped blob of cement into which a couple of incisor teeth of the kangaroo, rarely of the dingo, are fixed; the cement employed is that of the *Triodia* or *Grevillea*. There is an aperture in the base of the ornament through which a small lock of hair from over the centre of the forehead is passed and thus fixed, with the result that the tips of the two teeth rest midway between the

TABLE 6.6. Presence of sidelock pendants recorded in museum collections. **Bold** = museum presence; *italics* = ethnography indicated only.

REGION	SIDELOCK PENDANT TYPES RECORDED	OSSEOUS COMPONENT UTILISED
Kimberley	[none identified]	
Fitzmaurice	[none identified]	
North	[none identified]	
Arnhem	**Type 6**	macropod incisor; crocodile tooth
Desert	**Type 1; Type 2** *Type 4; Type 5*	macropod incisor; dingo bones; small animal long bones
Gulf	*Type ?*	macropod incisor
Torres Strait	[none identified]	
West Cape	[none identified]	
East Cape	[none identified]	
Rainforest	**Type 6**	macropod incisor
Northeast	[none identified]	
Southeast		macropod incisor; fish jaws; human teeth; fish teeth; dingo tail
Tasmania	*Type 3*	macropod incisor
Riverine	**Type 3 (?)** *Type 3*	macropod incisor
Spencer	[none identified]	
Eyre	**Type 1; Type 3; Type 4/; Type 5**	macropod incisor; small animal long bones; dingo bone; dingo tooth
Southwest	[none identified]	
Northwest	[none identified]	

> eyebrows. On occasion it is made to hang from a forehead band instead. Though used by both sexes as corrobborees and other festive occasions, it is manufactured by men only in the Upper Georgina, Leichhardt-selwyn, Cloncurry, Upper Diamantina, and portions of the Boulia districts. (Roth 1910b:25)

Curr seems to describe Type 2 or 3 Sidelock Pendants, stating that:

> the Yanda women wear, on occasions of corroboree, and ornament common in many parts of Australia ... it is made of the two front teeth of the kangaroo, which are fastened together at their butts with sinew and gum, and exited at an angle of 45 degrees. (Curr 1886:360)

Duncan-Kemp (1964:71) similarly describes women in the Eyre region of Queensland: 'above their ears and across their foreheads were fastened *miri-miri* nets, ornaments of

6. ORNAMENTS

kangaroo teeth hung rosette-fashion at the temples'. This description may be talking about a Type 2 Headband or the use of a headband and sidelock pendants.

Finally, only brief mentions are made for other regions of the continent. For Central Australia, Chewings (1936:111) describes how young Arunda (Arrernte) (Desert region) women wore:

> trinkets of kangaroo teeth set in spinifex resin from the hair or hung long necklaces of Stuart's beans . . . When in mourning they wear small bones dangling from the hair.

Roth (1910b:26) mentions that 'on Mornington Island, a double tooth-ornament is attached to the temporal hair of the females'. Also worth mentioning is a possible sidelock pendant made from a solitary crocodile tooth collected from the Arnhem region that may also be a forehead pendant. It is painted with red and white stripes, the tooth coated in white paint and attached with human hair string.

Finally, children are also specifically cited as wearing such adornments. An example of a sidelock ornament curated in the Australian Museum and collected from the Lachlan River (Riverine region) area is noted to have been worn by children, a note supported by Backhouse's (1967[1843]:517) observation for Adelaide (Spencer region): 'kangaroo's teeth are fastened to the locks of the children's hair, before and at the sides, as ornaments, and often tufts of feathers are appended behind'. Roth (1910b:26) similarly notes a 'single kangaroo-tooth ornament attached to the hair at the temples, but here used by children only' in the Burketown area (Gulf region).

Local names recorded for this ornament include the following.

Unspecified sidelock pendant:
- gna-oong (Port Jackson/Sydney area, Southeast region; Hunter 1963[1793])
- ma-na-ran (Port Jackson/Sydney area, Southeast region; Hunter 1963[1793]).

Type 1 Sidelock Pendant:
- yirrara (Koko-Lama-lama (Mbarrumbathama), Hinterland and coast of Princess Charlotte Bay, East Cape region; Roth 1910b)
- yirranggal (Maitakudi (Maithakari), Cloncurry area, Eyre region; Roth 1910b)
- milka (Pitta-Pitta, Boulia district, Eyre region; Roth 1910b).

Type 3 Sidelock Pendant:
- let-ter-rer (Riverine region; Eyre 1845).

Earrings

Examination of the museum collections found no pre-1970 examples of earrings collected from the Australian continent, probably reflecting the widespread choice not to pierce the earlobes. Palmer (1884:286) comments that for the people in the Gulf region, 'the septum of the nose was always bored through, in which they occasionally carried a stick, but the ears were never bored'. Similarly, Brough Smyth (1972[1876]a:274), when reporting observations for Gippsland (Riverine region), states that 'Mr. Bulmer says he has never seen any ear-ornaments. They never, he thinks, pierced the ears'. However, Curr (1886:346) notes in his observations that around the Burke River (Eyre region), 'pieces of the leg bones of birds' were worn as earrings (though how they were attached is unclear).

Cape York Peninsula appears to be the only area where ear piercings were a common way to decorate the human body. Jardine (1866:81) mentions that for Somerset on the very tip of Cape York, men would have 'large holes . . . made in the ears, and a piece of wood as large as a bottle-cork, and whitened with pipeclay, is inserted into them', while Roth (1910b:28) states that 'piercing of the ears would appear to be peculiar to the Cape York Peninsula. On the east coast it has been observed as far south as the Tully River' and that it was only seen on male individuals. He further notes that:

> On the Gulf side, e.g. Pennefather and Embly Rivers, the males also alone have both their ears pierced, and may wear ear-rings which could however be more correctly described as tubes, they being as much as two and a quarter inches external diameter and over four inches long. Such a tube (NGG. *Wà-amanu*) is made from the *Bombax malabaricum*, De Cand. (NGG. *Baiperi*), the core of which is hollowed out with a kangaroo-bone awl. (Roth 1910b:28)

He finishes by saying that:

> in the North-western Districts, but among the Cloncurry natives and then solely amongst some of the older men, ear-holes in which a kangaroo-bone is said to have been worn, were present. (Roth 1910b:28–9)

Nose bones
Description

As an ornament that is worn through the pierced nasal septum and almost exclusively made on bone, these items are commonly known as 'nose bones' in the Australian context. Such ornamentation is among the first to be specifically noted by early European observers. For example, former governor Arthur Phillip reported of the men he interacted with at Port Jackson on arrival in 1788:

> The perforation of the cartilage that divides the nostrils, and the strange disfiguring ornament of a long bone or stick thrust through it, was now observed . . . several very old men were seen in this excursion who had not lost the tooth, nor had their noses prepared to received that grotesque appending: probably, therefore, these are marks of distinction: ambition must have its badges, and where cloaths are not worn, the body itself must be compelled to bear them. (Phillip 1789:80)

Museums hold great collections of these facial adornments, reflecting both their ubiquity across much of the continent and their popularity with early collectors (Table 6.6). For the following discussion, nose bones have been here divided into nine types (see Figure 6.9):

> *Type 1*   Kangaroo fibula; natural end; long, acute or spatulate end—usually quite long, being around 15 centimetres in length.

6. ORNAMENTS

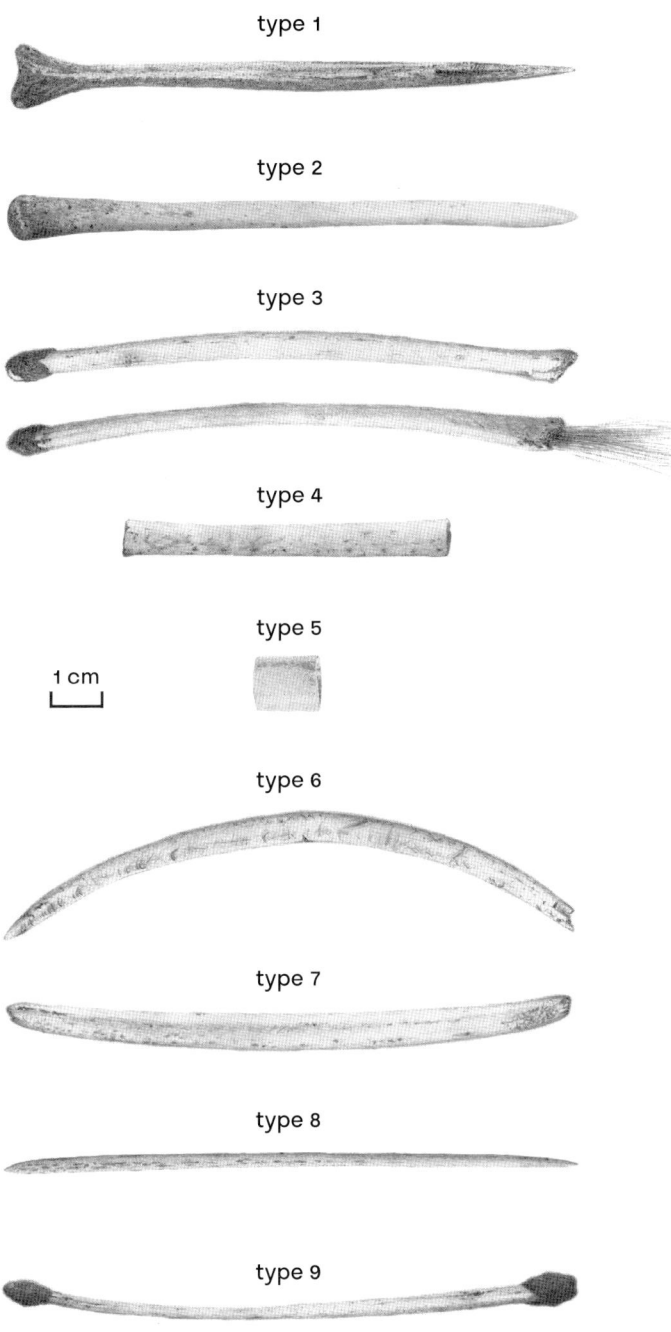

FIGURE 6.9. Types of nose bones found across the Australian continent. Most are made on macropod long bone or the wing bone of a large bird.

Type 2	Kangaroo fibula; end rounded, cut or otherwise shaped; some resin on end; long, acute or spatulate end; or blunt—usually quite long, being around 15 centimetres in length.
Type 3	Bird bone or other long hollow bone (rib?); can be decorated or not—this type can be very long, around 30 centimetres in length. Straight-cut ends are frequently observed.
Type 4	Shorter, but not full length—between 10 and 15 centimetres in length. Straight-cut ends frequently observed.
Type 5	Very short item, made on bird or kangaroo bone—less than 10 centimetres in length, sometimes as short as two centimetres. Some are straight-cut bone tube sections, while others are very small, stubby bipoints.
Type 6	Long and curved; made from rib bone
Type 7	Bone split in half with spatulate ends—these appear to be mostly (but not exclusively) made on bird radius. Some examples reach well over 20 centimetres in length. Extremities can have either more rounded or pointed finishes, and incised decorations and red ochre traces are common. Engravings are usually on the convex side.
Type 8	Quite long (above 15 centimetres) and straight
Type 9	Long piece of partially curved, long bone; resin knobs on each end

Sometimes the division between Type 1 and Type 2 Nose Bones is in shades of grey as the proximal end could conceivably be heavily worn from use and therefore become rounded, resulting in a typical Type 2 Nose Bone. Similarly, it is possible that Type 4 Nose Bones are really one of the previous three types that have been worn down through additional uses (see 'Awls' in Chapter 5). Likewise, some of the Type 1 and 2 Nose Bones have acute or spatulate distal tips, and it is currently unclear if these different tip forms are part of their design or simply reflect change over their use life. Certainly, their known multifunctionality must play a role in their physical appearance. Further study of these ornaments is required to provide more nuanced understandings of their design and change over time.

Manufacture and use

The vast majority of nose bones were made on macropod fibula, though the radius from large birds was also commonly selected. Identification of the specific bird species that were utilised include pelicans by the Arrernte (Desert region) and communities in the Eyre region; eagle (Ernabella, (Pukatja), Desert); hawk (Northeast region); bustard (Arrernte, Desert region); bush turkey (Sandy Blight Junction, Desert region); and emu (Desert, Riverine, and Southwest regions).

At least one type of nose bone is recorded for most regions of the continent, though the Desert and Southeast regions show significantly more variety than other regions (Table 6.7). Given that these two regions have been particularly studied by early European arrivals, surveyors, and collectors (etc.), this diversity in nose bone types may reflect sample size rather than a real phenomenon. In other words, such diversity in nose bone design may have been present in a number of the other regions, but our

6. ORNAMENTS

TABLE 6.7. Presence of nose bones recorded in museum collections. **Bold** = museum presence; *italics* = ethnography indicated only.

REGION	FOREHEAD PENDANT TYPES RECORDED	OSSEOUS COMPONENT UTILISED
Kimberley	**Type 8; Type 9; Type ?**	macropod fibula or tibia; large bird radius
Fitzmaurice	**Type 3**	large bird radius
North	*Type 3; Type 4; Type 8*	large bird radius
Arnhem	**Type 1; Type 2; Type ?** *Type 1; Type 2*	macropod fibula or tibia
Desert	**Type 1; Type 2; Type 3; Type 7; Type 8; Type ?** *Type 1; Type 4; Type 7*	macropod fibula or tibia; large bird radius; emu long bone (?)
Gulf	**Type 3** *present (unknown type)*	large bird radius
Torres Strait	[none identified]	
West Cape	*Type 3*	large bird radius
East Cape	**Type 2; Type 3** *Type 6*	macropod fibula or tibia; macropod rib (?); dugong bone
Rainforest	**Type 3; Type 6** *Type 3; Type 4*	macropod fibula or tibia; macropod (?) rib; large bird radius
Northeast	*Type 1 or 2; Type 3*	swan radius; hawk radius; macropod fibula
Southeast	**Type 1; Type 2; Type 5; Type 6** *Type 3; Type 8*	macropod fibula or tibia; emu bone (?)
Tasmania	*Type 1 or 2*	macropod fibula or tibia
Riverine	**Type 4; Type 5** *Type 5; Type 3 (?)*	macropod fibula or tibia; emu bone
Spencer	[none identified]	
Eyre	**Type 1; Type 3; Type ?** *present (unknown type)*	large bird radius
Southwest	**Type 5** *Type 8*	macropod fibula or tibia; emu (?) bone; large bird radius
Northwest	**Type 1; Type 4** *present (unknown type)*	macropod fibula or tibia; large bird radius

limited dataset currently does not reflect this possible reality. However, despite the variety present in the Desert region, an apparent preference for Types 3 and 7 Nose Bones in the available museum assemblages is seen.

Types of decorations seen in photographs or on museum-curated nose bones include engraved lines, which usually appear as short, sub-parallel lines spaced across the bone or in groups. These engravings are seen on Type 1, Type 2, and Type 4 Nose Bones. The well-represented Type 7 Nose Bones feature spatulate extremities and frequently display a series of sub-parallel lines on the convex surface, some with these lines found all the way along their length, while others have groups of lines gathered at either extremity. Insight into what these marks may represent is provided by Donald Thomson, who recorded that on a particular example he collected from Lake Hazlett in the Central Desert, the engraved lines were annual marks made by the owner (Item DT004507 notes, Museum Victoria). Cross-hatching appears on several Type 3 Nose Bones from the Desert region, as do groups of sub-parallel lines, with a couple of examples from the Gulf region featuring cross-hatched sections at each extremity. Single incised lines spiralling down the length of the tube were also noted and appear to be unique to the Kimberley region.

Attached decorations include the tips of rabbit-kangaroo or peragale tails (Desert region) or eagle or bright-coloured parrot (rosella, various cockatoos) feathers inserted into one hollow end (for Types 3 and 4) (Desert region). One example from the Arrernte features a tuft of 'dog tail' at one end. Knobs of resin are also commonly seen tipping the condyle (proximal) end of Type 1 or 2 Nose Bones and one or both ends of those made on hollow bone (such as Type 3). Red ochre residue consistent with incidental skin-to-ornament transfer, rather than intentional painted decoration, is also very commonly found on curated nose bones of all types.

Nose bones feature in early European descriptions of Indigenous Australians and provide a number of insights into not only who would wear these ornaments but when during their life they would acquire this ornament. Regarding the North and Arnhem regions, Basedow (1927:230–1) mentions that the Laragia (Larrakia) (North region) 'pinch a hole through the flesh with their finger nails' before a child can walk, while Campbell (1914:171), quoting Stoddart on Melville Island/Port Essington (North region), stated that 'the *septum nari* is invariably perforated; but it is on particular occasions only that they introduced a bone or piece of wood through it, and sometimes a feather'. While these authors suggest that both men and women had their nasal septum pierced, Earl (1846:240) found that on the Cobourg Peninsula and east coast (North region), it was only men that had this modification.

In western Arnhem Land, it appears that it was primarily (or only) women who had their nasal septa pierced. Berndt and Berndt (1964:183) recorded that here, 'when a girl is about seven or eight years of age her nasal septum is pierced', while Betty Meehan (1975) noted that bone awls were used for piercing the hole through the nasal septum, and Thomson (1946) mentions that nose bones (Type 1 and 2) were utilised by women to strike their scalp during mourning (see 'Awls' in Chapter 5).

Regarding the use of nose bones further south, Forrest (1876:317) comments of the peoples who live in Central Australia (Desert region) that 'boring their noses also is quite a ceremony with them, and once a year hundreds gather together in order to bore the noses of the younger men', while Berndt and Berndt (1964:185) state that in the Great Victorian Desert, 'there are minor excitements of a more formal kind in children's lives in some areas piercing of the nasal septum'. They mention both girls and boys undergoing this operation, as does Chewings for the Arrernte:

> The two former operations [cicatrices or keloids and boring of the nasal septum] are performed by male relatives when the boys and girls are twelve or thirteen years old.

6. ORNAMENTS

> Both are regarded as improvements to the appearance, or presence, and the young people readily submit to the operations. (Chewings 1936:112)

More detail is provided for the Arrernte and surrounding communities (Desert region), for whom Spencer and Gillen state that:

> To the north of the Arunta there do not appear to be any ceremonies attendant on the operation of boring the nasal septum. In the Arunta, Ilpirra, and Unmatjera tribes a boy, immediately after the operation, which is conducted by his father or elder brother, rips a piece of bark from a tree and throws it as far as he can in the direction of the Alcheringa camp of his mother, just as later on he throws his tooth. A girl, whose nose is first bored by her husband, takes a small pitchi, fills it with sand, and keeping her feet close together, jumps about moving the pitchi as if she were winnowing seed. In the Kaitish the operation is performed by an *ertwali* (wife's father), and is carried out during warm weather. In the Warramunga there is a tradition that the operation was first performed in the Alcheringa by an old crow who used his beak for the purpose. In all tribes a nose-bone or stick, or, during ceremonies, a bunch of leafy twigs, is often worn through the hole at the choice of the individuals, but these are much more frequently seen in the central tribes than in those on the coast. At the present day no significance of any kind is attached to the custom, the stick or bone being merely worn as an ornament. The only object of any real import worn through the hole is the mysterious *kupitja*, the mark of the medicine man amongst the Warramunga. (Spencer & Gillen 1904:615)

Chewings notes how nose bones were worn for special occasions:

> On the following day she is decorated as a bride: a cord, to which rat-tail tips are fastened, is wound round and round her head; her body, face, and arms are painted with red lines; and she wears a nose-bone in her nose. (Chewings 1936:102)

Regarding the use of nose bones further east into the Gulf region, Leichhardt describes a friendly interaction with several men between the Albert and Flinders rivers:

> They were altogether fine men. Three or four old men with grey beards were amongst them; and they introduced a young handsome lad to me, with a net on his head and a quill through his nose, calling him 'Yappar'. He was probably a youth of the Yappar tribe who had been sent forward as a messenger to inform them of our having passed through that country. (Leichhardt 1847:349)

Roth notes for North Queensland (Cape York Peninsula) that:

> The nose may be found pierced in both sexes, e.g. Pennefather, Middle Embley, Palmer, Endeavour, and Bloomfield Rivers, Cape Bedford, and whole North West Queensland; pierced in the males, sometimes in the females, e.g. Princess Charlotte Bay; in males alone, e.g. Cape Grafton and apparently in the Wellesley islands; sometimes in the males it being non-obligatory, e.g. Rockhampton . . . The implement used for the operation is either a pointed piece of bone or hardened wood. (Roth 1910b:29)

He continues by stating that 'nose-pins afford much variety in shape, size, and material' and that 'between the Mitchell and Staaten Rivers, amongst the Gunannni, the men alone make and use bone ones' (Roth 1910b:30).

Dalleburra (Dalla) people in North Queensland produced two kinds of bone awls, one of which (known as nooringyooroo) was made on bird bone and used for piercing the septum of the nose (Bennett 1927:410). Roth (1907, 1904:25) also noted the use of bone awls in piercing the nasal septum in North Queensland, with a Type 3 Nose Bone from Cape Bedford (East Cape region) noted to have been worn by both sexes in the accompanying museum note. Also found was a striking portrait taken by Thomson of a Wik Monkan (Wik Mungkan) (West Cape region) woman in mourning—she wears a long (approximately 15 centimetre), hollow Type 3 Nose Bone. The possible source of this long, curved nose bone is given by Jardine (1866:81), who describes for Somerset on the very tip of Cape York (East Cape region) that 'the septum of the nose is pierced, and the crescent-shaped tooth of the dugong is worn in it on state occasions'.

Regarding the use of nose bones further south by Turrbal people of the present-day Brisbane area, the perforation was made with the point of a spear:

> or the *Chepara* bored the septum of the nose with a pointed kangaroo bone, the perforation being kept open by a rounded piece of wood, which was frequently turned round in the hole, water being allowed to trickle through . . . These are only a few instances of a very wide Australian practice. (Howitt 2001[1904]:740–41)

Petrie (1904:48, 54–5) also describes how the nasal septum of young men was pierced at the time of initiation into manhood in the Moreton Bay area (Northeast region) and that:

> when about to have a corroboree . . . men always had their noses pierced (women never had), and it was considered a great thing to have a bone through one's nose! This bone was generally taken from a swan's wing, but it might be from a hawk's wing, or a small bone from the kangaroo's leg; and was supposed to be about four inches long. It was only worn during corrobborees or fights, and was called the '*buluwalam*'. (Petrie 1904:19–20)

He further describes how:

> the aborigines painted their bodies according to the tribe to which they belonged, so in a corrobboree or fight they were recognised at once by one another . . . And of course, the rest of the dress added to the spectacle—the native dogs' tails round their heads, the bones in their noses, and various belts and other arrangements. (Petrie 1904:21–2)

Interestingly, this record was yet another mention of dingo tails as a common accoutrement on special occasions.

Regarding the use of nose bones in southeastern Australia, Howitt (2001[1904]:636) described how boys were given their nose bone after initiation: 'after this the boys were dressed as men, with a red forehead band, a nose-peg, reed necklace, armlets, and with their faces marked with *naial*—that is, red ochre'. He further talks about how the perforation of the nasal septum 'was usually made when the boy was growing up, but some time before he was initiated' where:

6. ORNAMENTS

he lies down on his back, and his friend takes hold of the septum of his nose, extends it, moistens it with saliva, and then rapidly pierces it with a sharp bone instrument ... This proceeding is supposed to aid the *Ngrung-kong* in causing him to grow big and strong. A peg called *Gumbart* is left in until the wound is healed. The perforation in the septum of the nose in the Wurunjerri tribe was made when the child was about twelve years of age. It is called *Ilbi-jerri*. The old men performed the operation for the boys, and the old women for the girls, and it was in the winter-time that this was done. The parents would say to the child, 'you must get ready your bone; make it nice and sharp, so that a hole can be made in your nose'. After the bone had been pushed through the nose and left there, the child scraped a small hole in the ground, placed in it some stones heated in the fire, covered it with some earth, and poured water on it. It then held its head, covered with an opossum skin rug, over the steam until the peg became loose, and could be turned round. It did this every night and morning till the place was healed. The perforation was not made by the Yuin til the boy had been initiated, and was permitted to return to the camp from his probation in the bush. The nose-hole is called *Guraw*, and the nose-peg *Kurt-bagur*. (Howitt 2001[1904]:740–1)

Curr (1965[1883]:116) makes similar observations inland at Goulburn River in Victoria for the Bangerang people, that 'like the men, the women had the septum of the nose pierced' and that 'at ten or eleven years of age the boy was made a *kogomoolga*, gave up the name which he had hitherto borne ... the septum of his nose was pierced, and a bone stuck through it by way of ornament' (Curr 1965[1883]:117).

At Sydney Harbour, Collins recorded how:

between the ages of eight and sixteen, the males and females undergo the operation which they term *Gnah-noong*, viz that of having the *septum nasi* bored, to receive a bone or reed, which among them is deemed a great ornament, though I have seen many whose articulation was thereby rendered very imperfect. (Collins 1975[1798]:466)

In another account, he describes how:

Some boys who went away from us for a few days, returned dignified with this strange ornament, having, in the mean time, had the operation performed upon them; they appeared to be from twelve to fifteen years of age. The bone that they wear is the small bone in the leg of the kangaroo, one end of which is sharpened to a point. I have seen several women who had their noses perforated in this extraordinary manner. (Collins 1975[1798]:458)

Also, in Sydney from 1788, Hunter provides his own firsthand observations, stating that:

Some of the men wear a piece of wood or bone, thrust through the septum of the nose, which by raising the opposite sides of the nose, widens the nostril, and spreads the lower part very much; this, no doubt, they consider as a beauty. (Hunter 1968[1793]:41)

He also mentions:

two women were met with who had the septum on the nose perforated. One of them

> was Barangaroo, who now visited the settlement daily, in company with her husband, and seemed to be pleased as though she thought herself drest when her nose was occasionally ornamented with a small bone or a bit of stick. (Hunter 1968[1793]:317)

Some 50 years later, Backhouse (1967[1843]:434) saw how, at Kangaroo Ground, Cambewarra, 'all the men ... had the cartilages of their noses perforated, and bones, the thickness of a quill, and about four inches long, through them'.

In this region (Southeast region), it appears that nose bones were also an article of trade. Howitt describes that for Yuin people:

> At the termination of these ceremonies, when the novices had gone away into the bush for their time of probation, and when the people were about to separate, there was held a kind of market ... A complete set of articles is one *Ngulia* or belt opossum-fur string, four *Burrain* or men's kilts, one *Gumbrum* or bone nose-peg, and a complete set of corroboree ornaments. It was the rule that a complete set went together. (Howitt 2001[1904]:718)

Howitt (2001[1904]:525) describes how this set of a 'man's full ceremonial dress' is usually given to him by a relative or friend and, interestingly, that 'the wearing of this set is not confined to manhood, for small sets are sometimes made to please little boys'.

Bennett (1967[1834]:176), talking in general terms about the peoples of New South Wales he encountered as he travelled from Sydney through Yass and Canberra (Southeast and Riverine regions), states that 'both sexes have the *septum naris* perforated, in which a piece of straw, stick or emu-bone is worn'. He later specifies that 'the fibula bone of the leg [of the emu] is used [as] an ornament by the natives' (Bennett 1967[1834]:298).

Regarding the use of nose bones further inland in the Riverine region, Brough Smyth reported observations by Dr Gummow (of Swan Hill) in the Lower Murray (Riverine region). He thus speaks of the bone, Mellee-mellee-u, which is carried in the septum of the nose:

> Enclosed is a sort of awl made from the thigh-bone of the emu, called *Pin-kee*, which is used for boring the septum of the nostrils, also for perforating opossum skins when sewing them together to form rugs (*Pirri-wee*). The sinews of the kangaroo tail were used as thread, and called *Wirr-ran-nee*. After using the perforator called *Pin-kee* for piercing the septum of the nose, a piece of reed is slipped on to the point as a canal, and as the *Pin-kee* is withdrawn, the reed as a sheath, the latter is left to act as a tent, so as to dilate the opening. Gradually increasing the size of the reeds until the opening is sufficiently large, the *Mellee-mellee-u*—a piece of bone from the leg of the emu or the kangaroo—is finally inserted, and this remains in the septum for the nostrils of the males until the front teeth are knocked out. The females undergo the same treatment, and wear during their lives a ring of bone, cut from the wing of the bustard (*Naroo-vee*). The ring, called *Kolko*, is more than one-third of an inch in length, and the diameter is two-thirds of an inch. The aperture in the ring forms a foramen between the nostrils. (Brough Smyth 1972[1876]a:277)

This report is interesting, as it indicates that nose bones made on different raw materials may have been preferred or otherwise dictated between the sexes.

6. ORNAMENTS

The use of bone awls or needles to pierce the nasal septum is also noted along the Darling River:

> some boys, when about the age of ten, have a hole bored through the septum of the nose with bone needles (*peongeotah*), in which they can, when grown up, wear a bone about 6 inches long as an ornament at their dances. (Bonney 1884:126)

Sturt (1834:105) too saw that men are seen to wear nose bones on the Darling River—'bones through the cartilage of the nose'—while Mitchell (1965[1839]b:345) observed both sexes wearing nose bones while travelling the Darling and Murray rivers (Riverine region) and noted that 'when danger is apprehended, a small bone or piece of reed' was worn.

In Gippsland, this ornamentation appears to have been restricted to men, with Howitt noting for the Kurnai that:

> The perforation of the septum of the nose was usually made while the boy was growing up, but some time before he was initiated. It might be that some of the men would notice him as 'growing'. The young men, his friends, might say to him, 'You ought to have '*Ngrŭng*'; it wont hurt you'. He consents. He then lies down on his back, some friend takes hold of the septum of his nose, extends it, moistens it with saliva, and then rapidly pierces it with a sharp bone instrument. The patient must not show any sign of feeling pain. He then jumps up and extends his arms out quickly from the shoulder, and jerks each leg in succession. This proceeding being supposed to aid the '*Ngrŭng-Kong*' in causing him to grow big and strong. (Fison & Howitt 1991[1880]:191)

Also for Gippsland, Reverend Bulmer is reported as finding that:

> it was considered proper to bore the septum of the nose. Indeed it was ordained that the septum should be pierced, and that each person should wear in it a piece of bone, a reed, or the stalk of some grass, the name of the ornament being *Boon-joon*. The old men used to predict to those who were avert [sic] to this mutilation all kinds of evils. If it were omitted at the prior time, the sinner would suffer—not in this world, but in the next. (Brough Smyth 1972[1876]a:274)

Brough Smyth also records other names for the ornament in Victoria:

> The bone, or a piece of reed, worn in the septum of the nose, called *Noute-kower*. The bone of some animal—generally a bone somewhat curved three or more inches in length as passed through a hole made in the septum of the nose, and carried joyfully, as something to gain favour with both sexes. (Brough Smyth 1972[1876]a:271)

In another case, he states that:

> the ornaments worn by a female of the Yarra tribe were few and simple. In the septum of the nose was inserted a piece of the bone of the leg of a kangaroo, called *Ellejerr*. (Brough Smyth 1972[1876]a:273)

A RECORD IN BONE

Observations from around Melbourne made by both George Augustus Robinson and William Buckley are available. The latter described this ornamentation practice for the peoples he lived among west of Port Phillip, stating that:

> many of the women have rings made out of the bones of birds suspended from the inside of their nostrils, and the men have a small straight bone with a sort of knob at one end. Those who have the most ornaments are considered the most fashionable and attractive. (Flannery 2009:95)

This practice continued as Port Phillip grew, with Augustus Robinson entering in his journal for 4 June 1841 that:

> among the other ornaments and decorations for the dance, the native women thrust a large bone through a hole in the cartilage of their nose. These holes are perforated when young. I saw a young woman today make sad grimaces whilst she squeezed or thrust a large bone through the hole. I gave her, at the conclusion of the dance which lasted about an hour, a handkerchief for this bone which I consider as a curiosity and which I propose exhibiting to my fair countrywomen—not that I suppose they will imitate the example. I however deem it a curiosity. These bones are called *yal.lung. gub.boeng* and are scraped and prepared and made round—and some are sharp at each end (Clark 2000b:244).

Regarding the use of nose bones further west in Spencer, Wyatt commented that Aboriginal people of the Adelaide and Encounter Bay area had:

> other minor ceremonies or customs, such as the perforation of the septum of the nose for the reception of a bone or reed, said to be a token of mourning, for the death of a mother or near relative. (Wyatt 2009[1879]:164)

Here, the use of these ornaments appears to change between the communities of the Riverine and neighbouring Spencer regions.

A detailed description of how the Dieyeri (Diyari) (north of Adelaide, Spencer region) conducted the piercing, which is recorded as being called moodlawillpa, is as follows:

> This operation is inflicted on the boy or girl at the age of from five to ten years. The father generally proposes to the other denizens of the camp, to have his child's nose pierced, and one old man is selected to perform the ceremony, which is usually done at mid-day. A piece of wood, six inches long, from a tree called *Cooyamurra* (a species of acacia), is poised at one end sufficiently sharp to pierce the nose, the partition of which the operation takes in his left hand, while he pierces it with the right. A few minutes before, and during the operation, the men and women sing, believing that by singing a great deal of the pain is taken away from the child. The hole being made, a large quill about a quarter of an inch in diameter is placed in it to prevent it from closing up, and kept there until the wound is thoroughly healed. The word *Moodlawillpa* is derived from *moodla* (nose), and *willpa* (hole), hole in the nose. (Gason 2009[1879]:266).

6. ORNAMENTS

The only mention found in ethnographies regarding nose bones for the Eyre region is for people living at Cooper Creek, where Howitt noted that:

> a hole is bored through the cartilage of the nose, and in it is worn a long pointed bone, which has two uses—to extract thorns from the feet and to scratch the head. I sometimes have seen, instead of the bone, two feathers stuck through. (Howitt 1972[1876]:302)

More detail is available for the Southwest region, beginning with a detailed account by Hassell and Davidson:

> Just before the boys left the parent tribe to go away with another tribe as part of their invitations they had to go through the ceremony of *noilyet*, or the piercing of the septum of the nose. They were gathered together and each held by his father or next of kin, who firmly held the head between his hands while the *mulgar* pierced the septum with a sharp pointed stick and then inserted a piece of kangaroo bone. This was about two and one half inches long and one eight inch thick. The ends were finally ground to sharp points. One side was slightly rounded, the other flat. This bone, which was called *noilyet*, was worn until the boy returned from his leg visit. On his return and before he took a wife it was withdrawn by the *mulgar* in the presence of the entire tribe. He was then considered a man ... When the men went to war these bones are placed in the nose of each by the *mulgar* and were worn until peace was made. Should a native be sent on a peace errand he went along and wore his nose-bone with an upward turn. At all other times it was worn straight across his face. A messenger could thus be recognised by all who saw him. (Hassell E &Davidson 1936:685)

A similar name for the nose bone is provided for King George Sound in this same region: 'in the boys' noses, to admit the *Mulyat* when they arrive at years of puberty ... and sometimes it serves to extract teeth' (Moore 1884:23).

Regarding the use of nose bones in the Perth area (Southwest region), Chauncy reported that:

> the natives [along the Swan River] use a number of different kinds of ornaments, especially the men, who ... wear bunches of emu fathers on the arms, a wild dog's tail round the head just over the brow, and bunches of beautiful long feathers of the large black cockatoo or of the white cockatoo on the top of the head. The young men wear the small bone of the leg of the kangaroo through the cartilage of the nose as a sign of their having attained the age of puberty. (Chauncy 1972[1876]:251)

Breton (1834:22) at the Canning River states that 'many of them had thrust a feather, a bone, or a piece of wood through the septum of the nose'. Breton (1834:167) further mentions that 'their disfiguring themselves by thrusting a bone through the septum of the nose, and adorning their heads with feathers, is a practice which I understand prevails along the whole western coast'. Another general observation for Western Australia is given by Backhouse, who states that:

> In Western Australia, the blacks perforate the cartilage of the noses of the boys, when about twelve, or fourteen years of age; a kangaroo-bone, of the thickness of a goose-quill, is occasionally worn through the hole. (Backhouse 1967[1843]:542)

Finally, less information is available for Tasmania, though Bonwick (1870:37) includes an illustration of a Tasmanian dancer wearing a kangaroo nose bone and kangaroo incisor forelock pendants, suggesting that these ornaments were also present in at least some of these communities.

Of these ethnographic observations, Hassell and Davidson's (1936) account for the Southwest region is particularly interesting for the description of how wearing the nose bone in different manners transmitted different messages to the viewer. Comments regarding the importance of having the nasal septum pierced in some communities ('the old men used to predict to those who were avert to this mutilation all kinds of evils'; Brough Smyth 1972[1876]a:274) are also insightful, while authors for other regions appear to suggest that this alteration was purely for appearance. Whether or not the recorders were simply unaware of attitudes and beliefs in those places can only be known through further consultation with communities.

Archaeological finds of nose bones are currently rare. However, the oldest bone artefact thus far identified on the Australian continent (Carpenters Gap 1, the Kimberley) is identified as a probable nose bone owing to its morphology, use wear, and residues (Langley et al. 2016), as are more fragmentary finds dating to about 7500–7000 cal BP from Wee Jasper, located in the foothills of the Namadji Ranges (Theden-Ringl & Langley 2018). Mulvaney (1962:13) also suggested that one or more of the bone artefacts recovered from Aire River Shelter II, dating to 370 years or later, could have been nose bones. Finally, Lampert (1966) reports that 11 complete bipoints, which averaged 165 millimetres in length, were found at Port McDonnell, South Australia, and that 'all specimens in this last group are distinctly curved' (Lampert 1966:112), suggesting that they were nose bones rather than another artefact form.

Local names recorded for this ornament include the following.

Nose bone (unspecified):
- tjauwalla (Trial Bay, East Arnhem, Arnhem region; Item DT001060 notes, Museum Victoria)
- keeaala (Daly Waters, Desert region; Item A32562 notes, South Australian Museum)
- bunderi (Nggerikudi, West Cape region; Roth 1903b)
- rau-wòr-injala (Gunanni (Gonaniin), West Cape region; Roth 1910b)
- buluwalam (Moreton Bay, Northeast region; Petrie 1904)
- nang-oon (Port Jackson area, Southeast region; Hunter 1963[1793])
- gumbart (Kurnai, Southeast region; Howitt 2001[1904])
- kurt-bagur or gumbrum (Yuin, Southeast region; 2001[1904])
- yal.lung.gub.boeng (Port Phillip area, Riverine region; Clark 2000b)
- nautekauer (Victoria; Brough Smyth 1972[1876]a).

Type 1 Nose Bone:
- yungguyu ngakkara (East Arnhem, Arnhem region; Item DT001061 notes, Museum Victoria)

6. ORNAMENTS

- djmargulon (Lake Hazlett, Desert region; Item DT004507 notes, Museum Victoria)
- yauanda-munbarra (Northampton, Northwest region; Item X000866 notes, Museum Victoria).

Type 3 Nose Bone:
- lalkira or lalkera (Arrernte, Desert region; Chewings 1936)
- ti:lunba (Tomkinson Ranges, Desert region; Item A54770 notes, South Australian Museum)
- walawuru taruka (Ernabella, Musgrave Range, Desert region; Item A21731 notes, South Australian Museum)
- buluwalam (Brisbane, Northeast region; Petrie 1904).

Type 4 Nose Bone:
- kolko (Lower Murray River, Riverine region; item X001581 notes, Museum Victoria).

Type 5 Nose Bone:
- mili-mili-u or mellee-mellee-u (Lower Murray River, Riverine region; Brough Smyth (1972[1876]a:277).

Type 6 Nose Bone:
- pandari (Mapoon, West Cape region; Item E011800 notes, Australian Museum).

Type 7 Nose Bone:
- lalkira or lalkera (Arrernte, Desert region; Chewings 1936).

Masks
Description
Masks are full-face coverings with many components made from different organic materials.

Manufacture and use
The cultures of Torres Strait Islander peoples are the only cultures in the world to make turtle shell masks, known as krar (turtle shell) in the Western Islands and le-op (human face) in the Eastern Islands. The main section is made from turtle shell, with smaller additions made from turtle shell and other organic materials. The turtle shell is pierced or cut to be connected to the main section, as shown by two examples in the National Museum of Australia. These masks have perforations around the edge for attaching the various components. Decorative incisions into the mask appear to be painted over with white paint to highlight these details.

TABLE 6.8. Presence of necklace types recorded in museum collections. **Bold** = museum presence; *italics* = ethnography indicated only.

REGION	OSSEOUS COMPONENT UTILISED
Kimberley	**bird beaks; canine teeth; megafauna teeth; snake vertebrae**
Fitzmaurice	**macropod incisors**
North	*echidna quills*
Arnhem	**bird beaks; fish vertebrae; shark vertebrae** *bird beaks; canine teeth and bones; echidna quills; fish/shark vertebrae*
Desert	**eagle talons** *bandicoot tail tips; eagle talons; canine tail tips*
Gulf	*macropod incisors*
Torres Strait	**canine teeth**
West Cape	*macropod incisors; shark vertebrae*
East Cape	*shark vertebrae*
Rainforest	*eel rays*
Northeast	*macropod incisors*
Southeast	**macropod incisors** *canine teeth and bones; echidna quills; macropod incisors; crawfish 'antlers'; wombat claws*
Tasmania	**snake vertebrae; wombat claws** *wombat claws*
Riverine	*bird beaks; echidna quills; macropod incisors; lobster shell; bullock teeth; freshwater fishbones*
Spencer	[none identified]
Eyre	*eagle talons*
Southwest	[none identified]
Northwest	[none identified]

Ornaments worn around the neck

Necklaces of varying length and style are common in early photographs, though curated examples that include hard animal materials are quite rare. Presented below is the currently available data organised according to the type of animal material incorporated (Table 6.8).

Bandicoot

The bones and tail tips of 'rabbit-bandicoots'—including bilbies—saw use not only in the mourning chaplets described above under 'Circlets' but also on necklaces. Spencer and Gillen (1904:691) mention for the Arrernte (Desert region) that 'neck-band[s] with ornaments of small bones fixed in resin and rabbit bandicoot tail-tips [were] worn by men'. An interesting archaeological find that may represent a type of ornamentation was uncovered at the Victorian site of FM/1, located near Lake Alexander. There, an individual was found buried with 'a small heap of twenty-five bandicoot mandibles and other items clustered at the right shoulder' (Coutts & Witter 1977:64), which sounds like a mourning chaplet though this interpretation may never be confirmed.

Bird skulls and beaks

The skulls and beaks of birds see more use in neck ornaments than bandicoot parts, with two necklaces featuring 'water bird beaks' from the Kimberley region curated in the National Museum of Australia and a 'dance ornament' including a beak of a spoonbill from Milingimbi, Arnhem Land, in the Queensland Museum. This last necklace is recorded as having been worn by men. Interestingly, Kim Akerman (personal communication, 14 March 2022) observed that necklaces featuring the beaks of spoonbills, either as single pendants or as a series attached using beeswax, were worn by young people during specific teaching events in Arnhem Land.

Regarding the use of bird skulls and beaks on the other side of the continent, Worsnop (1897:158) wrote that 'on the Lower Murray I saw a necklace … on which were fastened downy feathers of the goose, shells, the mandible of a duck, the upper mandible of a black swan and tuffs of human hair'. Near Lake Alexandrina in this same area, Angas (1967[1847]:60) describes a four-year-old boy called Rimmelliperingery, whom he met with his parents: 'Rimmelliperingery is the pride of his tribe, and wears the upper mandible of the black swan round his neck; which is regarded as a *gunwarrie* or wizard charm'.

A 5500-year-old example of this type of ornament may be provided by Grave 108 at Roonka (Spencer region). Here the body of a small child was found with a bird skull pendant resting on their chest (Pretty 1977).

Bullock teeth

Mitchell (1965[1839]b:93) reports that on his 1836 (24 May) journey along the Darling River:

> we now ascertained through Piper, that the tribe had fled precipitately from the Darling last year, to the country westward, and did not return until last summer, when they found the two bullocks we left there; which, having become fat, they had killed and eaten. We also ascertained, that some of the natives then in the camp, wear the teeth of the slaughtered animals, and that they had much trouble in killing one of them, as it was remarkably fierce. (Mitchell 1965[1839]b:93)

This example provides an interesting case of the integration of materials from an introduced species into a community's ornamentation repertoire.

Canine teeth and bones

The teeth of dingos, and later camp dogs, appear to have been used in a number of regions. Isabelle McBryde (1974:12) describes that for the Hunter Valley and corresponding southeast coast, 'ornaments included shell pendants, necklaces of cane cut into lengths and strung like beads, dogs' teeth, and of coloured beans, all worn by the men, not the women' were utilised.

Regarding the use of canine teeth and bones further inland in the Arrernte lands (Desert regions), Spencer and Gillen talked about the following:

> the commonest form of neck-band in the Arunta tribe consists of a single thick strand of fur-string profusely coated with grease and red ochre so as to have a smooth surface. It is closely similar to the ordinary woman's headband. A second form frequently met with amongst the tribes consists of four or five strands united together at either end. Sometimes they form a flat, band-like structure, but more often . . . the strands are coiled upon one another. From each end passes off a string which serves to tie the band round the neck. Very often the ends of the strings are ornamented with tassels of feathers, birds' down, dingo or rabbit bandicoot tail-tips attached to a central stick. Neck-bands of this form are worn by both men and women, but the ornamented ones are more frequently seen on the former than on the latter. (Spencer & Gillen)

A single dingo molar almost entirely encased in resin—only the crown is exposed—and attached to a length of human hair string has been collected from Halls Creek in the Kimberley region. This item is recorded simply as a 'pendant' in the accompanying museum notes, so it could have been worn on the forehead, from the neck or both.

Finally, canine teeth are a popular choice for ornaments in the Torres Strait. Here, necklaces made of many dog incisors (some including more than 80 individual teeth) are made, with each incisor threaded one after the other and strung such that the teeth lay flat against the chest. Close examination of these adornments is required for more details about their attachment; however, it does appear that each of these teeth is perforated.

Dasyurid bones

Dasyurids include the Tasmanian devil, quolls, and numbats, as well as smaller marsupials. While some bones from these species may have been utilised in the making of mourning circlets described above, the only currently known example of their use in a necklace comes from the archaeological record. The skeleton of an infant found buried alongside an adult (Grave 63) at Roonka (Spencer region) was found with:

> two mandibular segments of a dasyurid (native cat) . . . in the pelvic region. They may have originally been higher up the body and fallen down. A neat attachment hole has been drilled in the ascending ramus of each mandible. (Pretty 1977:315)

Another archaeological find from a site known as FM/1 in Western Victoria (Riverine region) may provide a second example. Here, 'twenty-five bandicoot mandible and other items clustered at the right shoulder' of a buried individual may represent a mourning chaplet or another type of ornament (Coutts & Witter 1977:64).

Eagle talons

Talons from eagles and other large birds of prey see use in both the interior (Desert region) and Central Queensland (Eyre region). As in the sorcery charms described in Chapter 5, the talons were mounted in resin (no perforation or notching required)

6. ORNAMENTS

FIGURE 6.10. Eaglehawk talons are used as a feature piece on headbands and necklaces worn by women in Central Australia.

and attached to the ends of cords (Chewings 1936; Roth 1897; Spencer & Gillen 1904) (see Figure 6.10). The cords could be wound round the head or neck to serve either as a headband, with claws hanging, or as a necklace, with the talon pendants resting on the chest or back. The talons make a pleasant tinkling sound when they knock against each other.

Spencer and Gillen (1904:692) specify that the talons used in the Desert were from eaglehawks (see Figure 6.10), while Roth (1897) noted that eagle talons were traded to the Boulia district (Eyre region) from the north. Roth states that chest ornaments of:

> large eagle-hawk's claws, two of which are attached moon-shape-like into a piece of cement; two of such double-claw hoops may be fixed to the same neck-string. The claw is brought to Boulia from the north, both from the Georgina River, and down the Burke and Wills Rivers. (Roth 1910b:36)

He records that the Pitta-Pitta name for this ornament is 'mingkara', while the 'Kalkadun' (Kalkatungu) name is pi-ko.

Echidna quills

Echidna quills appear to have been used fairly widely, not only as medical instruments (see Chapter 5) but also to ornament necklaces and headpieces (see 'Forehead pendants' above). Unlike most elements used to create personal adornment on the Australian continent, echidna quills were perforated for stringing. Dawson (1981[1881]:25) describes how:

> in making necklaces of the quills of the porcupine ant-eater, the holes at the roots of the quills are burned through with a wooden pin made red-hot in the fire.

This firsthand account of artists in Western Victoria (Riverine region) matches the rare necklaces curated in Australian museums. The South Australian Museum curates an exceptional example—a full collar of echidna spines—collected from Lake Condah (Southeast region). A very similar-looking necklace is seen in a photograph by Fred Kruger illustrating 'a variety of implements and weapons at Coranderrk, Victoria, circa. 1877', while Edge-Partington (1969[1890–98]:Fig. 7) includes a drawing of this same type of necklace from the Alligator River in the Northern Territory. Those currently curated, as well as those illustrated, are perforated at the thicker extremity, which was originally embedded within the echidna's muscle, the dark-tipped sharp points pointing down and away from the string.

While such necklaces can use a couple of hundred individual quills to complete, a single large echidna could provide all the required materials.

Eel rays

The bony rays that support the gill membranes behind the lower jaw of the eel are noted to have been utilised on the Queensland coast, with Roth (1910b:Fig. 15) providing a drawing of eel rays cemented together with resin and attached to string worn at the Tully River, south of Cairns (Rainforest region) (see Figure 6.11). More detail is provided by Hamlyn-Harris (1918:9), who states that such pendants were:

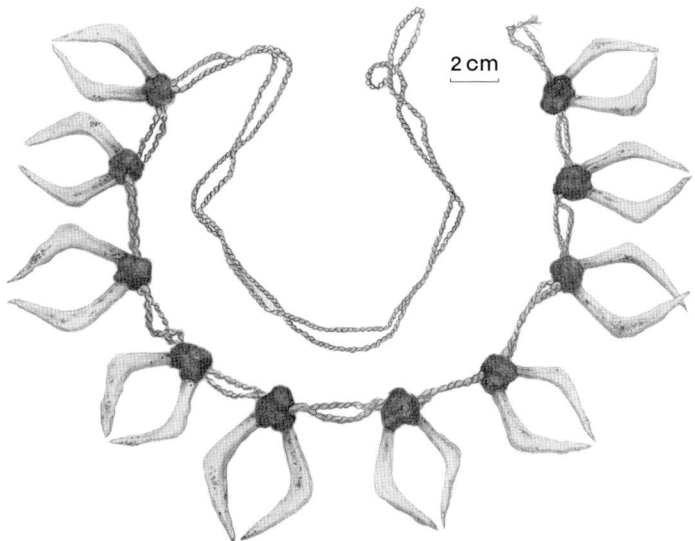

FIGURE 6.11. Eel rays create a neckline from the Rainforest region.

6. ORNAMENTS

in use by young boys when being initiated into manhood. They are worn hanging on the chest and the opposing tribe is supposed to throw spears at them during the ceremony.

Fish and lobster parts

While these necklaces would have been discounted from this work if adhering to the strict no shellfish rule, they have seen very little attention in the literature and so are included here. The available ethnographic works all pertain to the Murray River (Riverine region). Chauncy (1972[1876]:251) observed that 'the Murray River women make pretty but delicate necklaces with the small bones of the fresh-water lobster', while Augustus Robinson noted in his 1841 journal that a person from Port Phillip 'gave me a necklace called *too.ger.mun* made of the antlers of craw fish'. The rough sketch provided of this item shows what appears to be several individual threads onto which the crawfish antlers are strung, with the strings coming together on each side before a single thread creates the loop (Clark 2000b:71).

In terms of fishbones, Angas, when camping in the Lower Murray, mentions that:

> some of the girls had their cheeks painted bright red with *karkoo*, and one skinny little fellow, having an air of extreme gentility, wore a bunch of the head bones of a mucilaginous fish in his hair as an ornament. (Angas 1967[1847]:13)

More commonly seen in museum archives is the use of small, round vertebrae from fish, which are strung consecutively to form bands of bone beads (see Figure 6.12). These beads are frequently covered in red ochre and threaded on hair or plant fibre string. Strands can be either entirely or only partially covered with the vertebrae beads—that is, only half the strand is beaded, that which hangs over the chest. Several examples of choker-type arrangements with three or four strands of beads coloured red, yellow, and white from Milingimbi (Arnhem region) are held in the South Australian Museum,

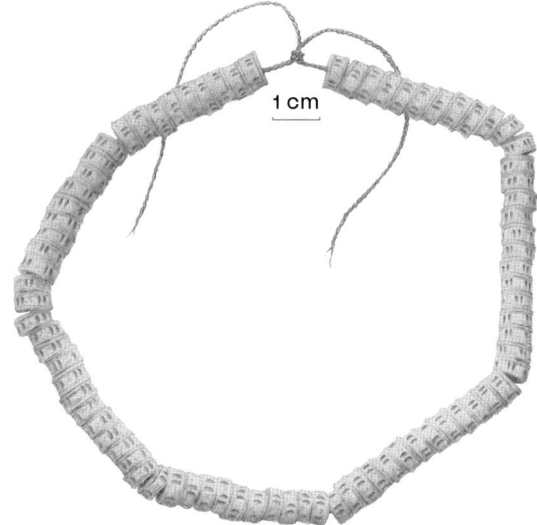

FIGURE 6.12. Fish vertebrae necklaces could be coloured with pigment or left plain.

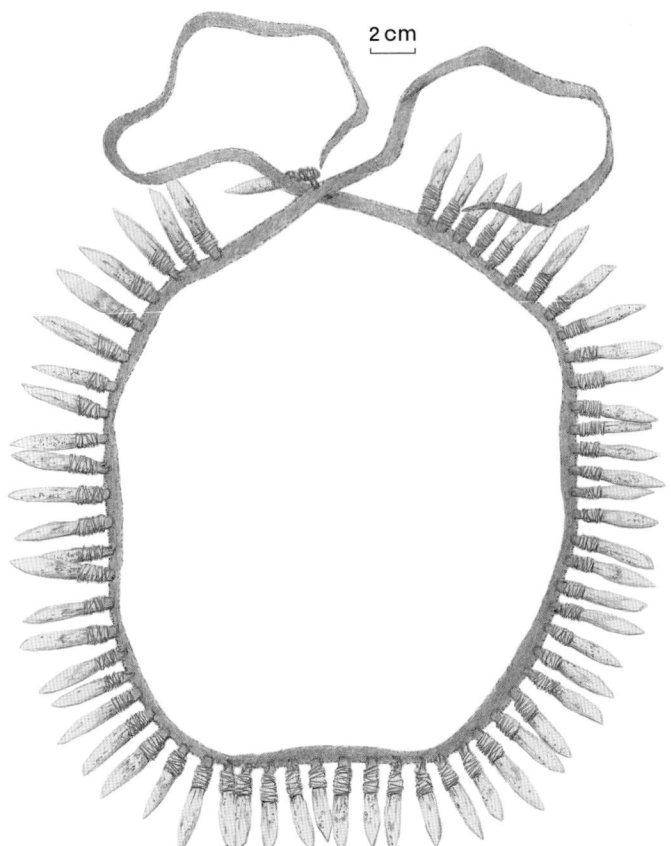

FIGURE 6.13. Macropod incisors are attached to the red leather band by folding short strips of leather over the tooth root and then wrapping the end over using sinew. The short leather pieces were threaded through a hole in the main band prior to being secured to each tooth.

and these strands are recorded as necklaces. Such necklaces collected from Arnhem can be painted or unpainted, and an archaeological example may be six small red-painted vertebrae beads discovered on Mirarr country of West Arnhem (Wright et al. 2016). These beads were originally identified as having come from a shark, but it is possible that they instead came from a large freshwater fish, a problem that needs further research to better distinguish between the vertebrae of fish and those of small sharks.

Macropod teeth

The most common type of necklace in both museum collections and early photographs incorporates multiple macropod lower incisors, macropod leather, and sinew or vegetable string. Each incisor is attached individually to the main strip of leather to form a spray of white points that fan out across the chest and over the shoulders (see figures 6.13 and 1.1). Instead of being pierced, a short strip of leather is folded over the root, and sinew or twine is then wrapped over the tooth and leather strip to bind it together. The shorter leather strip is passed through a small hole punctured in the larger collar strip. The leather frequently appears to be stained or rubbed with red ochre. This method of attachment has been described by several early observers (see below in this section), and this particular form of macropod incisor necklace appears to have some deep antiquity, with stencils of such necklaces seen in both the Arnhem region (Chaloupka 1993) and Carnarvon Gorge, Northeast region (Quinnell 1976).

Illustrations of these necklaces include Lesueur's 1824 image of ornaments from Port Jackson (Southeast region) (Bonnemains et al. 1988:89), as well as studio portraits of both men and women from the Southeast and Northeast regions. In writing, such necklaces are described by William Buckley for the peoples he lived among west of Port Phillip (Riverine region):

> They are very fond of ornaments—the women especially—and in their manufacture, are very ingenious. Their head-bands are netted like silk purses, and they do this kind of work without any needle or other instrument—using their fingers only. They make these bands as even as it could be done by the most experienced person with silk or thread, leaving a piece at each end to tie round the forehead, colouring them with ochre. Their neck ornaments are made like silk velvet guards. Upon these are strung a great number of pieces of shells, and of the teeth of the kangaroo, adding too, the feathers of the swan and emu; the strongest of which they split in the middle, in order to make them more pliable. (Flannery 2009:94–5)

Dawson (1981[1881]:81) described how:

> the usual necklace is formed of from eighty to one hundred kangaroo teeth, tied by theirs roots to a skin cord. This necklace hangs loosely round the neck and displays the teeth diverging towards the shoulder and breast.

Along similar lines, Brough Smyth includes an illustration of the macropod incisor necklace with the accompanying note that:

> this necklace . . . was very common many years ago; but the only examples I have seen have been obtained in the western districts of Victoria. It is formed of a long strip of well-dressed kangaroo skin, to which are attached the teeth (incisors) of the kangaroo. Each tooth is fastened to a small piece of skin by the tail sinews, and is neatly fixed to the long strip by knots based through incisions. The skin is stained with red-ochre; and the contrast of the colours is not unpleasing. (Brough Smyth 1972[1876]a:278)

A footnote on this page of Brough Smyth's volume states that 'Dr Gummow informs me that the incisor teeth of the lower-jaw of the kangaroo—such as are used for a necklace of this kind—are named *Lean-now*' (Brough Smyth 1972[1876]a:278). This comment by Brough Smyth suggests that some forms of ornamentation that were originally quite a common sight upon European settlement had become rare over a short period. This change is obviously the result of disruption to Aboriginal culture and, possibly, a subsequent change to the function of some ornaments. Indeed, it appears that Europeans were collecting these items early on, as exemplified by Augustus Robinson in his journal entry from Sunday 17 November 1839 at Port Phillip, where he notes that 'Billy Lonsdale called and brought a necklace of kangaroo teeth. Gave him one rug, one knife, and rice' (Clark 2000a:101).

Other forms of attaching macropod incisors are known from the Fitzmaurice and Riverine regions. In the Fitzmaurice region, each tooth is again individually set, but this time into resin, and then attached to the main band of fibre string. This form of necklace is noted to have the local name of larinjinnie. An unusual example of this form of necklace is curated in the British Museum, where instead of long lower incisors, the much shorter and squarer upper incisors have been utilised. Forty-nine wallaby upper incisors—each individually attached to the main leather band by their roots being wrapped in sinew and attached to a short strip of leather—make up this ornament. The accompanying note states that this necklace was 'made by Gunditjara and Kirrae Whurrong (Keeray Woorroong) peoples, collected by Augustus Strong, probably from St Marys, Warrnambool, in 1842–44' (Item Oc1847,0413.1 notes, British Museum).

Regarding the use of macropod teeth in ornaments worn around the neck in South West Victoria (Riverine region), Spencer and Gillen noted that plant fibre strings could be used instead of leather straps:

> a necklet with pendants of incisor teeth of kangaroos or wallabies is met with amongst the coastal tribes, and is called *quire* by the Mara. There is a central band made of a considerable number of vegetable-fibre strings somewhat loosely and irregularly bound round by a separate strand. A varying number of pendants is added, each made of a string with a lump of resin at either end into which a kangaroo incisor is fixed. The string is simply tied round the main band so that the pairs of teeth hang down, and lie upon the chest when the necklet is in use. The string is more or less red-ochred, and the teeth are usually coated, with pipe-clay so that they stand out very clearly on the dark skin of the natives. (Spencer & Gillen 1904:694)

Finally, a report of 'pendants worn at the neck include a cluster of macropod teeth set in pigmented gum mounted on string' (Best 2012:10) for the Wellesley Islands (Gulf region) sounds like the forehead pendants described above being also worn on the neck.

An archaeological find at Nawamoyn (North region) by Carmel Schrire (1982) indicates that, in the past, macropod incisors were sometimes perforated for stringing. Here she found just one example of a kangaroo (*Macropus antilopinus*) tooth, perforated through the root, which she suggests may have been an ornament. A second macropod incisor was also found, this one unperforated, which Schrire reports as displaying 'an unusually high gloss on the lingual surface' (Schrire 1982:128). This find in the north appears to mirror an extraordinary find of some 327 pierced kangaroo and wallaby incisors in a burial accidentally exposed at Cooma (Southeast region) in 1991 (Feary 1996). As it needed at least 126 individual animals to create, this beautiful ornament represents a significant amount of effort in its construction—both in the collection of raw materials and the piercing of the tooth roots for stringing. Another apparently similar example was found again as a headband in a burial at Kow Swamp, with this example dated to between 14,000 and 10,000 BP (Dortch 1979), and yet another at Nacurrie in a Terminal Pleistocene–aged burial (Brown 1989).

6. ORNAMENTS

Shark vertebrae

Necklaces made from shark vertebrae—known as nangana or ngaraka—have been collected from Elcho Island (Arnhem region) and are the same style as those made on fish vertebrae (described above). These necklaces are also known from mainland Arnhem (specifically Yirrkala) and include both painted and unpainted examples, as well as from West Cape York (Batavia River), where it is specified that the vertebrae came from young sharks (Roth 1910b:34). Thomson photographed men from the Edward River wearing these ornaments, while Roth (1903b:11) recorded that the Nggerikudi (West Cape region) name for a shark bone necklace was anga.

Snake vertebrae

Snake vertebrae were used to make bead necklaces, similar to fish or shark vertebrae. In the Kimberley, these necklaces consist of individual vertebrae threaded onto string through the intervertebral foramina (hole in the middle of each vertebra). A necklace from Looma has beads threaded only along half the length of the string so that only the part that falls directly across the chest is beaded. Another necklace of snake vertebrae, unpainted, is noted as having been collected from Tasmania (currently curated in the National Museum of Australia).

Again, Roonka (Spencer region) provides an archaeological example. On the body of the small child in Grave 108, 'a coiled mass of string upon string of reptile vertebrae, presumably the remains of a necklace' was found. This grave is dated to 5500 BP (Pretty 1977:305).

Tasmanian devil teeth

A unique archaeological find from Lake Nitchie in 1969 provides a glimpse at the use of Tasmanian devil (*Sarcophilus harrisii*) teeth some 6800 years ago (Macintosh et al. 1970; Macintosh 1971). Some 178 canine teeth from more than 100 Tasmanian devils were needed to make an impressive necklace found in the burial of a man who died when he was about 37 years old. Interestingly, each canine was perforated by thinning the tooth root before drilling, a technique that is very unusual for the Australian context.

Wombat claws

A magnificent necklace of wombat claws—each pierced through the root centre for stringing—is curated in the Tasmanian Museum and Art Gallery, with the museum noting that it was collected by George Augustus Robinson on 1 June 1830 at Sandy Cape, Tasmania. Augustus Robinson notes the following about finding the necklace: 'in a basket was the claws of some animal, which had been made into beads, and some yellow ochre' (Plomley 2008:198). This necklace is strung on a length of sinew and incorporates about 145 individual wombat claws, including at least a couple of double claws (from the back feet). With each animal having five claws on each front foot and four on each back foot, the construction of such a necklace would require all claws from at least eight wombats.

Significantly, Augustus Robinson, when acting as Chief Protector for Port Phillip, mentioned in 1839 that he 'got a necklace from Mr Hill of wombat claws and opossum twine', suggesting that the item in the Tasmanian Museum and Art Gallery is not a completely unique example (Clark 2000a:78).

Ornaments worn on the torso

Adornments that incorporate hard animal materials and are worn on the torso appear to be restricted to waistbands in museum collections, though archaeological finds provide more diverse insights. The use of bone materials in skin-marking will also be briefly discussed in this section.

Archaeological finds

The Spencer region site of Roonka provides some insights into ornamentation made some 4000–5000 years ago. First, the double burial of an adult male with a small child—known as Grave 108—displays bone awls down the midline of the adult's body, showing he was wrapped in a cloak that was pinned shut (Pretty 1977). A broad band of small bird bones found running along the left side of the body suggested to the excavators that this cloak was fringed with 'a band of bird feathers, possibly still partly incorporated as part-limbs, as a form of edging decoration' (Pretty 1977:305). Certainly, recent collections indicate that whole bird wings were utilised as fans (see 'Fans and fly-flicks' in Chapter 5), so it is possible that a similar approach was taken here to decorate the cloak.

In another interment at Roonka, Grave 109 was found with bands of notched marsupial incisors interspersed with 'broken lengths of bone as beads while the other appears to employ them as spacers' across the body (Pretty 1977:312). No further details about these finds are provided, though the three bone beads discovered at Devil's Lair (Southwest region) are brought to mind. The beads at Devil's Lair were recovered from contexts dating to about 12,000 years ago and appear to have been made on sections of kangaroo fibula or radius (Dortch 1979:39).

Waistbands

Apart from two rare examples of waistbands (also termed girdles or belts) made from fur string and decorated with macropod incisors from Hermannsburg (Desert region) and Newcastle Waters (Fitzmaurice region) (South Australian Museum), the only other known examples of waistbands that incorporate hard animal materials come from the Torres Strait. From Mer, dogs' teeth (canines) reappear, this time bound onto a line of plaited coconut root. This example is recorded as a dance belt worn by women and girls for ceremonial occasions.

Skin decorating tools

In 'Nose bones' above, it was shown that there are frequent mentions that bone points were used to pierce the nasal septum. In terms of the widespread practice of scarification, there are brief indications that bony materials were utilised as the tools to create these long-lasting markings. One such note is found on a photographic print that shows a close-up of an adult's arm and has the following printed on its reverse: 'This picture was taken to show the scars left by / the emu bone (*punyi*) that are inserted in the / folds of the skin *dur*'. This photograph is curated by the National Museum of Australia (Item 1985.0002.0847).

6. ORNAMENTS

Ornaments worn on the arms and hands

Ornaments for the arms and hands made solely from plant fibres or fur or hair string are common in photographs, but examples that incorporate hard animal materials are almost non-existent as far as is currently known. The only possible exception is a brief mention that bracelets were made from dingo tails in South West Western Australia (Meagher & Riede 1979:72), which presumably are in a similar style to the headbands described above and so only include a strip of the tail fur rather than any of the tail bones.

SUMMARY

- Great diversity in the use of hard animal materials to create body ornamentation across the Australian continent is evident.

- While some materials, such as macropod lower incisors, appear to have seen widespread use, other unique items in museum collections or that are briefly mentioned in ethnographic papers suggest that a wide range of hard animal parts have been used to ornament the human body over the past 65,000 or more years.

- Large gaps in our knowledge surrounding Indigenous body adornment throughout Australia's deep past remain.

- One of the most interesting aspects of the Indigenous Australian ornament traditions is the almost complete absence of perforated beads and pendants, with artists instead finding other methods for effective attachment. This alternative approach to ornamentation is important for archaeology in Australia and abroad, as traditionally, researchers have relied on the presence of perforations to identify ancient adornment. These Australian examples conclusively demonstrate that components do not need to be perforated for attachment and that a wide range of adornments can be designed and utilised without holes.

CHAPTER 7
FROM ARTEFACTS TO UNDERSTANDING THE HUMAN STORY IN AUSTRALIA

Introduction

The vast repertoire of bone and tooth technologies made on the Australian continent allows insights into the lives of all those who have made this place home over the past 65,000 or more years. However, while archaeologists have developed robust analytical and interpretative strategies for understanding the place of stone tools in the Australian landscape (see Holdaway & Stern 2004), technologies made on bone and tooth have been largely ignored in this context. This dichotomy is understandable when one considers that around 90 per cent of the archaeological record is made up of stone artefacts. Nevertheless, we need to remember that organic artefacts—those not made from stone—were originally more common in Australian toolkits. Only because stone is largely impervious to decay are these artefacts the mainstay of the archaeological record. Therefore, while bone and tooth tools might not be as archaeologically numerous, they nevertheless deserve the same amount of attention as their stone counterparts. Further, if we are to fully appreciate the diversity and richness of Indigenous Australian technologies over the millennia, bone and tooth tools and ornaments must be studied.

Below, recurring themes in the study of bone and tooth technology in Australia are highlighted, and pathways that may increase our understanding of these enigmatic living technologies are explored.

Recurring themes from Australian bone and tooth artefacts

Four major themes are evident from the study of Indigenous Australian bone and tooth artefacts: (1) the practice of reciprocity, (2) the impact of alternative 'ways of doing', (3) tool and ornament multifunctionality, and (4) the restricted distribution of long-lived ornaments on the human body.

First, let us discuss tool and ornament reciprocity. Several early European observers commented that it was common practice to exchange items of personal adornment on meeting with family, friends, and even friendly strangers on the Australian landscape. For example, Curr (1883:125), when talking about Bangerang people near Goulburn

7. FROM ARTEFACTS TO UNDERSTANDING

River, stated that 'frequently men of different tribes made exchanges of arms or articles of dress in token of good will; and women, in like manner, exchanged ornaments'. Curry too observed Bangerang people:

> neither kissing, shaking hands, nor any other salutation of the kind was used amongst the tribe, though frequently men of different tribes made exchanges of arms or articles of dress in token of goodwill; and women, in like manner, exchanged ornaments. (Curry 1965[1883]:125)

Similarly, when travelling along the Macarthur River, Leichhardt noted in his journal that:

> as soon as he saw that I intended to make him a present, he prepared one in return; and when I gave him some rings and buckles, he presented me with some of the ornaments he wore on his person. As our confidence in each other was thus established, some of my companions and several others of the natives came up, and we exchanged presents in a very amicable manner. (Leichhardt 1847[1996]:413)

Such observations of object exchange have significant implications for mapping the spatial distribution of ornaments and tools in the recent past, and this practice could stretch well back into archaeological periods depending on how long this tradition has been present among Indigenous Australian communities. As such, consideration of reciprocity practices involving material culture must not only be kept in mind but also be actively investigated to better reconstruct local changes to techno-complexes and the changing relationships between communities over time.

Next, the fact that almost all pieces of ornamentation on this continent were designed without the use of perforations has implications for archaeological interpretations abroad. Traditionally, the identification of early beads and pendants relied heavily on the archaeologist being able to identify an anthropogenic perforation or groove that allowed the item to be strung. Such evidence, when found in very deep time contexts, has changed our understanding of when the human mind reached 'modern' patterns and has been central to debates surrounding the abilities of non–*Homo sapiens* populations for decades.

The Australian material, however, clearly demonstrates that perforations and grooves are completely unnecessary for the creation of complex and beautiful necklaces, headbands, and many other types of body adornment. Here, the use of resins and wax to connect hard animal material elements to plant, fur and hair fibre strings or leather straps was mastered. Consequently, archaeologists can no longer rely on the presence of perforations or grooves to identify ornaments in all contexts. There are other 'ways of doing'.

Another lesson to be learned from Australian toolkits is the high degree of multi-functionality recorded for organic tools. Again, archaeologists working in Palaeolithic and other deep time contexts from Eurasia and Africa have tended to assign just one or two functions to a recovered implement form. However, the ethnographic evidence summarised herein demonstrates that very often, a tool form will have many, often quite different, functions—and conversely, one tool can either conduct all recorded functions or be kept for just one function. Thus, generalisations about tool function/s based on small assemblages could be significantly under-representing the behaviours of past peoples. While not a new idea by any means, these data are a timely reminder to those working in deep past contexts.

Finally, it was found that all the ornaments made from long-lasting hard animal materials were restricted to being worn from the chest (as necklaces) up towards the head. Kuhn and Stiner (2007b) argued that the invention and adoption of durable beads over less permanent ornamentation (such as body painting) allowed the messages that body adornment carries to become long lasting and loud. Specifically, durable beads could last beyond not only a single event but also a single lifetime. They could also be added indefinitely on top of one another to amplify their presence and be arranged first in one way before that arrangement is deconstructed and arranged in a new fashion, changing the message that they are transmitting. Durable beads and pendants could also be passed between individuals across space, transmitting their messages even when the maker/owner was not present themselves. This versatility and longevity have meant that durable beads were a powerful type of personal ornamentation throughout humanity's past.

With the exception of the beautiful fur cloaks seen over much of the continent, Indigenous Australians did not choose to create items that covered large parts of the body. The relatively warm environmental conditions certainly discouraged the creation of clothing that covered arms and legs (etc.), and as such, much of the body was visible most of the time. Theoretically, someone could wear an ornament anywhere on their person, and it would be highly visible to viewers. The restriction of hard animal material ornaments to the head and chest is then an interesting observation, for they were not restricted to this upper section because the lower parts were frequently covered (and were thus out of sight). Ornaments of softer materials (plant fibres and fur, feather and hair string) were worn on the lower body on a daily basis, however, and presumably, these adornments are no less significant in their presence.

The implication of this pattern of ornament use for archaeology is that the beads and pendants that are recovered from Australian sites are only going to give insights into how past peoples have decorated their upper body. The ornaments worn below the neck therefore remain largely 'invisible' unless this pattern of use has also changed significantly over time (and we may never know).

The future of Australian bone and tooth artefact studies

Researchers still have a long way to go if non-stone materials are to be meaningfully integrated into our understanding of Australia's past and present technological systems. From reviewing the Australian archaeological literature, it is evident that the amount of attention paid to bone and tooth artefacts was dependent on the size of the recovered artefact assemblage and the investigator's personal interest. As such, large regions of the continent and many forms of bone and tooth artefacts have gone unstudied, while others saw quite concentrated interest. Ironically, the part of Australia's bone and tooth toolkits that has been most intensively considered is the lack of bone technology in Tasmania after 3500 years ago (see Chapter 1). But even for this one hotly debated issue, archaeological discussions practically ceased more than 20 years ago.

7. FROM ARTEFACTS TO UNDERSTANDING

While conducting the research presented in this book, it was not uncommon for the author to receive comments from colleagues about how few bone artefacts are recovered in Australia. While stone tools are obviously much greater in number, it is hoped that this book has shown how ubiquitous osseous tools and ornaments were until very recently. Further, many items were hiding in plain sight. For example, AS Kenyon in 1904 commented that:

> My first experience on this strip was fifty years ago when the whole surface from Gorman's Lane South of Koroit and Tower Hill Lake was strewn with bone remains much decomposed and largely human. Amongst these, on the first occasion I picked up over one hundred bone implements discarding as many more as too fragmentary and decomposed. On later visits probably a dozen in all, I picked up more of the decayed specimens but always got several dozen. They were single and double pointed; I should estimate that altogether a thousand specimens have been picked up. The single points generally splint [sic] bones of kangaroos and small marsupials, whale, seal, dingo and human bones being also used, varied in length from three to eighteen inches. The points acute or needle shaped, blunt or obtuse, chisel and gouge edged. There does not seem to have been any particular use, i.e., no relationship between length and point can be found. As to double pointed bones, they range from 1 inches to about 6 inches in length, occasionally formed from hollow bones, points from blunt to sharp but never chisel pointed. Usually both points are alike in angle of point but not invariably. Certainly some were used as nose bones as the early settlers have recorded such use. The very small ones do not seem to be of possible use as spear points, the medium length ones predominate and they seem unsuitable as points. The longer ones, 4 inches to 6 inches, are very scarce and do not form more than one percent of the whole. (Mitchell 1958:197)

As such, it appears that a large number of bone artefacts has already been lost from changing coastlines and through urban development, but if looked for more closely, there is no doubt that many more will be found.

A second interesting avenue for future study revolves around the trade of both raw materials and finished artefacts. Specifically, bone for the production of awls appears to have been an item of trade in some areas, with Roth noting that the Cape Bedford (East Cape region) community:

> send out or export iron tomahawks, iron digging-sticks, nautilus-shell, different kinds of dilly-bag, pearl-shell chest ornaments and Melo-shells. In return, they obtain forehead-bands, kangaroo-tail sinew, kangaroo bones (of a certain kind to be specially used for making bone awls) . . . They travel in barter along the Northern Coast-line as far as, very probably, the Flinders River. (Roth 1910a:18)

Such also seems to have been the case in regard to tools, as Eyre (1845:214) mentions that:

> I have always found the natives ready to barter their nets, weapons, or other implements, for European articles, and sometimes they will give them unsolicited, and without any equivalent; amongst themselves they constantly do this.

This movement of bony raw materials for use in technology production is an area sorely in need of study.

Next, there is much that is not completely understood about why certain raw materials were selected and exactly how they were worked and used in daily life. Experimental programs undertaken with communities across the continent will provide a way to not only learn about these items archaeologically but also bring them into the light more broadly. Finally, looking through the museum archives, it was evident that more intensive and focused study of particular kinds of tools or ornamentation will no doubt find more nuanced spatial differences in their design and use. For example, a careful study of the overall form and painted designs on the forehead pendants is a very promising prospect for the future. In all, there are a very many projects waiting to be taken up by researchers and communities alike.

Conclusion

Osseous objects are witnesses to human occupation, cognitive capabilities, and collective identities, but also to individual expression and technical know-how. Their ability to be transformed into a huge array of tools and ornaments has allowed humanity to innovate and explore and has allowed archaeologists to trace the development of our minds, the movement of our peoples, and the creation of colourful cultures.

The Australian record is no different. The diversity and ubiquity of bone and tooth material culture across the continent provide an exceptional way to learn about the creativity and identity of the many nations that created them. It is hoped that this book will allow this record in bone to not only become more visible and understood but also be celebrated for its ingenuity and antiquity.

SUMMARY

- Bone and tooth artefacts were an important component of Indigenous Australian toolkits and continue to hold value for their respective communities.

- Much work remains to understand the spatial and temporal place of bone and tooth material culture across the Australian continent.

References

Abadía, OM & A Nowell 2015, 'Palaeolithic personal ornaments: historical development and epistemological challenges', *Journal of Archaeological Method and Theory* 22:952–79.

Abrams, G, SM Bello, K di Modica, S Pirson & D Bonjean 2014, 'When Neanderthals used cave bear (*Ursus spelaeus*) remains: bone retouchers from unit 5 of Scladina Cave (Belgium)', *Quaternary International* 326–327:274–87.

Aiston, G 1928, 'Chipped stone tools of the Aboriginal tribes east and northeast of Lake Eyre, South Australia', *Papers and Proceedings of the Royal Society of Tasmania* 1928:123–31.

Adams, W & E Adams 1991, *Archaeological typology and practical reality*, Cambridge University Press, Cambridge.

Akerman, K 1973, 'Two Aboriginal charms incorporating fossil giant marsupial teeth', *The West Australian Naturalist* 12:139–41.

—— 1995, 'The use of bone, shell and teeth by Aboriginal Australians' in E Johnson (ed.), *Ancient peoples and landscapes*, Museum of Texas, Lubbock, pp 173–83.

—— 2011, 'The use animal and human teeth in the material culture of Aboriginal Australians', *Ethnozootechnie* 89:133–42.

—— 2018, 'The esoteric and decorative use of bone, shell, and teeth in Australia' in MC Langley, M Litster, D Wright & SK May (eds), *The archaeology of portable art*, Routledge, Oxon, pp 199–219.

—— R Fullagar & A van Gijn 2002, 'Weapons and *wunan*: production, function and exchange of Kimberly points', *Australian Aboriginal Studies* 1:13–42.

Allain, J & A Rigaud 1986, 'Décor et fonction. Quelques exemples tirés du Magdalénien', *L'Anthropologie* 90:713–38.

Allen, J, R Cosgrove & S Brown 1988, 'New archaeological data from the southern forests region, Tasmania: a preliminary statement', *Australian Archaeology* 27:75–88.

—— B Marshall & D Ranson 1989, 'A note on excavations at the Maxwell River site, M86/2, Southwest Tasmania', *Australian Archaeology* 29:3–8.

Andrews, P & M Armour-Chelu 1998, 'Taphonomic observations of a surface bone assemblage in a temperate environment', *Bulletin de la Société Géologique de France* 169:433–42.

—— & J Cook 1985, 'Natural modifications to bones in a temperate setting', *Man* 20:675–91.

—— & EM Nesbit Evans 1983, 'Small mammal bone accumulations produced by mammalian carnivores', *Paleobiology* 9:289–307.

Angas, GD 1967[1847], *Savage life and scenes in Australia and New Zealand*, Smith, Elder and Co., London.

Anghelinu, M, M Mărgărit & L Niță 2017, 'A Paleolithic eyed needle from Bistricioara-Lutărie III (Ceahlău Basin, Northeastern Romania)', *Studii de Preistorie* 14:27–35.

Anzidei, AP 2001, 'Tools from elephant bones at La Polledrara di Cecanibbio and Rebibbia-Casal de' Pazzi' in

REFERENCES

G Cavarretta, P Gioia, M Mussi & MR Palombo (eds), *The world of elephants. Proceedings of the first international congress*, Consiglio Nazionale delle Ricerche, Rome, pp 415–18.

Armitage, SJ, SA Jasim, AE Marks, AG Parker, VI Usik & H-P Uerpmann 2011, 'The southern route "out of Africa": evidence for an early expansion of modern humans into Arabia', *Science* 331:453–56.

Arndt, S & MH Newcomer 1986, 'Breakage patterns on prehistoric bone points: an experimental study' in DA Roe (ed.), *Studies in the Upper Palaeolithic of Britain and Northwestern Europe*, British Archaeological Reports, International Series 269, Oxford, pp 165–73.

Attenbrow, V 2003, 'Habitation and land use patterns in the Upper Mangrove Creek catchment, New South Wales central coast', *Australian Archaeology* 57:20–31.

Averbouh, A 1999, 'Un fragment de percuteur sur partie basilaire de la grotte magdalénienne d'Enlène (Ariege)', *Bulletin de la Société Préhistorique Française* 96:497–504.

—— 2005, 'Collete du bois de renne et territoire d'exploitation chez les groups Magdaléniens des Pyrénées Ariégeoises' in D. Vialou, J. Renault-Miskovsky, M. Patou-Mathis (eds), *Comportements des hommes du Paléolithique moyen et supérieur en Europe: territoires et milieux*, CNRS, Paris, pp. 59–70.

Azema, M & F Rivère 2015, 'Animation in Palaeolithic art: a pre-echo of cinema', *Antiquity* 86:316–24.

Backhouse, J 1967[1843], *A narrative of a visit to the Australian colonies*, Johnson, New York.

Backwell, L & F d'Errico 2001, 'Evidence of termite foraging by Swartkrans early hominids', *Proceedings of the National Academy of Science* 98:1358–63.

—— & F d'Errico 2004, 'The first use of bone tools: a reappraisal of the evidence from Olduvai Gorge, Tanzania', *Palaeontologia Africana* 40:95–158.

—— & F d'Errico 2005, 'The origin of bone tool technology and the identification of early hominid cultural traditions' in F d'Errico & L Backwell (eds), *From tools to symbols: from early hominids to modern humans*, Wits University Press, Johannesburg, pp 238–75.

—— & F d'Errico 2008, 'Early hominid bone tools from Drimolen, South Africa', *Journal of Archaeological Science* 35:2880–94.

—— & F d'Errico 2016, 'Osseous projectile weapon from early to late Middle Stone Age Africa' in MC Langley (ed.), *Osseous projectile weaponry: towards an understanding of Pleistocene cultural variability*, VERT Series, Springer, Dordrecht, pp 15–29.

—— AH Parkinson, EM Roberts, F d'Errico & J-B Huchet 2012, 'Criteria for identifying bone modifications by termites in the fossil record', *Palaeogeography, Palaeoclimatology, Palaeoecology* 337–338:72–87.

Bahn, PG 1982, 'Inter-site and inter-regional links during the Upper Palaeolithic: the Pyrenean evidence', *Oxford Journal of Archaeology* 1:247–68.

Bailey, G 1993, 'Shell mounds in 1972 and 1992: reflections on recent controversies at Ballina and Weipa', *Australian Archaeology* 37:1–18.

Balme, J 1979, 'Artificial bias in a sample of kangaroo incisors from Devil's Lair, Western Australia', *Records of the Western Australian Museum* 7:229–44.

—— & S O'Connor 2019, 'Bead making in Aboriginal Australia from the deep past to European arrival: materials, methods, and meanings' *PaleoAnthropology* 2019:177–195.

Banfield, EJ 1910, *Confessions of a beachcomber*, T. Fisher Unwin, London.

Barker, BC 1991, 'Nara Inlet 1: coastal resource use and the Holocene marine transgression in the Whitsunday Islands, central Queensland', *Archaeology in Oceania* 26:102–09.

Barrington, G 1985, *A voyage to New South Wales*, View Productions, Sydney.

Barton, CM, GA Clark & A Cohen 1994, 'Art as information: explaining Upper Palaeolithic art in Western Europe', *World Archaeology* 26:186–207.

REFERENCES

Bartram, LE & CW Marean 1999, 'Explaining the "Klasies pattern": Kua ethnoarchaeology, the Die Kelders Middle Stone Age archaeofauna, long bone fragmentation and carnivore ravaging', *Journal of Archaeological Science* 26:9–29.

Basedow, H 1913, 'Notes on the natives of Bathurst Island, north Australia', *The Journal of the Royal Anthropological Institute of Great Britain and Ireland* 43:291–323.

—— 1927, 'Subincision and kindred rites of the Australian Aboriginal', *The Journal of the Royal Anthropological Institute of Great Britain and Ireland* 57:123–56.

Basiaco, AHH 2018, Worn to the bone: use-wear of bone points from the Madjedbebe rockshelter, Arnhem Land, unpublished PhD thesis, The University of Queensland, St Lucia, QLD.

Bassett-Smith, PW 1894, 'The Aborigines of north-west Australia', *The Journal of the Royal Anthropological Institute of Great Britain and Ireland* 23:324–31.

Bates, D 1985, *The native tribes of Western Australia*, National Library of Australia, Canberra.

Beaton JM 1985, 'Evidence for a coastal occupation time-lag at Princess Charlotte Bay (North Queensland) and implications for coastal colonisation and population growth theories for Aboriginal Australia', *Archaeology in Oceania* 20:1–20.

Beck, HC 1928, 'Classification and nomenclature of beads and pendants', *Archaeologia* 77:1–76.

Behrensmeyer, AK 1978, 'Taphonomic and ecological information from bone weathering', *Paleobiology* 4:150–62.

—— 1982, 'Time resolution in fluvial vertebrate assemblages', *Paleobiology* 8:69–77.

—— 1990, 'Bones' in DEG Briggs & PR Crowther (eds), *Palaeobiology: a synthesis*, Blackwell Scientific, Oxford, pp 232–235.

—— KD Gordon & GT Yanagi 1986, 'Trampling as a cause of bone surface damage and pseudocutmarks', *Nature* 319:768–71.

Bello, SM, SA Parfitt & C Stringer 2009, 'Quantitative micromorphological analyses of cut marks produced by ancient and modern handaxes', *Journal of Archaeological Science* 36:1869–80.

Bennett, G 1967[1834], *Wanderings in New South Wales, Batavia, Pedir Coast, Singapore, and China; being the journal of a naturalist in those countries, during 1832, 1833, and 1834, Vol. I*, Richard Bentley, New Burlington Street, London.

Bennett, MM 1927, 'Notes on the Dalleburra tribe of northern Queensland', *The Journal of the Royal Anthropological Institute of Great Britain and Ireland* 57:399–415.

Bergman, CA 1987, 'Hafting and use of bone and antler points from Ksar Akil, Lebanon' in D Stordeur-Yedid (ed.), *La main et l'outil: manches et emmanchements préhistorique*, Travaux de la Mainson de l'Orient No. 15, Lyon, pp 117–26.

Berndt, RM & CH Berndt 1964, *The world of the first Australians*, Ure Smith, Sydney.

—— & CH Berndt 1977, *The world of the first Australians*, Ure Smith, Sydney.

—— CH Berndt & JE Stanton 1993, *A world that was: the Yaraldi of the Murray River and the lakes, South Australia*, University of British Columbia Press, Vancouver.

Bertrand, A 1999, *Les armatures de sagaies Magdaléniennes en matière dure animale dans les Pyrénées*, Archaeopress, Oxford.

Best, A 2012, *Regional variation in the material culture of hunter-gatherers. Social and ecological approaches to ethnographic objects from Queensland, Australia*, British Archaeological Reports, International Series 1149, Oxford.

Beveridge, P 2008[1889], *On Aborigines of Victoria and Riverina*, Lowden Publishing, Melbourne.

Beyene, Y, S Katoh, G Wolde, WK Hart, K Uto, M Sudo, et al. 2013, 'The characteristics and chronology of the earliest Acheulean at Konso, Ethiopia', *Proceedings of the National Academy of Sciences* 110:1584–91.

Biddittu, I & P Celletti 2001, 'Plio-Pleistocene proboscidea and Lower Palaeolithic bone industry of Southern Latium

REFERENCES

(Italy)' in G Cavarretta, P Gioia, M Mussi & MR Palombo (eds), *The world of elephants. Proceedings of the first international congress*, Consiglio Nazionale delle Ricerche, Roma, pp 91–96.

Binford, LR 1981, *Bones: ancient men and modern myths*, Academic Press, New York.

Bird, JTS 1904, *The early history of Rockhampton, dealing chiefly with events up till 1870*, The Morning Bulletin Office, Rockhampton.

Bird, C & C Beeck 1980, 'Bone points and spatulae: salvage ethnography in southwest Australia', *Archaeology & Physical Anthropology in Oceania* 15:168–71.

Blasco, R, J Rosell, J Fernández Peris, I Cáceres & J María Vergès 2008, 'A new element of trampling: an experimental application on the Level XII faunal record of Bolomor Cave (Valencia, Spain)', *Journal of Archaeological Science* 35:1605–18.

Blumenschine, RJ 1988, 'An experimental model of the timing of hominid and carnivore influence on archaeological bone assemblages', *Journal of Archaeological Science* 15:483–502.

—— CW Marean & SD Capaldo 1996, 'Blind tests of inter-analyst correspondence and accuracy in the identification of cut-marks, percussion marks, and carnivore tooth marks on bone surfaces', *Journal of Archaeological Science* 23:493–507.

—— & MM Selvaggio 1988, 'Percussion marks on bone surfaces as a new diagnostic of hominid behavior', *Nature* 333:763–65.

Bocherens, H, DG Drucker, D Billiou, J-M Geneste & J van der Plicht 2006, 'Bears and humans in Chauvet Cave (Vallonpont-d'Arc, Ardèche, France): insights from stable isotopes and radiocarbon dating of bone collagen', *Journal of Human Evolution* 50:370–76.

Bonnardin, S 2009, *La parure funéraire au Néolithique ancien dans les Bassins parisiens et Rhénans et Rubané, Hinkelstein et Villeneuve-Saint-Germain*, Mémoire de la Société Préhistorique Française, Paris.

Bonnemains, J, E Forsyth & B Smith 1988, *Baudin in Australia waters: the artwork of the French voyage of discovery to the southern lands*, Oxford University Press, Melbourne.

Bonney, F 1884, 'On some customs of the Aborigines of the river Darling, New South Wales', *Journal of the Anthropological Institute of Great Britain and Ireland* 13:122–37.

Bonnichsen, R 1979, *Pleistocene bone technology in the Beringian refugium*, National Museum of Man Mercury Series, Archaeological Survey of Canada, Paper 89, Ottawa.

—— & RT Will 1980, 'Cultural modification of bone: the experimental approach in faunal analysis' in BM Gilbert (ed.), *Mammalian osteology*, Laramie, Wyoming, pp 7–30.

Bonwick, J 1870, *Daily life and origin of the Tasmanians*, Samson Low, Son, and Marston, London.

Bosinski, G 1991, Zur Technologie der junpaläolithischen Speerschleuder—Eine Studie auf der basis archäologischer, ethnologischer und experimenteller Erkenntnisse, unpublished PhD dissertation, Universität zu Köln, Cologne.

Bouchard, GP, SM Mentzer, J Riel-Salvatore, J Hodgkins, CE Miller, F Negrino, et al. 2019, 'Portable FTIR for on-site screening of archaeological bone intended for ZooMS collagen fingerprint analysis', *Journal of Archaeological Science: Reports* 26:101862.

Bouzzougar, A, N Barton, M Vanhaeren, F d'Errico, S Collcutt, T Higham, et al. 2007, '82,000-year-old shell beads from North Africa and implications for the origins of modern human behavior', *Proceedings of the National Academy of Science* 104:9964–69.

Bowdler, S 1975, 'Further radiocarbon dates from Cave Bay Cave, Hunter Island, north-west Tasmania', *Australian Archaeology* 3:24–6.

—— 1976, 'Hook, line and dilly bag: an interpretation of an Australian coastal shell midden', *Mankind* 10:248–258.

—— 1979, Hunter hill, Hunter island,

REFERENCES

unpublished PhD thesis, Australian National University, Canberra.

—— 1980, 'Fish and culture: a Tasmanian polemic', *Mankind* 12:334–40.

—— 1984 *Hunter hill, Hunter island*, Terra Australis 8, Department of Prehistory, Research School of Pacific Studies, Australian National University, Canberra.

Bradfield, J 2016, 'Bone point functional diversity: a cautionary tale from southern Africa' in MC Langley (ed.), *Osseous projectile weaponry: towards an understanding of Pleistocene cultural variability*, VERT Series, Springer, Dordrecht, pp 31–40.

—— 2019, 'Fishing with gorges: testing a functional hypothesis', *Journal of Archaeological Science: Reports* 24:593–607.

—— & T Brand 2015, 'Results of utilitarian and accidental breakage experiments on bone points', *Archaeological and Anthropological Science* 7:27–38.

—— & M Lombard 2011, 'A macro fracture study of bone points used in experimental hunting with reference to the South African Middle Stone Age', *South African Archaeological Bulletin* 66:67–76.

—— & S Wurz 2020, 'A functional assessment of the notched bone artefacts from Klasies River Main Site', *South African Archaeological Bulletin* 75:128–36.

Bradley, W 1969[1786], *A voyage to New South Wales, the journal of Lieutenant William Bradley, RN of HMS Sirius 1786–1792*, Public Library of New South Wales and Ure Smith, Sydney.

Breton, WH 1834, *Excursions in New South Wales, Western Australia and Van Dieman's Land, during the years 1830–33*, Bentley, London.

Brockwell, S & K Akerman 2007, 'Bone points from the Adelaide River, Northern Territory', *Australian Aboriginal Studies* 1:83–97.

Bromage, TG 1984, 'Interpretation of scanning electron microscopic images of abraded forming bone surface', *American Journal of Physical Anthropology* 64:161–78.

—— JM Bermúdez de Castro & Y Fernándes Jalvo 1991, 'The SEM in taphonomy research and its application to studies of cut-marks generally and the determination of hardness specifically', *Anthropologie* 29:163–69.

—— & A Boyde 1984, 'Microscopic criteria for the determination of directionality of cutmarks on bone', *American Journal of Physical Anthropology* 65:359–66.

Brooks, AS, DM Helgren, JS Cramer, A Franklin, W Hornyak, JM Keating, et al. 1995, 'Dating and context of three Middle Stone Age sites with bone points in the Upper Semliki Valley, Zaire', *Science* 268:548–53.

Brough Smyth, R 1972[1878]a, *The Aborigines of Victoria: with notes relating to the habits of the natives of other parts of Australia and Tasmania, Vol. I*, John Ferres, Government Printer, London.

—— 1972[1878]b, *The Aborigines of Victoria: with notes relating to the habits of the natives of other parts of Australia and Tasmania, Vol. II*, John Ferres, Government Printer, London.

Brown, P 1989, *Coobool Creek: a morphological and metrical analysis of the crania, mandibles and dentitions of a prehistoric Australian human population*, Terra Australis 13, Department of Prehistory, Research School of Pacific Studies, Australian National University, Canberra.

Brown, S 1993, 'Mannalargenna Cave: a Pleistocene site in Bass Strait' in MA Smith, M Spriggs & B Fankhauser (eds), *Sahul in review: Pleistocene sites in Australia, New Guinea and island Melanesia*, Department of Prehistory, Research School of Pacific Studies, Australian National University, Canberra, pp 258–271.

Brownlee, K 2005, Bone and antler tools from the Victoria Day site (Manitoba): building bridges with First Nation communities through experimental archaeology, unpublished Masters thesis, University of Manitoba, Manitoba.

Buc, N 2005, Análisis de microdesgaste en technologia osea. El case de pun zones y alisadores en el noroeste de la provincia de Buenos Aires (Humedal del Paraná inferior), unpublished PhD

REFERENCES

thesis, Universidad de Buenos Aires, Buenos Aires.

—— 2011, 'Experimental series and use-wear in bone tools', *Journal of Archaeological Science* 38:546–57.

Buckley, M, M Collins, J Thomas-Oates & JC Wilson 2009, 'Species identification by analysis of bone collagen using matrix-assisted laser desorption/ionisation time-of-flight mass spectrometry', *Rapid Communications in Mass Spectrometry* 23:3843–54.

—— SW Kansa, S Howard, S Campbell, J Thomas-Oates & M Collins 2010, 'Distinguishing between archaeological sheep and goat bones using a single collagen peptide', *Journal of Archaeological Science* 37:13–20.

Buffrénil, V & D Schoevaert 1998, 'On how the periosteal bone of the delphinium humerus becomes cancellous: ontogeny of a histological specialization', *Journal of Morphology* 198:149–64.

Cáceres, I, M Esteban-Nadal, M Bennàsar & Y Fernández-Jalvo 2011, 'Was it the deer or the fox?', *Journal of Archaeological Science* 38:2767–74.

Cameron, ALP 1885, 'Notes on some tribes of New South Wales', *The Journal of the Royal Anthropological Institute of Great Britain and Ireland* 14:344–370.

Campana, DV 1989, An analysis of the use-wear pattens on Natufian and Protoneolithic bone implements, unpublished PhD dissertation, Columbia University, New York.

Campbell, WB 1914, 'Description of a rock shelter with Aboriginal markings, and an indurated cast of a footprint at the Greenough River, and a cave dwelling at Narandagy Spring, Lockier River', *The Journal of the Natural History and Science Society of Western Australia* 5:9–14.

Camps-Fabrer, H 1975, 'Tendances actuelles des recherches sur l'industrie de l'os: Le premier colloque international sur l'industrie de l'os dans la prehistoire Abbaye de Sénanque (Vaucluse) Avril 1974', *Bulletin de la Société Préhistorique Française* 72:169–173.

—— & D Stodeur 1979, 'Orientation et définition des différentes parties de l'object' in H Camps-Fabrer (ed.), *Industrie de l'os Neolithique et de l'age des Metaux*, Éditions due Centre National de Recherche Scientifique, Paris, pp 9–11.

Capaldo, SD & RJ Blumenschine 1994, 'A quantitative diagnosis of notches made by hammerstone percussion and carnivore gnawing in bovid long bones', *American Antiquity* 59:724–48.

Carnegie, DW 1898, 'Explorations in the interior of Western Australia', *The Geographical Journal* 11:257–59.

Carter, M 2001, 'New evidence for the earliest human occupation in Torres Strait, northeastern Australia', *Australian Archaeology* 52:50–2.

Chaloupka, G 1993, *Journey through time*, Reed, Sydney.

Chauchat, C 1999, 'L'habitat Magalénien de la grotte du Bourrouilla à Arancou (Pyrénées-Atlantiques)', *Gallia Préhistoire* 41:1–151.

Chauncy, P 1972[1878], 'Notes and anecdotes of the Aborigines of Australia' in R Brough Smyth (ed.), *The Aborigines of Victoria and other parts of Australian and Tasmania, Vol. II*, John Curry, O'Neil, South Yarra, pp 221–84.

Chauvet, G 1910, *Os, ivoire et bois de renne ouvrés de la Charente. Hypothèses palethnographiques*, Bulletin de la Société archéologique et historique de la Charente, Angoulême.

Chauvière, F-X 2013, 'Dents' in L Mons, S Pean & R Pigeaud (eds), *Matières d'art: représetations préhistoriques et supports osseux, relations et contraintes. Industrie de l'os préhistoric*, Éditions Errance, Arles, pp 57–64.

Chewings, C 1936, *Back in the stone age: the natives of central Australia*, Angus & Robertson, Sydney.

Choi, K & D Driwantoro 2007 'Shell tool use by early members of *Homo erectus* in Sangiran, central Java, Indonesia: cut mark evidence', *Journal of Archaeological Science* 34:48–58.

Choyke, A 1983, 'An analysis of bone, antler

and tooth tools from Bronze Age Hungary', *Mitteilungen des Archäeologischen Instituts der UAW* 12:13–57.

—— 1997, 'The bone tool manufacturing continuum', *Anthropozoologica* 25-26:65–72.

Christensen, M 1999, *Technologie de l'ivoire au paléolithique supérieur. Caractérisation physico-chimique du matériau et analyse fonctionnelle des outils de transformation*, British Archaeological Reports, International Series 751, Oxford.

Clark, GA 1993, 'Paradigms in science and archaeology', *Journal of Archaeological Research* 1:203–34.

Clark, ID (Ed.) 2000a, *The journals of George Augustus Robinson, Chief Protector, Port Phillip Aboriginal Protectorate, Volume one: 1 January 1839 – 30 September 1840*, Heritage Matters, Ballarat.

—— (Ed.) 2000b, *The journals of George Augustus Robinson, Chief Protector, Port Phillip Aboriginal Protectorate, Volume two: 1 October 1840 – 31 August 1841*, Heritage Matters, Ballarat.

—— (Ed.) 2000c, *The journals of George Augustus Robinson, Chief Protector, Port Phillip Aboriginal Protectorate, Volume three: 1 September 1841 – 31 December 1983*, Heritage Matters, Ballarat.

—— (Ed.) 2000d, *The journals of George Augustus Robinson, Chief Protector, Port Phillip Aboriginal Protectorate, Volume four: 1 January 1844 – 24 October 1845*, Heritage Matters, Ballarat.

—— (Ed.) 2000e, *The journals of George Augustus Robinson, Chief Protector, Port Phillip Aboriginal Protectorate, Volume five: 25 October 1845 – 9 June 1849*, Heritage Matters, Ballarat.

Clark, JGD & MW Thompson 1953, 'The groove and splinter technique of working antler in Upper Palaeolithic and Mesolithic Europe', *Proceedings of the Prehistoric Society* 19:148–160.

Clark, PM 1987, *Willandra Lakes world heritage archaeology resource study*, Report to the New South Wales Department of Planning and the Western Land Commission of NSW, Sydney.

Clifford, E & P Bahn 2018, 'If the cat fits . . . A new look at the so-called lion man from Hohlenstein-Stadel', *Die Kunde* 69:99–120.

Cogger, H 2014, *Reptiles and amphibians of Australia*, CSIRO Publishing, Collingwood.

Cole, K 1979, *The Aborigines of Arnhem Land*, Rigby, Adelaide.

Collins, D 1975[1798], *An account of the English colony in New South Wales, Vol. I*, AH & AW Reed in association with the Royal Australian Historical Society, Sydney.

—— 1975[1802], *An account of the English colony in New South Wales, Vol. II*, AH & AW Reed in association with the Royal Australian Historical Society, Sydney.

Collins, MJ, CM Nielsen-Marsh, J Hiller, CI Smith, JP Roberts, RV Prigodich, et al. 2002, 'The survival of organic matter in bone: a review', *Archaeometry* 44:383–94.

Colliver, FS & FD Woolston 1975, 'The Aborigines of Stradbroke Island', *Proceedings of the Royal Society of Queensland* 86:91–104.

Conard, N 2009, 'A female figurine from the basal Aurignacian of Hohle Fels Cave in southwestern Germany', *Nature* 459:248–252.

Conkey, MW 1980, 'The identification of prehistoric hunter-gatherer aggregation: the case of Altamira', *Current Anthropology* 21:609–30.

Connah, G 1975, 'Current research at the department of prehistory and archaeology, University of New England', *Australian Archaeology* 3:28–31.

Cook, J 1986, 'The application of scanning electron microscopy to taphonomic and archaeological problems' in DA Roe (ed.), *Studies in the Upper Palaeolithic of Britain and Northwest Europe*, British Archaeological Report, International Series 296, Oxford, pp 143–63.

Cortés-Sánchez, M, FJ Jiménez-Espejo, MD Simón-Vallejo, C Stringer, MC Lozano Francisco, A García-Alix, et al. 2019, 'An early Aurignacian arrival into southwestern Europe', *Nature: Ecology & Evolution* 3:207–12.

Cosgrove, R 1993, 'Hunters on the edge of the Tasmanian ice' in G Burenhult (ed.), *The first humans: human origins*

REFERENCES

and history to 10,000 BC, University of Queensland, St Lucia, pp 166–67.
—— 1995, 'Late Pleistocene behavioural variation and time trends: the case from Tasmania', *Archaeology in Oceania* 30:83–104.
—— 1999, 'Forty-two degrees south: the archaeology of late Pleistocene Tasmania', *Journal of World Prehistory* 13:357–402.
—— & E Raymont 2002, 'Jiyer Cave revisited: preliminary results from northeast Queensland rainforest', *Australian Archaeology* 54:29–36.
Courtenay, LA, MA Maté-González, J Aramendi, J Yravedra, D González-Aguilera & M Domínguez-Rodrigo 2018, 'Testing accuracy in 2D and 3D geometric morphometric methods for cut mark identification and classification', *PeerJ* 6:e5133.
Coutts, PJF 1976, 'The prehistory of Victoria: a review', *Records of the Victorian Archaeological Survey* 2.
—— & DC Witter 1977, 'New radiocarbon dates for Victoria archaeological sites', *Records of the Victoria Archaeological Survey* 4:59–73.
—— DC Witter & DM Parsons 1977, 'Impact of European settlement on Aboriginal society in Western Victoria', *Records of the Victorian Archaeological Survey* 4:17–58.
Cristiani, E & D Borić 2012, '8500-year-old Mesolithic garment embroidery from Vlasac (Serbia): technological, use-wear and residue analyses', *Journal of Archaeological Science* 39:3450–89.
—— I Živaljević & D Borić 2014, 'Residue analysis and ornament suspension techniques in prehistory: cyprinid pharyngeal teeth beads from Late Mesolithic burials at Vlasac (Serbia)', *Journal of Archaeological Science* 46:292–310.
Crowther, WL 1924, 'Notes on the habits of the extinct Tasmanian race. (1) The uses and manufacture of bone implements', *Papers of the Royal Society of Tasmania* 1924:136–39.
—— 1926, 'The uses and manufacture of implements by Tasmanian Aborigines' in G Lightfoot (ed.), *Proceedings of the Pan-Pacific Science Congress, Australia, 1923, Vol. I*, Government Printer, Melbourne, pp 264–66.
Cruz-Uribe, K 1991, 'Distinguishing hyena from hominid bone accumulations', *Journal of Field Archaeology* 18:467–86.
Curr, EM 1883, *Recollections of squatting in Victoria*, George Robertson, Melbourne.
—— 1886, *The Australian race: its origin, languages, customs, place of landing in Australia, and the routes by which it spread itself over that continent, Vol. One*, John Fames, Government Printer, Melbourne.
Currey, JD 2002, *Bones: structure and mechanics*, Princeton University Press, Princeton.
Curry, EM 1965[1883], *Recollections of squatting in Victoria, then called the Port Phillip District, (from 1841–1851)*, Cambridge University Press/George Robertson, London/Melbourne.
Daly, H 1887, *Digging, squatting and pioneering life in the Northern Territory of South Australia*, Sampson, Low, Marston, Searle and Rivington, London.
Davidson, DS 1937, 'Transport and receptacles in Aboriginal Australia', *Journal of the Polynesian Society* 46:175–205.
—— & FD McCarthy 1957, 'The distribution and chronology of some important types of stone implements in Western Australia', *Anthropos* 52:390–458.
Davis, JM 1972[1878], 'Notes relating to the Aborigines of Australia' in R Brough Smyth (ed.), *The Aborigines of Victoria and other parts of Australian and Tasmania, Vol. II*, John Curry, O'Neil, South Yarra, pp 310–22.
Davis, KL 1985, A taphonomic approach to experimental bone fracturing and applications to several South African Pleistocene sites, unpublished PhD thesis, State University of New York, Binghamton.
Dawson, J 1981[1881], *Australian Aborigines the languages and customs of several tribes of Aborigines in the Western District of Victoria*, Robertson, Melbourne.
d'Errico, F 1993, 'La vie sociale de l'art mobilier paléolithique. Manipulation,

transport, suspension des objets on os, bois de cervidés, ivoire', *Oxford Journal of Archaeology* 12:145–74.

—— & LR Backwell 2003a, 'Possible evidence of bone tool shaping by Swartkrans early hominids', *Journal of Archaeological Science* 30:1559–76.

—— & LR Backwell 2003b, 'Additional evidence on the early hominid bone tools from Swartkrans with reference to spatial distribution of lithic and organic artefacts', *South African Journal of Science* 99:259–67.

—— G Giacobini, J Hather, AH Powers-Jones & AM Radmilli 1995, 'Possible bone threshing tools from the Neolithic levels of the Grotta dei Piccioni (Abruzzo, Italy)', *Journal of Archaeological Science* 22:537–549.

—— G Giacobini & PF Puech 1984, 'Varnish replica: a new method for the study of worked bone surfaces', *Ossa* 9–10:29–51.

—— C Henshilwood, M Vanhaeren & K Van Niekerk 2005, '*Nassarius kraussianus* shell beads from Blombos Cave: evidence for symbolic behaviour in the Middle Stone Age', *Journal of Human Evolution* 48:3–24.

—— P Jardón-Giner & B Soler-Mayor 1993, 'Critères à base expérimentale pour l'étude des perforations naturelles et intentionnelles sur coquillages' in PC Anderson, S Beyries, M Otte & H Plisson (eds), *Traces et fonction: les gestes retrouvés. Actes du colloque international de Liège Vol I*, Service de Préhistoire, Liège, pp 255–67.

—— M Julien, D Lilies, M Vanhaeren & D Baffier 2003, 'Many awls in our argument. Bone tool manufacture and use in the Châtelperronian and Aurignacian levels of the Grotte du Renne at Arcy-sur-Cure' in J Zilhão & F d'Errico (eds), *The chronology of the Aurignacian and the transitional technocomplexes—Dating, stratigraphies, cultural implications*, Instituto Português de Arqueologia, Lisbon, pp 247–70.

—— & P Villa 1997, 'Holes and grooves: the contribution of microscopy and taphonomy to the problem of art origins', *Journal of Human Evolution* 33:1–31.

Dibble, HL 1995, 'Middle Paleolithic scraper reduction: background, clarification, and review of the evidence to date', *Journal of Archaeological Method and Theory* 2:299–368.

Dobosi, VT 2001, 'Ex Proboscideis-Proboscidean remains as raw material at four Palaeolithic sites, Hungary' in G Cavarretta, P Gioia, M Mussi & MR Palombo (eds), *The world of elephants. Proceedings of the first international congress*, Consiglio Nazionale delle Ricerche, Rome, pp 429–31.

Dobres, M-A & CR Hoffman 1994, 'Social agency and the dynamics of prehistoric technology', *Journal of Archaeological Method and Theory* 1:211–58.

Domínguez-Rodrigo, M & A Piqueras 2003, 'The use of tooth pits to identify carnivore Tara in tooth-marked archaeofaunas and their relevance to reconstruct hominid carcass processing behaviours', *Journal of Archaeological Science* 30:1385–1891.

Dortch, CE 1979, 'Australia's oldest known ornaments', *Antiquity* 53:39–43.

—— & D Merrilees 1973, 'Human occupation of Devil's Lair, Western Australia during the Pleistocene', *Archaeology and Physical Anthropology in Oceania* 8:89–115.

Dortch, J 1996, 'Late Pleistocene and recent Aboriginal occupation of Tunnel Cave and Witchcliffe Rock Shelter, southwestern Australia', *Australian Aboriginal Studies* 2:51–60.

Duncan-Kemp, AM 1964, *Where strange paths go down*, WR Smith and Patterson, Brisbane.

Durrand, WJ 1940, 'Notes on the Torres Islands', *Oceania* 10:389–403.

Earl, GW 1846, 'On the Aboriginal tribes of the northern coast of Australia', *Journal of the Royal Geographical Society* 16:239–51.

Edge-Partington, J 1969[1890–98], *An album of weapons, tools, ornaments, articles of dress etc., of the natives of the Pacific Islands*, facsimile published by Holland Press, London.

REFERENCES

Edwards, R 1968, 'An Aboriginal bone sheathed point from Fromm's Landing, South Australia', *Mankind* 6:690–91.

Eickhoff, S & B Herrmann 1985, 'Surface marks on bones from a Neolithic collective grave (Odagsen, Lower Saxony). A study on differential diagnosis', *Journal of Human Evolution* 14:263–74.

Ewart, E 2012, 'Making and unmaking Panará beadwork—or, how to overcome the fixity of material things', *Anthropology and Humanism* 37:177–90.

Eyre, EJ 1845, *Journals of expeditions of discovery into central Australia. In the years 1840–1 including an account of the manners and customs of the Aborigines and the state of their relations with Europeans*, T and W Boone, London.

Feary, S 1996, 'An Aboriginal burial with grave goods near Cooma, New South Wales', *Australian Archaeology* 43:40–2.

Felts, WJL & FA Spurrell 1965, 'Structural orientation and density in cetacean humeri', *American Journal of Anatomy* 116:171–203.

Fernández-Jalvo, Y & P Andrews 2016, *Atlas of taphonomic identifications*, Springer, Dordrecht.

—— P Andrews, D Pesquero, C Smith, D Marín-Monfort, B Sánchez, et al. 2010, 'Early bone diagenesis in temperate environments: part 1: surface features and histology', *Palaeogeography, Palaeoclimatology, Paleoecology* 288:62–81.

Fisher, DC 1981, 'Crocodilian scatology, microvertbrate concentrations, and enamel-less teeth', *Paleobiology* 7:262–75.

Fisher, JW 1995, 'Bone surface modifications in zooarchaeology', *Journal of Archaeological Method and Theory* 2:7–68.

Fison, L & AW Howitt 1991[1880], *Kamilaroi and Kurnai*, Aboriginal Studies Press, Canberra.

Flanagan, RJ 1888, *The Aborigines of Australia*, Flanagan and Robertson, Sydney.

Flannery, T 2009, *The life and adventures of William Buckley. Thirty-two years a wanderer amongst the Aborigines of the then unexplored country around Port Phillip*, Text Publishing, Melbourne.

Flenniken, JJ 1978, 'The experimental replication of Paleo-Indian eyed needles from Washington', *Northwest Anthropological Research Notes* 12:61–71.

Flood, J 1974, 'Pleistocene man at Clogg's Cave: his tool-kit and environment', *Mankind* 9:175–88.

Forrest, J 1876, 'On the natives of central and Western Australia', *The Journal of the Anthropological Institute of Great Britain and Ireland* 5:316–22.

Francis, P 1982, 'Experiments with early techniques for making whole shells into beads', *Current Anthropology* 23:713–14.

Francis, V 2002, 'Twenty interesting points: an analysis of bone artefacts from Platypus Rockshelter', *Queensland Archaeological Reports* 13:63–70.

Frankel, D 1986, 'Excavations in the lower southeast of South Australia: November 1985', *Australian Archaeology* 22:75–87.

Fraser, J 1892, *The Aborigines of New South Wales*, Charles Potter, Government Printer, Sydney.

Frison, G 1982, 'Bone butchering tools in archaeological sites', *Canadian Journal of Anthropology* 2:159–67.

—— & GM Zeimens 1980, 'Bone projectile points: an addition to the Folsom cultural complex', *American Antiquity* 45:231–37.

Fullagar, R 1986, Use-wear and residues on stone tools: functional analysis and its application to two southeastern Australian archaeological assemblages, unpublished PhD thesis, La Trobe University, Melbourne, VIC.

—— 1991, 'The role of silica in polish formation', *Journal of Archaeological Science* 18:1–24.

Gallus, A 1970, 'The Keilor project', *The Artefact* 18:1–8.

—— & ED Gill 1973, 'Aboriginal bone fish hooks with Aboriginal skeletons at Wallpolla Creek, west of Mildura, Victoria, Australia', *Memoirs of the National Museum of Victoria* 34:215–16.

Gamble, C 1980, 'Information exchange in the Palaeolithic', *Nature* 283:522–23.

—— 1982, 'Interaction and alliance in Palaeolithic society', *Man* 17:92–107.

REFERENCES

Gason, S 2009[1879], 'The manners and customs of the Dieyerie Tribe of Australian Aborigines' in JD Woods (ed.), *The native tribes of South Australia*, State Library of South Australia, Adelaide, pp 257–307.

Gates St-Pierre, C 2007, 'Bone awls of the St. Lawrence Iroquonians: a microwear analysis' in C Gates St-Pierre & RB Walker (eds), *Bones as tools: current methods and interpretations in worked bone studies*, British Archaeological Reports, International Series 1622, Oxford, pp 107–118.

—— 2018, 'Needles and bodies: a micro wear analysis of experimental bone tattooing instruments', *Journal of Archaeological Science: Reports* 20:881–87.

Gaudzinski, S 1999, 'Middle Palaeolithic bone tools from the open-air site Salzgitter-Lebenstedt (Germany)', *Journal of Archaeological Science* 26:125–41.

—— E Turner, AP Anzidei, E Álvarez-Fernández, J Arroyo-Cabrales, et al. 2005, 'The use of Proboscidean remains in every-day Palaeolithic life', *Quaternary International* 126–28:179–94.

Gill, ED 1974, 'Aboriginal menus and cooking methods as inferred from archaeological sites in southeast Australia', *The Artefact* 35:1–8.

—— & MR Banks 1956, *Cainozoic history of Mowbray Swamp and other areas of north-western Tasmania*, Records of the Queen Victoria Museum, Launceston, New Series, No. 6, The Queen Victoria Museum, Launceston.

Gilligan, I 2007, 'Clothing and modern human behaviour: prehistoric Tasmania as a case study', *Archaeology in Oceania* 42:102–11.

Girya, EY & GA Khlopachev 2018, 'Experimental data on the spitting and knapping of mammoth tusks and reindeer antlers' in M Christensen & N Goutas (eds), *À coup d'éclats! La fracturation des matières osseuses en préhistoire*, Société Préhistorique Française, Paris, pp 325–40.

Go, MC 2018, 'A case of human bone modification by ants (Hymenoptera: Formicidae) in the Philippines', *Forensic Anthropology* 1:117–23.

Goede, A, P Murray & R Harmon 1978, 'Pleistocene man and megafauna in Tasmania: dated evidence from cave sites', *The Artefact* 3:139–149.

Greenfield, HJ 1999, 'The origins of metallurgy: distinguishing stone from metal cut-marks on bones from archaeological sites', *Journal of Archaeological Science* 26:797–801.

—— 2006, 'Slicing cut marks on animal bones: diagnostics for identifying stone tool type and raw material', *Journal of Field Archaeology* 31:147–63.

Grey, G 1841, *Journals of two expeditions of discovery in north west and western Australia during the years 1837, 38, and 39*, Boon, London.

Guthrie, RD 1983, 'Osseous projectile points: biological considerations affecting raw material selection and design among Paleolithic and Paleoindian peoples' in J Clutton-Brock & C Grigson (eds), *Animals and archaeology*, British Archaeological Reports, International Series 163, Oxford, pp 273–94.

Guzzo Falci, C, J Cuisin, A Delpuech, A van Gijn & CL Hofman 2019, 'New insights into use-wear development in bodily ornaments through the study of ethnographic collections', *Journal of Archaeological Method and Theory* 26:755–805.

Haagen, C 1994, *Bush toys. Aboriginal children at play*, Aboriginal Studies Press, Canberra.

Haddon, AC 1912, *Reports of the Cambridge anthropological expedition to Torres Straits, Vol. 4: arts and crafts*, Cambridge University Press, Cambridge.

Hagelberg, E & JB Clegg 1991, 'Isolation and characterisation of DNA from archaeological bone', *Proceedings of the Royal Society B* 244:45–50.

Haglund, L 1976, *An archaeological analysis of the Broadbeach Aboriginal burial ground*, University of Queensland Press, St Lucia.

Hale, HM & NB Tindale 1930, 'Notes on some human remains in the Lower

REFERENCES

Murray Valley, South Australia', *Records of the South Australian Museum* 4:145–218.

—— & NB Tindale 1933, 'Aborigines of Princess Charlotte Bay, north Queensland', *Records of the South Australian Museum* 5:63–116.

Hamlyn-Harris, R 1918, 'Queensland ethnological notes 2', *Memoirs of the Queensland Museum* 6:4–12.

Hamm, G, P Mitchell, LJ Arnold, GJ Prideaux, D Questiaux, NA Spooner et al. 2016, 'Cultural innovation and megafauna interaction in the early settlement of arid Australia', *Nature* 539:280–283.

Hammond, JE 1933, *Winjan's People: the story of the south west Australian Aborigines*, Imperial Printing, Perth.

Hardy, BL, M-H Moncel, C Kerfant, M Lebone, L Bellot-Gurlet & N Mélard 2020, 'Direct evidence of Neanderthal fibre technology and its cognitive and behavioral implications', *Scientific Reports* 10:4889.

Harmand, S, JE Lewis, CS Feibel, CJ Lepre, S Prat, A Lenoble et al. 2015, '3.3-million-year-old stone tools from Lomekwi 3, west Turkana, Kenya', *Nature* 521:310–315.

Harney, WE & AP Elkin 1943, 'Melville and Bathurst islanders: a short description', *Oceania*, 13:228–34.

Harrison, R 2009, 'The archaeology of Port Headland coastal plain and implications for understanding the prehistory of shell mounds and middens in north-western Australia', *Archaeology in Oceania* 44:81–98.

Hassell, E & DS Davidson 1936, 'Notes on the ethnology of the Wheelman tribe of south-western Australia', *Anthropos* 31:679–711.

Hassell, K 1966, *The relations between the settlers and Aborigines in South Australia, 1836–1860*, Libraries Board of South Australia, Adelaide.

Haydon, GH 1846, *Five years experience in Australia Felix*, Hamilton, Adams and Company, London.

Haynes, G 1983, 'A guide for differentiating mammalian carnivore taxa responsible for gnaw damage to herbivore limb bones', *Paleobiology* 9:164–72.

—— 1988, 'Longitudinal studies of African elephant death and bone deposits', *Journal of Archaeological Science* 15:131–57.

—— 1991, *Mammoths, mastodons, and elephants: biology, behavior, and the fossil record*, Cambridge University Press, Cambridge.

—— & D. Stanford 1984, 'On the possible utilization of *Camelops* by early man in North America', *Quaternary Research* 22:216–230.

Head, L 1985, 'Pollen analysis of sediments from the Bridgewater Caves archaeological site, southwestern Victoria', *Australian Archaeology* 20:1–15.

Heckel, C 2009a, Widening the lens: physical science research and microscopy in the archaeological study of mammoth ivory, unpublished Master's thesis, New York University, New York.

—— 2009b, 'Physical characteristics of mammoth ivory and their implications for ivory work in the Upper Palaeolithic', *Mitteilungen der Gesellschaft fur Urgeschichte* 18:71–91.

—— & S Wolf 2014, 'Ivory debitage by fracture in the Aurignacian: experimental and archaeological examples', *Journal of Archaeological Science* 42:1–14.

Hedges, REM, AR Millar & AWG Pike 1995, 'Measurements and relationships of diagenetic alteration of bone from three archaeological sites', *Journal of Archaeological Science* 22:201–09.

Henshilwood, CS, F d'Errico, CW Marean, RG Milo & R Yates 2001, 'An early bone tool industry from the Middle Stone Age at Blombos Cave, South Africa: implications for the origins of modern human behaviour, symbolism and language', *Journal of Human Evolution* 41:631–78.

—— KL van Niekerk, S Wurz, A Delagnes, SJ Armitage, RF Rifkin et al. 2014, 'Klipdrift shelter, southern cape, South Africa: preliminary report on the Howiesons Poort layers', *Journal of Archaeological Science* 45:284–303.

REFERENCES

Hiscock, P 2008, *Archaeology of ancient Australia*, Routledge, London.

Hockett, BS 1996, 'Corroded, thinned and polished bones created by golden eagles (*Aquila chrysaetos*): taphonomic implications for archaeological interpretations', *Journal of Archaeological Science* 23:587–91.

Hodder, I 1990, 'Style as historical quality' in MW Conkey & C Hastorf (eds), *The uses of style in archaeology*, Cambridge University Press, Cambridge, pp 44–51.

Hoffman, BW 2002, 'Broken eyes and simple grooves: understanding eastern Aleut needle technology through experimental manufacture and use of bone needles' in L Frank, RS Shepard & GA Reinhardt (eds), *Many faces of gender*, University Press of Colorado, Boulder, pp 151–64.

Hohenstein, UT, E Gargani & M Bertolini 2020, 'Use-wear analysis of bone and antler tools from Farneto (Bologna, Italy) and Sa Osa (Oristano, Italy) archaeological sites', *Journal of Archaeological Science: Reports* 32:102386.

Holdaway, S & N Stern 2004, *A record in stone. The study of Australia's flaked stone artefacts*, Museum Victoria/Aboriginal Studies Press, Melbourne/Canberra.

Horton, D 1994, *The encyclopaedia of Aboriginal Australia: Aboriginal and Torres Strait Island history, society and culture*, Aboriginal Studies Press, Canberra.

Hunter, J 1968[1793], *An historical journal of events at Sydney and at sea 1787–1792*, John Bach, Sydney.

Hounslow, O, J Simpson, L Whalley & M Collins 2013, 'An introduction to ZooMS (zooarchaeology by mass spectrometry) for taxonomic identification of worked and raw materials' in A Choyke & S O'Connor (eds), *From these bare bones: raw materials and the study of worked osseous objects*, Oxbow Books, Oxford, pp 201–07.

Howitt, AW 1972[1878], 'Notes on the Aborigines of Cooper's Creek' in R Brough Smyth (ed.), *The Aborigines of Victoria and other parts of Australia and Tasmania, Vol. II*, John Curry, O'Neil, South Yarra, pp 300–09.

—— 2001[1904], *The native tribes of south-east Australia*, Aboriginal Studies Press, Canberra.

Hutson, JM, CC Burke & G Haynes 2013, 'Osteophagia and bone modifications by giraffe and other large ungulates', *Journal of Archaeological Science* 40:4139–49.

Hutchinson, S 2012, Them bones, them bones. A technological and functional analysis of the faunal bone artefacts from Ngaut Ngaut (Devon Downs), South Australia, unpublished Honours dissertation, Department of Archaeology, La Trobe University.

Isaacs, J 1987, *Bush food: Aboriginal food and herbal medicine*, New Holland, Sydney.

Jardine, J 1866, 'Description of the neighbourhood of Somerset, Cape York, Australia', *Journal of the Royal Geographical Society* 36:76–85.

Jochim, MA 1983, 'Palaeolithic art in ecological perspective' in G Bailey (ed.), *Hunter-gatherer economy in prehistory: a European perspective*, Cambridge University Press, Cambridge, pp 212–19.

Johnston, H & P Clark 1998, 'Willandra Lakes archaeological investigations 1968–98', *Archaeology in Oceania* 33:105–119.

Jones, PR 1980, 'Experimental butchery with modern stone tools and its relevance for Palaeolithic archaeology', *World Archaeology* 12:153–65.

Jones, R 1971, Rocky Cape and the problem of the Tasmanians, unpublished PhD thesis, Faculty of Arts, University of Sydney, Sydney.

Jorgenson, J 1829, *History of the origin, rise, and progress, of the Van Diemen's Land Company*, Robson, Blades, London.

Juana de, S, AB Galán & M Domínquez-Rodrigo 2010, 'Taphonomic identification of cut marks made with lithic handaxes: an experimental study', *Journal of Archaeological Science* 37:1841–50.

Julien, M 1977 'Harpons unilatéraux et bilatéraux: evolution morphologique ou adaptation différenciée?' in

REFERENCES

H Camps-Fabrer (ed.), *Méthodologie appliquée a l'industrie de l'os préhistorique*, Éditions du Centre National de la Recherche Scientifique, Paris, pp 177–189.

—— 1982, *Les harpons magdaléniens, supplement a Gallia Préhistoire 17*, Éditions du Centre National de la Recherche Scientifique, Paris.

Kaiser, GW 2007, *The inner bird: anatomy and evolution*, UBC Press, Vancouver.

Kamminga, J 1978, Journey into the microcosms: a functional analysis of certain classes of prehistoric Australian stone tools, unpublished PhD thesis, University of Sydney, Sydney, NSW.

—— & H Allen 1973, *Report of the archaeological survey, Alligator rivers environmental fact-finding study*, Government Printer, Darwin.

Keddie, G 2012, 'Ulna bone tools: identifying their function', *The Midden* 44:23–8.

Keeley, LH 1980, *Experimental determination of stone tool uses*, University of Chicago Press, Chicago.

Kirby, J 1894, *Old times in the bush of Australia*, James Curtis, Ballarat.

Knecht, H 1991a, Technological innovation and design during the early Upper Paleolithic: a study of organic projectile technologies, unpublished PhD dissertation, New York University, New York.

—— 1991b, 'The role of innovation in changing Early Upper Paleolithic organic projectile technologies', *Techniques et Culture* 17–18:115–144.

—— 1993, 'Early Upper Paleolithic approaches to bone and antler projectile technology' in G Larsen Peterkin, HM Bricker & P Mellars (eds), *Hunting and animal exploitation in the Later Palaeolithic and Mesolithic of Eurasia*, Archaeological Papers of the American Anthropological Association No. 4, pp 33–47.

—— 1997, 'Projectile points of bone, antler, and stone: experimental explorations of manufacture and use' in H Knecht (ed.), *Projectile technology*, Plenum Press, New York, pp 191–212.

Kohen, JL, ED Stockton & MAJ Williams 1984, 'Shaws Creek KII Rockshelter: a prehistoric occupation site in the Blue Mountains Piedmont, eastern New South Wales', *Archaeology in Oceania* 19:57–73.

Krueger, KL, JC Willman, GJ Matthews, J-J Hublin & A Pérez-Pérez 2019, 'Anterior tooth-use behaviors among early modern humans and Neandertals', *PLoS One* 14:e0224573.

Kuhn, SL & MC Stiner 2007a, 'Body ornamentation as information technology: towards an understanding of the significance of early beads' in P Mellars, K Boyle, O Bar-Yosef & C Stringer (eds), *Rethinking the human revolution: new behavioural and biological perspectives on the origin and dispersal of modern humans*, McDonald Institute for Archaeological Research, Cambridge, pp 45–54.

—— & MC Stiner 2007b, 'Paleolithic ornaments: implication for cognition, demography and identity', *Diogenes* 54:40–8.

Kumbani, J, J Bradfield, N Rusch & S Wurz 2019, 'A functional investigation of southern Cape Later Stone Age artefacts resembling aerophones', *Journal of Archaeological Science: Reports* 24:693–711.

Lampert, RJ 1966, 'An excavation at Durras North, NSW', *Archaeology and Physical Anthropology in Oceania* 1:83–118.

—— 1971, *Burrill Lake and Currarong; coastal sites in southern New South Wales, Terra Australis 1*, Department of Prehistory, Australian National University, Canberra.

Langley, MC 2015, 'Investigating maintenance and discard behaviours for osseous projectile points: a Middle to Late Magdalenian (c.19,000 to 14,000 cal. BP) example', *Journal of Anthropological Archaeology* 40:340–60.

—— 2018, 'Establishing a typology for Australian pointed bone implements', *Australian Archaeology* 84:164–80.

—— 2020, 'Re-analysis of the "engraved" Diprotodon tooth from Spring Creek, Victoria, Australia', *Archaeology in Oceania* 55:33–41.

REFERENCES

—— 2021, Analysis of osseous technologies from Madjedbebe, unpublished report prepared for Gundjeihmi Aboriginal Corporation.

—— J Balme & S O'Connor 2021a, 'Bone artefacts from Riwi Cave, south-central Kimberley: reappraisal of the timing and role of osseous artefacts in northern Australia', *International Journal of Osteoarchaeology* 31(5):673–82.

—— O Carriage & the Walbunga Custodian Elders 2021b, 'Insights from a small sea cave: re-analysis of the bone technology from Durras North, Yuin country, coastal New South Wales, Australia', *Australian Archaeology* 88:18–30.

—— & S O'Connor 2015, '6500-year-old Nassarius shell appliqués in Timor-Leste: technological and use wear analyses', *Journal of Archaeological Science* 62:175–92.

—— & S O'Connor 2016, 'An enduring shell artefact tradition from Timor-Leste: Oliva bead production from the Pleistocene to Late Holocene at Jerimalai, Lene Hara, and Matja Kuru 1 and 2', *PLoS One* 11:e0161071.

—— S O'Connor & K Aplin 2016, 'A >46,000-year-old macropod bone implement from Carpenter's Gap 1: challenging past perspectives of Pleistocene Australia', *Quaternary Science Reviews* 154:199–213.

—— & T Suddendorf 2020, 'Mobile containers in human cognitive evolution studies: understudied and underrepresented', *Evolutionary Anthropology* 29:299–309.

—— L Wallis, M Nango, D Djandjomerr, C Nadjamerrek, R Djandjul & R Gamarrawu 2023, 'Fishhooks, fishing spears, and weaving: The bone technology of Madjedbebe, Northern Autralia', *International Journal of Osteoarchaeology* DOI:10.1002/oa.3201.

Lartet, E & H Christy 1864, *Reliquae aquitanicae: being a contribution to the archaeology and paleontology of the Perigord and adjoining provinces of southern France*, Ruper Jones, London.

Lave, J & E Wenger 1991, *Situated learning: legitimate peripheral participation*, Cambridge University Press, Cambridge.

Lbova, L & P Volkov 2016, 'Processing technology for the objects of mobile art in the Upper Palaeolithic of Siberia (the Malta site)', *Quaternary International* 403:16–22.

Leakey, MD 1971, *Olduvai Gorge, Vol. 3, Excavations in Beds I and II*, Cambridge University Press, Cambridge.

Leder, D, R Hermann, M Hüls, G Russo, P Hoelzmann, R Nielbock, et al. 2021, 'A 51,000-year-old engraved bone reveals Neanderthals' capacity for symbolic behaviour', *Nature Ecology & Evolution* 5:1273–82.

Leichhardt, L 1847, *Journal of an overland expedition in Australia from Moreton Bay to Port Essington*, T. and W. Boone, London.

Legrand, A 2007, *Fabrication et utilisation de l'outillage en matières osseuses du Meolithiques de Chypre: Khirokitia et Cap Andreas-Kastros*, British Archaeological Reports, International Series 1678, Oxford.

LeMoine, GM 1989, 'Use wear analysis of bone tools', *Archaeozoologia* 3:211–24.

—— 1991, Experimental analysis of the manufacture and use of bone and antler tools among the Mackenzie Inuit, unpublished PhD thesis, University of Calgary, Calgary.

—— 1994, 'Use wear on bone and antler tools from the Mackenzie Delta, Northwest Territories', *American Antiquity* 59:316–34.

—— 1997, *Use wear analysis on bone and antler tools of the Mackenzie Inuit*, British Archaeological Reports International Series, Oxford.

Lemonnier, P 1993, *Technological choices: transformation in material culture since the Neolithic*, Routledge, London.

Li, F, CJ Bae, CB Ramsey, F Chen & X Gao 2018, 'Re-dating Zhoukoudian Upper Cave, northern China and its regional significance', *Journal of Human Evolution* 121:170–77.

Lillios, KT 1999, 'Objects of memory: the ethnography and archaeology of

REFERENCES

heirlooms', *Journal of Archaeological Method and Theory* 6:235–62.

Lockyer, M 1923, 'Expedition sent from Sydney in 1826 to found a settlement at King George's Sound, Western Australia' in HP Moore (ed.), *Notes on the early settlers in South Australia prior to 1836*, Royal Geographical Society of Australia, South Australia.

López-González, F, A Grandal-d'Anglade & JR Vidal-Romaní 2006, 'Deciphering bone depositional sequences in caves through the study of manganese coatings', *Journal of Archaeological Science* 33:707–17.

Lourandos, H 1976, 'Archaeological fieldwork in south-western Victoria 1974/1975', *Australian Archaeology* 4:9–10.

Lumholtz, C 1889, *Among cannibals: an account of four years travels in Australia and of camp life with the Aborigines of Queensland*, Murray, London.

Lyman, RL 1984, 'Broken bones, bone expediency tools, and bone pseudotools: lessons from the blast zone around Mount St. Helens, Washington', *American Antiquity* 49:315–33.

—— 1994, *Vertebrate taphonomy*, Cambridge University Press, Cambridge.

—— 2021, 'On the importance of systematics to archaeological research: the covariation of typological diversity and morphological disparity', *Journal of Palaeolithic Archaeology* 4:3.

—— & GL Fox 1989, 'A critical evolution of bone weathering as an indication of bone assemblage formation', *Journal of Archaeological Science* 16:293–317.

—— MJ O'Brien & V Hayes 1998, 'A mechanical and functional study of bone rods from the Richey-Roberts Clovis cache, Washington, U.S.A.', *Journal of Archaeological Science* 25:887–906.

MacGregor, A 1985, *Bone, antler, ivory & horn. The technology of skeletal materials since the Roman period*, Croom Helm, London.

Macintosh, NWG 1971, 'Analysis of an Aboriginal skeleton and a pierced tooth necklace from Lake Nitchie, Australia', *Anthropologies* 9:49–62.

—— KN Smith & AB Bailey 1970, 'Lake Nitchie skeleton: unique Aboriginal burial', *Archaeology & Physical Anthropology in Oceania* 5:85–100.

Mackaness, G 1941, 'George Augustus Robinson's journal into south-eastern Australia, 1844', *Journal of the Royal Australian Historical Society* 27:318–49.

Maigrot, Y 1997, 'Tracéologie des outils tranchants en os des Ve et IVe millénaires Av. J.-C. en Bassin Parisien: Essai méthodologique et application', *Bulletin de la Société Préhistorique Française* 94:198–216.

Maloney, T, S O'Connor, D Vannieuwenhuyse, J Balme & J Fyfe 2016, 'Re-excavation of Djuru, a Holocene rockshelter in the southern Kimberley, North Western Australia', *Australian Archaeology* 82:80–85.

Mania, D & U Mania 2005, 'The natural and sociocultural environment of *Homo erectus* at Bilzingsleben, Germany' in C Gamble & M Porr (eds), *The hominin individual in context: archaeological investigations of Lower and Middle Palaeolithic landscapes, locales and artifacts*, Routledge, London, pp 98–114.

Marean, CW, M Bar-Matthews, J Bernatchez, E Fisher, P Goldberg, AIR Herries, et al. 2007, 'Early human use of marine resources and pigment in South Africa during the Middle Pleistocene', *Nature* 449:905–08.

Mărgărit, M 2016, 'Testing the endurance of prehistoric adornments: raw materials from the aquatic environment', *Journal of Archaeological Science* 70:66–81.

—— V Radu, A Boroneant & C Bonsall 2018, 'Experimental studies of personal ornaments from the Iron Gates Mesolithic', *Archaeological and Anthropological Sciences* 10:2095–2122.

Marshall, B & R Cosgrove 1990, 'Tasmanian devil (*Sarcophilus harrisii*) scat-bone: signature criteria and archaeological implications', *Archaeology in Oceania* 25:102–13.

Martellotta, EF, J Wilkins, A Brumm & MC Langley 2021, 'New data from old collections: retouch-induced marks on

REFERENCES

Australian hardwood boomerangs', *Journal of Archaeological Science: Reports* 37:102967.

Martín, MB, GIM Appel & GP Roldán 2018, 'Needles made of human bones from Xochimilco', *Quaternary International* 472:149–59.

Martisius, NL, F Welker, T Dogandžić, MN Grote, W Rendu, V Sinet-Mathiot, et al. 2020, 'Non-destrucion ZooMS identification reveals strategic bone raw material selection by Neandertals', *Scientific Reports* 10:7746.

Marun, LH 1972, The Morning and their predecessors on the coastal Nullarbor Plain, unpublished PhD thesis, University of Sydney, Sydney.

Mason, HGB 1909, *Darkest West Australia*, Hacking and co, Kalgoorlie.

Massola, A 1956, 'Australian fish hooks and their distribution', *Memories of the National Museum of Victoria* 22:1–17.

—— 1961, 'A Victorian skull-cap drinking bowl', *Mankind* 5:415.

Mathews, RH 1901, 'Ethnological notes on the Aboriginal tribes of the Northern Territory', *Queensland Geographical Journal* 16:69–90.

Matisoo-Smith, E & KA Horsburg 2012, *DNA for archaeologists*, Left Coast Press, California.

Matthews, JM 1966, 'The Hoabinhian affinities of some Australian assemblages', *Archaeology and Physical Anthropology in Oceania* 1:5–22.

McBryde, I 1968, 'Archaeological investigations in the Graman district', *Archaeology and Physical Anthropology in Oceania* 3:77–93.

—— 1974, *Aboriginal prehistory in New England*, Sydney University Press, Sydney.

McCarthy, FD 1936, 'The geographical distribution theory and Australian material culture', *Mankind* 2:12–6.

—— 1939, '"Trade" in Aboriginal Australia, and "trade" relationships with Torres Strait, New Guinea and Malaya', *Oceania* 9:405–38.

—— 1940, 'The bone point, known as muduk, in eastern Australia', *Records of the Australian Museum* 20:313–19.

—— 1948, 'The Lapstone Creek excavation: two culture periods revealed in eastern New South Wales', *Records of the Australian Museum* 22:1–34.

—— 1949, 'The prehistoric cultures of Australia', *Oceania* 29:305–319.

—— 1952, 'Some new records of tanged implements and pounders in eastern Australia', *Mankind* 4:361–64.

—— 1953, 'A circumcision ceremony and stone arrangement on Groote Eylandt', *Records of the Australian Museum* 23:97–103.

—— 1961, 'Report on Australian and Melanesia', *Asian Perspectives* 5:141–155.

—— 1965, 'The Aboriginal past: archaeological and material equipment' in RM Berndt & CH Berndt (eds), *Aboriginal man in Australia: essays in honour of Emeritus Professor A.P. Elkin*, Angus and Robertson, Sydney, pp 71–100.

—— 1976, *Australian Aboriginal stone implements*, The Australian Museum Trust, Sydney.

—— & FM Setzler 1960, 'The archaeology of Arnhem Land' in CP Mountford (ed.), *Records of the American-Australian scientific expedition to Arnhem Land, Vol. 2, anthropology and nutrition*, Melbourne University Press, Melbourne, pp 215–95.

McCourt, T 1975, *Aboriginal artefacts*, Rigby, Adelaide.

McDonald, J & A Ross 1990, 'Helping the police with their inquiries: archaeology and politics at Angophora Reserve Rockshelter, N.S.W.', *Archaeology in Oceania* 25:114–121.

McGrath, K, K Rowsell, C Gates St-Pierre, A Tedder, G Foody, C Roberts, et al. 2019, 'Identifying archaeological bone via non-destructive ZooMS and the materiality of symbolic expression: examples from Iroquoian bone points', *Scientific Reports* 9:11027.

McNiven, IJ & A Bedingfield 2008, 'Past and present marine mammal hunting rates and abundances: dugong (*Dugong dugon*) evidence from Dabangai Bone Mound, Torres Strait', *Journal of Archaeological Science* 35:505–15.

REFERENCES

—— J Crouch, M Weisler, N Kemp, L Clayton Martínez, J Stanisic, et al. 2008, 'Tigershark Rockshelter (Baidamau Mudh): seascape and settlement reconfigurations on the sacred islet of Pulu, Western Zenadh Kes (Torres Strait)', *Australian Archaeology* 66:15–32.

Meagher, SJ & WDL Riede 1979, 'Use of natural resources by the Aborigines of south-western Australia' in RM Berndt & CH Berndt (eds), *Aborigines of the west: their past and their present*, University of Western Australia Press, Perth, pp 66–80.

Meehan, B 1975, *Shell bed to shell midden*, unpublished PhD thesis, Australian National University, Canberra.

Megaw, JVS 1969, 'Trail excavations in Captain Cook's Landing Place Reserve, Kurnell, N.S.W.', *The Artefact* 1969:3–6.

—— & RVS Wright 1966, 'The excavation of an Aboriginal rock shelter on Gymea Bay, Port Hacking, N.S.W.', *Archaeology and Physical Anthropology in Oceania* 1:23–50.

Memmott, P 2007, *Gunya, goondie and wurley: the Aboriginal architecture of Australia*, University of Queensland Press, St Lucia.

Merritt, SR 2012, 'Factors affecting Early Stone Age cut mark cross-sectional size: implications from actualistic butchery trials', *Journal of Archaeological Science* 39:2984–94.

Meston, AL 1956, 'Miscellaneous notes on the culture of the Tasmanian Aboriginal', *Memoirs of the National Museum of Victoria* 20:1–9.

Meyer, HEA 1846, *Manners and customs of the Aborigines of the Encounter Bay Tribe, South Australia*, George Dehane, King William-Street, Adelaide.

Mitchell, SR 1958, 'An Aboriginal bone industry', *Mankind* 5:194–99.

Mitchell, TL 1965[1839]a, *Three expeditions into the interior of Eastern Australia; with descriptions of the recently explored region of Australia Felix, and of the present colony of New South Wales. Volume I*, T. & W. Boone/Libraries Board of South Australia, New Bond Street/Adelaide.

—— 1965[1839]b, *Three expeditions into the interior of Eastern Australia; with descriptions of the recently explored region of Australia Felix, and of the present colony of New South Wales. Volume II*, T. & W. Boone/Libraries Board of South Australia, New Bond Street/Adelaide.

Moore, DR 1976, 'Archaeological research in the Department of Anthropology, Australian Museum, Sydney', *Australian Archaeology* 5:7.

Moore, GF 1842, *A descriptive vocabulary of the language in common use amongst the Aborigines of Western Australia*, William S. Orr, London.

—— 1884, *Diary of ten years of an early settler in Western Australia; and also a descriptive vocabulary of the language of the Aborigines*, M Walbrook, London.

Morlan, RE 1980, *Taphonomy and archaeology in the Upper Pleistocene of the Northern Yukon territory: a glimpse of the peopling of the New World*, Musée National de Homme, Ottawa.

—— 1983, 'Spiral fractures on limb bones: which ones are artificial?' in GM LeMoine & AS MacEachern (eds), *Carnivores, human scavengers & predators: a question of bone technology*, Archaeological Association of the University of Calgary, Calgary, pp 241–69.

—— 1984, 'Toward the definition of criteria for the recognition of artificial bone alterations', *Quaternary Research* 22:160–71.

Morley, I 2013, *The prehistory of music. Human evolution, archaeology, and the origins of musicality*, Oxford University Press, Oxford.

Morwood MJ & LM Godwin 1982, 'Aboriginal sites in the Hughenden Region, North Queensland highlands', *Australian Archaeology* 15:49–53.

Müller, K & I Reiche 2011, 'Differentiation of archaeological ivory and bone materials by micro-PIXE/PIGE with emphasis on two Upper Palaeolithic key sites: Abri Pataud and Isturitz, France', *Journal of Archaeological Science* 38:3234–43.

Mulvaney, DJ 1960, 'Archaeological excavations at Fromm's Landing on the lower

REFERENCES

Murray River, South Australia', *Proceedings of the Royal Society of Victoria* 72:53–85.

—— 1962, 'Archaeological excavations on the Air River, Otway Peninsula, Victoria', *Proceedings of the Royal Society of Victoria* 75:1–15.

—— 1974, 'Summary report on first Mungo project season', *The Artefact* 32:4–5.

—— & J Kamminga 1999, *Prehistory of Australia*, Allen and Unwin, Sydney.

Murray-Wallace, CV & SM Colley 1997, 'Amino acid racemisation and radiocarbon dating of a contact period midden, Greenglade rockshelter, New South Wales', *Archaeology in Oceania* 32:163–169.

Newcomer, MH 1974, 'Study and replication of bone tools from Ksar Akil (Lebanon)', *World Archaeology* 6:138–53.

—— 1977, 'Experiments in Upper Paleolithic bone work' in H Camps-Fabrer (ed.), *Methodologie appliqué a l'industrie de l'os préhistorique*, Éditions du Centre National du Recherche Scientific, Paris, pp 293–301.

Nind, S 1831, 'Description of the Natives of King George's Sound (Swan River colony) and adjoining country', *The Journal of the Anthropological Institute of Great Britain and Ireland* 1:21–51.

Nivens, JR 2020, Coloring materials in the Vézère Valley (France): insights into early Aurignacian intra-regional variability, unpublished PhD thesis, New York University, New York.

Noe-Nygaard, N 1989, 'Man-made trace fossils on bones', *Human Evolution* 4:461–91.

O'Brien, MJ, RL Lyman, B Buchanan & M Collard 2016, 'A review of the late Pleistocene North America bone and ivory tools' in MC Langley (ed.), *Osseous projectile weaponry: towards an understanding of Pleistocene cultural variability*, VERT Series, Springer, Dordrecht, pp 221–235.

O'Connell, JF 1995, 'Ethnoarchaeology needs a general theory of behavior', *Journal of Archaeological Research* 3:205–55.

O'Connor, S 1992, 'The timing and nature of prehistoric island use in northern Australia', *Archaeology in Oceania* 27:49–60.

Odell, GH 1975, 'Micro-wear in perspective: a sympathetic response to Lawrence H Keeley', *World Archaeology* 7:226–40.

—— 1977, The application of micro-wear analysis to the lithic component of an entire prehistoric settlement: methods, problems and functional reconstructions, unpublished PhD dissertation, Harvard University, Cambridge.

—— 1981, 'The mechanics of use-breakage of stone tools: some testable hypotheses', *Journal of Field Archaeology* 8:197–209.

Oliver, JS 1989, 'Analogues and site context: bone damages from Shield Trap Cave (24CB91), Carbon County, Montana, U.S.A.' in R Bonnichsen & MH Sorg (eds), *Bone modification*, Centre for the Study of the First Americans, Orono, pp 73–98.

—— 1994, 'Estimates of homing and carnivore involvement in the FLK Zinjanthropus fossil assemblage: some socioecological implications', *Journal of Human Evolution* 27:267–94.

Olsen, SL 1979, 'A study of bone artifacts from Grasshopper Pueblo, AZ P:14:1', *Kiva* 44:341–73.

—— 1980, 'Bone artifacts from Kinishba Ruin: their manufacture and use', *Kiva* 46:39–67.

—— 1984, Analytical approaches to the manufacture and use of bone artifats in prehistory, unpublished doctoral thesis, University of London, London.

—— 1988, 'The identification of stone and metal tool marks on bone artifacts' in SL Olsen (ed.), *Scanning electron microscopy in archaeology*, British Archaeological Reports International Series 452, Oxford, pp 337–60.

—— & P Shipman 1988, 'Surface modification on bone: trampling versus butchery', *Journal of Archaeological Science* 15:535–53.

Orton, J 2008, 'Later Stone Age ostrich eggshell bead manufacture in the Northern Cape, South Africa', *Journal of Archaeological Science* 35:1765–75.

Osgood, C 1940, *Ingalik material culture*, Yale University Publications in Anthropology, New Haven.

REFERENCES

Osipowicz, G, G Piličiauskienė, J Orłowską & G Piličiauskas 2020, 'An occasional ornament, part of clothes or just a gift for ancestors? The results of traceological studies of teeth pendants from the Subneolithic sites in Šventoji, Lithuania', *Journal of Archaeological Science: Reports* 29:102130.

Ossa, P, B Marshall & C Webb 1995, 'New Guinea II cave: a Pleistocene site on the Snowy River, Victoria', *Archaeology in Oceania* 30:22–35.

Owen, TD & FD Pate 2014, 'A Kaurna burial, Salisbury, South Australia: further evidence for complex late Holocene Aboriginal social systems in the Adelaide region', *Australian Archaeology* 79:45–53.

Palmer, E 1884, 'Notes on some Australian tribes', *The Journal of the Anthropological Institute of Great Britain and Ireland* 13:276–347.

Pante, M, I de la Torre, F d'Errico, J Njau & R Blumenschine 2020, 'Bone tools from beds II–IV, Olduvai Gorge, Tanzania, and implications for the origins and evolution of bone technology', *Journal of Human Evolution* 148:102885.

Pardoe, C 1993, 'Wamba Yadu, a later Holocene cemetery of the Central River Murray', *Archaeology in Oceania* 28:77–84.

Pargeter, J & J Bradfield 2012, 'The effects of class I and II bovids on macro fracture formation and tool displacement: results of a trampling experiment in a southern African Stone Age context', *Journal of Field Archaeology* 37:238–51.

Parr, J 1999, 'Once, twice maybe, but not three times: reheating *Xanthorrhoea australis* resin', *Australian Archaeology* 49:23–27.

Peltier, A 1992, 'Fiche générale bâtons percés' in H Barge-Mahieu, H Camps-Fabrer, V Feruglio, A Peltier & D Ramseyer (eds), *Fiches typologiques de l'industrie osseuse Prehistoric, Cahier V, Bâtons percés, baguettes*, Éditions du CEDARC, Treignes, pp 7–34.

Pennycuick, CK 1967, 'The strength of the pigeon's wing bones in relation to their function', *Journal of Experimental Biology* 46:219–33.

Perez, VR, LR Godfrey, M Nowak-Kemp, DA Burney, J Ratsimbazafy & N Vasey 2005, 'Evidence of butchery of giant lemurs in Madagascar', *Journal of Human Evolution* 49:722–42.

Perston, YL, M Moore, Suryatman, MC Langley, B Hakim, AA Oktaviana, et al. 2021, 'A standardised classification scheme for the mid-Holocene Toalean artefacts of south Sulawesi, Indonesia', *PLOS One* 16:e0251138.

Pétillon, J-M 2005, 'Tir experimental de pointes a base fourchue en bois de renne' in V Dujardin (ed.), *Industrie osseuse et parures du Solutréen au Magdalénien en Europe*, Société Préhistorique Française, Paris, pp 243–56.

—— 2006, *Des magdaléniens en arms. Technologie des armatures de projectile en bois de cervidé du magdalénien supérieur de la Grotte d'Isturitz (Pyrénées-Atlantiques)*, Centre d'Etudes et de Documentation Archeologique, Treignes.

—— & S Ducasse 2012, 'From flakes to grooves: a technical shift in antler working during the last glacial maximum in southwest France', *Journal of Human Evolution* 62:435–65.

Petrie, CC 1904, *Tom Petrie's reminiscences of early Queensland (dating from 1837)*, Watson, Ferguson & Company, Brisbane.

Pickering, TR, M Domínguez-Rodrigo, CP Egeland & CK Brain 2004, 'Beyond leopards: tooth marks and the contribution of multiple carnivore taxa to the accumulation of the Swartkrans Member 3 fossil assemblage', *Journal of Human Evolution* 46:595–604.

—— & CP Egeland 2006, 'Experimental patterns of hammerstone percussion damage on bones: implications for inferences of carcass processing by humans', *Journal of Archaeological Science* 33:459–69.

Pitman, HT & LA Wallis 2012, 'The point of spinifex: Aboriginal uses of spinifex grasses in Australia', *Ethnobotany Research and Applications* 10:109–31.

Plomley, NJB 2008, *Friendly mission: the Tasmanian journals of George Augustus*

REFERENCES

Robinson, Queen Victoria Museum, Launceston.

Pobiner, BL & DR Braun 2005, 'Strengthening the inferential link between cut mark frequency data and Oldowan hominid behavior: results from modern butchery experiments', *Journal of Taphonomy* 3:107–20.

Pokines, J 1998, 'Experimental replication and use of Cantabrian Lower Magdalenian antler projectile points', *Journal of Archaeological Science* 25:875–86.

—— & CJH Ames 2015, 'Weathering and dispersal of a cattle (*Bos taurus*) carcass in the desert of eastern Jordan over a six-year interval', *Journal of Taphonomy* 13:17–31.

—— & M Krupa 1997, 'Self-barbed antler spearpoints and evidence of fishing in the Late Upper Paleolithic of Cantabrian Spain' in H Knecht (ed.), *Projectile technology*, Plenum Press, London, pp 241–62.

Pomi, LH & ED Tonni 2011, 'Termite traces on bones from the Late Pleistocene of Argentina', *Ichnos* 18:166–71.

Porteus, SD 1931, *The psychology of a primitive people*, Edwin Arnold, London.

Potts, R & P Shipman 1981, 'Cutmarks made by stone tools on bones from Olduvai Gorge, Tanzania', *Nature* 291:577–80.

Pretty, GL 1977, 'The cultural chronology of the Roonka Flat' in RVS Wright (ed.), *Stone tools as cultural markers*, Australian Institute of Aboriginal Studies, Canberra, pp 288–331.

Quinnell, MC 1976, Aboriginal rock art in Carnarvon Gorge, south central Queensland, unpublished Master's thesis, University of New England, Armidale, NSW.

Radmilli, AM & G Boschian 1996, *Gli scavi a Castel di Guido. Il piu antico giacimento di cacciatori del Paleolitico Inferiore nell'agro Romano*, Istituto Italiano di Preistoria e Protostoria, Firenze.

Redmond, BG & KB Tankersley 2005, 'Evidence of Early Paleoindian bone modification and use at the Sheriden Cave Site (33WY252), Wyandot Country, Ohio', *American Antiquity* 70:503–26.

Reiche, I, L Favre-Quattropani, T Calligaro, J Salomon, H Bocherens, L Charlet, et al. 1999, 'Trace element composition of archaeological bones and post-mortem alteration in the burial environment', *Nuclear Instruments and Methods in Physics Research B* 150:656–62.

—— K Müller, A Staude, J Goebbels & H Riesemeir 2011, 'Synchrotron radiation and laboratory micro X-ray computed tomography—useful tools for the material identification of prehistoric objects made of ivory, bone or antler', *Journal of Analytical Atomic Spectrometry* 9:1802–12.

Rensberger, JM & HB Krentz 1988, 'Microscopic effects of predator digestion on the surfaces of bones and teeth', *Scanning Microscopy* 2:1541–51.

Richter, D, R Grün, R Joannes-Boyau, TE Steele, F Amani, M Rue, et al. 2017, 'The age of the hominin fossils from Jebel Irhoud, Morocco, and the origins of the Middle Stone Age', *Nature* 546:293296.

Rick, TC 2002, 'Eolian processes, ground cover, and the archaeology of coastal dunes: a taphonomic case study from San Miguel Island, California, U.S.A.', *Geoarchaeology* 17:811–33.

Rigaud, S, S Costamagno, J-M Pétillon, P Chalard, V Laroulandie & M Langalis 2019, 'Settlement dynamic and beadwork: new insights on Late Upper Paleolithic craft activities', *PaleoAnthropology* 2019:137–55.

—— M Vanhaeren, A Queffelec, G Le Bourdon & F d'Errico 2014, 'The way we wear makes the difference: residue analysis applied to Mesolithic personal ornaments from Hohlenstein-Stadel (Germany)', *Archaeological and Anthropological Sciences* 6:133–44.

Roberts, E, R Rogers & BZ Foreman 2003, 'An experimental approach to identifying and interpreting dermestid (Insecta, Coleoptera) bone modification', *Journal of Vertebrate Paleontology* 23:89A.

Roberts, M & S Parfitt, S 1999, *A Middle Pleistocene hominid site at Eartham Quarry, Boxgrove, West Sussex*, English Heritage, London.

REFERENCES

Rodríguez-Hidalgo, A, JI Morales, A Cobra, LA Courtenay, JL Fernández-Marchena, G García-Argudo, et al. 2019, 'The Châtelperronian Neanderthals of Cova Foradada (Calafell, Spain) used imperial eagle phalanges for symbolic purposes', *Science Advances* 5:10.1126/sciadv.aax1984.

Romandini, M, M Peresani, V Laroulandie, L Metz, A Pastoors, M Vaquero et al. 2014, 'Convergent evidence of eagle talon used by late Neanderthals in Europe: a further assessment on symbolism', *PloS One* 9:e1011278.

—— E Cristiani & M Peresani 2015, 'A retouched bone shaft from the Late Mousterian at Fumane cave (Italy). Technological, experimental and micro-wear analysis', *Comptes Rendus Palevol* 14:63–72.

Rosell, J, R Blasco, G Campeny, JC Díez, RA Alcalde, L Menéndez, JL Arsuaga, JM Bermúdez de Castro & E Carbonell 2011, 'Bone as a technological raw material at the Gran Dolina site (Sierra de Atapuerca, Burgos, Spain)', *Journal of Human Evolution* 61:125–131.

—— R Blasco, JF Peris, E Carbonell, R Barkai & A Gopher 2015, 'Recycling bones in the Middle Pleistocene: some reflections from Gran Dolina TD10-1 (Spain), Bolomor Cave (Spain) and Qesem Cave (Israel)', *Quaternary International* 361:297–312.

Roth, WE 1897, *Ethnological studies among the north west central Queensland Aborigines*, Government Printer, Brisbane.

—— 1901 *Food: its search, capture, and preparation, North Queensland ethnography, Bulletin no. 3*, Government Printer, Brisbane.

—— 1902, *Games, sports and amusements, North Queensland ethnography, Bulletin no. 4*, Government Printer: Brisbane.

—— 1903a, *Superstition, magic, and medicine, North Queensland ethnography, Bulletin no. 5*, Government Printer, Brisbane.

—— 1903b, *An elementary grammar of the Nggerikudi language, North Queensland ethnography, Bulletin no. 6*, Government Printer, Brisbane.

—— 1904, *Domestic implements, arts and manufactures, North Queensland ethnography, Bulletin no. 7*, Government Printer, Brisbane.

—— 1907, *Burial customs, and disposal of the dead, North Queensland ethnography, Bulletin no. 9*, The Australian Museum, Sydney.

—— 1909a, *On certain initiation ceremonies, North Queensland ethnography, Bulletin no. 12*, The Australian Museum, Sydney.

—— 1909b, *Fighting weapons, North Queensland ethnography, Bulletin no. 13*, The Australian Museum, Sydney.

—— 1910a, *Transport and trade, North Queensland ethnography, Bulletin no. 14*, The Australian Museum, Sydney.

—— 1910b, *Decoration, deformation and clothing, North Queensland ethnography, Bulletin no. 15*, The Australian Museum, Sydney.

Rozoy, JG 1992, 'Experimentation de lancer de sagaies avec le propulseur', *Bulletin de la Société Royale Belge d'Études Geologiques et Archeologiques—Les Chercheurs de la Wallonie* 32:169–84.

Runnings, A, C Gustafson & D Bentley 1989, 'Use-wear on bone tools: a technique for study under the scanning electron microscope' in R Bonnichsen & M Sorg (eds), *Bone modification*, Centre for the Study of the First Americans, Orono, pp 259–266.

Rybczynski, N, JC Gosse, CR Harington, R Wogelius, A Hidy & M Buckley 2013, 'Mid-Pliocene warm-period deposits in the High Arctic yield insight into camel evolution', Nature Communications 4:1550.

Sackett, JR 1973, 'Style, function and artifact variability in Palaeolithic assemblages' in C Renfrew (ed.), *The explanation of culture change*, University of Pittsburgh Press, Pittsburgh, pp 317–325.

Sano, K, Y Beyene, S Katoh, D Koyabu, H Endo, T Sasaki et al. 2020, 'A 1.4-million-year-old bone handaxe from Konso, Ethiopia, shows advanced tool technology in the early Acheulean', *Proceedings of the National Academy of Sciences* 117:18393–400.

REFERENCES

Sayre, MP, MJ Miller & SA Rosenfeld 2016, 'Isotopic evidence for the trade and production of exotic marine mammal bone artifacts at Chavín de Huántar, Peru', *Archaeological and Anthropological Science* 8:403–417.

Schiffer, M 1987, *Formation processes of the archaeological record*, University of New Mexico Press, Albuquerque.

Schrire, C 1982, *The Alligator rivers prehistory and ecology in western Arnhem Land, Terra Australis 7*, Department of Prehistory, Research School of pacific Studies, The Australian National University, Canberra.

Schürmann, CW 2009[1879], 'The Aboriginal tribes of Port Lincoln in South Australia, their mode of life, manners, customs, etc.' in JD Woods (ed.), *The native tribes of South Australia*, State Library of South Australia, Adelaide, pp 209–51.

Schwartz, FJ 2008, 'A survey of the tail spine characteristics of stingrays frequenting Indo-Pacific ocean areas between the international date line and the Chagos Archipelago-Maldive Islands', *Journal of the North Carolina Academy of Science* 124:27–45.

—— 2009, 'Ways to identify stingrays of the world possessing or lacking serrated stinging tail spines', *Journal of the North Carolina Academy of Science* 125:107–09.

Semenov, SA 1964, *Prehistoric technology*, Cory, Adams and Mackay, London.

Shahack-Gross, R, O Bar-Yosef & S Weiner 1997, 'Black-coloured bones in Hayonim Cave, Israel: differentiating between burning and oxide staining', *Journal of Archaeological Science* 24:439–46.

Shahom, D & A Belfer-Cohen 2017, 'The Natufian audio-visual bone pendants from Hayonim Cave' in D Bar-Yosef Mayer, C Bonsall & A Choyke (eds), *Not just for show: the archaeology of beads, beadwork and personal ornaments*, Oxbow Books, Oxford, pp 95–102.

Sheppard Brennand, M 2018, 'Hunter-gatherer economies along the Newcastle coastline: an analysis of a shell midden site from the Late Holocene', paper presented to the Australian Archaeological Association/New Zealand Archaeological Association joint conference, Auckland, New Zealand, 27 November – 1 December 2018.

Shine, D, D Wright, T Denham, K Aplin, P Hiscok, K Parker & R Walton 2013, 'Birriwilk rockshelter: a mid- to late Holocene site in Manilikarr Country, southwest Arnhem Land, Northern Territory', *Australian Archaeology* 76:69–78.

Shipman, P 1981, 'Applications of scanning electro microscopy to taphonomic problems', *Annals of the New York Academy of Sciences* 376:357–86.

—— G Foster & M Schoeninger 1984, 'Burnt bones and teeth: an experimental study of color, morphology, crystal structure and shrinkage', *Journal of Archaeological Science* 11:307–25.

—— & J Rose 1983a, 'Early hominid hunting, butchering, and carcass-processing behaviors: approaches to the fossil record', *Journal of Anthropological Archaeology* 2:57–98.

—— & J Rose 1983b, 'Evidence of butchery and hominid activities at Torralba and Ambrona: an evolution using microscopic techniques', *Journal of Archaeological Science* 10:465–74.

—— & J Rose 1984, 'Cutmark mimics on modern and fossil bovid bones', *Current Anthropology* 25:116–17.

—— & J Rose 1988, 'Bone tools: an experimental approach' in SL Olson (ed.), *Scanning electron microscopy in archaeology*, British Archaeological Reports, International Series, Oxford, pp 303–335.

Shipton, C, P Roberts, W Archer, SJ Armitage, C Bita, J Blinkhorn et al. 2018, '78,000-year-old record of Middle and Later Stone Age innovation in an East African tropical forest', *Nature Communications* 9:1832.

Shunkov, MV, AY Fedorchenko, MB Kozlikin & AP Derevianko 2020, 'Initial Upper Palaeolithic ornaments and formal bone tools from the East Chamber of Denisova Cave in the Russian Altai', *Quaternary International* 559:47–67.

REFERENCES

Slack, M, M Fillios & R Fullagar 2009, 'Aboriginal settlement during the LGM at Brockman, Pilbara Region, Western Australia', *Archaeology in Oceania* 44:32–39.

Slon, V, F Mafessoni, B Vernot, C de Filippo, S Grote, B Viola et al. 2018, 'The genome of the offspring of a Neanderthal mother and a Denisovan father', *Nature* 561:113–16.

Smith, MA 2000, 'The opening chapter of the romance of excavation in Australia': reflections on Norman Tindale's archaeology', *Historical Records of Australia Science* 13:151–60.

Soressi, M, SP McPherron, M Lenoir, T Dogandžić, P Goldberg, Z Jacobs et al. 2013, 'Neandertals made the first specialized bone tools in Europe', *Proceedings of the National Academy of Science* 110:14186–190.

Spencer, B 1914, *Native tribes of the Northern Territory of Australia*, Macmillan, London.

—— 1922, *Guide to the Australian ethnological collection exhibited in the National Museum of Victoria*, Melbourne Government Printer, Melbourne.

—— & FJ Gillen 1899, 'Some remarks on totemism as applied to Australian tribes', *The Journal of the Anthropological Institute of Great Britain and Ireland* 28:275–80.

—— & FJ Gillen 1904, *The northern tribes of Central Australia*, Macmillan and Company, London.

—— & FJ Gillen 1927, *The Arunta*, MacMillan and Co., London.

Spennemann, DHR 1986, 'Experimental butchery with bamboo knives', *Bulletin of Experimental Archaeology* 7:3.

—— 1987, 'Cannibalism in Fiji: the analysis of butchering marks on human bones and the historical record, with an appendix on experimental butchering with bamboo blades', *Domodomo* 5:29–46.

Speth, JD & E Tchernov 2002, 'Middle Paleolithic tortoise use at Kebara Cave (Israel)', *Journal of Archaeological Science* 29:471–83.

Stiner, MC 2014, 'Finding a common bandwidth: causes of convergence and diversity in Paleolithic beads', *Biological Theory* 9:51–64.

Stockdale, J 1950[1789], *The voyage of Governor Phillip to Botany Bay, with an account of the establishment of the colonies of Port Jackson and Norfolk Island compiled from authentic papers*, Australiana Society, Adelaide.

Stockton, E 1973, 'Shaw's Creek Shelter: human displacement of artifacts and its significance', *Mankind* 9:112–17.

—— 1977a, 'Middens of the central coast, New South Wales', *Australian Archaeology* 7:20–31.

—— 1977b, 'Pre-microlithic industries in south-eastern Australian', *The Artefact* 2:209–19.

Stodiek, U 1990, 'Drei jungpaläolithische rengeweih schlägel aus Solutré, Dép: Saône-et-Loire, Frankreich', *Archäologisches Korrespondenzblatt* 20:363–71.

—— 1991, 'Erste Ergebnisse experimenteller Untersuchungen von gewiehgeschoßspitzen des Magdalenien', *Archäologische Mitteilungen aus Nordwestdeutschland Beiheft* 6:245–56.

—— 2000, 'Preliminary results of an experimental investigation of Magdalenian antler points' in C Bellier, P Cattelain & M Otte (eds), *La chasse dans la préhistoire*, Société Royale Belge d'Anthropologie et de Préhistoire/Service de Préhistoire de l'Université de Liège, Bruxelles, pp 70–8.

Stone, EA 2011, Through the eye of the needle: investigations of ethnographic, experimental, and archaeological bone tool use from perishable technologies, unpublished doctoral thesis, The University of New Mexico, Albuquerque.

Stordeur-Yedid, D 1979, *Les aiguilles a chas au Paléolithique, XIII supplement a Gallia Préhistoire*, Éditions du CNRS, Paris.

Stormon, EJ 1977, *The Salvado memoirs*, University of Western Australia Press, Perth.

Strathern, M 1979, 'The self in self-decoration', *Oceania* 49:241–57.

Sturt, C 1834, *Two expeditions into the interior of southern Australia*, Smith, Elder and Co, London.

REFERENCES

Sullivan, ME 1984, 'A shell midden excavation at Pambula Lake on the far south coast of New South Wales', *Archaeology in Oceania* 19:1–15.

Sutton, P 1994, 'Material culture traditions of the Wik people, Cape York Peninsula', *Records of the South Australian Museum* 27:31–52.

Szpak, P 2011, 'Fish bone chemistry and ultrastructure: implications for taphonomy and stable isotope analysis', *Journal of Archaeological Science* 38:3358–72.

Taborin, Y 1993, *La parure en coquillage au Paléolithique*, CNRS Éditions, Paris.

Taplin, G 2009[1879], 'The Narrinyeri. An account of the tribes of south Australian Aborigines inhabiting the country around the lakes Alexandrina, Albert, and Coorong, and the lower part of the River Murray: their manners and customs also, an account of the mission at point Macleay' in JD Woods (ed.), *The native tribes of South Australia*, State Library of South Australia, Adelaide, pp 1–156.

Tappen, M 1994, 'Bone weathering in the tropical rain forest', *Journal of Archaeological Science* 21:667–73.

Tartar, E & R White 2013, 'The manufacture of Aurignacian split-based points: an experimental challenge', *Journal of Archaeological Science* 40:2723–45.

Tátá, F, J Cascalheira, J Marreiros, T Pereira & N Bicho 2014, 'Shell bead production in the Upper Paleolithic of Vale Boi (SW Portugal): an experimental perspective', *Journal of Archaeological Science* 42:29–41.

Tejero, J-M, R Yeshurun, O Barzilai, M Goder-Goldberger, I Hershkovitz, R Lavi et al. 2016, 'The osseous industry from Manot Cave (Western Galilee, Israel): technical and conceptional behaviours of bone and antler exploitation in the Levantine Aurignacian', *Quaternary International* 403:90–106.

Texier P-J, G Porraz, J Parkington, J-P Rigaud, C Poggenpoel, C Miller et al. 2010, 'A Howiesons Poort tradition of engraving ostrich eggshell containers dated to 60,000 years ago at Diepkloof rock shelter, South Africa', Proceedings of the National Academy of Science 107:6180–85.

Theden-Ringl, F & MC Langley 2018, 'At the margins of the high country: a terminal Pleistocene to late Holocene occupation record from Wee Jasper, southeastern Australia', *Australian Archaeology* 84:145–63.

Thomas, NW 1906, *Natives of Australia: the native races of the British Empire*, Archibald Constable and Company, London.

Thomson, DF 1936, 'Notes on some bone and stone implements from north Queensland', *The Journal of the Royal Anthropological Institute of Great Britain and Ireland* 66:71–4.

—— 1946, 'Names and naming in the Wik Monkan Tribe', *The Journal of the Royal Anthropological Institute of Great Britain and Ireland* 76:157–68.

Threlkeld, L 1855, Manuscript at the Australian Institute of Aboriginal Studies, Canberra.

Tindale, NB 1938, 'Prupe and Koromarange: a legend of the Tanganekald, corona, South Australia', *Transactions of the Royal Society of South Australia* 62:18–23.

Tostevin, GB 2007, 'Social intimacy, artefact visibility and acculturation. Models of Neanderthal—Modern Human interaction' in P Mellars, KV Boyle, O Bar-Yosef & C Stringer (eds), *Rethinking the human revolution*, McDonald Institute for Archaeological Research, Cambridge, pp 341–57.

Tyzzer, EE 1936, 'The "simple bone point" of the shell-heaps of the northeastern Algonkian Area and its probable significance', *American Antiquity* 1:261–79.

Van Baal, J 1963, 'The cult of the bull-roarer in Australia and southern New Guinea', *Bijdragen tot de Taal-, Landen Volkenkunde Deel* 119:201–14.

Vanderwal, RL 1978, 'Adaptive technology in southwest Tasmania', *Australian Archaeology* 8:107–126.

Van Gijn, A 2005, 'A functional analysis of some late Mesolithic bone and antler implements from the Dutch coastal zone' in H Luik, A Choyka, C Batgey &

REFERENCES

L Lougas (eds), *From hooves to horns, from mollusc to mammoth, manufacture and use of bone artifacts from Prehistoric Times to the Present. Proceedings of the 4th Meeting of the (ICAZ) Worked Bone Research Group*, Eesti Teaduste Akadeemia, Tallinn, pp 47–66.

Vanhaeren, M 2005, 'Speaking with beads: the evolutionary significance of bead making and use' in F d'Errico & L Backwell (ed.), *From tools to symbols. From early hominids to modern humans*, Wits University Press, Johannesburg, pp 525–53.

—— & F d'Errico 2006, 'Aurignacian ethnolinguistic geography of Europe revealed by personal ornaments', *Journal of Archaeological Science* 33:1105–28.

—— F d'Errico, KL van Niekerk, CS Henshilwood & RM Erasmus 2013, 'Thinking strings: additional evidence for personal ornament use in the Middle Stone Age at Blombos Cave, South Africa', *Journal of Human Evolution* 64:500–17.

Veth, P, K Ditchfield & F Hook 2014, 'Maritime deserts of the Australian northwest', *Australian Archaeology* 79:156–166.

Vettese, D, R Blasco, I Cáceres, S Gaudzinski-Windheuser, M-H Moncel, UT Hohenstein et al. 2020, 'Towards an understanding of hominin marrow extraction strategies: a proposal for a percussion mark terminology', *Archaeological and Anthropological Sciences* 12:48.

Villa, P & F d'Errico 2001, 'Bone and ivory points in the Lower and Middle Paleolithic of Europe', *Journal of Human Evolution* 41:69–112.

—— & E Mahieu 1991, 'Breakage patterns of human long bones', *Journal of Human Evolution* 21:27–48.

Vinnicombe, P 1987, 'Salvage archaeology of the Burrup Peninsula', *Australian Archaeology* 25:53–79.

Voss, VR 1952, *The Morey papers*, National Library of Australia, Canberra.

Wade, JP 1967, 'The excavation of a rockshelter at Connell's Point, New South Wales', *Archaeology and Physical Anthropology in Oceania* 2:35–40.

Watson, JA & HM Abbey 1986, 'The effects of termites (Isoptera) on bone: some archaeological implications', *Sociobiology* 11:245–54.

Webb, C & J Allen 1990, 'A functional analysis of Pleistocene bone tools from two sites in southwest Tasmania', *Archaeology in Oceania* 25:75–8.

Weniger, G-C 1995, *Widerhaken spitzen des magdalenien westeuropas*, Ein Vergleich mit Ethnohistorischen Jägergruppen Nordamerikas, Mainz.

Werner, JJ & JM Miller 2018, 'Distinguishing stone age drilling techniques on ostrich eggshell beads: an experimental approach', *Journal of Archaeological Science: Reports* 22:108–14.

West, JA & J Louys 2007, 'Differentiating bamboo from stone tool cut marks in the zooarchaeologial record, with a discussion on the use of bamboo knives', *Journal of Archaeological Science* 34:512–18.

White, C 1967, 'The prehistory of the Kakadu people', *Mankind* 6:426–43.

White, J 1962[1790], *Journal of a voyage to New South Wales*, Angus & Robertson, Sydney.

White, R 1992a, 'Beyond art: toward an understanding of the origins of material representation in Europe'. *Annual Review of Anthropology* 21:537–64.

—— 1997, 'Systems of personal ornamentation in the early Upper Palaeolithic: methodological challenges and new observations' in P Mellars, K Boyle, O Bar-Yosef & C Stringer (eds), *Rethinking the human revolution*, McDonald Institute Monographs, Cambridge, pp 287–302.

—— 2002, 'Observations technologiques sur les objets de parure', *Gallia Préhistoire* 34:257–66.

—— 2007, 'Systems of personal ornamentation in the early Upper Palaeolithic: Methodological challenges and new observations', in P. Mellars (ed.), *Rethinking the human revolution*, McDonald Institute Monographs, Cambridge, pp 287–302.

REFERENCES

White, TD 1992b, *Prehistoric cannibalism at Mancos 5MTUMR-2346*, Princeton University Press, Princeton.

—— & N Toth 1989, 'Engis: preparation damage, not ancient cutmarks', *American Journal of Physical Anthropology* 78:361–67.

Wiessner, P 1982, 'Risk, reciprocity and social influence on !Kung San economics' in E Leacock & R Lee (eds), *Politics and history in band societies*, Cambridge University Press, Cambridge, pp 61–84.

—— 1983, 'Style and social information in Kalahari San projectile points', *American Antiquity* 48:253–76.

—— 1984, 'Reconsidering the behavioral basis for style: a case study among the Kalahari San', *Journal of Anthropological Archaeology* 3:190–234.

—— 1985, 'Style or isochrestic variation? A reply to Sackett', *American Antiquity* 50:160–66.

Wilke, PJ, JJ Flennen & TL Ozbun 1991, 'Clovis technology at the Anzick site, Montana', *Journal of California and Great Basin Anthropology* 13:242–72.

Wobst, MH 1977, 'Stylistic behavior and information exchange' in CE Cleland (ed.), *For the director: research essays in honor of James B. Griffin*, Museum of Anthropology, University of Michigan, Ann Arbor, pp 317–42.

Wojtczak, D & M Kerdy 2018, 'They left traces. Preliminary analyses of microwear traces on bone and antler tools from Sutz-Lattrigen Assen, lake Bienne, Switzerland', *Journal of Archaeological Science: Reports* 17:798–808.

Worgan, GB 1978[1788], *Journal of a first fleet surgeon, William Dixson Foundation Publication 16*, Library Council of New South Wales in association with the Library of Australian History, Sydney.

Worsnop, T 1897, *The prehistoric arts, manufactures, works, weapons etc. of the Aborigines of Australia*, CE Bristow, Government Printer, Adelaide.

Wright, D, MC Langley, SK May, I Johnston & L Allen 2016, 'Painted shark vertebrate beads from the Djawumbu-Madjawarrnja Complex, Western Arnhem Land', *Australian Archaeology* 82:43–54.

Wright, RVS 1971, 'Prehistory in the Cape York Peninsula' in DJ Mulvaney & J Golson (eds), *Aboriginal man and environment in Australia*, ANU Press, Canberra, pp 133–140.

Wroe, S, JH Field, M Archer, DK Grayson, GJ Price, J Louys et al. 2013, 'Climate change frames debate over the extinction of megafauna in Sahul (Pleistocene Australia-New Guinea)', *Proceedings of the National Academy of Science* 110:8777–91.

Wyatt, JP 2009[1879], 'Some amount of the manners and superstitions of the Adelaide and Encounter Bay Aboriginal tribes with a vocabulary of their languages, names of persons and places, etc.' in JD Woods (ed), *The native tribes of South Australia*, State Library of South Australia, Adelaide, pp 159–81.

Yerkes, RW & PN Kardulias 1993, 'Recent developments in the analysis of lithic analysis', *Journal of Archaeological Research* 1:89–119.

Zutovski, K & R Barkai 2016, 'The use of elephant bones for making Acheulian handaxes: a fresh look at old bones', *Quaternary International* 406:227–38.

Index

NOTE: Page locators followed by an '*i*' indicate an illustration; page locators followed by a '*t*' indicates a table'; figures in the colour section are indicated by 'CS' and the figure number followed by a '*f*'.

abrasion of osseous artefacts, CS 2.9*f*
   lying on the ground, 37
   while in the ground, 40
active edge of tools, 58*i*, 59
Akerman, Kim, 15
Allen, Jim, 13, 14
archaeological sites in Australia, bone or tooth artefact finds, 5–6, 6*i*, 7–11*t*, 11–12
archaeozoology, 20–21
arm ornaments, 205
attack points, 69, CS 4.2*f*
awls
   characteristics, 76–77*t*
   as cloak pins or fasteners, 120
   description, 74–75
   hafting of, 75*i*, 83
   local names recorded for, 86–87
   manufacture and use, 75, 77–86
   in men's bags, 84
   as murder weapons, 116
   trade of bony raw material for, 85–86
   types, 74–75, 75*i*
   unusual examples, 86
   in women's bags, 83–84

Balme, Jane, 14
bandicoot bones and tail tip necklaces, 194–95
beads
   description, 65
   major attributes, 66*t*
   metrics, 69–70
   orientation, 68
   raw material, 67
   terms for describing, 68*i*
bird beak
   characteristics and properties, 24
   use in necklaces, 195
bird feather quills, use as needles, 119, 119*i*
bird skulls, use in necklaces, 195
birds, characteristics and properties of bones, 23*i*, 24
bone, characteristics and properties, 22–24
bone and tooth artefact studies
   ethnographic analogies, 45
   experimental programs, 45–46, 47–53
   form and style, 42–44
   future of, 208–10
   identifying raw material, 46, 53–54
   microtraces, 54–56
bone and tooth artefacts
   identifying, 26
   overview of Australian finds, 5–15
   overview through deep time, 2–5
   recurring themes in Australia, 206–8
   types of materials worked, 15–17
   see also ornaments; tools
bone artefacts, identifying, 26
bone flaking, 30–32, 31*t*
bone tool analysis, 17–18

INDEX

damage caused during excavation and analysis, 42
natural processes and agents affecting artefacts lying on the ground effects, 37–40
natural processes and agents affecting artefacts while in the ground, 40–41
raw material properties, 21–26
separating real artefacts from pseudotools, 37
types of bone- and tooth-working, 26–33
undertaking a new analysis, 21
use wear and damage, 33–37
bone whistles, 118
bone-working, 26–28
   chop marks, 28
   cut marks, 28–30
   drilling, 30
   flaking, 30–32
   grinding, 32
   polishing, 32
   sawing, 33
   scraping, 33
Bowdler, Sandra, 13–14
Buckley, Mike, 53
bull roarers, 118, 119
bullock teeth necklaces, 195
burnishers, 87

camel bone, 114
canine teeth and bone necklaces, 195–96
carnivores, tooth marks on bone surfaces, 39
cassowary casques, CS 2.2f
   characteristics and properties, 25
   as forehead pendants, 173
ceremonial tools, 88
charms, 88–90, 89i, 145–46
Chauvet, Gustave, 43
chemical erosion of osseous artefacts, 41
chisels, 137–38, 143
chop marks in osseous materials, 28, CS 2.4f
Christy, Henry, 42–43
circlets
   description, 158
   local names recorded for, 161
   manufacture and use, 159, 160–61

presence in museum collections and ethnographies, 153t, 160
types, 159, 159i
clap sticks, 118
claws, characteristics and properties, 24–25
cloak pins, 120, 121
combs, 90
containers
   fasteners for, 91
   made from human bone, 144–45
Cosgrove, Richard, 13
cut marks in osseous materials, 28–30, CS 2.4f, CS 2.7f
cutting tools, use wear and damage, 33–34

dasyurid bone necklaces, 196
death pointers
   characteristics, 93t
   description, 92
   local names recorded for, 95
   manufacture and use, 92, 93–95
denticulating tools, 135
digestion of bones, evidence of, 37–38, CS 2.9f
digging tools, use wear and damage, 34
dingo teeth and bone necklaces, 195–96
drilling in osseous materials, 30, CS 2.5f
drills, 96, 97i

eagle talon necklaces, 196–97, 197i
earrings, 179–80
eating utensils, 98, 99i
echidna quills
   characteristics and properties, 25
   in necklaces, 197–98
   use as spear points, 125
eel rays, 198–99
elongated tools, terms for describing, 60t
emu bones, 16, 17i
engraving tools, 139–41, 143, 144
ethnographic analogies, 45
exchange of artefacts, 206–7
experimental archaeology, 45–46, 47–53

fans, 99
fasteners, 120–22
faunal analysis, 20

INDEX

fighting tools, 100–102
fish vertebrae necklaces, 199, 199*i*, 200
fishbone
    characteristics and properties, 24
    use as fishhooks, 109
fishhooks
    bird talon hooks, 108
    bone hooks, 104*i*, 105–6, CS 3.5*f*
    composite hooks, 104*i*, 106–8, 108*i*
    description, 102
    fishbone hooks, 109
    local names recorded for, 109
    mammal incisor hooks, 108–9
    manufacture and use, 102, 103–9
    overview of non-marine shell fishhooks, 103*t*
    shell hooks, 109
    terms for describing, 60*t*, 62*i*
    turtle shell hooks, 103–4, 104*i*, 105
flaked bones, 30–32
flaking in osseous materials, CS 2.5*f*, CS 2.6*f*
fly-flicks, 99
forehead pendants
    cassowary casques, 173
    description, 168
    local names recorded for, 174, 175
    manufacture and use, 169, 170, 171–74
    presence in museum collections and ethnographies, 153*t*, 171*t*
    type 1, 168, 169, 170*i*, 174
    type 2, 168, 170, 170*i*, 171, 174
    type 3, 168, 170*i*, 171–72, 174
    type 4, 169, 170*i*, 172, 174
    type 5, 169, 170*i*, 172, 174
    type 6, 169, 170*i*, 172
    type 7, 169, 170*i*, 172
    type 8, 169, 170*i*, 173, 175
    types, 168–69
fossiles directeurs, 43
fractures in bones, from natural processes and agents, 38
freshwater animals, 16–17

gnawing of bones, CS 2.9*f*
    evidence of, 38
gougers, 137–39, 143–44
grinding of osseous materials, CS 2.5*f*, 32

groovers, 109–10, 109*i*

hafted tools, 58*i*, 59
hafting of osseous tools, use wear and damage, 35, CS 2.7*f*
hair pins
    description, 153
    forms, 155*i*
    local names recorded for, 158
    manufacture and use, 154, 156–58
    presence in museum collections and ethnographies, 153*t*, 156*t*
Hale, Herbert, 5–8, 11
hand ornaments, 205
handheld tools, 58*i*, 59
handles, 110–11
handling of tools, use wear and damage, 34, CS 2.7*f*
hard animal materials, defined, 22
harpoons, 111–12, 111*i*
head ornaments
    broad forms, 152*i*
    presence in museum collections and ethnographies, 153*t*
    regional representation in museums, 152*i*
    types, 151
    see also specific forms, e.g. nose bones
headbands
    description, 163
    dingo tails headbands, 165–66
    local names recorded for, 168
    manufacture and use, 163, 164–68
    presence in museum collections and ethnographies, 153*t*
    type 1, 163
    type 2, 163, 164–67
    type 3, 167–68
    types, 162*i*, 163
herbivores, evidence of chewing of bones, 38
housing, 112
human bone
    containers, 144–45
    interpersonal weapons, 145–46
    material culture made on, 144–50
    medicines and medical tools, 146–47
    mementos of loved ones, 147–50
    tools, 149

INDEX

toys, 149
weapons, 149–50

impact fractures, CS 2.8*f*, CS 3.2*f*
information exchange theory, 43, 44
insect activity, effects on bones, 38
interpersonal weapons
    human-bone charms used against others, 145–46
    poison bones, 145

Jones, Rhys, 13, 14

kangaroo bones, 16, 16*i*
keratin artefacts, identifying, 26
keyholing, 71–72, CS 4.2*f*
knives, 60
    bone knives, 114
    fighting knives, 100, 101–2, 101*i*
    macropod scapula knives, 113, 113*i*, 114
    manufacture and use, 113–14
    turtle shell knives, 113*i*
    yam knives, 113*i*

Lampert, Ron, 13
Lartet, Edouard, 42–43
lobster bone necklaces, 199
Lourandous, Harry, 13

macropod incisor necklace, 2*i*
macropod teeth necklaces, 200–202, 200*i*, CS 2.2*f*
Malapuwinarana (Tasmanian man), CS 5.16*f*
manganese staining, CS 2.10*f*
marine animals, 16–17
marine mammals, characteristics and properties of bones, 23–24
masks, 193, 194*t*
McCarthy, Frederick, 11–12
medical or surgical tools
    description, 114
    human bones, 146–47
    local names recorded for, 115–16
    manufacture and use, 114–15
medicines, whole or ground human bones, 146–47
megafauna, 15–16, 88–89, 89*i*

mementos of loved ones, 147–50
microtraces, 26–27, 54–56, 62, 63*i*
murder weapons
    description, 116
    local names recorded for, 118
    manufacture and use, 116–18
musical instruments, 117, 118

necklaces
    bandicoot bones and tail tips, 194–95
    bird skulls and beaks, 195
    bullock teeth, 195
    canine teeth and bones, 195–96
    dasyurid bones, 196
    eagle talons, 196–97, 197*i*
    echidna quills, 197–98
    eel rays, 198–99
    fish and lobster parts, 199–200, 199*i*
    macropod teeth, 200–202, 200*i*
    shark vertebrae, 203
    snake vertebrae, 203
    Tasmanian devil teeth, 203
    wombat claws, 203
needles, 119–20, 119*i*
netting needles, 120
nose bones
    193, type 7
    description, 180
    local names recorded for, 192–93
    manufacture and use, 182, 183–92
    presence in museum collections and ethnographies, 153*t*, 183*t*
    type 1, 180, 181*i*, 184, 192–93
    type 2, 181*i*, 182, 184
    type 3, 181*i*, 182, 183, 184, 186, 193
    type 4, 181*i*, 182, 184, 193
    type 5, 181*i*, 182, 193
    type 6, 181*i*, 182, 193
    type 7, 181*i*, 182, 183, 184
    type 8, 181*i*, 182
    type 9, 181*i*, 182

organic artefacts, 206
    see also bone and tooth artefacts
ornaments
    attachment mode, 70, 71*i*
    distinguished from tools, 17–18

INDEX

distribution on the body, 208
exchange of, 206–7
manufacturing traces, 69–70
metrics, 69
orientation, 68
perforations and grooves, 207
raw material, 67
shape, 67–68
terms for describing, 65, 67
use traces, 70–72
see also specific types e.g. head ornaments
osseous artefact studies *see* bone and tooth artefact studies
osseous material, defined, 22

pendants
    description, 66, 67
    major attributes, 66t
    manufacturing traces, 69–70
    metrics, 69
    orientation, 68
    raw material, 67
    terms for describing, 68i
    see also forehead pendants; sidelock pendants
piercing tools, use wear and damage, 35–36, CS 2.8f
pipes (musical instrument), 118
pipes (smoking), 123
plant-working tools, identifying, 35–37, CS 3.6f
pointed bone tools, terms for describing, 61i, 64t
polishing of osseous materials, 32, CS 2.5f
pressure-flakers
    local names recorded for, 136
    manufacture and use, 135
    use wear and damage, 34
projectile points
    determining distal and proximal extremities, CS 3.2f
    use wear and damage, 35, CS 3.2f

raw material
    identifying, 53–54, 58
    properties, 21–26
rodents, evidence of gnawing of bones, 38

root etching of osseous artefacts, 4, CS 2.10f

saw marks in osseous materials, 33, CS 2.4f
scraping of osseous materials, 33, CS 2.4f
Semenov, Sergei, 55
shark vertebrae necklaces, 203
sidelock pendants
    description, 175
    local names recorded for, 179
    manufacture and use, 175–77, 178–79
    presence in museum collections and ethnographies, 153t, 178t
    type 1, 175, 175i, 177, 178, 179
    type 2, 175, 175i, 178–79
    type 3, 175, 175i, 176, 177, 178–79
    type 4, 175, 175i
    type 5, 175, 175i
    type 6, 175, 175i
skin decorating tools, 204
skin-working tools
    description, 122
    identifying, CS 3.6f
    manufacture and use, 122–23
    use wear and damage, 36–37
smoking pipes, 123
smoothing boards, 109–10, 109i
snake vertebrae necklaces, 203
social interaction theory, 43–44
spear points
    characteristics, 124–25t
    description, 123, 125
    echidna quills, 125
    human bone, 149
    local names recorded for, 132–33
    manufacture and use, 125–32
    multi-pronged spears, 127i, 128–30, 132–33
    multi-pronged stingray barb spears, 131–32, 133
    single-point spears, 126, 132
    single-point spears with barb, 126–28, 127i
spears
    fighting spears, 100–101, 102
    fishing spears, 102
spearthrower pegs
    description, 133–34
    manufacture and use, 134–35
spoons, 99i

INDEX

stilettos *see* awls
stingray barbs, CS 2.2f
   characteristics and properties, 25
   use as spear points, 131–32, 133
stone artefacts, 206
stone tools, 206
stone-working tools, 135–36
surgical tools *see* medical or surgical tools

Tasmanian devil teeth necklaces, 203
teeth, characteristics and properties, 25
terrestrial mammals, characteristics and properties of bones, 23*i*
Tindale, Norman, 5–8, 11
tools
   active edge, 58*i*, 59
   creation and use life, 27*i*
   cross-section, 61
   defining 'types', 63, 73
   distinguished from ornaments, 17–18
   exchange of, 206–7
   hafted or handheld, 59
   identifying raw material, 58
   microtraces, 62, 63*i*
   multi-functionality, 207–8
   orientation, 59, 60
   regional represented in museum collections, 74*i*
   terms for describing, 57, 60*t*, 61*i*
   see also bone tool analysis; stone tools; *types of tools*, e.g. awls
tooth marks on bone surfaces, CS 2.9f
torso ornaments, 204
toys, 136, 149
trampling fractures, CS 2.10f
trampling of artefacts, 40–41
turtle shell
   characteristics and properties, 26
   use as fishhooks, 103–4, 104*i*, 105
   use as knives, 113*i*, 114

use wear analysis, 26–28, 54
use wear and damage, CS 2.7f
   cutting tools, CS 2.7f, 33–34
   digging tools, 34
   direct pressure, 34
   hafting, CS 2.7f, 35

handling, CS 2.7f, 34
impact, 35
impact fractures, CS 2.8f
piercing, 35–36, CS 2.8f
skin-working tools, 36–37

waistbands, 204
wallaby
   claws, CS 2.2f
   incisors, CS 2.2f
weapons *see* fighting tools; interpersonal weapons; murder weapons
wear and damage from use *see* use wear and damage
weathering, 39–40
Webb, Catherine, 14
whalebone, use as structural frames for shelters, 112, CS 5.11f
wombat claw necklaces, 203
woodworking tools
   chisels, 137–38
   gougers, 137–39
   local names recorded for, 143–44
   manufacture and use, 137–41, 143
   in museum collections and ethnographies, 142*t*
   tooth-based engravers, 139–41, 143
   types, 137

zooarchaeology, 20–21
   zooarchaeology by mass spectrometry (ZooMS), 53

About the author

Associate Professor Michelle C Langley FSA is is an archaeologist in the Australian Research Centre for Human Evolution at Griffith University, Brisbane, Australia. She studied archaeology at The University of Queensland before earning her PhD in Palaeolithic archaeology at the University of Oxford. Her work focuses on the use of antler, bone, ivory, tooth, and shell in creating tools and ornaments by communities the world over. She is equally passionate about human cognitive evolution and the identification of children's behaviour in archaeological contexts.

She has been published in specialist and academic journals, including *Nature Communications*, *Antiquity*, *Quaternary Science Reviews* and the *Journal of Human Evolution*. She has written for and appeared regularly in the media, including *National Geographic*, *New Scientist*, *Archaeology Magazine*, NITV, SBS and the ABC. She was a recipient of the 2018 Queensland Young Tall Poppy Science Award and was a finalist in Women in Technology Research Leaders in Science 2021. She is a Fellow of the Society of Antiquaries of London.